Regular Verbs

-er Verbs

PARLER: to speak

Past participle: parlé

Commands: Parle! Parlons! Parlez!

Subject	Present	Imperfect	Future	Conditional	Subjunctive
je	parle	parlais	parlerai	parlerais	parle
tu	parles	parlais	parleras	parlerais	parles
il, elle, on	parle	parlait	parlera	parlerait	parle
nous	parlons	parlions	parlerons	parlerions	parlions
vous	parlez	parliez	parlerez	parleriez	parliez
ils, elles	parlent	parlaient	parleront	parleraient	parlent

-ir Verbs

FINIR: to finish

Past participle: Fini

Commands: Finis! Finissons! Finissez!

Subject	Present	Imperfect	Future	Conditional	Subjunctive
je	finis	finissais	finirai	finirais	finisse
tu	finis	finissais	finiras	finirais	finisses
il, elle, on	finit	finissait	finira	finirait	finisse
nous	finissons	finissions	finirons	finirions	finissions
vous	finissez	finissiez	finirez	finiriez	finissiez
ils, elles	finissent	finissaient	finiront	finiraient	finissent

-re Verbs

VENDRE: to sell

Past participle: vendu

Commands: Vends! Vendons! Vendez!

Subject	Present	Imperfect	Future	Conditional	Subjunctive
je	vends	vendais	vendrai	vendrais	vende
tu	vends	vendais	vendras	vendrais	vendes
il, elle, on	vend	vendait	vendra	vendrait	vende
nous	vendons	vendions	vendrons	vendrions	vendions
vous	vendez	vendiez	vendrez	vendriez	vendiez
ils, elles	vendent	vendaient	vendront	vendraient	vendent

tear here

Useful Abbreviations

French Abbreviation	Stands For	English
av.	avenue	avenue
bd.	boulevard	boulevard
CEE	Communauté économique européenne (Marché commun)	Common Market
Cie.	compagnie	company
EU	États-Unis	United States
F	francs	francs
h.	heures	o'clock
M.	Monsieur	Mr., sir
Mlle	Mademoiselle	Miss
MM	Messieurs	sirs
Mme	Madame	Mrs.
n^o	numéro	number
P et T	Postes et Télécommunications	telephone company
RATP	Régie Autonome des Transports Parisiens	Paris transport system
SI	Syndicat d'initiative	tourist information
SNCF	Société Nationale des Chemins de Fer	French railway system
s.v.p.	s'il vous plaît	please
UE	Union Européenne	European Union

In Case of an Emergency

Phrase	French	Pronunciation
Be careful!	Soyez prudent(e)!	*swah-yay prew-dahN(t)*
Get out!	Sortez!	*sohr-tay*
Help!	Au secours!	*o skoor*
Help me!	Aidez-moi!	*eh-day mwah*
Hurry up!	Dépêchez-vous!	*day-peh-shay voo*
Look!	Regardez!	*ruh-gahr-day*
Listen!	écoutez!	*ay-koo-tay*
Quickly!	Vite!	*veet*
Wait!	Attendez!	*ah-tahN-day*
Watch out!	Attention!	*ah-tahN-syohN*

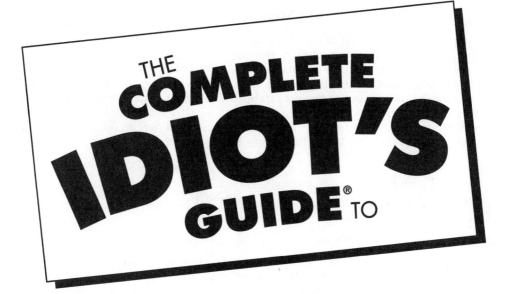

THE **COMPLETE IDIOT'S GUIDE®** TO

Learning French

Second Edition

by Gail Stein

**alpha
books**

Macmillan USA, Inc.
201 West 103rd Street
Indianapolis, IN 46290

A Pearson Education Company

International Standard Book Number: 0-02863229-X
Library of Congress Catalog Card Number: 99-65479

01   00   8   7   6   5   4   3   2

Interpretation of the printing code: The rightmost number of the first series of numbers is the year of the book's printing; the rightmost number of the second series of numbers is the number of the book's printing. For example, a printing code of 99-1 shows that the first printing occurred in 1999.

Printed in the United States of America

Alpha Development Team

Publisher
Marie Butler-Knight

Editorial Director
Gary M. Krebs

Associate Managing Editor
Cari Shaw Fischer

Acquisitions Editors
Randy Ladenheim-Gil
Amy Gordon

Development Editors
Phil Kitchel
Amy Zavatto

Assistant Editor
Georgette Blau

Production Team

Development Editor
Alexander Goldman

Production Editor
Suzanne Snyder

Copy Editor
John Sleeva

Cover Designer
Mike Freeland

Photo Editor
Richard H. Fox

Illustrator
Floyd Hughes

Book Designers
Scott Cook and Amy Adams of DesignLab

Indexer
Maro Riofrancos

Layout/Proofreading
Darin Crone, Marie Kristine Parial-Leonardo,
Julie Trippetti

Contents at a Glance

Contents

Appendix

Foreword

A few short years ago, I become the first American Director of the French Institute Alliance Française, (FIAF), New York's French Cultural Center. I was a novice at learning French then but my position demanded that I attain some proficiency in this beautiful language. While I would have loved to study in a class, or even have taken private lessons without pause, I'm afraid the pace of my job kept getting in the way. I needed an easy guide and reference check so that I might reinforce what I was learning and continue on my own during those hectic periods. *The Complete Idiot's Guide to Learning French on Your Own* could not have come out at a better time.

It was the perfect primer for someone with a busy schedule or a serious study guide for someone who wants greater depth at more intensive intermediate levels. Most importantly, it was written in 'user-friendly' terms. I was pleased to endorse the book when it first appeared. I am delighted that pains were taken to update and add to this valuable resource.

In fact, a whole new chapter has been added related to business French, two additional sidebars have been added providing quick tips and shortcuts to learning the language and more exercises have been added to every chapter. Don't miss the appendix either— there you'll find a list of twenty sentences you must know and a list of common mistakes that can be easily avoided with some basic study.

All in all, this is the primer that can give you the guideposts you'll need to learn this beautiful tongue. Whether you fear mastering the accent, or the dreaded subjunctive, there are tips to enlighten you and rules written in a vernacular that any American or English reader can understand.

Images of France can be gleaned through these pages as the sounds and rhythms of the French language come to life. Cultural references abound reinforcing those images that draw us to the country, its art, its literature, its wine and its culinary delights.

At FIAF, we immerse our students in French language training, complemented by French films and cultural programs, an independent learning center staffed by native French tutors, and arguably the largest and most beautiful all-French library in the country. One of the new programs we have is Café Philosophique where one can discuss issues and differences between our cultures either in French or in English. If your desire is to participate in French, then hope is but a few pages away. Whether you're a beginner or more advanced, this updated *Complete Idiot's Guide to Learning French* continues to make the basics basic and the harder stuff simpler. Best of all, it does so in a language you can understand and one that you can learn from.

David S. Black
Executive Director
French Institute Alliance Française

Introduction

You have at your fingertips a completely updated, user-friendly book that will help you enjoy your language learning experience to the fullest. This book's light, simple, clear-cut approach will give you all the confidence you need to start communicating almost instantly with a reasonable amount of success and an encouraging sense of achievement.

Learning French will allow you to broaden your horizons and will open a path to endless opportunities, intriguing experiences, exotic adventures, and exciting challenges. Just open your eyes, ears, heart, and soul to the new cultures, creative ideas, varying perspectives, and unique situations that await you all over the world. A knowledge of French is a handy and useful tool that will serve you well when you least expect it.

This book was designed for people from all walks of life, with wide and varied interests: from travel to business to a pure and simple love for learning. Seize the chance to put the French-speaking world at your doorstep. Do it now!

Why and How This Book Is Meant for You

This book will take you from the most basic material to a broader understanding of the structural patterns of the French language and, finally, to a higher level of expertise and proficiency. This book is not a phrase book, a dictionary, a grammar text, or a tour guide. It is unique in that it is a combination of the four all wrapped up into one. It's goal is to teach you to communicate effectively in common, everyday situations. You'll be able to socialize, ask for information, express your opinions, and be persuasive—plain and simply: to get what you want and need. Whether you are a student, tourist, businessperson, or lover of languages, the simple, easy-to-use format of this book will provide you with the knowledge and skills you need. Each thematically constructed chapter ties together vocabulary, useful phrases, and grammar, and furnishes authentic materials and activities that will give you a thorough understanding of French-speaking people and their culture. Here's what you can expect to find in this book:

Part 1, "The Bare Basics," begins with a discussion of the importance of French in today's world, is followed by an easy-to-use phonetic pronunciation guide designed for the shy and easily intimidated speaker, and then proceeds to demonstrate your pre-existing knowledge of many French words, phrases, and expressions. Don't agonize over grammar; basic elementary terms and rules are presented painlessly along with idioms, slang, and typical gestures. From the outset you'll be able to ask and answer simple questions and engage in basic conversations.

Part 2, "Travel Time," provides useful information and tips on how to plan a trip to a French-speaking country and get the most out of it. You'll learn how to meet and greet others, and introduce and speak about yourself and your traveling companions. For the curious type, asking questions will be quite easy. There are chapters to help you navigate the airport, obtain ground transportation, and even rent a car. You'll also become proficient at giving and receiving directions. Finally, this section helps you acquire a room with the creature comforts you prefer.

Part 3, "Fun Time," helps you have a fantastic, fun-filled time. Everything that makes that dream vacation a reality is featured in this section: food, shopping, sports, tourist attractions, musical events, and leisure activities. You'll learn to plan your activities around the weather, to offer suggestions, and to express your opinions and preferences. The chapters about food ensure that your appetite is satisfied and your diet maintained. If you love to shop, there's a chapter that enables you to buy anything from haute couture fashions to souvenirs for the crowd back home.

Part 4, "Time Out: Problems," helps you deal with simple, minor inconveniences, as well as those of a more serious nature. Turn to this section when you need your hair cut, a spot removed, your camera repaired, a replacement contact lens, new heels on your shoes, a prescription filled, or your mail sent. You'll even be able to explain what happened in the past.

Part 5, "It's Time for Business," was written to meet the needs of those who want to conduct business transactions at the bank. You'll learn how to make deposits and withdrawals, open a checking account, and take out a loan. You'll also learn tasks such as sending faxes, making photocopies, and using the computer. This section includes mini-dictionaries for banking-, computer-, business- and stock market-related terms. When you're through, you'll be able to buy or rent property abroad and to express your present and future needs.

If you are truly committed to learning French, by the time you've completed this book, you will have studied and practiced skills that will enable you to feel confident in both social and business situations. With time, patience, and the willingness to make a sincere effort, you will be able to communicate successfully in a beautiful language in a relatively short period of time.

Extras

In addition to all the vocabulary lists, useful phrases and expressions, and grammatical explanations, this book provides many interesting and informative facts set apart from the text in sidebars. These useful tools will speed up and enhance your acquisition of French in an interesting and clear-cut manner. Look for the following icons that set these tidbits apart:

Memory Enhancer

Consult these boxes for a speedy refresher course of grammar or a quick understanding of new rules.

Attention!

These warnings will help you avoid unnecessary or embarrassing mistakes.

Un deux trois

These sidebars feature tips for learning and perfecting your French in a fast, fun way.

En 10 Minutes

You'll be on the road to success if you spend just 10 minutes a day reviewing the highlights of the most important material contained in the chapter.

Culture Capsule

Refer to these boxes for useful facts and an increased cultural understanding of the customs of the French-speaking world. These useful tidbits will certainly make your travel experience more fulfilling.

Trademarks

All terms mentioned in this book that are known to be or are suspected of being trademarks or service marks have been appropriately capitalized. Alpha Books and Macmillan USA, Inc. cannot attest to the accuracy of this information. Use of a term in this book should not be regarded as affecting the validity of any trademark or service mark.

Acknowledgments

I would like to acknowledge the contributions, input, support, and interest of the following people:

Natercia Alves, Marie-Claire Antoine, Monika Bergenthal, Vivian Bergenthal, Richard Calcasola (of Maximus Hair Salon), Nancy Chu, Trudy Edelman, Richard Edelman, Marc Einsohn, Raymond Elias, Werner K. Elias, Barbara Gilson, Robert Grandt, François Haas (of the Office of the French Treasury), Martin Hyman, Roger Herz (of Roger Herz, Inc.), Martin Leder, Christina Levy, Nancy Lasker (of L'Oréal), Max Rechtman, Marie-Madeleine Saphire, and Barbara Shevrin.

Special Thanks to the Technical Reviewer

The Complete Idiot's Guide to Learning French, Second Edition was reviewed by an expert who double-checked the accuracy of what you'll learn here, to help us ensure that this book gives you everything you need to know about French. Special thanks are extended to Stephanie Rosenfeld.

Dedication

This book is dedicated to:

➤ My wonderfully patient and supportive husband, Douglas

➤ My incredibly loving and understanding sons, Eric and Michael

➤ My proud parents, Jack and Sara Bernstein

➤ My superior consultant and advisor, Roger H. Herz

➤ My mentor from the very beginning, Yetta Rosenblum

➤ The memory of a very special gentleman, Ernest Rothschild—a true professional

Part 1
The Bare Basics

Learning simple, basic grammar is the fastest, easiest, most efficient way to pick up French effortlessly. All it takes is a quick study of a few simple rules. Be honest: Does the thought of grammar turn you off? Surprise! As you'll learn in Part 1, the rules are easy and don't test your memorization skills in the slightest. You'll also learn to speak idiomatically so that you'll be mistaken for a native! Just dive right in and, before you know it, you'll be communicating in French with ease and confidence.

Chapter 1

The Top Ten Reasons You Should Study French

In This Chapter

➤ Why French?

➤ Where you can use French

➤ Developing a workable learning strategy

➤ Have no fear

You've picked up this book, and as you're leafing through it you're probably wondering, "Should I or shouldn't I?" Undoubtedly, you're asking yourself if it will be difficult, if you'll have the time, if it's going to be worth the effort, and if you'll stick with it. My name may not be Dave, but here are my top ten reasons why you need to study French:

10. You can't put down Colette's romance novels.

9. You'd like to root for the Montréal Canadiens in French.

8. You loved the musical *Les Misérables* so much that you decided to read the original version in its entirety—all 600 plus pages.

7. You want to avoid ordering francs with mustard and sauerkraut.

6. You never know when you're going to run into Catherine Deneuve.

5. You want to impress your date at a French restaurant.

4. You love French movies but find the subtitles too distracting.

3. They won't let you onto the topless beach in Martinique without it.

2. Two words: French fries.

And finally, the best reason of all:

1. You want to meet St. Exupéry's *Little Prince*.

Are you totally convinced that French is the language for you? If you're still a little doubtful, let's look at some more down-to-earth, realistic reasons why you should study French.

Reality Check

The following are some serious and credible reasons why this book is for you:

10. **You're a musician, and France is a country where culture is taken seriously.** You long to go to *L'Opéra* and admire its sculptured façade, its magnificent marble staircase, and its elegant foyer. You really like classical music (although you'd never admit it to your friends) and would like to enjoy the operas you love in their native language: *Carmen*, by Bizet; *Faust*, by Gounod; *Manon*, by Massenet; *Samson et Dalila*, by Saint-Saëns. Yes, you want to take your studies further.

9. **You're an *artiste*.** Your dream is to sit in the *Place du Tertre* in Montmartre and paint watercolor scenes of Paris, or do charcoal portraits of the tourists who stop by your easel to admire your work.

Culture Capsule

Paris has many museums: the Musée du Louvre, with its *Mona Lisa* and *Vénus de Milo*; the Musée d'Orsay, with its impressionist collection; the Centre Georges-Pompidou, with its fabulous modern art museum; the well-hidden Musée Picasso; and many more. You can have a picnic lunch at the Musée Rodin while you sit and admire *Le Penseur* (*The Thinker*) or *Le Baiser* (*The Kiss*). In Paris, art is respected and loved.

8. **You love French movies and long to understand the actors without the distraction of poorly translated subtitles.** You know that those subtitles don't tell it all and you want to know what's really happening. You are also aware that this is a good way to pick up some up-to-date slang expressions.

7. **You're not greedy, but you do want to make more money.** France, a leading nation in the European Union, has the fourth largest economy in the world, and you'd like to take advantage of that. *Haute couture* (high fashion), perfume,

leather goods, precision instruments, automobiles, chemical and pharmaceutical products, and jewelry are all thriving French industries.

6. **You want to prove you're smart.** The French language has the reputation of being difficult to learn. This myth dates back to a time when only the smartest junior-high school students were offered French. Of course, anyone who's ever studied French knows that it really isn't any more difficult than any other foreign language.

5. **You want to live in a French-speaking country.** You love the language, you love the people, or maybe you've been relocated by your company. Whatever the reason, if you're going to be staying in a French-speaking country for an extended period of time, you've got to learn the language.

4. **You love to cook and have a special passion for fabulous dishes and desserts.** You want to go to the original sources to understand all the food terms and culinary techniques. If you decide to take a cooking course in France, you want to know what's going on.

3. **You love to eat.** Are you a gourmet? Even if you love food but don't study it, a basic knowledge of French, especially the culinary terms, is a must. Whether you prefer *nouvelle, haute,* or traditional cuisine, Cajun specialties, regional or native dishes, French cooking is the world's greatest. Whether you eat in Paris or New Orleans, Algeria or Port-au-Prince, the city or the country, you can be sure that the food you are served is fresh and appetizing, and that it has been expertly and lovingly prepared by a chef who takes great pride in his or her work. And a good French wine can improve even the best meal.

Culture Capsule

Remember that champagne is made only from the grapes grown in the Champagne valley in France. So if you crave the real bubbly, make sure it's from France.

2. **You want to be totally irresistible, and you believe that speaking French will attract that special someone.** You're probably right. French, more than any other language, has the reputation of being "the language of love." It doesn't even matter what you say. Just whisper any of the beautiful, flowing, song-like phrases in someone's ear to "Wow!" them and to make their heart beat faster. It's practically foolproof.

Un deux trois

You don't have to go far to speak French: Louisiana, Maine, New Hampshire, Vermont, Massachusetts, Canada. Or, you could go across the globe to distant, exotic lands in Africa or Asia. More than 60 million tourists visit France each year. The possibilities and opportunities are endless.

1. **You love to travel.** In addition to France, there are more than 40 French-speaking countries in the world, where more than 100 million people speak French on a daily basis. Whether you travel for business or pleasure, romance or adventure, excitement or relaxation, your choices include: sensuous tropical islands with white, sandy beaches; lush rain forests with luxuriant, native vegetation; tempting snow-covered mountains perfect for winter sports; sweaty, sultry jungles where special thrills lurk everywhere; fortified ancient villages where history comes to life; or bustling, modern cities where the future rapidly unfolds.

Fast Forward

The best, most foolproof way to become proficient in something is to plunge right in. Immerse yourself in anything and everything that is French. Have a love affair with the language and the culture. Follow these suggestions to ensure an enduring and fulfilling relationship:

➤ **Examine your goals, honestly evaluate your linguistic abilities, and pace yourself accordingly.** Take your time, don't rush, and set aside special time each day that you devote only to French.

➤ **Invest in or borrow a good bilingual dictionary.** Pocket varieties (usually running between $6 and $15) may suit the needs of some learners but prove somewhat deficient for others. Carefully peruse what is available in your local bookstore or library before making a decision on what is best for you. Current popular dictionaries that are easy to use and that provide a comprehensive listing of modern, colloquial vocabulary words are published by a number of companies. The best include those by Simon and Schuster and Larousse. They can be found in any bookstore to fit any size pocketbook.

➤ **Take advantage of all available opportunities to listen to the language.** Rent French movies and try not to read the English subtitles. If broadcast in your area, listen to public service radio or television stations that provide French programs. Search bookstores and public or college libraries for language tapes that will help you hear and master the French sound system. Create your own tapes and use them to perfect your accent. Ask to use language laboratories and computer programs that are available in many high schools and universities.

➤ **Read everything you can get your hands on.** Fairy tales, children's books, comic books (*Astérix* is my personal favorite), newspapers (*Le Monde, France-Soir, Le Figaro, Libération, Le Dauphiné Libéré*), magazines (*Paris Match, Elle, L'Express, Marie-Claire*). If you're not too bashful, read aloud to practice your pronunciation and comprehension at the same time.

➤ **Surf the Net.** There are so many places you can go and things you can see at home on your computer. Take advantage of all the things the Web has to offer.

Un deux trois

If you're planning a trip to France, why not visit the official website of the French Government Tourist Office: **www.Frenchtourism.com**

Create *un coin français* (a French corner) in a convenient spot in your home. Decorate it with posters or articles. Label items whose names you want to learn and display them for easy viewing. Keep all your materials together and organized in this special French spot.

Forget Your Fear

Some people are truly afraid to study a foreign language. They think that it'll be too much work, too hard, too time-consuming. In reality, if you take it slow and don't allow yourself to become overly concerned with grammar and pronunciation, you will manage very well. To help you feel more at ease, try to remember the following:

➤ **Don't be intimidated by the grammar.** Everyone makes mistakes—even native speakers. And besides, you usually need only one or two correct words (especially verbs) to be understood.

➤ **Don't be intimidated by the pronunciation.** Put on your best French accent. Don't be shy and speak, speak, speak. In any country, there are many different regional accents. Certainly yours will fit in somewhere!

➤ **Don't be intimidated by the French.** They are perfectly lovely people and accept anyone who makes a sincere attempt to communicate.

➤ **Don't be intimidated when people tell you that French is difficult.** As you will see, almost immediately, French is easy and fun.

Bonne chance! (*Bohn shahNs!*) (Good luck!)

Let's begin *tout de suite* (*toot sweet*) (immediately)!

The Least You Need to Know

➤ Anyone and everyone, from all walks of life, can profit from studying French.

➤ French is very useful to know because it is an international language spoken daily throughout the world.

➤ You'll always get by, despite imperfections in your grammar and pronunciation.

➤ Fear not! Learning French is really easier than you think.

➤ To become a *francophone* (French speaker), you must first be a *francophile* (lover of French).

Chapter 2

Pronounce It Properly

In This Chapter

➤ When there's stress involved

➤ Go with the flow

➤ Perfecting your accent

➤ Phonetically fine

When you speak French, you want to sound like they do in the movies: irresistible, romantic, sexy, sophisticated, chic. It's only natural. So lose your inhibitions, put on your best French accent, and repeat and practice the sounds of the language. Although different from English, these sounds are not too difficult to master. Just follow the rules, learn the proper pronunciation of the phonetic symbols, be patient, and you're on your way!

This is a *work* chapter. It's not terribly exciting; it's not particularly fun; and it's not especially amusing—but don't be reluctant to see it through. Just like anything you might have to learn (a sport, a hobby, a trade, or a profession), there's work involved, and you must be committed to putting in a certain amount of effort and energy. Think of learning a language as a mental fitness routine. Start slowly and carefully work up to a pace that suits you. Remember, you don't want to burn yourself out at the first workout. So give it your best shot and practice, practice, practice. Oh là là, you'll be sounding like a native in no time!

Attention!

Avoid overstressing letters. Do not overemphasize letters, words, or syllables. Doing so ruins the sound of the language.

Memory Enhancer

Liaison links a final consonant with a beginning vowel. Elision eliminates a final pronounced *a* or *e* and replaces it with an apostrophe before a beginning pronounced vowel.

The Stress of It All

In French, each syllable of a word has just about equal stress. When speaking, try to pronounce each syllable of a word with equal emphasis. When you remember, place a slightly stronger emphasis on the last syllable of a group of words. Speak smoothly, speak musically, and speak evenly. My best advice: For maximum results, stay on an even keel.

Not Dangerous Liaisons— Elisions

Liaison (linking) and *elision* (sliding) are two elements of the French language that give it its fluidity and melodious beauty by smoothing out rough spots.

Liaison

Liaison refers to the linking of the final consonant of one word with the beginning vowel of the next word. There are many rules in French explaining when a liaison is mandatory, optional, and forbidden. I could go on for pages boring you with rules you'll probably never remember. Instead, simply follow the pronunciation guide provided in this chapter and the phonetic keys for words and phrases throughout the book. Make a liaison when you see that the pronunciation of the last consonant sound of one word precedes the beginning vowel of the next word. Look at the first example to get a better idea. The first word is *vous*, pronounced *voo*. Its final *s* (pronounced *z*) is linked to the beginning of the next word, *arrivez*. The pronunciation of this word is now *zah-ree-vay,* and the necessary liaison has been painlessly achieved. When in doubt, follow the guide.

Words	Liaison
Vous arrivez	*voo zah-ree-vay*
Mon ami	*mohN nah-mee*

Elision

Elision occurs when there are two pronounced vowel sounds: one at the end of a word, and the other at the beginning of the next word. The first vowel is dropped and replaced by an apostrophe. To pronounce the words, simply slide them together. If you try to say them separately, the vowel sounds will clash, and you will probably feel like you have a word stuck in your throat. Elision is a very natural device and gives the language fluidity. The following is an example of elision:

Words	Elision	Pronunciation
Je arrive	J'arrive	*zah-reev*
Le hôtel	l'hôtel	*lo-tehl*

Add a Little Accent Here

If this is your first experience with a foreign language, you'll probably be mystified by accent marks. Just think of them as pronunciation guideposts that help you speak like an old pro.

Working on Your Own Personal Accent

For some, French pronunciation is a breeze. If you are lucky enough to have been born with a "good ear," chances are you can carry a tune or play a musical instrument. You'll imitate the lilt, intonation, and stress without a problem.

For most of us, however, pronunciation is not without problems. If this is you, you're in good company. Consider my former college French literature teacher, a Rhodes scholar from Oxford University, who later went on to become chairman of the Romance Language Department. He was charming, interesting, sweet, very, very intellectual, well-read, and knowledgeable. He also had the worst French accent I have ever heard. He pronounced every word, every syllable, every letter so harshly and with such stress and emphasis that the students would sit in class squinting in pain. He butchered the pronunciation so much that it was memorable.

In my more naïve days, I often wondered why he would teach a language he obviously had so much trouble speaking. When I think back, I realize that it really didn't matter at all. Why? Because we all understood him despite his terrible pronunciation. And that, *débutant(e)s*, is a very valuable lesson for us all. No matter what you sound like (and you couldn't sound any worse than this teacher), if you use the correct vocabulary, you will be able to make yourself understood. That should be your goal. Nobody is going to laugh at you; they might just say "Pardon" more than usual. In the end, your level of competence in pronunciation is no big deal. So relax, try your best, and, above all, don't be discouraged.

Memory Enhancer

Remember: The accent grave over the *a* (*à*) doesn't change the pronunciation, whereas the *â* is given a longer sound.

Accent Marks

There are five different accent marks in French that may be used to change the sounds of letters (*é* versus *è*, *a* versus *â*, and so on), to differentiate between the meanings of two words whose spellings are otherwise the same (a *has* and à *to, at*, ou *or* and où *where*, and so on), or to replace an *s* that was part of the word many centuries ago in old French.

An *accent aigu* (´) is seen only on an *e* (*é*).

é produces the sound (*ay*), as in *day*.

An *accent grave* (`) is used with *a* (*à*), *e* (*è*), and *u* (*ù*).

On an *e*, an accent grave produces the sound of (*eh*), as in the *e* in the English word *met*.

It doesn't change the sound of the *a* (*à*) or *u* (*ù*).

An *accent circonflexe* can be used on all vowels: *â*, *ê*, *î*, *ô*, *û*. The vowel sounds are longer for *â* and *ô*, are slightly longer for *ê*, and are practically imperceptible on *î* and *û*.

A *cédille* (ç) is used only on a *c* (*ç*). When the *c* comes before *a*, *o*, or *u*, it means that you pronounce the letter as a soft *c* (the sound of *s*).

> **Memory Enhancer**
>
> The circumflex also often replaces an *s* from old French. Simply stick a mental *s* in the word to see if the meaning jumps out at you. For example: *arrêter* (as in *arrest*) or *fête* (as in *feast, festival*).

A *tréma* (¨) occurs on a second vowel in a series. This accent indicates that the two vowels are pronounced separately, each having its own distinct sound: Haïti (*ay-ee-tee*), Noël (*noh-ehl*).

> **Culture Capsule**
>
> The *é* may replace an *s* that used to exist in the word in old French. Adding a mental *s* immediately after *é* may enable you to easily determine the meaning of a word. See if the meaning jumps out at you:
>
> *éponge* (as in *sponge*)
>
> *étranger* (as in *stranger*)

Vowel Sounds Simplified

French vowels are a bit complicated. Why? In general, each vowel has a number of different sounds, and there are specific rules and accent marks that help you determine how a vowel is to be pronounced. I've included some practice exercises to help you. Some of the sentences are pretty silly, but they will help you learn how to pronounce the vowel sounds.

Memory Enhancer

Keep the following in mind:

H and *Y* are usually considered vowels in French.

French Letter	Symbol	Pronunciation Guide
a, à, â	ah	Say *a* as in *spa*

Open wide (but not too wide) and say *ahhh....*

ça	la	ma	sa	ta	va	papa	Canada
sah	*lah*	*mah*	*sah*	*tah*	*vah*	*pah-pah*	*kah-nah-dah*

French Letter	Symbol	Pronunciation Guide
é final *er* and *ez*; *es* in some one-syllable words; a few *ai, et* combinations	ay	Say *ay* as in *day*

é, final *er,* and *ez* are always pronounced *ay*. Instead of driving yourself crazy trying to remember the rules (which are vague), just look at the following guide:

bébé	télé	météo	été	René
bay-bay	*tay-lay*	*may-tay-o*	*ay-tay*	*ruh-nay*
danser	arriver	désirer	parler	tourner
dahN-say	*ah-ree-vay*	*day-zee-ray*	*pahr-lay*	*toor-nay*
chez	nez	allez	passez	assez
shay	*nay*	*ah-lay*	*pah-say*	*ah-say*
des	les	mes	tes	ces
day	*lay*	*may*	*tay*	*say*
ai	gai	et		
ay	*gay*	*ay*		

13

French Letter	Symbol	Pronunciation Guide
e in one-syllable words or in the middle of a word followed by a single consonant	uh	Say *e* as in *the*

Again, this is another rule that requires too much thought for simple conversational French. Consult the pronunciation guide until the rule becomes second nature.

ce	je	le	ne	de
suh	*zhuh*	*luh*	*nuh*	*duh*

regarder	venir	repasser	demander	prenons
ruh-gahr-day	*vuh-neer*	*ruh-pah-say*	*duh-mahN-day*	*pruh-nohN*

French Letter	Symbol	Pronunciation Guide
è, ê, and *e* (plus two consonants or a final pronounced consonant) *et, ei, ai*	eh	Say *e* as in *met*

At this point, don't overwhelm yourself with rules. When in doubt, let the guide do the work for you. With practice, you'll get the hang of it.

très	mère	père	achète	bibliothèque
treh	*mehr*	*pehr*	*ah-sheht*	*bee-blee-oh-tehk*
fête	tête	être	même	prêter
feht	*teht*	*ehtr*	*mehm*	*preh-tay*
est	sept	rester	concert	Suzette
eh	*seht*	*reh-stay*	*kohN-sehr*	*sew-zeht*
quel	sel	chef	cher	cette
kehl	*sehl*	*shehf*	*shehr*	*seht*
ballet	bonnet	jouet	complet	cabinet
bah-leh	*bohN-neh*	*zhoo-eh*	*kohN-pleh*	*kah-bee-neh*

seize	treize	Seine	peine	pleine
sehz	*trehz*	*sehn*	*pehn*	*plehn*
aider	jamais	chaise	mais	américaine
eh-day	*zhah-meh*	*shehz*	*meh*	*ah-may-ree-kehn*

French Letter	Symbol	Pronunciation Guide
i, î, y, ui	ee	Say *i* as in *magazine*

Smile and show your teeth when you say ee.

il	ici	midi	timide	visiter
eel	*ee-see*	*mee-dee*	*tee-meed*	*vee-zee-tay*
Sylvie	lycée	mystère	dîne	île
seel-vee	*lee-say*	*mee-stehr*	*deen*	*eel*
huit	nuit	qui	guide	bruit
weet	*nwee*	*kee*	*geed*	*brwee*

French Letter	Symbol	Pronunciation Guide
I+ll, il when preceded by a vowel	y	Say *y* as in *your*

For the *ill*, *ail*, or *eil* combinations, remember to keep the *l* silent.

fille	famille	gentille	billet	travail
fee-y	*fah-mee-y*	*zhahN-tee-y*	*bee-yeh*	*trah-vahy*
soleil	oeil	détail		
soh-lehy	*uhy*	*day-tahy*		

French Letter	Symbol	Pronunciation Guide
i + ll in these words only	eel	Say the word *eel*

Every rule has an exception; or in this case, because there aren't too many, the words might be worth memorizing—especially because they're used frequently.

| ville | village | mille | million | tranquille |
| *veel* | *vee-lahzh* | *meel* | *mee-lyohN* | *trahN-keel* |

French Letter	Symbol	Pronunciation Guide
o (before *se*), *o* (last pronounced sound of word), *ô, au, eau*	o	Say *o* as in *no*

Keep your lips rounded to pronounce this very open *o* sound. Once again, for o, there are many letter combinations you will have to eventually learn. For the time being, follow the pronunciation guide.

radio *rah-dyo*	trop *tro*	mot *mo*	stylo *stee-lo*	vélo *vay-lo*
hôtel *o-tehl*	allô *ah-lo*	tôt *to*	bientôt *byaN-to*	hôpital *o-pee-tahl*
au *o*	aussi *o-see*	jaune *zhon*	autre *otr*	auteur *o-tuhr*
eau *o*	beau *bo*	cadeau *kah-do*	gâteau *gah-to*	manteau *mahN-to*

French Letter	Symbol	Pronunciation Guide
o when followed by a pronounced consonant other than *s*	oh	*o* as in *love*

This *o* sound is not nearly as rounded and open as the one before. It may take some practice to distinguish between the two. If you can't, don't worry—chances are no one is listening that closely anyway. As you practice, try to hear the difference.

notre *nohtr*	pomme *pohm*	donner *doh-nay*	téléphone *tay-lay-fohn*	octobre *ohk-tohbr*

French Letter	Symbol	Pronunciation Guide
ou, où, oû	oo	Say *oo* as in *tooth*

Round your lips to say *oo*.

toujours *too-zhoor*	écouter *ay-koo-tay*	douze *dooz*	doux *doo*	beaucoup *bo-koo*
où *oo*	goût *goo*			

French Letter	Symbol	Pronunciation Guide
oy, oi	wah	Say *w* as in *watch*

moi	trois	soir	froid	voiture	pourquoi
mwah	*trwah*	*swahr*	*frwah*	*vwah-tewr*	*poor-kwah*
voyage	voyez				
vwah-yahzh	*vwah-yay*				

French Letter	Symbol	Pronunciation Guide
u, û	ew	No equivalent

There really is no English sound that is equivalent to the French *u* sound. Try the following for best results: Say the sound *oo* as in *Sue* while trying to say *ee* as in *see*. As you try to make the sound, concentrate on puckering your lips as if you just ate a very sour pickle. That's about as close as you can get. If you say *oo*, don't worry, you'll be understood. This is a foreign sound that requires concentration and practice.

super	sur	tu	du	une	salut
sew-pehr	*sewr*	*tew*	*dew*	*ewn*	*sah-lew*

You're Supposed to Sound Nasal!

You must use your nose and your mouth to produce a French nasal sound. Here's how it's done: Hold your nose, then use your mouth to say the vowel sound. It's that simple. Of course you're not going to walk around with your hand on your nose. That's just a technique to get you started and to make you aware of what a nasal sound should sound like. We are so accustomed to English pronunciation that we never stop to consider how we produce sounds. When learning a foreign language, it's necessary to pause and think about the sounds we want to make.

Attention!

Be careful: There is no nasal sound in the following combinations:

vowel + MM, vowel + M + vowel, vowel + NN, vowel + N + vowel

For example:

homme is pronounced *ohm*

bonne is pronounced *bohn*

Nasal sounds occur when a vowel is followed by a single *N* or *M* in the same syllable. In the pronunciation guide, you will see a vowel sound followed by *N*. This indicates that you must make a nasal sound.

French Nasal	Symbol	Pronunciation Guide
an (am), en (em)	ahN	Similar to *on* with little emphasis on *n*

Now hold your nose, say **on,** and you'll quickly get the hang of it. Watch for the N indicating the vowel sound.

Français	dans	anglais	grand	lampe
frahN-seh	*dahN*	*ahN-gleh*	*grahN*	*lahNp*
maman	ambiance	ambition	en	encore
mah-mahN	*ahN-byahNs*	*ahN-bee-syohN*	*ahN*	*ahN-kohr*
souvent	attendre	décembre	temps	sembler
soo-vahN	*ah-tahNdr*	*day-sahNbr*	*tahN*	*sahN-blay*
employé				
ahN-plwah-yay				

French Nasal	Symbol	Pronunciation Guide
in (im), ain (aim)	aN	Similar to *an* with little emphasis on *n*

Hold your nose again and practice the sounds:

cinq	Martin	cousin	demain	américain
saNk	*mahr-taN*	*koo-zaN*	*duh-maN*	*ah-may-ree-kaN*
simple	important	impossible	impatient	faim
saNpl	*aN-pohr-tahN*	*aN-poh-seebl*	*aN-pah-syahN*	*faN*

French Nasal	Symbol	Pronunciation Guide
oin	waN	Similar to *wa* of *wag*

You should be getting the hang of nasals by now. Try these:

loin	coin	moins	point	soin
lwaN	*kwaN*	*mwaN*	*pwaN*	*swaN*

French Nasal	Symbol	Pronunciation Guide
ien	yaN	Similar to *yan* of *Yankee*

Try these sounds:

bien	rien	vient	italien	Lucien
byaN	*ryaN*	*vyaN*	*ee-tahl-yaN*	*lew-syaN*

French Nasal	Symbol	Pronunciation Guide
on (om)	ohN	Similar to *on* as in *long*

Here are some more to try:

on	bon	sont	non	onze
ohN	*bohN*	*sohN*	*nohN*	*ohNz*

pardon	tomber	bombe	comprendre	compter
pahr-dohN	*tohN-bay*	*bohNb*	*kohN-prahNdr*	*kohN-tay*

combien				
kohN-byaN				

French Nasal	Symbol	Pronunciation Guide
un (um)	uhN	Similar to *un* as in *under*

Be patient for the last of the nasal sounds:

un	brun	lundi	parfum	emprunter
uhN	*bruhN*	*luhN-dee*	*pahr-fuhN*	*ahN-pruhN-tay*

Consonants Are Easy!

Most final consonants are not pronounced except for final *c, r, f,* and *l.* A final *s* is not pronounced in French, so avoid the temptation. Doing so will quickly unveil your amateur status.

Éric	Luc	avec	parc	amour
ay-reek	*lewk*	*ah-vehk*	*pahrk*	*ah-moor*

bonjour	tour	cour	neuf	sauf
bohN-zhoor	*toor*	*koor*	*nuhf*	*sof*

chef	actif	il	Michel	journal
shehf	*ahk-teef*	*eel*	*mee-shehl*	*zhoor-nahl*

cheval				
shuh-vahl				

But

salut	dessert	beaucoup	minutes
sah-lew	*duh-sehr*	*bo-koo*	*mee-newt*

French Letter	Symbol	Pronunciation Guide
b, d, f, k, l, m, n, p, s, t, v, z	The same	Same as English

These letters are all so easy because they are pronounced exactly the same in French and in English. You will, however, have to follow the rules for the pronunciation of other consonants.

French Letter	Symbol	Pronunciation Guide
c (hard sound before *a, o, u*, or consonant) *qu*, final *q*	k	Say *c* as in *card*

carte *kahrt*	court *koor*	document *doh-kew-mahN*	classe *klahs*	qui *kee*
quoi *kwah*	quatre *kahtr*	pourquoi *poor-kwah*	cinq *saNk*	

French Letter	Symbol	Pronunciation Guide
c (soft sound before *e, i, y*), *ç, s* at beginning of word, *s* next to a consonant, *tion* (*t*), *x* (only in the words given)	s	*cent*

As you can see, there are lots of ways to get the *s* sound. Practice them all:

ce *suh*	cinéma *see-nay-mah*	Nancy *nahN-see*	ça *sah*	nation *nah-syohN*
attention *ah-tahN-syohN*	invitation *aN-vee-tah-syohNn*	action *ahk-syohN*	six *sees*	dix *dees*
soixante *swah-sahNt*				

French Letter	Symbol	Pronunciation Guide
ch	sh	Say the *ch* in *machine*

We've all had practice with this sound—especially those of us with children. *Shhh.*

chanter	chocolat	sandwich	toucher
shahN-tay	*shoh-koh-lah*	*sahNd-weesh*	*too-shay*

French Letter	Symbol	Pronunciation Guide
g (hard sound before *a, o, u,* or consonant), *gu* (before *i, e, y*)	g	Say the *g* in *good*

These words should present no problem:

garçon	goûter	glace	légume
gahr-sohN	*goo-tay*	*glahs*	*lay-gewm*
Guy	bague	fatigué	guide
gee	*bahg*	*fah-tee-gay*	*geed*

French Letter	Symbol	Pronunciation Guide
g (soft sound before *e, i, y*), *ge* (soft before *a, o*), *j*	zh	Say the *s* as in *pleasure*

This might take a little practice before you get used to it:

garage	girafe	Gisèle	Égypte
gah-razh	*zhee-rahf*	*zhee-zehl*	*ay-zheept*
âge	orange	manger	voyageons
ahzh	*oh-rahNzh*	*mahN-zhay*	*vwah-yah-zhohN*
je	jour	jaune	jupe
zhuh	*zhoor*	*zhon*	*zhewp*

French Letter	Symbol	Pronunciation Guide
gn	ny	Say the *n* as in *union*

This sound will take some practice, too. Be careful not to overemphasize it:

montagne	Espagne	gagner	accompagner
mohN-tah-nyuh	*ehs-pah-nyuh*	*gah-nyay*	*ah-kohN-pah-nyay*

French Letter	Symbol	Pronunciation Guide
h		Always silent

We've come to the easiest letter of all. *H* is always silent. Most of the time, it is used as a vowel and, therefore, requires elision with a vowel that might precede it: *l'homme* (*the man*). In other instances, *h* is used as a consonant and does not require elision with the preceding vowel: *le héros*. To tell how *h* is being used, you must look in a dictionary, where the consonant *h* is usually indicated with an *.

huit	hôtel	heure	homme
weet	*o-tehl*	*uhr*	*ohm*

French Letter	Symbol	Pronunciation Guide
r	r	No equivalent

The French *r* requires the participation of your throat. First, drop your tongue to the bottom of your mouth and rest it against your teeth. Keep it pressed there, out of your way. Now clear your throat or gargle and say "r" at the back of your throat at the same time. That's it; you've got the French *r*. A few words of advice: Do not roll your *r*; that's what they do in Spanish. Do not roll your tongue; that's what we do in English. This will require a fair amount of practice on your part until you get it down pat.

merci	au revoir	parler	rentrer
mehr-see	*o ruh-vwahr*	*pahr-lay*	*rahN-tray*

French Letter	Symbol	Pronunciation Guide
s (between vowels), *sion*	z	Say *z* as in *zero*

This sound is easy:

musée	musique	cousin	télévision
mew-zay	*mew-zeek*	*koo-zaN*	*tay-lay-vee-zyohN*

French Letter	Symbol	Pronunciation Guide
th	t	Say *t* as in *to*

There is no **th** sound in French. Native French speakers have a tremendous amount of difficulty with our words *the*, *this*, and *there* because they pronounce *th* as *t*. You, of course, will want to say *th*. Don't. Your nationality will be showing again.

Catherine	thé	théâtre	sympathique
kah-treen	*tay*	*tay-ahtr*	*saN-pah-teek*

French Letter	Symbol	Pronunciation Guide
x	ks	Say *xc* as in *excel*

This last sound (that's right, we've finally reached the end) is a little tricky. Practice it well:

extra	mixte	excellent	exprimer
ehks-trah	*meekst*	*ehk-seh-lahN*	*ehks-pree-may*

Wow Them With Your Accent

Now that you are an expert, put on your best accent and practice pronouncing these names that were taken from a Parisian phone book:

1. Éric Le Parc
2. Colette Lapierre
3. Michel Lechien
4. Alain Lechat
5. Agnès Leloup
6. Roland Lamouche
7. Patrick Leboeuf
8. Solange Laforêt
9. Philippe Lebec
10. Florence Lavigne
11. Monique Le Pont
12. Dominique Lafontaine
13. Daniel La Tour
14. Jean Levache
15. Jeanne Larivière
16. Hubert La Fleur

En 10 Minutes

Chapter 1 suggested that you collect newspaper articles. Now is the time to put them to use. Sit in front of a mirror. If possible, record yourself. Read one paragraph from an article that interests you. Watch your face and the movement of your lips and tongue.

Culture Capsule

Many French family names begin with *Le* and *La* and are taken from elements in nature. It really does lend an extra beauty to the language when the people are named for beautiful things. However, I am sure that Jean Lavache (*John the Cow*) would probably have been happier had his ancestors been associated with something different.

The Least You Need to Know

➤ Reading aloud from French newspapers, magazines, and literature will help you lose your inhibitions and perfect your accent.

➤ While speaking the language, allow yourself to slide the sounds together by using liaison and elision.

➤ Even if your accent isn't up to snuff, you'll still be understood and your attempts will be appreciated.

➤ Practice and good listening skills will improve your accent.

➤ Use your nose correctly to pronounce French nasal sounds.

Chapter 3

The French You Know

In This Chapter

➤ Cognates help with comprehension

➤ Tricks that work

➤ French words used in English

➤ Avoiding mistakes

Café, *restaurant*, *amateur*, *boutique*, *bureau*—you already know many French words. You see, you really do know a lot of French. You don't realize it yet, but your vocabulary is filled with French words and phrases. And there are plenty of French words and expressions that you will find very easy to use and understand with a minimal amount of effort. By the end of this chapter, you will be well on your way to producing simple but intelligent sentences that allow you to express feelings, thoughts, and opinions.

I Know This Already!

There is absolutely nothing on television. After watching the French news on a local cable station, my husband (who has no French blood coursing through his veins) takes off for the local video rental store to choose some entertainment for the evening. An hour later he returns with a wide grin on his face and cheerfully exclaims: "Oiseau ([*wah-zo*] that's French for bird, his term of endearment for me), I've got a surprise for you." I wait in eager anticipation to hear that he rented a hot, new release fresh from the theater. Instead, he informs me that he picked out the latest French film.

As a francophile, I should be jumping for joy. But he can read the disappointment on my face. Truth be told, I find French movies lacking in adventure, and I don't love character studies. The subtitles are extremely distracting. He, on the other hand, can't wait to get the film into the VCR, and I can't understand why. It's true that he had two years of college French, but that was over 30 years ago. And I did all his homework. The Cs he passed with were certainly not an indication of a love affair with the language. So why French films? He likes exotic movies, he loves to hear the language, and, believe it or not, he can understand what the actors and actresses are saying. How can that be? He never listened as a student. How does the man do it?

The answer is *cognates*. What are they? Quite simply, a *cognate* is a word that is spelled exactly the same, or almost the same, as a word in English and that has the same meaning. Sometimes we've actually borrowed the word from the French, letter for letter, and have incorporated it into our own vocabulary. Sure, the cognates are pronounced differently in each language, but the meaning of the French word is quite obvious to anyone who speaks English.

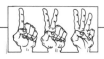

Un deux trois

There is no way to easily determine the gender of a French noun, so it is best to learn the noun with its corresponding article. See Chapter 6, "French—The Sexy Language," for a more detailed explanation. For now, just remember:

le is for masculine singular nouns.

la is for feminine singular nouns.

l' is for any singular noun that begins with a vowel.

A Perfect Match

The table below contains a list of cognates, which are words that have exactly the same meaning in both French and English. Take your time pronouncing the French words and compare them to their English equivalents. Your goal is to sound French.

All French nouns (people, places, things, ideas) have an assigned gender. This might seem strange to you at first, because we do not have anything similar in English. For now, just remember that if you want to say that French is easy, you must use the definite article: "Le français est facile."

When you look at the following list, notice that most French nouns are listed under a specific definite article: *le* or *la*. These articles both mean "the" and indicate the gender of the noun (masculine or feminine, respectively). If you are very observant, you will see that *l'* is used with nouns beginning with a vowel.

Perfect Cognates

Adjectives		Nouns		
	Le	*La*	*L'*	
blond	ballet	blouse	accident	
blohN	*bah-leh*	*blooz*	*ahk-see-dahN*	
certain	chef	date	ambulance	
sehr-taN	*shehf*	*daht*	*ahN-bew-lahNs*	
content	client	dispute	animal	
kohN-tahN	*klee-yahN*	*dees-pewt*	*ah-nee-mahl*	
horrible	hamburger	note	olive	
oh-reebl	*ahm-bewr-gehr*	*noht*	*oh-leev*	
immense	journal	photo	orange	
ee-mahNs	*zhoor-nahl*	*foh-to*	*oh-rahnzh*	

You Understand So Much Already!

I'd venture to guess that, by now, you're in the same league as my husband. The following sentences should be a snap to understand, and the pronunciation should be no problem if you patiently follow the key. Don't be shy! Give it your best effort.

Read the following sentences in French. What are you saying? (*Est* means *is* in French.)

1. La blouse est orange.
   lah blooz eh toh-rahNzh

2. Le service est horrible.
   luh sehr-vees eh toh-reebl

3. Le sandwich est immense.
   luh sahN-weesh eh tee-mahNs

4. Le chef est excellent.
   luh shehf eh tehk-seh-lahN

5. Le client est certain.
   luh klee-yahN eh sehr-taN

Now try a few with some new words:

1. Le pull-over est rose.
   luh pewl-oh-vehr eh roz

2. Le film est important.
   luh feelm eh taN-pohr-tahN

3. La question est unique.
   lah kehs-tyohN eh tew-neek

Attention!

All adjectives in French must agree in number and gender with the nouns they modify. The rules governing the agreement of adjectives will be discussed in detail in Chapter 9.

4. Le voyage est urgent.
   luh vwah-yahzh eh tewr-zhahN

5. Le guide est intelligent.
   luh geed eh taN-teh-lee-zhahN

An Almost Perfect Match

The following table lists the cognates that are nearly the same in both French and English. Take your time pronouncing the French words and compare them to their English equivalents. Remember: Your goal is to sound French.

Near Cognates

Adjectives		Nouns	
	Le	*La*	*L'*
amusant *ah-mew-zahN*	cinéma *see-nay-mah*	cathédrale *kah-tay-drahl*	agence *ah-zhahNs*
ancien *ahN-syaN*	dictionnaire *deek-syoh-nehr*	chambre *shahNbr*	anniversaire *ah-nee-vehr-sehr*
bleu *bluh*	dîner *dee-nay*	couleur *koo-luhr*	appartement *ah-pahr-tuh-mahN*
confortable *kohN-fohr-tahbl*	docteur *dohk-tuhr*	famille *fah-mee-y*	éléphant *ay-lay-fahN*
délicieux *day-lee-syuh*	jardin *zhahr-daN*	fontaine *fohN-tehn*	employé *ahN-plwah-yay*
difficile *dee-fee-seel*	lampe *lahNp*	exemple *ehks-zahNpl*	hôtel *o-tehl*
élégant *ay-lay-gahN*	mécanicien *may-kah-nee-syaN*	lettre *lehtr*	oncle *ohNkl*
fatigué *fah-tee-gay*	papier *pah-pyay*	marchandise *mahr-shahN-deez*	opticien *ohp-tee-syaN*
intéressant *aN-tay-reh-sahN*	moteur *moh-tuhr*	musique *mew-zeek*	orchestre *ohr-kehstr*
magnifique *mah-nyee-feek*	président *pray-zee-dahN*	nationalité *nah-syoh-nah-lee-tay*	
occupé *oh-kew-pay*	professeur *proh-feh-suhr*	personne *pehr-sohn*	
populaire *poh-pew-lehr*	programme *proh-grahm*	pharmacie *fahr-mah-see*	

Adjectives		Nouns	
	Le	*La*	*L'*
riche *reesh*	supermarché *sew-pehr-mahr-shay*	salade *sah-lahd*	
sérieux *say-ryuh*	téléphone *tay-lay-fohn*	soupe *soop*	
sincère *saN-sehr*	théâtre *tay-ahtr*	télévision *tay-lay-vee-zyohN*	
splendide *splahN-deed*	touriste *too-reest*	tomate *toh-maht*	
superbe *sew-pehrb*	vendeur *vahN-duhr*		

Versatile Verbs

Many French verbs (words that show action or a state of being) are so similar to their English counterparts that you will recognize their meaning almost immediately. The majority of French verbs fall into one of three families: the *er* family, the *ir* family, and the *re* family. This concept is foreign to us, since English has borrowed so much from so many different languages that no "verb families" exist. For now, you will see that the largest French family, by far, is the *er* family. Any verbs belonging to a family are considered *regular*, while those that do not belong to a family are designated as *irregular*. Each family has its own set of rules, which are explained in Chapter 7. All irregular verbs must be memorized.

Attention!

Verbs in French are conjugated to agree with their subjects. The rules governing verb conjugation are explained in Chapter 7.

Look at the three major families and see if you can determine the meanings of the verbs presented in the following table.

Verb Families

The ER Family			
accompagner	*ah-kohN-pah-nyay*	inviter	*aN-vee-tay*
adorer	*ah-doh-ray*	marcher	*mahr-shay*
aider	*eh-day*	modifier	*moh-dee-fyay*
blâmer	*blah-may*	observer	*ohb-sehr-vay*

continues

Verb Families (cont.)

The ER Family

changer	*shahN-zhay*	pardonner	*pahr-doh-nay*
chanter	*shahN-tay*	passer	*pah-say*
commander	*koh-mahN-day*	payer	*peh-yay*
commencer	*koh-mahN-say*	persuader	*pehr-swah-day*
danser	*dahN-say*	porter	*pohr-tay*
décider	*day-see-day*	préférer	*pray-fay-ray*
déclarer	*day-klah-ray*	préparer	*pray-pah-ray*
demander	*duh-mahN-day*	présenter	*pray-zahN-tay*
désirer	*day-zee-ray*	prouver	*proo-vay*
dîner	*dee-nay*	recommander	*ruh-koh-mahN-day*
échanger	*ay-shahN-zhay*	refuser	*ruh-few-zay*
embrasser	*ahN-brah-say*	regarder	*ruh-gahr-day*
entrer	*ahN-tray*	regretter	*ruh-greh-tay*
hésiter	*ay-zee-tay*	remarquer	*ruh-mahr-kay*
ignorer	*ee-nyoh-ray*	réparer	*ray-pah-ray*
signer	*see-nyay*	réserver	*ray-zehr-vay*
tourner	*toor-nay*	vérifier	*vay-ree-fyay*

The IR Family

accomplir	*ah-kohN-pleer*
applaudir	*ah-plo-deer*
finir	*fee-neer*

The RE Family

défendre	*day-fahNdr*
répondre	*ray-pohNdr*
vendre	*vahNdr*

You've Got It!

As a matter of fact, this is so easy that you can easily read and understand these sentences without any problem at all:

Un deux trois

Note that many French verbs belong to the ER family. Become familiar with ER verbs first.

1. Le docteur aide le bébé.
    luh dohk-tuhr ehd luh bay-bay

2. Maman prépare de la soupe et de la salade.
    mah-mahN pray-pahr duh lah soop ay duh lah sah-lahd

3. Le mécanicien répare le moteur.
    luh may-kah-nee-syaN ray-pahr luh moh-tuhr

4. La famille regarde la télévision.
    lah fah-mee-y ruh-gahrd lah tay-lay-vee-zyohN

5. Le touriste réserve la chambre.
    luh too-reest ray-sehrv lah shahNbr

6. Le guide recommande le café.
    luh geed ruh-koh-mahNd luh kah-fay

7. L'employé vend la marchandise.
    l'ahN-plwah-yay vahN lah mahr-shahN-deez

8. L'enfant adore la musique moderne.
    lahN-fahN ah-dohr lah mew-zeek moh-dehrn

9. L'acteur préfère l'opéra italien.
    lahk-tuhr pray-fehr l'oh-pay-rah ee-tah-lyaN

10. Le professeur présente le programme.
    luh proh-feh-suhr pray-zahNt luh proh-grahm

What Do You Think?

Imagine that you are a tourist in a French-speaking country. Use what you've learned to express the following opinions to a fellow tourist:

1. The garden is splendid.
2. The fountain is superb.
3. The artist is popular.
4. The music is splendid.
5. The restaurant is elegant.

Un deux trois

Prepare several flash cards with an English word on one side and its equivalent French cognate, along with the proper pronunciation, on the other. Practice looking at the English and giving the correct French pronunciation. Try not to peek!

6. The theater is old.

7. The cathedral is magnificent.

8. The actor is tired.

9. The hotel is elegant.

10. The opera is amusing.

Some special tricks on pronunciation have already been mentioned in Chapter 2. When you look at the following table, you will see how adding an *s* after an accent circonflexe (ˆ) and how substituting an *s* for an *é* or adding one after it will help you figure out the meanings of many words.

Special Tricks

accent (ˆ)	English	é	English
arrêter *(ah-ruh-tay)*	to arrest	écarlate *(ay-kahr-laht)*	scarlet
bête *(beht)*	beast	échapper *(ay-shah-pay)*	to escape
conquête *(kohN-keht)*	conquest	école *(ay-kohl)*	school
coûter *(koo-tay)*	to cost	épars *(ay-pahr)*	sparse
croûte *(kroot)*	crust	épellation *(ay-puh-lah-syohN)*	spelling
fête *(feht)*	feast	épice *(ay-pees)*	spice
forêt *(foh-reh)*	forest	épier *(ay-pyay)*	to spy
hôpital *(o-pee-tahl)*	hospital	éponge *(ay-pohNzh)*	sponge
hôte *(ot)*	host	épouser *(ay-poo-zay)*	to espouse

Now see if you can complete the list:

accent (ˆ)	English	é	English
hôtesse *(o-tehs)*	_____	état *(ay-tah)*	_____
île *(eel)*	_____	étrange *(ay-trahNzh)*	_____
intérêt *(aN-teh-reh)*	_____	étude *(ay-tewd)*	_____
pâte *(paht)*	_____	répondre *(ray-pohNdr)*	_____

What We've Borrowed

Are you a *gourmet* cook or a *chef*? Do you live near a large *avenue* or *boulevard*? Do you enjoy *ballet*? In America, a truly multi-cultural society, we readily borrow and accept things from other backgrounds that suit our wants and needs and that make our life more meaningful, fulfilling, and interesting. And so we've borrowed a great many words from the French that we use on a daily basis. We've adopted these words and have made them a part of our everyday vocabulary. We even assume, incorrectly, that these words are English when they are not.

Culture Capsule

The French are very resistant to the infiltration of American words, politely called *franglais,* into their language. Many of our words have, indeed, slowly crept into French: *le jean, le fax, le walkman, le C.D., le club, le jazz, le steak,* and *le week-end,* for example. The French government, through the Académie Française, tries to limit their use as much as possible by prohibiting foreign words in official texts, advertisements, and announcements for employment opportunities.

French Awareness

The following French words and expressions are widely used by most of us. Define as many of them as you can:

1. à la carte
2. à la mode
3. bon voyage
4. c'est la vie
5. carte blanche
6. chic
7. coup d'état
8. crème de la crème
9. de rigueur
10. débutante
11. déjà vu
12. esprit de corps
13. fait accompli
14. faux pas
15. gourmet

16. joie de vivre
17. naïve
18. objet d'art
19. pièce de résistance
20. R.S.V.P.
21. rendez-vous
22. vis-à-vis

Attention!

The meanings of some words, called *cognates*, are obvious because they are identical, or very close, to their English equivalents. These words must be pronounced with your very best French accent. Be on the lookout, however, for French words that look like English words but that have a completely different meaning, which are known as *false friends*.

False Friends (*Faux Amis*)

Just when you think you know it all, exceptions pop up to prevent you from becoming overly confident. *Faux amis* (false friends) are words spelled exactly the same or almost the same in both French and English, but which have very different meanings in each language and might even be different parts of speech. Don't fall into the trap of thinking that every French word that looks like an English one is automatically a cognate. It's not quite that simple. Beware of the *faux amis* listed in the following table.

False Friends

English	Part of speech	French	Part of speech	Meaning
attend	verb	attendre *(ah-tahNdr)*	verb	to wait
bless	verb	blesser *(bleh-say)*	verb	to wound
comment	noun	comment *(koh-mahN)*	adverb	how
figure	noun	la figure *(lah fee-gewr)*	noun	face
library	noun	la librairie *(lah lee-breh-ree)*	noun	bookstore
liver	noun	le livre *(luh leevr)*	noun	book
occasion	noun	l'occasion *(loh-kah-zyohN)*	noun	opportunity
prune	noun	la prune *(lah prewn)*	noun	plum
raisin	noun	le raisin *(luh reh-zaN)*	noun	grape
rest	verb	rester *(rehs-tay)*	verb	to remain
sale	noun	sale *(sahl)*	adjective	dirty
sang	verb	le sang *(luh sahN)*	noun	blood
sensible	adjective	sensible *(sahN-seebl)*	adjective	sensitive
stage	noun	le stage *(luh stahzh)*	noun	training course

English	Part of speech	French	Part of speech	Meaning
store	noun	le store *(luh stohr)*	noun	shade
travel	verb	travailler *(trah-vah-yay)*	verb	to work

You Are Well Read

The famous French literary titles listed here all contain cognates. Give their English equivalents:

Anouilh—*Le Sauvage*

Balzac—*La Comédie humaine*

Baudelaire—*Les Paradis artificiels*

Camus—*L'Étranger*

Cocteau—*La Machine Infernale*

Cocteau—*Les Enfants terribles*

Colette—*La Vagabonde*

Flaubert—*L'Éducation sentimentale*

Gide—*La Symphonie pastorale*

Hugo—*Les Misérables*

Laclos—*Les Liaisons dangereuses*

Malraux—*La Condition humaine*

Molière—*Le Malade imaginaire*

Prévert—*Spectacle*

Rousseau—*Confessions*

Sartre—*La Nausée*

Voltaire—*Lettres Philosophiques*

Zola—*La Joie de Vivre*

Culture Capsule

Literature plays a very important role in the intellectual life in France. For centuries, world-renowned writers have been held in the highest esteem and considered national heroes. Many have received the prestige and respect of a national funeral and are buried in the Panthéon, where the inscription on the front portal reads: "Aux grands hommes, la patrie reconnaissante" (To the great men, the fatherland is grateful).

Now You're a Pro

You can identify the sections of the newspaper shown below because you really do know a lot of French already. Give the English meaning and explain what the articles are about:

ACTUALITÉ
Les vertus thérapeutiques du champagne

SPORT
Cyclisme: Milan–San Remo

SCIENCES ET MÉDECINE
La Tuberculose, première cause de mortalité chez les adultes

INTERNATIONAL
Québec: le référendum sur l'indépendance
La question en question

The Least You Need to Know

➤ Cognates are words that look exactly or almost the same in English and French and that have the same meaning in both languages. They allow you to express yourself in French with a minimal amount of effort.

➤ We use many French words and expressions in English every day.

➤ Beware of false friends—words spelled the same or almost the same in both languages—that have different meanings in each language. Don't let them trap you into mistakes.

Chapter 4

Idiomatically Speaking

In This Chapter

➤ What are idioms and how do we use them?

➤ What is slang and should we use it?

➤ Using body language to express yourself

Idioms are very important to a complete and correct understanding of the language. Imagine a beautiful young woman walking along the Champs-Élysées, an elegant, tree-lined avenue in Paris. Two men approach from the opposite direction and look her up and down. She hears one man casually say to the other "Oh là là. Elle a du chien." The young lady, having taken a year or two of French in school hears *elle* (she) and *chien* (dog). She immediately puts two and two together and thinks these men have called her a "dog." If she is extraordinarily brazen, perhaps she even smacks one across the face. She has just made a terrible mistake. What she doesn't understand is the idiomatic expression *avoir du chien*, which in English means *to be alluring, sexy.* The English equivalent of what the men said was really: "Boy, is she attractive."

Idioms Aren't for Idiots!

So what exactly is an idiom? In any language, an *idiom* is a particular word or expression whose meaning cannot be readily understood by either its grammar or the words used. Examples of some common English idioms are:

To look on the bright side.   To fall head over heels.

On the other hand.   To be down and out.

Idioms Versus Slang

What's the difference between an idiom and slang? *Slang* refers to colorful, popular words or phrases that are not part of the standard vocabulary of a language. Slang is considered unconventional. Many of these words evolved as needed to describe particular things or situations. Here are some examples of English slang:

Give me a break!   Get real!

Tough luck!   Get a life!

Idioms are acceptable in oral and written phrases, whereas slang, although freely used in informal conversations, generally is considered substandard in formal writing or speaking. Much slang is, at best, x-rated.

Take Your Pick

Take a look at some of these popular expressions used in sentences. I'm sure you will immediately realize that it would be impossible to translate them into French. Certainly they couldn't be translated word for word. Which are they, idioms or slang?

You drive me crazy!   Keep your shirt on!

Don't jump the gun!   I'm always on the go.

It's raining cats and dogs!   We'll just have to kill some time.

I'm going to call your bluff.   Did you fall for it?

Did you recognize that these are idiomatic expressions we use in English all the time? Good for you. Now compare those sentences with the following:

That's tacky!   What a cop out!

She just flipped out!   Don't dis my friend.

Do you notice how these slang sentences differ from the idiomatic ones? Excellent! You probably won't be using much French slang, but the idioms sure will come in handy.

There are many idioms in French. In this chapter, we will look at six categories of idioms that you might find helpful: travel and transportation, time, location and direction, expressing opinions, physical conditions, and weather conditions. Other idiomatic expressions will appear in their appropriate chapters.

Getting Off to a Fast Start

Let's say you are taking a trip. We might ask: "Are you going on a plane or on a boat?" The French word for *on* is *sur* (sewr). If you said: "Je vais sur l'avion," however, that would imply you were flying on the exterior of the plane, which is truly impossible. It is well worth your time to learn the idiomatic expressions covered in the table below.

Memory Enhancer

The preposition *en* is usually used when you are traveling inside of something, such as a subway. Use *à* when you expect to feel your hair blowing in the breeze.

Idioms for Travel and Transportation

Idiom	Pronunciation	Meaning
à bicyclette	*ah bee-see-kleht*	by bicycle
à cheval	*ah shuh-vahl*	on horseback
à moto	*ah moh-to*	by scooter
à pied	*ah pyeh*	on foot
en automobile	*ahN no-toh-moh-beel*	by car
en avion	*ahN nah-vyohN*	by plane
en bateau	*ahN bah-to*	by boat
en bus	*ahN bews*	by bus
en métro	*ahN may-tro*	by subway
en taxi	*ahN tahk-see*	by taxi
en train	*ahN traN*	by train
en voiture	*ahN vwah-tewr*	by car

Using Your Idioms I (or And You're Off)

Tell how you would get to the following places:

Example: the drugstore   à pied

1. Your place of business or school
2. The movies
3. Your doctor
4. The nearest hospital
5. Europe
6. The park
7. A tropical island
8. A fishing trip
9. A museum
10. The library

Culture Capsule

Only some areas in France provide bus service (*cars de ramassage*) for students. Most French students, who must provide their own means of transportation to school, drive a moped (*une mobylette*) after the age of 14. Buses, on the whole, are not a very popular means of transportation in the country, because subway and rail systems are extraordinarily clean, comfortable, efficient, and fast.

Memory Enhancer

Use the preposition *à* to express *until* before a time period when you expect to see someone at a later time. For example: *à lundi* (until Monday).

It's That Time

For some travelers, time is of the essence. They make sure they get that wake-up call bright and early in the morning. They want to be on the go as soon as possible. For others, it's not important at all. They don't even wear a watch. They're on vacation, and time is simply unimportant. Whether you're time-conscious or not, the idioms in the following table will serve you well.

Time Expressions

Idiom	Pronunciation	Meaning
à bientôt	*ah byaN-to*	see you soon
à ce soir	*ah suh swahr*	until this evening
à demain	*ah duh-maN*	until tomorrow
à l'heure	*ah luhr*	on time
à la fois	*ah lah fois*	at the same time
à samedi	*ah sahm-dee*	until Saturday
à temps	*ah tahN*	on time
à tout à l'heure	*ah too tah luhr*	see you later
au bout de	*o boo duh*	at the end of
au revoir	*o ruh-vwahr*	goodbye
de bonne heure	*duh boh nuhr*	early
de jour en jour	*duh zhoor ahN zhoor*	from day to day
de temps à autre	*duh tahN zah o-truh*	from time to time
de temps en temps	*duh tahN zahN tahN*	from time to time

Idiom	Pronunciation	Meaning
du matin au soir	*dew mah-taN o swahr*	from morning until evening
en même temps	*ahN mehm tahN*	at the same time
en retard	*ahN ruh-tahr*	late
il y a (+ time)	*eel yah*	ago (+ time)
par jour (semaine, mois)	*pahr zhoor (suh-mehn, mwah)*	by day, week, month
tout à l'heure	*too tah luhr*	in a while
tout de suite	*toot sweet*	immediately

Using Your Idioms II (or What Time Is It?)

What French idioms of time would you use in the following situations?

1. When you leave a friend for the day you would say:

2. If your boss wants something done right away, he wants it done:

3. If you have an interview at 9 a.m. and you arrive at 10 a.m., you arrive:

4. If you have an interview at 9 a.m. and you arrive at 8 a.m., you arrive:

5. If you are going to see a friend later today, you will see him/her:

6. If you go to the movies every once in a while, you go:

7. If you work all day long, you work:

8. If you are leaving a friend for today but know that you will see him/her tomorrow, you would say:

Memory Enhancer

"Tard" (*tahr*) means "late in the day or evening," whereas "en retard" (*ahN ruh-tahr*) means "late in arriving."

Un deux trois

Note that idoms with *à* are often about time.

Where To?

Probably among the most useful idioms are those telling you how to get where you want to go. Most men, of course, would never dream of asking for directions. They have to prove that they can find it themselves. So when my husband and I find ourselves off the beaten path, I'm the one who goes into the nearest gas station. I like to know exactly where I'm going and, if I get lost, I want precise directions. The idioms of location and direction in the following table are quite important for any traveler, don't you think? (This list is for men, too.)

Idioms Showing Location and Direction

Idiom	Pronunciation	Meaning
à côté (de)	*ah ko-tay (duh)*	next to, beside
à droite (de)	*ah drawht (duh)*	to the right (of)
à gauche (de)	*ah gosh (duh)*	to the left (of)
à l'étranger	*ah lay-trahN-zhay*	abroad
à la campagne	*ah lah kahN-pahN-nyuh*	in the country
à la maison	*ah lah meh-zohN*	at home
à part	*ah pahr*	aside
à travers	*ah trah-vehr*	across, through
au loin	*o lwaN*	in the distance
au milieu (de)	*o mee-lyuh (duh)*	in the middle (of)
au-dessous de	*o duh-soo duh*	beneath, below
au-dessus de	*o duh-sew duh*	above, over
de l'autre côté (de)	*duh lohtr ko-tay (duh)*	on the other side (of)
du côté de	*dew ko-tay duh*	in the direction of, toward
en bas (de)	*ahN bah (duh)*	at the bottom (of)
en face (de)	*ahN fahs (duh)*	opposite, facing
en haut (de)	*ahN o (duh)*	at the top (of)
en plein air	*ahN pleh nehr*	in the open air, outdoors
en ville	*ahN veel*	downtown
le long de	*luh lohN duh*	along
par ici (là)	*pahr ee-see (lah)*	this way (that way)
tout droit	*too drwah*	straight ahead
tout près	*too preh*	nearby

Culture Capsule

No one in France is going to tell you how many blocks away a certain tourist attraction is located. The concept of "blocks" is strictly American. When giving directions in France, the average man or woman in the street will tell you the number of streets (rues—*rew*) or traffic lights (feux—*fuh*) you will encounter.

Using Your Idioms III (or Getting There in One Piece)

You can get there. Below is a small map of a city street. There are six buildings to identify:

la pharmacie Legrand	le cinéma Rex
le café Lebrun	le restaurant Bonaparte
le théâtre Odéon	le musée de l'art moderne

Read the directions and label the buildings on le boulevard Victor Hugo:

À gauche de la pâtisserie il y a le théâtre Odéon. Et à côté du théâtre il y a le café Lebrun. En face du café se trouve le restaurant Bonaparte. À droite de la pâtisserie, il y a la pharmacie Legrand. De l'autre côté du boulevard, en face, est le cinéma Rex. À gauche du cinéma et tout droit devant le théâtre se trouve le musée de l'art moderne.

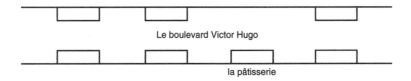

So, What's Your Opinion?

Everyone, at one time or another, has an opinion about something. Some people are certainly more expressive than others. Whether you're talking about your flight, the food you ate, the movie you watched, the people you met, or life in general, you will need to know how to properly express your feelings. The following table should help.

Expressing Your Opinions with Idioms

Idiom	Pronunciation	Meaning
à mon avis	*ah mohN nah-vee*	in my opinion
à vrai dire	*ah vreh deer*	to tell the truth
au contraire	*o kohN-trehr*	on the contrary
bien entendu	*byaN nahN-tahN-dew*	of course
bien sûr	*byaN sewr*	of course
bon marché	*bohN mahr-shay*	cheap
c'est-à-dire	*seh-tah-deer*	that is to say
cela m'est égal	*suh-lah meh tay-gahl*	that's all the same to me (I don't care.)
cela ne fait rien	*suh-lah nuh feh ryaN*	that doesn't matter
d'accord	*dah-kohr*	agreed, okay
de mon côté	*duh mohN ko-tay*	as for me, for my part
jamais de la vie	*zhah-meh duh lah vee*	never, out of the question
n'importe	*nahN-pohrt*	it doesn't matter
ressembler à	*ruh-sahN-blay ah*	to resemble
sans doute	*sahN doot*	without a doubt
tant mieux	*tahN myuh*	so much the better
tant pis	*tahN pee*	too bad
tout à fait	*too tah feh*	entirely
tout de même	*too dmehm*	all the same

Un deux trois

For a quick and easy study of these useful expressions, write each one on a separate index card. Attach the cards to your refrigerator with magnets. Everytime you go for a snack, take one card and memorize it. The next time a friend makes a suggestion to you, think of the appropriate French response.

Using Your Idioms IV (or Being Totally Up Front)

Your friend has proposed some afternoon activities. Indicate a willingness to go along with his/her suggestions. Show that you are unwilling to go along with him/her.

Are You All Right?

Let's say you are freezing cold. So you say to your French host: "Je suis froid," and he cracks up laughing. Why? In English we use adjectives to describe how we are feeling, thus you've chosen (so you think): "I am cold." The French say: "I have cold" (which doesn't mean that they are sick and have a cold). Your French host would literally interpret what you said as that you are cold to the touch of a hand. Of course this sounds very strange and silly to us. Just remember, our idioms sound very off-beat to others.

You will notice that all the following idioms begin with the verb *avoir,* which means *to have.* Of course, it will be necessary to conjugate *avoir* as the subject of the sentence changes, but that will be discussed further in Chapter 9. For now, concentrate on how you feel—*J'ai* (zhay, I have)—using the expressions for physical conditions in the following table.

Memory Enhancer

Always use the verb *avoir* (to have) to express your physical condition (even though the English uses the verb "to be").

Idiomatic Physical Conditions

Idiom	Pronunciation	Meaning
avoir besoin (de)	*ah-vwahr buh-zwaN (duh)*	to need
avoir chaud	*ah-vwahr sho*	to be hot (person)
avoir envie (de)	*ah-vwahr ahN-vee (duh)*	to need
avoir faim	*ah-vwahr faN*	to be hungry
avoir froid	*ah-vwahr frwah*	to be cold (person)
avoir honte (de)	*ah-vwahr ohNt (duh)*	to be ashamed (of)
avoir l'air (+ adj.)	*ah-vwahr lehr*	to seem, look
avoir l'air de (+ inf.)	*ah-vwahr lehr duh*	to seem to, look as if
avoir mal à	*ah-vwahr mahl ah*	to have an ache in
avoir peur (de)	*ah-vwahr puhr (duh)*	to be afraid (of)
avoir quelque chose	*ah-vwahr kehl-kuh shohz*	to have something wrong
avoir raison	*ah-vwahr reh-zohN*	to be right
avoir soif	*ah-vwahr swahf*	to be thirsty
avoir sommeil	*ah-vwahr soh-mehy*	to be sleepy
avoir tort	*ah-vwahr tohr*	to be wrong
avoir...ans	*ah-vwahr...ahN*	to be ___ years old

Using Your Idioms V (or What's Happening?)

Express how you feel, using idioms.

1. sleepy
2. hot
3. hungry
4. thirsty
5. being wrong
6. on your 30th birthday
7. being correct
8. cold

Memory Enhancer

Weather conditions are always expressed impersonally with the expression *il fait...* (it's...) even though English uses the verb "to be." *Faire* can be used with other subject nouns and pronouns but not when discussing the weather.

Baby, It's Cold Outside

Travelers tend to be obsessed with weather, which makes sense given that many plans are contingent on it. The French way of discussing weather differs from ours. If you said to your French host: "Il est chaud," he or she would assume that you were speaking about something that was warm to the touch. The French use the verb *faire* (to make, to do) to describe most weather conditions. We wouldn't use the verbs *make* and *do* to express ourselves in English; we'd be laughed at. But in France, do as the French do as you study the following table.

Idiomatic Weather Expressions

Idiom	Pronunciation	Meaning
faire beau	*fehr bo*	to be nice weather
faire chaud	*fehr cho*	to be hot weather
faire des éclairs	*fehr day zay-klehr*	to be lightning
faire doux	*fehr doo*	to be mild
faire du soleil	*fehr dew soh-lehy*	to be sunny
faire du tonnerre	*fehr dew toh-nehr*	to be thundering
faire du vent	*fehr dew vahN*	to be windy
faire frais	*fehr freh*	to be cool
faire froid	*fehr frwah*	to be cold
faire jour	*fehr zhoor*	to be daytime, light
faire mauvais	*fehr mo-veh*	to be bad weather
faire nuit	*fehr nwee*	to be night, dark
Quel temps fait-il?	*kehl tahN feh-teel*	What is the weather?

Culture Capsule

The weather in France is very similar to the weather in the northeastern United States. So expect a warm, rainy spring, a hot summer, a cool autumn, and a cold winter—and dress appropriately.

Using Your Idioms VI (or How's the Weather?)

Look at a weather map of France for the day. Tell what the weather will be in each of the following cities:

1. À Paris il fait _____.

2. À Nice il fait _____.

3. À Bordeaux il fait _____.

4. À Strasbourg il fait _____.

5. À Toulouse il fait _____.

Culture Capsule

Never use *faire* when speaking about snow or rain:

Il neige.	*eel nehzh*	It's snowing.
Il pleut.	*eel pluh*	It's raining.

It's in Your Hands

The French are very expressive people and tend to speak a lot with their hands. Facial expressions and body language are also an important part of communicating feelings and emotions. Many gestures perfectly convey certain French slang expressions without the use of words. These gestures play an important role in the French language.

In many instances it is unwise to attempt to translate word for word from English to French. This can backfire and cause embarrassment, especially in situations where specific idiomatic expressions are necessary.

When you can't think of the words you need, do not hesitate to use body language and gestures to convey your thoughts and feelings.

Attention!

Although idioms are an accepted form of expression in any language, slang is not.

The Least You Need to Know

➤ Idioms are expressions that can't be translated word for word from one language to another.

➤ Idioms, not slang, will help you speak the language the way it should be spoken.

➤ Proper body language can help you communicate without even uttering a word.

Chapter 5

Grasp That Grammar!

In This Chapter

➤ A crash course in very basic grammar

➤ Using a bilingual dictionary

Today's approach to learning a foreign language is certainly much different than it was in the past. There's been a de-emphasis on grammatical rules and an emphasis on communication. So if you really want to speak like a Frenchman/woman, you will be happy to know that speaking a foreign language doesn't mean you'll mentally have to translate word for word from one language to the other or concentrate on memorizing endless pages of rules. Sure, that's how they tried to teach you in school way back when (and it was pure drudgery). But the powers that be have finally come to realize that communicating doesn't mean walking around with a dictionary under your arm. On the contrary, it means learning to use the language and its patterns the way a native speaker does. To do this, you need to know basic grammar as well as the idioms and colloquialisms used by native speakers.

If grammar is a weak spot for you, don't despair. Today's focus is strictly on your communicative skills. So if you're lacking in one area, make up for it in another: Use body language, facial gestures, common sense, and a dictionary to get your point across.

Grappling with Grammar

When you hear the word *grammar*, do you get a sinking feeling in the pit of your stomach like when someone mentions *math?* Did you ever have the pleasure of diagramming a sentence? I still have very vivid memories of many seemingly useless grammatical terms. You don't have to be an expert grammarian to learn a foreign language. All you really need is a basic understanding of four simple parts of speech: nouns, verbs, adjectives, and adverbs. Now don't get all nervous. You'll see how simple it really is.

En 10 Minutes

Nouns refer to people, places, things, or ideas. All French nouns have a gender (masculine or feminine) and a number (singular or plural). Special articles help determine the gender and number of nouns.

Nouns

Nouns refer to people, places, things, or ideas. Just like in English, nouns can be replaced by pronouns (he, she, it, they). Unlike English, however, all nouns in French have a gender. That means that all nouns have a SEX. That ought to grab your attention. Sorry to disappoint you, but in this case SEX refers to the masculine or feminine designation of the noun. In French, all nouns also have a number (singular or plural). Little articles (words that stand for "the" or "a") serve as noun markers and usually help to indicate gender and number. But even if you can't figure out the gender of a noun, you will still be understood, as long as you use the correct word. You will learn more about gender in Chapter 6.

En 10 Minutes

Verbs show an action or a state of being. French verbs are conjugated (in much the same way as English verbs are) to agree with their subject.

Verbs

Verbs are words that show action or a state of being. In both English and French, we conjugate verbs. That word "conjugate" sounds a lot scarier than it really is. In English, conjugating is so automatic (because we've been doing it practically since birth) that we don't even realize that we are doing it. I had a friend who took four years of high school French and never understood the concept of verb conjugation. (She was absent that day.) I explained it to her, and she realized that it's really quite simple. *Conjugating* means giving the correct form of the verb so that it agrees with the subject. For example: In English, we say *I am* but *you are*, *he is*, and so on; *I look* but *she looks*. It just doesn't work to mix and match the subjects and verb forms whether you are speaking English or French. Imagine how silly it would sound to you if a French person said, "I are." You will have to strive to give the form of the verb that matches the subject. But don't despair. Even if you use the wrong verb form, you will be understood. Surely you would understand a foreigner who said, "You is very nice."

That's enough for now. Verb conjugation will be explained in greater depth in Chapter 7.

Adjectives

Adjectives help to describe nouns. Unlike English, in French all adjectives agree in number and gender (sex) with the nouns they modify. In other words, in a French sentence, all the words have to match. If the noun is singular, then its adjective must also be singular. If the noun is feminine, then you must be sure to give the correct feminine form of the adjective you are using.

In English, adjectives are generally placed before the nouns they modify: for example, *the blue house*. In French, most adjectives come after the nouns they describe: for example, *la maison bleue*. Don't get nervous. If you make a mistake, you will still be understood. You will find out more about adjectives in Chapter 9.

En 10 Minutes

Adjectives describe nouns or pronouns. In French, they must agree in gender (masculine or feminine) and number (singular or plural) with the words they modify. Unlike in English, most French adjectives follow the nouns they modify.

Adverbs

Adverbs are words that describe verbs, adjectives, or other adverbs. In English, most adverbs end in *-ly*: for example, *He dances slowly*. In French, they end in *-ment*: *Il danse lentement*. Adverbs will probably pose few problems as you learn the language. Adverbs are discussed in greater detail in Chapter 18.

En 10 Minutes

Adverbs modify verbs, adjectives or other adverbs. English adverbs often end in *-ly*; French adverbs generally end in *-ment.*

I'm No Idiot—Using a Bilingual Dictionary Is Easy

Sure you know how to use an *English* dictionary. Even if you don't know how to spell the word you're looking up, you usually stumble across it eventually. But using a bilingual dictionary requires a certain, albeit minimal, amount of grammatical expertise. Believe it or not, an open-book dictionary test is probably harder than any test you would have to study for.

Attention!

To use a bilingual dictionary successfully, you must know and be aware of the differences between the various parts of speech. Using a noun instead of a verb, for example, is a mistake.

Your Bilingual Dictionary— A Crash Course

The very first thing you should do is open to the front of your dictionary and find the list of abbreviations. Generally, there is a rather long, comprehensive list. There are only a few abbreviations that are truly essential and that need attention. They are:

➤ *adj.*   adjective.

➤ *adv.*   adverb.

➤ *f.*   indicates a *feminine* noun. The gender of nouns will be explained in Chapter 6.

➤ *n.*   noun (sometimes an *s* is used). The *n.* designation is generally used only if the noun can be either masculine or feminine.

➤ *m.*   indicates a *masculine* noun.

➤ *pl.*   indicates a *plural* noun. More on plural nouns in Chapter 6.

➤ *p.p.*   indicates the *past participle* of a verb. A past participle is necessary when a verb is used in the past tense. An explanation follows in Chapter 21.

➤ *v.i.*   indicates an *intransitive* verb, which can stand alone: *I eat*.

➤ *v.t.*   indicates a *transitive* verb that may be followed by a direct object: *He removes his hat* (*removes* may not stand alone) or may be used in the passive, where the subject is acted upon: *I was seen*.

➤ *v.r.*   indicates a *reflexive* verb, where the subject acts upon itself: *I brush my teeth*. Reflexive verbs will be treated in Chapter 20.

Now, let's see how well you can do with your bilingual French-English, English-French dictionary. We'll start with the English word *mean*. Consider the following sentences and how the meaning of the word *mean* changes:

That man is **mean**. (adjective)

What can that **mean**? (verb)

What is the **mean** (average)? (noun)

If you change *mean* to the plural, its meaning changes:

What is the **means** of transportation? (noun)

Look up the word *mean*, and you see:

mean [min] *vt* signifier; *adj* (miserly) radin, (nasty) méchant, (vicious) sauvage; *n* (math) moyenne *f*; (method) moyen; *m* means ressources *fpl*

Now try completing the following sentences with the correct form of the word mean:

1. *That man is **mean**.* Determine the part of speech. Did you choose an adjective? Good! Now complete the French sentence: *Cet homme est _____.* The correct choice is *méchant.*

2. *What can that **mean**?* In this sentence, did you select ***mean*** as a verb? You got it! The French sentence would read: *Qu'est-ce que ça peut _____.* I hope you chose *signifier.*

3. *What is the **mean**?* This term refers to the *average* of two numbers. Because the correct word is feminine, you will have to use the article *la* before the noun you choose. Articles will be discussed in Chapter 6. The French is: *Quelle est la _____.* The answer is *moyenne.*

4. *What is the **means** of transportation? **Means*** is plural in English but masculine, singular in French. Use *le* before the noun you choose. The French is: *Quel est _____ de transport.* The answer is *le moyen.*

As you can see, to successfully look up the meanings of the word you want to use, you must do three things:

1. Check to make sure that you are using the correct part of speech: noun, verb, adjective, or adverb.

2. Check your work by looking up the French word you have chosen and by verifying that the English meaning given is the one you want.

3. Check that you are using the correct form of the word: the right number (singular or plural) and the right gender (masculine or feminine).

Attention!

Some verbs can be used transitively and intransitively according to their meaning. Be careful to use a direct object when a transitive verb is indicated.

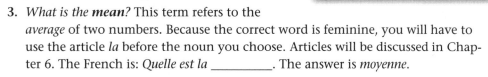

Un deux trois

Select a common English word that can be used as different parts of speech (as a noun, as a verb, as an adjective, and/or as an adverb). Try the word "check" or "well," for example. Find as many French equivalent words as you can and take note of how these words are used.

Just Look It Up

Use a bilingual dictionary to see if you can find the correct word to complete each of the following French sentences. For now, I've supplied the proper articles. *Write all verbs in the infinitive form.* We'll move on to conjugation later, in Chapter 7.

1. Look at the fire!   Regarde le _____.

2. The boss is going to fire the   Le patron va _____ l'employé.
   employee.

3. I see the light.   Je vois la _____.

4. I am going to light the barbecue.   Je vais _____ le barbecue.

5. There is water in the well.   Il y a de l'eau dans le _____.

6. He sings well.   Il chante _____.

7. The land is fertile.   La _____ est fertile.

8. The plane is going to land.   L'avion va _____.

9. He dances better than you.   Il danse _____ que toi.

10. The chocolate cake is better.   Le gâteau au chocolat est _____.

11. The children are going to play.   Les enfants vont _____.

12. I would love to see the play.   J'aimerais voir la _____.

The Least You Need to Know

➤ The parts of speech are the same in both French and English.

➤ To use a bilingual dictionary effectively, you must know the different parts of speech.

➤ You must use both sides of a bilingual dictionary to obtain the proper definition of a word.

Chapter 6

French—The Sexy Language

In This Chapter

➤ Determining gender

➤ Switching gender

➤ Going from singular to plural

Unlike in English, where girls are girls, and boys are boys, and everything else is neuter, every single noun (person, place, thing, or idea) in French is designated as *masculine* or *feminine*, *singular* or *plural*. How is this determination made? Sometimes it's obvious, sometimes there are clues, and sometimes it's just downright tricky. This chapter will teach you to make the right connections.

The Battle of the Sexes

If you're speaking about a man or a woman, gender is obvious. But what if you want to talk about a lovely boutique you passed by the other day? There is no obvious clue to you as yet, telling you the gender of the word *boutique*. Do you assume that it's feminine because women like to go to boutiques? In this day and age, that's a dangerous thing to do. There are, however, tricks for determining gender that you will learn as you read and study the chapter.

For instance, the word *boutique* ends in *que*; most French words with this ending are feminine.

Suppose that you want to purchase a tie that you saw in the boutique. It would be normal to assume that *cravate* is masculine because men wear ties more often than women do. But you would be wrong in your assumption. In fact, *cravate* is a feminine word. "Why?" you're probably asking yourself. "That really doesn't make any sense." You're right. It doesn't. And unfortunately, there are no clues and no tricks to help you with this word and many others like it. So what do you do? You learn which endings are usually masculine and which are feminine; for the others, you try to learn the word with its *noun marker* (le [un] or la [une]). If you forget the noun marker, you can always resort to a good French dictionary. Just remember: Even if you make a gender mistake, as long as you have the correct vocabulary word, you'll be understood.

Noun Markers

Noun markers are articles or adjectives that tell you whether a noun is *masculine* (m.) or *feminine* (f.), *singular* (sing.) or *plural* (pl.). The most common markers, shown in the table below, are *definite articles* expressing "the" and *indefinite articles* expressing "a," "an," "one," or "some."

Singular Noun Markers

	Masculine	Feminine
the	le (l') (*luh*)	la (l') (*lah*)
a, an, one	un (*uhN*)	une (*ewn*)

Singular Nouns

The nouns in the table below are very easy to mark because they obviously refer to males or females:

Gender-Obvious Nouns

Masculine Noun	Pronunciation	English	Feminine Noun	Pronunciation	English
le père	*luh pehr*	father	la mère	*lah mehr*	mother
le grand-père	*luh grahN-pehr*	grandfather	la grand-mère	*lah grahN-mehr*	grandmother
le garçon	*luh gahr-sohN*	boy	la fille	*la fee-y*	girl
l'ami	*lah-mee*	friend (m.)	l'amie	*lah-mee*	friend (f.)
un homme	*uhN nohm*	man	une femme	*ewn fahm*	woman
un oncle	*uhN nohN-kluh*	uncle	une tante	*ewn tahNt*	aunt
un cousin	*uhN koo-zaN*	cousin (m.)	une cousine	*ewn koo-zeen*	cousin (f.)
un ami	*uhN nah-mee*	friend (m.)	une amie	*ewn nah-mee*	friend (f.)

All nouns must be identified as either masculine or feminine. Use *le* to express the definite article (the) and *un* to express the indefinite article (a, an, or one) before a masculine singular noun. Use *la* to express the definite article (the) and *une* to express the indefinite article (a, an, or one) before a feminine singular noun. Use *l'* before any singular noun that begins with a vowel, regardless of gender.

Mark Your Nouns

Choose the correct definite article noun marker (le, la) when referring to these people:

Example:

reine (*rehn*) queen

C'est la reine.

It's the queen.

Memory Enhancer

The *e* is never dropped from the indefinite article *une*. The final *e* does, however, change the sound of the word *un* (uhN) to *une* (ewn).

1. _____ fils (*fees*) son
2. _____ vendeur (*vahN-duhr*) salesman
3. _____ princesse (*praN-sehs*) princess
4. _____ mari (*mah-ree*) husband
5. _____ soeur (*suhr*) sister
6. _____ neveu (*neh-vuh*) nephew
7. _____ actrice (*ahk-trees*) actress
8. _____ prince (*praNs*) prince
9. _____ nièce (*nyehs*) niece
10. _____ frère (*frehr*) brother
11. _____ femme (*fahm*) woman, wife
12. _____ roi (*rwah*) king

Some nouns can be either masculine or feminine. To indicate whether you are speaking about a male or female, simply change the marker to suit the identity of the person, as listed in the following table:

Example:

Le touriste (male) prend (is taking) des photos.

La touriste (female) aussi prend des photos.

When you come across these words in a dictionary, you will not see a simple *m.* or *f.* Some dictionaries will designate them with an *n.* for noun or *s.* for substantive (which stands for noun) or will simply show *m/f.*

This means that you must choose the correct marker according to the person you are speaking about.

Nouns for Both Sexes

Word	Pronunciation	Meaning
artiste	*ahr-teest*	artist
camarade	*kah-mah-rahd*	friend
concierge	*kohN-syehrzh*	concierge
élève	*ay-lehv*	student
enfant	*ahN-fahN*	child
malade	*mah-lahd*	sick person
secrétaire	*seh-kray-tehr*	secretary
touriste	*too-reest*	tourist

Let's take a look at an interesting sentence:

Jacques Cousteau est une personne importante.

Did you notice the use of the feminine indefinite article *une?* Are you perplexed? After all, Jacques Cousteau is a man. Shouldn't the indefinite article reflect this? Not really. The answer is simple, although somewhat unsatisfactory for men and women alike.

Whether we agree or not, some nouns are always masculine or feminine no matter what the sex of the person to whom you are referring. Notice that the "Always Masculine" list, which generally refers to professions, is much longer than the "Always Feminine" list.

Attention!

When you come across French words that can be either masculine or feminine, your dictionary will say *m/f.*

Always Masculine	Always Feminine
agent de police (*ah-zhahN duh poh-lees*)/ police officer	connaissance/acquaintance (*koh-neh-sahNs*)
bébé (*bay-bay*)/baby	personne/person (*pehr-sohn*)
chef (*shehf*)/chef, head	star (*stahr*)/star
dentiste (*dahN-teest*)/dentist	vedette (*vuh-deht*)/star
écrivain (*ay-kree-vaN*)/writer	victime (*veek-teem*)/victim
ingénieur (*aN-zhay-nyuhr*)/engineer	
mannequin (*mahn-kaN*)/model	
médecin (*mayd-saN*)/doctor	
pompier (*pohN-pyeh*)/firefighter	
peintre (*paNtr*)/painter	
professeur (*proh-feh-suhr*)/teacher	

The endings in the following table can be helpful in determining the gender of the noun and can make marking easier. This will require some memorization and practice on your part. When in doubt, always consult your dictionary for the gender of a word. An *m* . or an *f.* will always appear. Make sure to look carefully in case the gender is in doubt.

Masculine and Feminine Endings

Masculine Endings	Example	Feminine Endings	Example
-acle	spectacle (*spehk-tahkl*)	-ade	limonade (*lee-moh-nahd*)
-age*	garage (*gah-rahzh*)	-ale	cathédrale (*kah-tay-drahl*)

continues

Masculine and Feminine Endings (cont.)

Masculine Endings	Example	Feminine Endings	Example
-al	animal (*ah-nee-mahl*)	-ance	chance (*shahNs*)
-eau**	château (*shah-to*)	-ence	essence (*eh-sahNs*)
-et	ticket (*tee-keh*)	-ette	chaînette (*sheh-neht*)
-ier	papier (*pah-pyay*)	-ie	magie (*mah-zhee*)
-isme	cyclisme (*see-kleez-muh*)	-ique	boutique (*boo-teek*)
-ment	changement (*shahNzh-mahN*)	-oire	histoire (*ees-twahr*)
		-sion	expression (*ehks-preh-syohN*)
		-tion	addition (*ah-dee-syohN*)
		-ure	coiffure (*kwah-fewr*)

* except page (pahzh) (f.); plage (plahzh) (f.) beach

** except eau (o) (f.) water; peau (po) (f.) skin

Un deux trois

Endings that are generally feminine include:

–ade, –ale, –ance, –ence, –ette, –ie, –ique, –oire, –sion, –tion, –ure

En 10 Minutes

Endings that are generally masculine include:

–acle, –age, –al, –eau, –et, –ier, –isme, –ment

Mark More Nouns

You are looking around a gift shop. In order to tell the salesperson what you would like, use the indefinite article noun marker *un* or *une*. After #4, you're on your own:

Example:

chaînette (f.) (*sheh-neht*) chain

Je voudrais une chaînette, s'il vous plaît.

(*zhuh voo-dreh*) I would like (*seel voo pleh*) please

1. _____ écharpe (f.) (*ay-shahrp*) scarf
2. _____ tee-shirt (m.) (*tee-shehrt*) tee shirt
3. _____ affiche (f.) (*ah-feesh*) poster
4. _____ c.d. (m.) (*say day*) compact disk
5. _____ cassette (*kah-seht*) cassette
6. _____ tableau (*tah-blo*) picture
7. _____ collier (*koh-lyeh*) necklace
8. _____ ceinture (*saN-tewr*) belt
9. _____ bougie (*boo-zhee*) candle

10. _____ gilet (*zhee-leh*) vest
11. _____ bracelet (*brahs-leh*) bracelet
12. _____ journal (*zhoor-nahl*) newspaper

Gender Benders

Marking some nouns is as easy as adding an *e* to the masculine form to get the corresponding feminine form. When you do this, there will be a change in the pronunciation of any feminine noun ending in a *consonant*. For the masculine noun, the final consonant is not pronounced. When the *e* is added to form the feminine, the consonant must then be pronounced. Another change is that the final nasal sound of a masculine *in* ending (aN) loses its nasality when the feminine ending becomes *ine* (een). Observe these changes in the following table.

Gender Benders

Le (L'), Un	La (L'), Une
ami (*ah-mee*)/friend	amie (*ah-mee*)/friend
avocat (*ah-vo-kah*)/lawyer	avocate (*ah-vo-kaht*)/lawyer
client (*klee-yahN*)/client	cliente (*klee-yahNt*)/client
cousin (*koo-zaN*)/cousin	cousine (*koo-zeen*)/cousin
employé (*ahN-plwah-yay*)/employee	employée (*ahN-plwah-yay*)/employee
étudiant (*ay-tew-dyahN*)/student	étudiante (*ay-tew-dyahNt*)/student
voisin (*vwah-zaN*)/neighbor	voisine (*vwah-zeen*)/neighbor

Some masculine noun endings (usually referring to professions) very conveniently have a corresponding feminine ending. Most of the feminine endings sound different, as you will notice in the table below.

More Gender Benders

Masculine Ending	Feminine Ending
-an	paysan (*peh-ee-zahN*)/peasant
-anne	paysanne (*peh-ee-zahn*)/peasant
-el	contractuel (*kohN-trahk-tew-ehl*)/traffic enforcer
-elle	contractuelle (*koh-trahk-tew-ehl*)/traffic enforcer
-er	pâstissier (*pah-tee-syay*)/pastry chef
-ère	pâstissière (*pah-tee-syehr*)/pastry chef
-eur	vendeur (*vahN-duhr*)/salesman
-euse	vendeuse (*vahN-duhz*)/saleswoman

continues

More Gender Benders (cont.)

Masculine Ending	Feminine Ending
-ien	mécanicien (*may-kah-nee-syaN*)/mechanic
-ienne	mécanicienne (*may-kah-nee-syehn*)/ mechanic
-on	patron (*pah-trohN*)/boss
-onne	patronne (*pah-trohn*)/boss
-teur	spectateur (*spehk-tah-tuhr*)/spectator
-trice	spectatrice (*spehk-tah-trees*)/spectator

What's Their Line?

Review what you've learned so far and then complete the list with the missing professions. Be very careful before you choose an ending. Remember, some nouns do not change.

Il est	Elle est	Il est	Elle est
avocat	_____	infirmier	_____
_____	dentiste	pompier	_____
coiffeur	_____	_____	patronne
_____	factrice	mannequin	_____
boucher	_____	_____	pâtissière
_____	étudiante	médecin	_____
_____	chef	_____	ouvrière

Attention!

It is unnecessary to use *un* or *une* before a person's profession unless it is modified: *Il est docteur. Il est un bon docteur.*

If you did well in this exercise, then it's time to continue. The good news is: There are no more rules. However, because most nouns in French do not follow any specific set of rules, you should learn them with their markers. You'll see that you'll get the hang of it in no time. And if you make a gender mistake, it's really not that serious; as long as you've chosen the correct noun, you'll be understood.

When There's More Than One

When a French noun refers to more than one person, place, thing, or idea, just like in English, it must be made plural. But it is not enough to simply change the noun; the marker must be made plural, as well. As you study the following table, you will see that in the plural, the masculine and feminine noun markers for *the* and *some* are exactly the same.

Memory Enhancer

Only singular noun markers show the gender of the noun.

Plural Noun Markers

	Masculine	Feminine
the	les	les
some	des	des

What does this mean? Because *le, la,* and *l'* all become *les* in the plural, and *un* and *une* become *des*, using a plural noun marker does not enable you to determine the gender of any noun. Plural noun markers indicate only that the speaker is referring to more than one noun. This means that you must learn each noun with its singular noun marker.

Plural Nouns

Forming the plural of most nouns in French is really quite easy. All you have to do is add an *unpronounced s* to the singular form:

Un deux trois

In a mixed group of males and females, the masculine plural form always prevails. *Les amis,* for example, can refer to male friends or a group of male and female friends. If there are only females present, use *les amies.*

le garçon (*luh gahr-sohN*),	les garçons (*lay gahr-sohN*),
un garçon (*uhN gahr-sohN*)	des garçons (*day gahr-sohN*)
la fille (*lah fee-y*),	les filles (*lay fee-y*),
une fille (*ewn fee-y*)	des filles (*day fee-y*)
l'enfant* (*lahN-fahN*),	les enfants** (*lay zahN-fahN*)
un enfant**	des enfants**
(*uhN nahN-fahN*)	(*day zahN-fahN*)

Remember *elision and **liaison? Use the pronunciation guide and *slide the sounds joined by the apostrophe: *l'homme* (*lohm*) and *j'écoute* (*zhay-koot*), and **link the sound of the final consonant with the beginning vowel: *les hôtels* (*lay zo-tehl*) and *nous arrivons* (*noo zah-ree-vohN*). Don't pronounce the final *s* if you want your French to sound authentic.

The letters *s*, *x*, and *z* are all letters that are used to make plurals in French. So what happens if you have a French noun that ends in one of these letters? Absolutely nothing!

le prix (*luh pree*)/the price, prize   les prix (*lay pree*)

le fils (*luh fees*)/the son   les fils (*lay fees*)

le nez (*luh nay*)/the nose   les nez (*lay nay*)

Common words that end in *s:*

l'ananas (*lah-nah-nah*)/pineapple   le héros (*luh ay-ro*)*/hero

l'autobus (*lo-toh-bews*)/bus   le mois (*luh mwah*)/month

le bas (*luh bah*)/stocking   le jus (*luh zhew*)/juice

le bras (*luh brah*)/arm   le palais (*luh pah-leh*)/palace

le colis (*luh koh-lee*)/package   le pardessus (*luh pahr-duh-sew*)/overcoat

le corps (*luh kohr*)/body   le pays (*luh pay-ee*)/country

le dos (*luh do*)/back   le repas (*luh ruh-pah*)/meal

la fois (*lah fwah*)/time   le tapis (*luh tah-pee*)/rug

Common words that end in *x:*

la croix (*lah krwah*)/cross   la voix (*lah vwah*)/voice

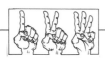

Un deux trois

Set up *un coin français* (a French corner) in your home that is reserved for your study of French. Label the items you keep there: photos, stationery items, books, and so on. Practice identifying the objects and the people using *le, la, l'*, and *les*. Then switch to *un, une*, and *des*. Also try changing all the singular nouns to plural and vice versa.

More Than One

Chances are that when you travel, you're going to see more than one château, museum, church, and so forth. If you choose to discuss or describe these things, you'll want to make sure that you've got your plurals down pat. Practice makes perfect, so try to express that you see more than one of the things in the following list.

Example (hero):
Je vois des héros (*zhuh vwah day ay-ro*)/I see heroes.

boutique   automobile

croix   tapis

restaurant   magazine

palais   autobus

Other Plurals

The letter *x* is used in French to make plurals.

➤ For nouns ending in *eau*:

le bateau (*luh bah-to*)/boat	les bateaux
le bureau (*luh bew-ro*)/office, desk	les bureaux
le cadeau (*luh kah-do*)/gift	les cadeaux
le chapeau (*luh shah-po*)/hat	les chapeaux
le château (*luh shah-to*)/castle	les châteaux
le couteau (*luh koo-to*)/knife	les couteaux
l'eau (*lo*) (f.)/water	les eaux
le gâteau (*luh gah-to*)/cake	les gâteaux
le manteau (*luh mahN-to*)/coat	les manteaux
le morceau (*luh mohr-so*)/piece	les morceaux
l'oiseau (*lwah-zo*)/bird	les oiseaux
le rideau (*luh ree-do*)/curtain	les rideaux
le tableau (*luh tah-blo*)/picture, chalkboard	les tableaux

➤ For nouns ending in *eu*, except *le pneu* (*luh pnuh*)/tire: *les pneus*:

le cheveu (*luh shuh vuh*)/hair	les cheveux
le jeu (*luh zhuh*)/game	les jeux
le lieu (*luh lyuh*)/place	les lieux
le neveu (*luh nuh-vuh*)/nephew	les neveux

➤ For nouns ending in *al*, change *al* to *aux* except for *le bal* (*luh bahl*)/ball: *bals*; *le festival* (*luh fehs-tee-vahl*)/festival: *festivals*:

l'animal (*lah nee mahl*)/animal	les animaux
le cheval (*luh shuh-vahl*)/horse	les chevaux
l'hôpital (*lo-pee-tahl*)/hospital	les hôpitaux
le journal (*luh zhoor-nahl*)/ newspaper	les journaux

Attention!

Although you can refer to one hair in French as *un cheveu*, (for example, if there were a hair in your food), *hair*, in general, is always plural and is referred to as *les cheveux*.

➤ For some nouns ending in *ou,* add *x* to form the plural:

le bijou (*luh bee-zhoo*)/jewel   les bijoux

le caillou (*luh kah-yoo*)/pebble   les cailloux

le genou (*luh zhuh-noo*)/knee   les genoux

le joujou (*luh zhoo-zhoo*)/toy   les joujoux

➤ Just as we have some words in English that are always plural (*pants, sunglasses, shorts, news*), so do the French. Here are some nouns that might prove useful to you:

les ciseaux (m.) (*lay see-zo*)/scissors   les lunettes (f.) (*lay lew-neht*)/eyeglasses

les gens (m.) (*lay zhahN*)/people   les vacances (f.) (*lay vah-kahNs*)/vacation

Learning a foreign language wouldn't be a challenge if there weren't some irregularities. Here are some irregular plurals you might find useful:

l'oeil (m.) (*luhy*)/eye   les yeux (*lay zyuh*)

le travail (*luh trah-vahy*)/work   les travaux (*lay trah-vo*)

madame (*mah-dahm*)/Mrs.   mesdames (*may-dahm*)

mademoiselle (*mahd-mwah-zehl*)/Miss   mesdemoiselles (*mayd-mwah-zehl*)

monsieur (*muh-syuh*)/Mr.   messieurs (*meh-syuh*)

Some compound nouns (nouns made up of two nouns usually joined by a hyphen) do not change in the plural—only their markers do:

le gratte-ciel (*luh graht-syehl*)   les gratte-ciel/skyscrapers

le hors d'oeuvre* (*luh ohr-duhvr*)   les hors d'oeuvre/appetizers (*lay ohr-duhvr*)

le rendez-vous (*luh rahN-day-voo*)   les rendez-vous/appointments

There is no elision or liaison with *h* as indicated in the dictionary: *le homard* (*luh oh-mard*) and *les hors-d'oeuvre* (*lay ohr-duhvr*). If the noun already ends in *s, x,* or *z,* no additions are needed to form the plural.

The letter *x* is used to make most nouns ending in *eau* and *eu,* and some nouns ending in *ou* plural.

Most nouns ending in *al* change *al* to *aux* to form the plural.

The words *ciseaux m.* (scissors); *gens m.* (people); *lunettes f.* (glasses), and *vacances f.* (vacation) are always plural.

The few words with completely irregular plurals must be memorized:

l'oeil	les yeux	eyes
le travail	les travaux	works
madame	mesdames	ladies
mademoiselles	mesdemoiselles	misses
monsieur	messieurs	gentleman

En 10 Minutes

All markers of plural nouns must be made plural. Most nouns in French are made plural by adding an *s*.

Compound nouns—nouns made up of two nouns and generally joined by a hyphen—invariably remain in the plural.

Practice with Plurals

If you're anything like me, you're always looking for something because you're either (a) very absent-minded or (b) totally lacking a sense of direction. Try your luck at telling someone what you are looking for:

Example: boats

Je cherche (*zhuh shehrsh*/I am looking for) les bateaux.

1. castles
2. eyeglasses
3. people
4. newspapers
5. packages
6. palaces
7. scissors
8. toys

What Have You Learned About Gender?

Read the following employment ads that were taken from an actual French newspaper and check whether the employer is looking for a male or female employee:

FILIALE
D'UN IMPORTANT
GROUPE
IMMOBILIER

recherche

**HOTESSE
COMMERCIALE**

**SECRÉTAIRES
MEDICALES**

Un poste fixe et un C.D.D.

INFIRMIER

Création de poste.

**RETOUCHEUSE
QUALIFIEE**

P.A.P. FEMININ
JEUDI, VENDREDI, SAMEDI
se prés. à partir de 14H

The Least You Need to Know

➤ You can change some nouns from masculine to feminine by adding an *e* or by changing the ending of the word.

➤ You must memorize the gender of most nouns.

➤ Certain endings are almost always masculine (*acle, age, al, eau, et, ier, isme, ment*); others are almost aways feminine (*ade, ale, ance, ence, ette, ie, ique, oire, sion, tion, ure*).

➤ Most nouns can be made plural by adding *s*.

➤ Some nouns ending in *eau, eu,* and *ou* can be made plural by adding *x*.

➤ Nouns ending in *al* change to *aux* in the plural.

➤ Singular and plural nouns sound the same—only the markers change in spelling and pronunciation.

On the Move!

In the preceding chapter, you learned about nouns: how to determine their gender and how to make them plural. Nouns, and the pronouns used to replace them, are very important because you can use them as the subject of a sentence. In this chapter, you will see how you can communicate your thoughts in French by using nouns or pronouns and the verbs that convey the actions that are being performed.

Planning and taking an imaginary trip to a French-speaking country will teach you how to get along in most everyday situations where you would need French. Picture the places you could go: the bustling cities, the sandy beaches, the medieval towns. Imagine the sites you could see: the museums, the cathedrals, the parks, the gardens; and the people you could meet: French, Canadians, Haitians, Africans. The possibilities are endless. Let's start with the basics.

Who's the Subject?

You're on a group tour and everyone involved seems to have his or her own agenda. *You* would like to take pictures of the beautiful stained-glass windows of Notre Dame. The woman next to you, *she* insists on the Eiffel Tower. The couple to your right, *they* would prefer to spend the day shopping. And the tour guide, well, *he's* just disgusted at this point. In order to express the things people do, you need to learn about verbs. Verbs require a *subject*, whether it is stated, as in:

> *I* would like to go to the Louvre.
>
> *The guide* is waiting for us.

or understood, as in a command:

> *Go* to the Pompidou Center. (The subject is understood to be *you*.)

A subject can be a noun or a pronoun that replaces the noun:

> *The artist* is painting a landscape.
>
> *He (she)* is painting a landscape.

Subject Pronouns

Just as in English, the French subject pronouns in the following table are given a person and a number (singular or plural):

Subject Pronouns

Person	Singular		Plural	
first	je* (*zhuh*)	I	nous (*noo*)	we
second	tu** (*tew*)	you	vous*** (*voo*)	you
third	il (*eel*)	he	ils****(*eel*)	they
	elle (*ehl*)	she	elles (*ehl*)	they
	on (*ohN*)	one, you, we, they		

* The subject pronoun je requires elision and becomes j' before a vowel or vowel sound (h, y). In English, the subject pronoun I is always capitalized, regardless of its position in the sentence. In French, je is capitalized only at the beginning of a sentence, just like any other word.

** The subject pronoun tu is used when speaking to a single (one) friend, relative, child, or pet. Tu is called the familiar form. The u from tu is never dropped for elision: tu arrives.

*** The subject pronoun vous is used in the singular to show respect to an older person or when speaking to someone you don't know very well. Vous is always used when speaking to more than one person, regardless of familiarity. Vous is referred to as the polite form.

**** The subject pronoun ils is used to refer to more than one male or a combined group of males and females.

Tu or Vous?

Would you use *tu* or *vous* when speaking to the following people? A doctor? Your cousin? Your friend? A salesman? A woman waiting in line for a bus? Two friends? A policeman from whom you are asking directions? Your friends?

Culture Capsule

Tu is used by the French when speaking to their pets, who are considered family members and are held in very high regard. It is not unusual to see a family accompanied by its dog in a French restaurant. No, the dog doesn't sit at the table. It eats on the floor, as usual, out of its own bowl. And, believe it or not, there are special take-out restaurants catering strictly to the family canine.

Pronouns are very useful because they allow you to speak fluidly without having to constantly repeat the noun. Imagine how tedious it would be to hear: Luc is French; Luc is from Paris; Luc would make a wonderful guide. A better version would be: Luc is French; *he*'s from Paris and *he*'d make a wonderful guide. Use pronouns to replace *proper nouns* (the name of a person or persons), as follows:

Noun	Pronoun
Lucien	Il
Marie-Claire	Elle
Philippe et Claude	Ils
Marie et Anne	Elles
Raymond et Georgette	Ils

Culture Capsule

Compound first names are popular in France. Boys names generally begin with Jean: Jean-Luc, Jean-Pierre, Jean-Paul. Girls names generally begin with Marie: Marie-Hélène, Marie-France, Marie-Madeleine. Don't get confused by them when you have to determine whether the subject is singular or plural.

You can also use pronouns to replace the name of a common noun referring to a person, place, thing, or idea:

Noun	Pronoun
le restaurant	il
la boutique	elle
le restaurant et le café	ils
la boutique et la poste	elles
le restaurant et la boutique	ils

Who's Who?

Are you like me, an incurable gossip? Imagine that you've just attended a fabulous party and now you're driving your best friend home. Of course, the two of you can't wait to talk about all the *invités* (guests). Which pronoun would you use when speaking about: Charles? Lucie et Sylvie? Berthe? Pierre? Luc et Henri? Robert et Suzette? Janine, Charolotte, Michèle, et Roger? Paul, Roland, et Annick?

Un deux trois

When in doubt, use *vous*.

And which pronoun would you substitute for these nouns, subjects which came up in your conversation about the festivities? La fête? Le bal costumé? La musique et le décor? Les vêtements? Le travail et le coût? La cuisine et la nourriture? L'ambiance? L'hôte et l'hôtesse?

Moving Along with Verbs

Do you like to bungee jump? Participate in ballroom dancing competitions? Skydive? Or are you a couch potato attracted to activities like reading a book or watching television? No matter what your preferences, you'll have to learn to use verbs to express any action, motion, or state of being. Verbs are referred to as *regular* if they follow a set pattern of rules and *irregular* if they don't. This chapter will look at regular verbs only.

Regular Verbs

Verbs are generally shown in the infinitive, the basic "to" form of the verb: to live, to laugh, to love. An infinitive, whether in French or English, is the form of the verb before it has been conjugated. We conjugate verbs all the time in English without even paying attention to the fact that we're doing it. *Conjugation* refers to changing the ending of a regular verb so that it agrees with the subject. For example, think of the verb *dance*. The infinitive is *to dance*, and it is conjugated as follows:

I dance	We dance
You dance	You dance
He/she dances	They dance

With irregular verbs, such as the verb *to be*, the entire verb form changes:

I am	We are
You are	You are
He/she is	They are

Regular verbs in French belong to one of three large families: verbs whose infinitives end in *er*, *ir*, or *re*. The verbs within each family are all conjugated in exactly the same manner, so after you've learned the pattern for one family, you know them all.

When they stand alone, verbs are generally written in their infinitive form. If you want to express what someone is doing, you must choose a subject pronoun and then learn the conjugations.

The er Verb Family

Let's start with the biggest and easiest family. This will give you an introduction to conjugation that will put you at ease right from the start. To conjugate *er* verbs, drop *er* from the infinitive and then add the following endings:

Pronoun	Verb Ending
je	-e
tu	-es
il, elle, on	-e
nous	-ons
vous	-ez
ils, elles	-ent

Let's take a look at how this is done to the verb parler (to speak). Drop the -er from the infinitive and add the proper ending:

Singular Forms	Plural Forms
Je parle, I speak	Nous parlons, We speak
Tu parles, You speak	Vous parlez, You speak
Il parle, He speaks	Ils parlent, They speak
Elle parle, She speaks	Elles parlent, They speak
On parle, One, We, They speak(s)	

Now you can conjugate any *er* verb that belongs to the family. So, if you want to brag about your accomplishments to impress a member of the opposite sex, the sky's the limit.

Je gagne beaucoup d'argent.	I earn a lot of money.
Je joue très bien aux sports.	I play sports very well.
Je dîne dans les restaurants les plus élégants.	I dine in the finest restaurants.

See how easy it is?

Conjugation 101

Use the correct form of the verb to express what each individual is doing on vacation:

For example, (*regarder*): Je *regarde* le spectacle.

1. (traverser) Il _____ la rue.
2. (demander) Elles _____ l'adresse.
3. (chercher) Nous _____ le musée.

4. (accompagner) J'_____
    ma famille.

5. (louer) Vous _____
    un appartement.

6. (présenter) Sylvie et Luc _____
    leurs amis à leurs parents.

7. (réserver) Robert _____
    une chambre d'hôtel.

8. (monter) Tu _____ à la tour.

9. (parler) Marie _____ avec
    ses amis.

10. (poser) Jean et Robert _____
    des questions.

Memory Enhancer

A subject can be followed by two consecutive verbs. When this occurs, conjugate only the first verb. The second verb remains in the infinitive: Je désire danser. (I want to dance.) Il aime jouer au tennis. (He loves to play tennis.)

The *ir* Verb Family

To conjugate *ir* verbs, drop *ir* from the infinitive and then add the endings:

Pronoun	Verb ending
je	is
tu	is
il, elle, on	it
nous	issons
vous	issez
ils, elles	issent

Let's take a look at the conjugated forms of *choisir* (to choose):

Singular Forms	Plural Forms
Je choisis, I choose	Nous choisissons, We choose
Tu choisis, You choose	Vous choisissez, You choose
Il choisit, He chooses	Ils choisissent, They choose
Elle choisit, She chooses	Elles choisissent, They choose
On choisit, One, We, They choose(s)	

Conjugation 102

It's time to see if you're up to the challenge. Be careful with infinitives, such as *choisir* and *réussir*, that already have *i*'s and *s*'s in them. By the time you're finished conjugating them, they may look a little strange (Nous réussissons, Tu choisis), but they are correct. Be confident and give the correct form of the verb and express what each tourist does:

1. Nous/finir _____ à huit heures.

2. On/réfléchir _____ .

3. Ils/jouir _____ de tout.

4. Tu/applaudir _____ au théâtre.

5. Elle/réussir _____ à parler français.

6. Je/choisir _____ un bon tour.

7. Vous/agir _____ bien.

8. Alice et Berthe/remplir _____ les formulaires.

The *re* Verb Family

The *re* verb family is, by far, the smallest. The verbs *attendre* (to wait for), *entendre* (to hear), and *vendre* (to sell) are high-frequency verbs that you'll be using and hearing on a regular basis. So, it will be necessary to commit this conjugation to memory. To conjugate *re* verbs, drop *re* from the infinitive and then add the endings:

Memory Enhancer

You're in luck. There is no ending for the third person singular form (*il, elle, on*) of *re* verbs: Il (*Elle, On*) répond/He, She, One answers.

Pronoun	Verb ending
je	*s*
tu	*s*
il, elle, on	
nous	*ons*
vous	*ez*
ils, elles	*ent*

Note the conjugated forms of *attendre* (to wait for).

Singular Forms	**Plural Forms**
J'attend**s**, I wait	Nous attend**ons**, We wait
Tu attend**s**, You wait (fam. sing.)	Vous attend**ez**, You (pol. sing. and plur.) wait
Il attend, He waits	Ils attend**ent**, They wait
Elle attend, She waits	Elles attend**ent**, They wait
On attend, One, We, They wait	

Conjugation 103

People on vacation do all sorts of different things. Use your knowledge of *re* verbs to describe their actions. In the following, choose the verb that best completes the sentence. Then, provide the correct verb form to explain what each tourist is doing:

attendre (to wait for)	perdre (to lose)	descendre (to go down)
rendre (to return)	entendre (to hear)	répondre (to answer)

1. Tu _____ le métro.
2. Elles _____ en ville.
3. Nous _____ notre plan de la ville.
4. Vous _____ à des questions.
5. Il _____ les nouvelles (the news).
6. Je _____ les documents.

To review, all regular verbs follow a pattern of conjugation consistent with their infinitive endings. Simply drop the final *er*, *ir*, or *re* and add the ending that corresponds to the subject, as shown in the table below:

Un deux trois

Leaf through a family album and use pronouns to identify the people you see. Try to express in French what the different people are doing.

Review of Regular Verbs

	-er verbs	-ir verbs	-re verbs
je	-e	-is	-s
tu	-es	-is	-s
il, elle, on	-e	-it	(no ending)
nous	-ons	-issons	-ons
vous	-ez	-issez	-ez
ils, elles	-ent	-issent	-ent

Go Ahead! Ask Me a Question!

When planning a trip, you'll find a lot of questions that you'll want to ask. Let's concentrate on the easy ones—those that require a simple Yes or No answer.

There are four ways to show that you're asking a question:

1. intonation
2. the tag *n'est-ce pas* (isn't that so?)
3. *Est-ce que* at the beginning of your phrase
4. inversion

It's Okay to Raise Your Voice

The easiest way to show that you're asking a question is to simply change your intonation and raise your voice at the end of the sentence. To do this, place an imaginary question mark at the end of your statement and speak with a rising inflection.

Attention!

Subject pronouns must always be used in French, except when giving a command.

| Tu penses au voyage? | Are you thinking about the trip? |

Notice how your voice starts out lower and gradually keeps rising until the end of the sentence.

When using the same sentence as a statement of fact, notice how your voice rises and then lowers by the end of the sentence.

| Tu penses au voyage. | You are thinking about the trip. |

The n'est-ce pas? Tag

Another simple way to ask a question is to add the tag *n'est-ce pas* (*nehs pas*/isn't that so?) at the end of the sentence.

> Tu penses au voyage, n'est-ce pas?

Est-ce que

Yet another way to ask the same question is to put *Est-ce que* (*ehs-kuh*) at the beginning of the sentence. *Est-ce que* is not translated but does indicate that a question follows:

> Est-ce que tu penses au voyage?

Attention!

Est-ce que becomes *Est-ce qu'* before a vowel or vowel sound (*h, y*): Est-ce qu'il pense au voyage?

Doing an About Face

The last way to form a question is by inversion, which is used far more frequently in writing than in conversation. *Inversion* means reversing the word order of the *subject pronoun* and the *conjugated verb form*. Several rules govern inversion, which can get tricky. Don't despair, however. If you feel more comfortable using one of the other three methods mentioned, by all means, use them. You will still be speaking perfectly correct French, you will be understood, and your question will be answered. For those who are up to the challenge, the rules are as follows:

Attention!

You can only invert a verb with a subject pronoun. If you try to do this with a noun, you will sound like an amateur. If you find this rule hard to remember, use one of the other 3 easier ways to ask a question.

➤ **Avoid inverting with *je*.** It's awkward and is very rarely used.

➤ **You can ONLY invert subject pronouns with conjugated verbs. DO NOT INVERT with nouns!** Look at some examples to see how inversion works with the subject pronouns:

Tu penses au voyage.	Penses-tu au voyage?
Nous expliquons bien.	Expliquons-nous bien?
Vous parlez français.	Parlez-vous français?
Ils commandent du vin.	Commandent-ils du vin?
Elles habitent à Paris.	Habitent-elles à Paris?

➤ **A *-t-* must be added with *il* and *elle* to avoid having two vowels together.** This usually happens only with verbs in the *er* family. For the *ir* and *re* families, the *il* and *elle* verb forms end in a consonant:

Il travaille aujourd'hui.	Travaille-**t**-il aujourd'hui?
Elle contacte l'agent.	Contacte-**t**-elle l'agent?
Il finit son dessert.	Finit-il son dessert?
Elle attend le bus.	Attend-elle le bus?

➤ **When you have a noun subject and you want to use inversion, you MUST replace the noun with the appropriate pronoun.** You may retain the noun at the beginning of the question, but then you must invert the corresponding pronoun with the conjugated verb form. For example:

Le chanteur **est-il** français? The pronoun *il* was chosen because *le chanteur* (the singer) is a singular, masculine noun. No *-t-* was necessary because the verb ends in a consonant.

La robe **est-elle** trop petite? The pronoun *elle* was chosen because *la robe* (the dress) is a feminine, singular noun. Again, no *-t-* was necessary because the verb ends in a consonant.

Le docteur et le dentiste **travaillent-ils** aujourd'hui? The pronoun *ils* was chosen because we are referring to more than one male noun.

Les brochures **sont-elles** à notre disposition? The pronoun *elles* was chosen because we are referring to a feminine, plural noun.

Le gâteau et la mousse **sont-ils** excellents? The pronoun *ils* was chosen because when referring to two nouns of different genders, the male noun is *always* given precedence.

Attention!

Remember that a masculine pro-noun is always used when referring to a subject that contains masculine and feminine nouns.

Remember that whether you are using intonation, *est-ce que*, *n'est-ce pas*, or inversion, you are asking for exactly the same information: a yes/*oui* (*wee*) or no/*non* (*nohN*) answer:

Tu poses des questions intelligentes?

Est-ce que tu poses des questions intelligentes?

Tu poses des questions intelligentes, n'est-ce pas?

Poses-tu des questions intelligentes?

Ask Me—I Dare You

Imagine that you're sitting on a bus with your tour group. Unfortunately, you're stuck in horrible traffic on the autoroute and you and your fellow travelers are bored beyond belief. To keep yourselves occupied, you decide to ask questions about everyone on board, including yourselves. Using the subjects and actions listed, write questions in as many ways as you can.

1. nous/parler trop
2. il/descendre souvent en ville
3. vous/accomplir beaucoup
4. Marie/téléphoner toujours à sa famille

5. tu/attendre toujours les autres
6. les garçons/jouer au tennis
7. elles/écouter le guide
8. Luc et Anne/sembler heureux

And the Answer Is...

If you're an upbeat person who enjoys doing a lot of things, you'll surely want to know how to answer "yes." To answer affirmatively (yes), use *oui* (*wee*) and then give your statement:

Vous dansez?   Oui, je danse.

To answer yes to a negative quesion, use *si*.

Tu ne danses pas bien?   Si, je danse bien.

Memory Enhancer

There are two ways to say "yes" in French:

Use *oui* to answer an affirmative question.

Use *si* to answer a negative question.

Perhaps you're in a foul mood and everyone and everything is getting on your nerves. Or maybe "no" is just an honest answer. To answer negatively (no), use *non* (*nohN*) and then add *ne* and *pas* (not), respectively, before and after the conjugated verb form. Remember, if there are two verbs, only the first is conjugated:

Vous fumez?   Non, je ne fume pas.   Non, je ne désire pas fumer.

You can easily vary your negative answers by putting the following negative phrases before and after the conjugated verb:

ne...jamais (*nuh...zhah-meh*)	never
Je ne fume jamais.	I never smoke.
Ne...plus (*nuh...plew*)	no longer
Je ne fume plus.	I no longer smoke. (I don't smoke anymore.)
ne...rien (*nuh...ryaN*)	nothing, anything
Je ne fume rien.	I'm not smoking anything.

It's All About You

What are your good or bad habits? Do you have hobbies? Are there activities you really enjoy doing to relax? Read the following list and answer with a yes or no sentence. (Sample responses are located in the Answer Key in Appendix A.)

Fumer?

Crier?

Jouer au tennis?

Danser bien?

Parler français?

Bavarder avec des amis?

Dîner tôt?

Aimer réussir?

Attention!

Never use a double negative in French. Use *ne* + one other negative word only: *pas*, or *jamais*, or *plus*, or *rien*.

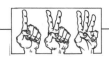

Un deux trois

The word *non* means "no."

Questions may be asked by:

1. Raising the intonation of your voice at the end of a sentence.
2. Adding the *n'est-ce pas?* tag to the end of a sentence.
3. Placing *Est-ce que* at the beginning of a sentence.
4. Reversing the order of the subject pronoun and the verb.

Questions may be answered affirmatively as follows:

1. Use *oui* in response to an affirmative question.
2. Use *si* in response to a negative question.

Questions may be answered negatively by using *ne* + verb + one of the following: *pas* (not), *jamais* (never), *plus* (no longer), or *rien* (nothing).

Verb Tables

If you want to increase your vocabulary quickly, you'll need to have as many verbs as possible on the tip of your tongue. The following three tables provide you with practical lists of the most frequently used *er*, *ir*, and *re* verbs; these are the ones that you'll need the most in any given situation.

Common *er* Verbs

Verb	Pronunciation	Meaning
aider	*eh-day*	to help
annoncer	*ah-nohN-say*	to announce
bavarder	*bah-vahr-day*	to chat
changer	*shahN-zhay*	to change
chercher	*shehr-shay*	to look for
commencer	*koh-mahN-say*	to begin
danser	*dahN-say*	to dance
demander	*duh-mahN-day*	to ask
dépenser	*day-pahN-say*	to spend (money)
donner	*doh-nay*	to give
écouter	*ay-koo-tay*	to listen (to)
étudier	*ay-tew-dyay*	to study
expliquer	*eks-plee-kay*	to explain
exprimer	*eks-pree-may*	to express
fermer	*fehr-may*	to close
fonctionner	*fohNk-syohN-nay*	to function
garder	*gahr-day*	to keep, watch
habiter	*ah-bee-tay*	to live (in)
indiquer	*aN-dee-kay*	to indicate
jouer	*zhoo-ay*	to play
laver	*lah-vay*	to wash
manger	*mahN-zhay*	to eat
marcher	*mahr-shay*	to walk
nager	*nah-zhay*	to swim
oublier	*oo-blee-yay*	to forget
parler	*pahr-lay*	to speak
penser	*pahN-say*	to think
préparer	*pray-pah-ray*	to prepare
présenter	*pray-zahN-tay*	to present, introduce
quitter	*kee-tay*	to leave, remove
regarder	*ruh-gahr-day*	to look at, watch
regretter	*ruh-gruh-tay*	to regret
rencontrer	*rahN-kohN-tray*	to meet
retourner	*ruh-toor-nay*	to return

continues

Common *er* Verbs (cont.)

Verb	Pronunciation	Meaning
sembler	*sahN-blay*	to seem
signer	*see-nyay*	to sign
téléphoner	*tay-lay-foh-nay*	to telephone
travailler	*trah-vah-yay*	to work
voyager	*vwah-yah-zhay*	to travel

Common *ir* Verbs

Verb	Pronunciation	Meaning
agir	*ah-zheer*	to act
avertir	*ah-vehr-teer*	to warn
blanchir	*blahN-sheer*	to bleach, whiten
choisir	*shwah-zeer*	to choose
finir	*fee-neer*	to finish
guérir	*gay-reer*	to cure
jouir	*zhoo-eer*	to enjoy
maigrir	*meh-greer*	to become thin
obéir	*oh-bay-eer*	to obey
punir	*pew-neer*	to punish
réfléchir	*ray-flay-sheer*	to reflect, think
réussir	*ray-ew-seer*	to succeed

Common *re* Verbs

Verb	Pronunciation	Meaning
attendre	*ah-tahNdr*	to wait for
descendre	*deh-sahNdr*	to go (come) down
entendre	*ahN-tahNdr*	to hear
perdre	*pehrdr*	to lose
répondre	*ray-pohNdr ah*	to answer
vendre	*vahNdr*	to sell

Your Trip Awaits

You're finally going to take that dream trip. Read the following ads for travel agencies and match them with the services you think they provide.

1. This agency caters to a younger crowd. _____

2. This agency provides for an exchange of residences. _____

3. This agency will take you home, if you live in Paris. _____

4. This agency caters to an athletic crowd. _____

Attention!

The third person singular forms of *rompre* (to break) and *interrompre* (to interrupt) are slightly irregular:

il/elle rompt   il/elle interrrompt

a)   MAISON DE VOYAGES

VOYAGES EN GROUPES
FORFAIT INDIVIDUEL
BILLETS ET LOCATIONS
LIVRAISON À DOMICILE (PARIS)

b)   SPORTS ET LOISIRS
TOUS LES
VOYAGES POUR TOUS
LES SPORTS

Jeux olympiques
Football
Rugby "5 Nations"
Marathons, Formule 1
Basketball, Volleyball
Tennis, Voile
Sports loisirs
Stages tous sports

c)

LOISIRS ET VACANCES

DES VACANCES PARTOUT DANS LE MONDE AVEC UNE SEULE CLEF

AVEC LE DROIT DE SÉJOUR

ÉCHANGEABLE

Consultez l'Annuaire électronique
11 Nom: LOISIRS ET VACANCES
Loc: BOULOGNE
Dept: 92

d)

VOYAGES de la JEUNESSE
Jeunes 18/35
voyagez à des
prix exceptionnels
séjours, circuits
expéditions…club 18/35

The Least You Need to Know

➤ Subject pronouns can be used to replace any subject noun.

➤ Any verb that follows a subject noun or pronoun must be properly conjugated.

➤ There are different rules for conjugating verbs belonging to the *er*, *ir*, and *re* families.

➤ There are four ways to ask a question in French: intonation, using the *n'est-ce pas* tag, using *est-ce que*, and inversion.

➤ Use *ne* + verb + *pas* (not), *jamais* (never), *plus* (no longer) or *rien* (never) to answer a question negatively.

Part 2
Travel Time

You never know where life will take you and whom you'll meet along the way. In an ever-growing, multicultural society—where foreign travel is not only a luxury but has become a business necessity—you might easily find yourself in a French-speaking country one day soon. Undoubtedly, your French will serve you well around the globe.

Being able to introduce yourself and your traveling companions will help you to meet new people from different cultures and will allow you to pick up useful travel tips before the plane has landed. Upon arrival, you'll be able to get around the airport so that there's no delay in reaching your destination. Your comfort, of course, will also be very important to you.

The highlights of Part 2 include how to get where you're going in a timely fashion, and how to procure some necessary creature comforts once you've arrived.

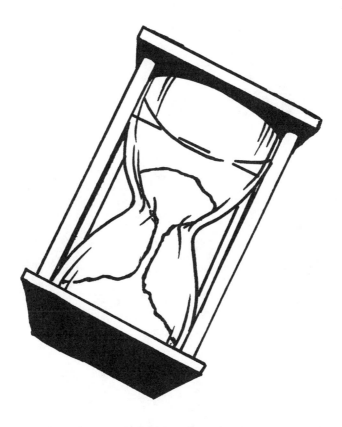

Chapter 8

Greetings and Salutations

In This Chapter

➤ Hellos and good-byes

➤ The irregular verb *être* (to be)

➤ Jobs and professions

➤ When you need information

The time has come to put what you've learned to good use. Now that you can create simple French sentences (using subject nouns, pronouns, and regular verbs) and ask yes-no questions, you're ready to engage in a short conversation.

While you're sitting on the plane on your way to a glorious vacation in a French-speaking country, you might want to strike up a conversation with the person sitting next to you. If that person speaks French, you're in luck. This is an excellent opportunity for you to introduce yourself and, perhaps, to get a few helpful hints and recommendations about places to visit, restaurants to go to, and things to do in the country you're visiting.

Becoming Friends

Even though you've read every travel book in your local bookstore, you may still be a little nervous about your trip. What you really need to do is speak to someone from the country—someone who lives there and can fill you in on everything you can do and see and everywhere to go. Where can you find this person? Probably sitting right next to you on the plane! There's plenty of time before you arrive at your destination, so why not strike up a conversation?

Culture Capsule

Out of respect, older women in France are generally addressed as *Madame* (Mrs.), whether they are married or not. At what age is one considered "older"? It's hard to say. When in doubt, use *Madame*. *Mademoiselle* (Miss, Ms.) is used for younger women.

It's considered quite a *faux pas* to address someone informally if a strong friendship or relationship has not been established. One would not *tutoyer* (use *tu*) a new business acquaintance or a stranger. Never use the familiar form *tu* when speaking to someone you don't know well. It's considered very rude and insulting. Since you don't know the person at all, a formal approach is *de rigueur* (mandatory). A typical opening conversation might start with many of the phrases :

Bonjour	*bohN-zhoor*	Hello.
Bonsoir	*bohN swahr*	Good evening.
monsieur	*muh-syuh*	Sir.
madame	*mah-dahm*	Miss, Mrs.
mademoiselle	*mahd-mwah-zehl*	Miss.
Je m'appelle	*zhuh mah-pehl*	My name is (I call myself).
Comment vous appelez-vous?	*kohN-mahN voo zah-play voo*	What is your name?
Comment allez-vous?	*kohN-mahN tah-lay voo*	How are you?
Très bien.	*treh byaN*	Very well.
Pas mal.	*pah mahl*	Not bad.
Comme ci comme ça.	*kohm see kohm sah*	So so.

When you're ready to leave, remember to say *au revoir* (*o ruh-vwahr*), "good-bye." If you plan on seeing the person sometime soon use à + the period of time: *à demain*—see you tomorrow; *à tout à l'heure*—see you soon; *à lundi*—see you Monday. During an informal opening conversation (between young people or friends), you might use the phrases:

Salut!	*sah-lew*	Hi!
Je m'appelle.	*zhuh mah-pehl*	My name is (I call myself).
Comment t'appelles-tu?	*kohN-mahN tah-pehl tew*	What's your name?
Ça va?	*sah vah*	How's it going?
Ça marche?	*sah mahrsh*	How's it going?
Ça va.	*sah vah*	O.K.
Ça marche.	*sah mahrsh*	O.K.

Memory Enhancer

Salut is a familiar way of saying "hello" as well as "good-bye."

To Be or Not to Be

If you'd really like to get to know the person you are talking to, ask him or her a few questions about himself or herself: Where he or she is from, for example. You'll also want to respond correctly when others ask where you are from. To do this, you will need the verb *être* (to be). Just as it is in English, the verb *to be* (*être*) is irregular, and all of its forms must be memorized. Because you will be using this verb so frequently, make it a top priority to memorize its forms. Compare the conjugations in the following table. As you will see, there are more irregular forms in French than there are in English.

The Verb *être* (to be)

je suis	*zhuh swee*	I am
tu es	*tew eh*	you are
il, elle, on est	*eel (ehl) (ohN) eh*	he, she, one is
nous sommes	*noo sohm*	we are
vous êtes	*voo zeht*	you are
ils, elles sont	*eel (ehl) sohN*	they are

Do you detect an unfamiliar accent when speaking to an acquaintance? Get ready to satisfy your curiosity by using the verb être to ask about a person's origins. You're ready to proceed:

Formal use:

Vous êtes d'où?	*voo zeht doo*	Where are you from?

Informal use:

Tu es d'où?	*tew eh doo*	Where are you from?
Je suis de _____ (city).	*zhuh swee duh*	I am from _____ (city).

To express the city or state you come from, keep the following in mind:

Use *de* (from) for all cities and feminine states; that is, any state ending in *e* and for any state whose name has an adjective:

> Je suis de Maine.

> Je suis de New York.

Use *du* (from) for all masculine states; that is, states ending in any letter other than *e*:

> Je suis du Vermont.

Use *des* (from) to say that you come from the United States:

> Je suis des États-Unis.

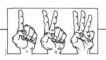

Un deux trois

Try looking at a map and using all the different forms of *être* to practice saying where different people you know, or don't know, come from. You might want to pick people in the news and express where they are from.

Idioms with *être*

Imagine that you are on the phone with your French relative, Uncle Gaston. You think you hear him say to you, "Je suis en train de préparer le dîner." Hearing the cognates *train*, *preparer*, and *diner*, you immediately assume that Uncle Gaston is a chef on one of France's trains, perhaps on the T.G.V. (Train à Grande Vitesse—a very modern and fast train). But how could this be? The last you heard, he was a nephrologist at a leading teaching hospital in Paris. Did he have a change of heart? If you think you hear something that sounds wildly implausible, chances are you're right. Just when you think you have a handle on the language, *idioms*, those linguistic bugaboos, are ready to trip you up. In this case, your Uncle was using an idiomatic expression that means he's busy preparing dinner (bouillabaisse perhaps?). The following table will show you some new idioms with *être*.

Idioms with *être*

être à	*ehtr ah*	to belong to
être d'accord (avec)	*ehtr dah-kohr*	to agree (with)
être de retour	*ehtr duh ruh-toor*	to be back
être en train de + infinitive	*ehtr ahN traN duh*	to be in the act of, busy
être sur le point de + infinitive	*ehtr sewr luh pwaN duh*	to be on the verge of

Make sure to conjugate the verb when you use it in context:

Ce journal est à moi.	This newspaper is mine.
Je suis d'accord.	I agree.
Est-il de retour?	Is he back?
Nous sommes en train de manger.	We are busy eating.
Es-tu sur le point de finir?	Are you on the verge of finishing?

Using *être*

Complete the sentence with the correct form of **être** and the idiom that fits:

être à

être de retour

être d'accord

être en train de

être sur le point de

1. Je travaille. Je _____ préparer le dîner.
2. Je dis "oui." Tu dis "oui." Nous _____.
3. Les filles arrivent dans six minutes. Elles _____ arriver.
4. Le sac bleu _____ M. Dupont.
5. Vous _____ depuis quand (since when?)

What's Your Line?

You can also use *être* to ask about a person's job or to talk about your own job. The feminine forms are given in parentheses in the following table. Some occupations have only masculine or feminine forms despite the gender of the person employed.

Un deux trois

Other professions use the same word for masculine and feminine employees, but require the gender-appropriate noun marker (le [un] or la [une]).

Attention!

The indefinite article *un* (*une*) is not used with someone's profession (*Je suis professeur. Elle est artiste*), unless the profession is qualified by an adjective (*Je suis un bon professeur. Elle est une artiste célèbre*).

Formal use:

Quel est votre métier?	*kehl eh vohtr may-tyay*	What is your profession?

Informal use:

Quel est ton métier?	*kehl eh tohN may-tyay*	What is your profession?
Je suis…	*zhuh swee…*	I am…

Professions

Profession	French	Pronunciation
accountant	comptable	*kohn-tahbl*
actor (actress)	acteur (actrice)	*ahk-tuhr (ahk-trees)*
artist	artiste m. or f.	*ahr-teest*
business man (woman)	homme (femme) d'affaires	*ohm (fahm) dah-fehr*
cashier	caissier (caissière)	*kehs-yay (kehs-yehr)*
dentist	dentiste m.	*dahN-teest*
doctor	docteur m., médecin m.	*dohk-tuhr, mayd-saN*
electrician	électricien(ne)	*ay-lehk-tree-syaN (ay-lehk-tree-syehn)*
engineer	ingénieur m.	*aN-zhay-nyuhr*
firefighter	pompier m.	*pohN-pyay*
gov't employee	fonctionnaire m.	*fohNk-syoh-nehr*
hairdresser	coiffeur (coiffeuse)	*kwah-fuhr (kwah-fuhz)*
jeweler	bijoutier (bijoutière)	*bee-zhoo-tyay (bee-zhoo-tyehr)*
lawyer	avocat(e)	*ah-voh-kah(t)*
manager	gérant(e)	*zhay-rahN(t)*
mechanic	mécanicien(ne)	*may-kah-nee-syaN (may-kah-nee-syehn)*
musician	musicien(ne)	*mew-zee-syaN (mew-zee-syehn)*
nurse	infirmier (infirmière)	*aN-feer-myay (ahN-feer-myehr)*

Profession	French	Pronunciation
optician	opticien(ne)	*ohp-tee-syaN (ohp-tee-syehn)*
owner	propriétaire m. or f.	*proh-pree-ay-tehr*
photographer	photographe m. or f.	*foh-to-grahf*
pilot	pilote m.	*pee-loht*
police officer	agent de police m.	*ah-zhahN duh poh-lees*
postal worker	facteur (factrice)	*fahk-tuhr (fahk-trees)*
programmer	programmeur (programmeuse)	*proh-grah-muhr (proh-grah-muhz)*
salesperson	vendeur (vendeuse)	*vahN-duhr (vahN-duhz)*
secretary	secrétaire m. or f.	*seh-kray-tehr*
student	étudiant(e)	*ay-tewd-yahN (ay-tew-dyahNt)*
teacher	professeur m.	*proh-feh-suhr*
waiter	garçon m., serveur m.	*gahr-sohN, sehr-vuhr*
waitress	serveuse f.	*sehr-vuhz*

An Introductory Conversation

You're sitting on the plane reading your traveler's guide to France when your seatmate decides to get talkative. How would you repond when she says the following? (Sample responses can be found in the Answer Key in Appendix A.)

1. Bonjour.
2. Comment vous appelez-vous?
3. Comment allez-vous?
4. Vous êtes-d'où?
5. Quel est votre métier?

Curiosity Killed a Cat... but Not You

Picture this: That sublime hunk/babe in seat 6B—you think he's/she's cute. What phrases do you need to probe more deeply and develop the relationship of your dreams? You have a million questions and you want thorough answers. You're going to have to ask *information questions* to find

Memory Enhancer

To refer to a woman in a profession that always uses the masculine word form, simply add the word *femme* (*fahm*/woman) before the job title: Elle est femme pilote/She's a woman pilot.

Un deux trois

Imagine you are going to meet a long-lost, distant French family member for the first time. Prepare a brief speech to introduce yourself in French.

out all the relevant facts you seek. Whatever the situation or problem, you'll be able to see it through with the words and expressions in the following table:

Questions

Word/Phrase	Pronunciation	Meaning
à quelle heure	*ah kehl uhr*	at what time
à qui	*ah kee*	to whom
à quoi	*ah kwah*	to what
avec qui	*ah-vehk kee*	with whom
avec quoi	*ah-vehk kwah*	with what
de qui	*duh kee*	of, about, from whom
de quoi	*duh kwah*	of, about, from what
combien (de + noun)	*kohN-byaN (duh)*	how much, many
comment	*kohN-mahN*	how
où	*oo*	where
d'où	*doo*	from where
pourquoi	*poor-kwah*	why
quand	*kahN*	when
qui	*kee*	who, whom
que	*kuh*	what
qu'est-ce que	*kehs-kuh*	what
quoi	*kwah*	what

Getting Information 1-2-3

You're ready to make your move. What's your opening line? Something corny like, "Excuse me, where are you from?" Or, "Where are you going?" Or perhaps you have a more interesting question to break the ice. No matter how you choose to pursue your line of questioning, you'll find that the easiest way to ask for information is to put the question word immediately after the verbal phrase or thought. Here are some questions you might want to ask a traveling companion:

Attention!

Note that French does not have separate words for *who* (subject) and *whom* (object). The word *qui* serves as both.

> Vous voyagez (Tu voyages) **avec qui?**
>
> Vous voyagez (Tu voyages) **pourquoi?**
>
> Vous voyagez (Tu voyages) **comment?**
>
> Vous parlez (Tu parles) **de qui? de quoi?**

Vous regardez (Tu regardes) **quoi**?

Vous êtes (Tu es) **d'où**?

Vous habitez (Tu habitez) **où** en France?

Le vol (the flight) arrive **quand**? **à quelle heure**?

Un soda coûte **combien**?

Getting Information Using *est-ce que*

Information questions can also be asked by using *est-ce que*. This is done by putting the question word at the very beginning of the sentence and then adding *est-ce que* before the verbal phrase or thought:

> **Avec qui** est-ce que vous voyagez (tu voyages)?
>
> **Pourquoi** est-ce que vous voyagez (tu voyages)?
>
> **Comment** est-ce que vous voyagez (tu voyages)?
>
> **De qui**? **De quoi** est-ce que vous parlez (tu parles)?
>
> Qu'est-ce que vous regardez (tu regardes)?
>
> **D'où** est-ce que vous êtes (tu es)?
>
> **Où** est-ce que vous habitez (tu habites) en France?
>
> **Quand**? **À quelle heure** est-ce que le vol (the flight) arrive?
>
> **Combien** est-ce qu' un soda coûte?

En 10 Minutes

You can get information by using question words at the end of a thought with intonation, before *est-ce que*, or before an inverted verb form.

Attention!

Quoi becomes *que (qu')* before *est-ce que*:

Tu veux faire quoi?

Qu'est-ce que tu veux faire? What do you want to do?

Getting Information Using Inversion

Finally, you can use inversion to ask information questions. Put the question word(s) (as listed in the previous table) before the inverted subject pronoun and conjugated verb form:

Avec qui voyagez-vous (voyages-tu)?

Pourquoi voyagez-vous (voyages-tu)?

Comment voyagez-vous (voyages-tu)?

De qui? De quoi parlez-vous (parles-tu)?

Que regardez-vous (regardes-tu)?

D'où êtes-vous (es-tu)?

Où habitez-vous (habites-tu) en France?

Quand? À quelle heure le vol (the flight) arrive-t-il?

Combien coûte-t-il un soda?

Attention!

Quoi becomes *que (qu')* when inversions is used: Tu veux faire *quoi?* Que veux-tu *faire?*

You will probably ask for information in a variety of different ways. No doubt you'll choose the way that feels more comfortable and seems to flow. Most of the time, however, you will probably tack the question word or phrase onto the end of your statement (Vous êtes d'où?). Why not? It's easy and it works. Using *est-ce que* may be your choice on occasion, especially if you have a noun subject (A quelle heure est-ce que l'avion arrive?). At other times, you might find it preferable to invert (Que cherches-tu?). Whichever way you choose, you will be perfectly understood and will get the information you need.

Getting the Scoop

Read each of the following paragraphs. Ask as many questions as you can, based on the information given to you in each selection. In paragraph A, you are asking about Robert. In paragraph B, you must ask Georgette questions about herself:

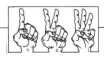

Un deux trois

Be imaginative. Pretend that right now you are sitting next to an interesting person in an airplane bound for Martinique. Think of five questions you would ask that person to get to know him better.

➤ A. Robert est des États-Unis. Il voyage avec sa famille en France en voiture. Ils passent deux mois en France. Is désirent visiter tous les villages typiques. Ils retournent à Pittsburgh en septembre.

➤ B. Je m'appelle Georgette. Je suis de Nice. Je cherche une correspondante américaine parce que je désire pratiquer l'anglais. Je parle anglais seulement quand je suis en classe. J'adore aussi la musique. Je suis sérieuse.

The Least You Need to Know

➤ Choose your words carefully! The greeting words you use depend upon your familiarity with that person.

➤ The verb *être* is one of the most useful verbs in French. It is essential to memorize it because it is irregular.

➤ You can ask yes/no questions by using intonation, the tag *n'est-ce pas, est-ce que* at the beginning of a sentence, and inversion.

➤ You can get information easily by learning a few key words and phrases, and by placing them at the end of the thought, before *est-ce que* at the beginning of the sentence, or before an inverted question form.

Chapter 9

I'd Like to Get to Know You

In This Chapter

➤ Family members

➤ Showing possession

➤ Introducing family and friends

➤ The irregular verb *avoir* (to have)

➤ Describing people and things

If you've successfully used the linguistic tools provided in the preceding chapter, then you should be well on your way to introducing yourself and making new friends. You certainly don't want to appear rude, so how about introducing your family members to your new acquaintances? Perhaps you, too, will meet a new friend and be introduced to members of his or her family. Whatever the circumstances, it helps to be prepared.

Let's say there is someone in particular you would like to meet. But before you make your introduction, you'd like to find out a few things about this person. This chapter will give you the tools you need to find out what your potential pal is really like.

Here's the Clan

How many times have you opened your mouth during the course of a conversation only to find that you've done a magnificent job of sticking your foot in it? If you're anything like me, it's probably happened more often than you care to remember. Have you ever (as I have done) mistaken someone's father for his grandfather? Or worse yet, someone's wife for his mother? I've learned not to make any assumptions when I meet someone. The following table will help you to avoid a potentially embarrassing situation.

Family Members

Male	Pronunciation	Meaning	Female	Pronunciation	Meaning
le père	*luh pehr*	father	la mère	*lah mehr*	mother
le grand-père	*luh grahN-pehr*	grandfather	la grand-mère	*lah grahN-mehr*	grandmother
le beau-père	*luh bo-pehr*	father-in-law	la belle-mère	*lah behl-mehr*	mother-in-law
l'enfant	*lahN-fahN*	child	l'enfant	*lahN-fahN*	child
le frère	*luh frehr*	brother	la soeur	*lah suhr*	sister
le demi-frère	*luh duh-mee frehr*	step-brother	la demi-soeur	*lah duh-mee suhr*	step-sister
le beau-fils	*luh bo-fees*	stepson, son-in-law	la belle-fille	*lah behl-fee-y*	step-daughter
le fils	*luh fees*	son	la fille	*lah fee-y*	daughter
l'oncle	*lohNkl*	uncle	la tante	*lah tahNt*	aunt
le cousin	*luh koo-zahN*	cousin	la cousine	*lah koo-zeen*	cousin
le neveu	*luh nuh-vuh*	nephew	la nièce	*lah nyehs*	niece
le mari	*luh mah-ree*	husband	la femme	*lah fahm*	wife
le gendre	*luh zhahNdr*	son-in-law	la belle-fille	*lah behl-fee-y*	daughter-in-law
le petit ami	*luh puh-tee tah-mee*	boyfriend	la petite amie	*lah puh-tee tah-mee*	girlfriend

So, you've got a large family. How much easier it is to group our kids, parents, and grandparents together when we speak about them. Here are some useful plurals and their spellings:

les enfants	*lay zahN-fahN*	the children
les parents	*lay pah-rahN*	the parents
les grands-parents	*lay grahN-pah-rahN*	the grandparents
les beaux-parents	*lay bo pah-rahN*	the in-laws

Culture Capsule

Families in France tend to be very close-knit. Today, however, the family unit is weakening and shrinking as young people leave in pursuit of employment opportunities and as French women join the work force and have fewer children. To fight this change, the French government gives monthly financial assistance for each minor child (under 18) and provides an excellent daycare system.

You Belong to Me

Don't be upset, but you're probably possessed. That is, you're somebody's somebody: your mother's child, your friend's friend, your brother's sister, or your sister's brother. There are two ways to show possession in French: by using the preposition *de* and by using possessive adjectives.

Possession with *de*

To show possession in English, we put *'s* or *s'* after a noun. But there are no apostrophes in French. In order to translate *Roger's mother* into French, a speaker would have to say *The mother of Roger = la mère de Roger*. The preposition *de* means *of* and is used to express possession or relationship. *De* is repeated before each noun and becomes *d'* before a vowel:

> C'est le père de Jean et d'Anne.

> He's John and Anne's father.

If the possessor is referred to not by name but by a common noun, such as *the boy* or *the parents* (*He is the boy's father:* The father of the boy; or *That's the parents' car:* The car of the parents), then *de* contracts with the definite articles *le* and *les* to express *of the,* as shown below.

Contractions with *de*

de+le	du
de+les	des

Ce sont les parents *du* garçon.

Ce sont les parents *des* jeunes filles.

No changes are necessary for **de + la** or **de + l'**.

Ce sont les parents *de la* fille.

Ce sont les parents *de l'*homme.

A Sense of Belonging

Now that you understand how to use *de* to express possession, how would you say the following?

---

1. Michael's mother

   _____

2. André and Marie's father

   _____

3. The girls' grandparents

   _____

4. The boy's uncle

   _____

5. The family's grandfather

   _____

6. The child's brother

   _____

French does not use the English possessive construction *'s* or *s'* to show possession. Instead use the following formulas:

Thing/person possessed + de + proper name of possessor:

la mère de Roger

Thing/person possessed + de + definite article + noun:

le père de la fille

l'oncle du garçon

la grand-mère des enfants

Possessive Adjectives

The possessive adjectives *my, your, his, her,* and so on, show that something belongs to someone. In French, possessive adjectives agree with the nouns they describe (the person or thing that is possessed) and not with the subject (the person possessing them). See how this compares with English:

English	French
He loves *his* mother.	Il aime *sa mère.*
She loves *her* mother.	Elle aime *sa mère.*
He loves *his* father.	Il aime *son père.*
She loves *her* father.	Elle aime *son père.*

Son and *sa* both mean *his* or *her* because the possessive adjective agrees with the noun it modifies, not with the subject. Therefore, *her father = son père* because *son* agrees with the word *père*, which is masculine; and *his mother = sa mère* because *sa* agrees with the word *mère*, which is feminine. This difference makes French very tricky to English speakers. Just remember that it is important to know the gender (masculine or feminine) of the noun possessed. When in doubt, look it up! The following table summarizes the use of possessive adjectives:

Attention!

There is no elision with possessive adjectives because there are no final vowels to drop. Never use *m', t',* or *s'* to express *his* or *her*.

Possessive Adjectives

Used before masculine singular nouns or feminine singular nouns beginning with a vowel	Used before feminine singular nouns beginning with a consonant only	Used before all plural nouns
mon (*mohN*) my	ma (*mah*) my	mes (*may*) my
ton (*tohN*) your (fam.)	ta (*tah*) your (fam.)	tes (*tay*) your (fam.)
son (*sohN*) his, her	sa (*sah*) his, her	ses (*say*) his, her
notre (*nohtr*) our	notre (*nohtr*) our	nos (*no*) our
votre (*vohtr*) your (pol.)	votre (*vohtr*) your (pol.)	vos (*vo*) your (pol.)
leur (*luhr*) their	leur (*luhr*) their	leurs (*luhr*) their

Memory Enhancer

The French use *mon, ton,* and *son* before feminine nouns beginning with a vowel to prevent a clash between two pronounced vowel sounds:

mon ami—my male friend

mon amie—my female friend

It's a Matter of Preference

Do you have a favorite song, color, restaurant, vacation spot? We all have our own individual preferences. What are yours? Express them by using the correct possessive adjective (mon, ma, mes).

Examples:

acteur favori	Mon acteur favori est Danny DeVito.
acteurs favoris	Mes acteurs favoris sont Mel Gibson et Patrick Swayze.

1. actrices favorites _____ .
2. restaurants favoris _____ .
3. couleur favorite _____ .
4. chanson (song) favorite _____ .
5. sport favori _____ .
6. film favori _____ .

A French possessive adjective agrees in gender and number with the noun it modifies, and not with the subject. The masculine singular form of the possessive adjective is used before any noun that begins with a vowel, regardless of gender.

Totally Possessed

Give the possessive adjective you would use to talk about these people:

1. (their) _____ parents

2. (his) _____ soeur

3. (your) (fam.) _____ enfant

4. (my) _____ père

5. (your) (pol.) _____ cousins

6. (his) _____ amie

7. (her) _____ grands-parents

8. (their) _____ cousine

9. (her) _____ frère

10. (our) _____ famille

Attention!

Remember that *son* expresses *his* or *her* and agress with the noun that follows it, not with the possessor.

Introductions

Let me introduce myself. My name is Gail. And I'd love for you to meet my husband, Doug, who's helped me tremendously with this book. Do you know my sons Eric and Michael? Eric is a computer wiz. This manuscript couldn't have been typed without him. And Michael, well, he's my source of moral support and a terrific salesman. Now, let's make some introductions in French:

Let me introduce myself. My name is _____.

Permettez-moi de me présenter. Je m'appelle _____

Pehr-meh-tay mwah duh muh pray-zahN-tay. Zhuh mah-pehl _____.

You might ask about a companion:

Do you know my cousin, Roger?

Vous connaissez (Tu connais) mon cousin, Roger?

voo koh-neh-say (tew koh-neh) mohN koo-zahN roh-zhay?

If the answer is *no* (*non*), you would say:

Let me introduce my cousin, Roger.

Je vous présente (Je te présente) mon cousin, Roger.

zhuh voo pray-zahNt (zhuh tuh pray-zahNt) mohN koo-zahN roh-zhay.

or

This is my cousin, Roger.

C'est mon cousin, Roger.

seh mohN koo-zahN roh-zhay.

To express pleasure at having met someone, you might say:

Formally

I am glad (happy, delighted) to know you.

Je suis content(e) [heureux (heureuse), enchanté(e)] de vous connaître.

zhuh swee kohN-tahN [zuh-ruh(z), zahN-shahN-tay] duh voo koh-nehtr.

Informally

Delighted. It's a pleasure.

Enchanté(e), C'est un plaisir.

ahN-shahN-tay, seh tuhN pleh-zeer.

The correct reply to an introduction is

The pleasure is mine.

Moi de même.

mwah dmehm.

Un deux trois

If you want to know a person's address and phone number, simply ask:

Quelles sont tes coordonnées?

kehl sohN tay koh-ohr-doh-nay

What's your address and phone number?

You Can Do It

Are you interested in initiating a conversation and getting your family or traveling companion involved? If so, see if you can do the following in French:

1. Introduce yourself to someone.
2. Ask someone if they know a member of your family.
3. Introduce a member of your family to someone.
4. Express pleasure at having met someone.
5. Respond to someone who says how glad they are to have met you.

Taking the Conversation a Little Further

Perhaps you would like to discuss how many children you have or your age; or you might want to describe family members or friends who aren't present. A verb that you will find most helpful is *avoir* (to have). Like the verb *être* (to be), *avoir* is an irregular verb, and all of its forms (as seen in the table below) must be memorized.

The Verb *avoir* (to have)

j'ai	*zhay*	I have
tu as	*tew ah*	you have
il, elle, on a	*eel,(ehl),(ohN) ah*	he, she, one has
nous avons	*noo zah-vohN*	we have
vous avez	*voo zah-vay*	you have
ils, elles ont	*eel, (ehlz) ohN*	they have

Idioms with *avoir*

In Chapter 4, you were given many idioms with *avoir* that express physical conditions. To refresh your memory, review Chapter 4.

Now you are ready for some new *avoir* idioms. Perhaps you would like to thank a family for giving you the *opportunity* to stay in their home. You might be tempted to give a French twist to our word *opportunity*. After all, *opportunité* does have a French ring to it. When you look up your creation (*opportunité*) in a bilingual dictionary, you will find that the word does exist, but it doesn't mean what you had hoped. (In fact, it means *expediency*, *advisability*, *fitness*.) To avoid other mistakes, study the *avoir* idioms in the following table.

Un deux trois

Using the verb *avoir*, talk about your family members and those of your friends. Take the exercise a little further and use the verb *être* to state their professions, as follows: J'ai une soeur. Elle est artiste. Raymond a un père. Il est comptable.

Idioms with *avoir*

avoir l'occasion de	*ah-vwahr loh-kah-zyohN duh*	to have the opportunity to
avoir de la chance	*ah-vwahr duh lah shahNs*	to be lucky
avoir l'habitude de	*ah-vwahr lah-bee-tewd duh*	to be accustomed to
avoir l'intention de	*ah-vwahr laN-tahN-syohn duh*	to intend to
avoir le temps de	*ah-vwahr luh tahN duh*	to have the time to
avoir lieu	*ah-vwahr lyuh*	to take place

Make sure to conjugate the verb when you use it in context:

J'ai l'occasion de voyager.	I have the opportunity to travel.
Tu as de la chance.	You're lucky.
J'ai l'habitude de dîner à six heures.	I'm accustomed to dining at six o'clock.

Avez-vous l'intention de partir bientôt?	Do you intend to leave soon?
Ils n'ont pas le temps d' attendre.	They don't have the time to wait.
Le rendez-vous a lieu à midi.	The meeting is taking place at noon.

Using avoir

Avoir is a verb that you'll be constantly using. Now that you've taken the time to learn all of its forms and useful idiomatic expressions, see if you can properly complete the following thoughts:

avoir de la chance	avoir l'occasion de
avoir l'habitude de	avoir le temps de
avoir l'intention de	avoir lieu

1. Tu ne travailles pas. Alors tu _____ aider tes parents.

2. Il regarde la télévision tous les jours. Il _____ regarder la télévision.

3. Vous avez gagné (won) la loterie. Vous _____.

4. Elles sont riches. Elles _____ visiter la France chaque année (every year).

5. J'étudie le français. Un jour j'_____ d'aller (to go) à Paris.

6. La cérémonie _____ aujourd'hui (today).

Memory Enhancer

Avoir + noun is also used to describe certain physical conditions that are expressed in English with *to be + adjective*:

J'ai chaud. I'm hot.

For a refresher course, refer back to Chapter 4.

What's He/She Like?

I've been blabbing about myself for several chapters now. Are you curious to know what I'm like? Do you have a mental picture of what a French author looks like? Did you guess brunette (thank you, L'Oréal), brown eyes, 5'4", thin, and young at heart? (I'd tell you my real age, but my students might be curious enough to read this book and discover the answer to a very well-kept secret.) That's me.

If you want to describe a person, place, thing, or idea in detail, you must use adjectives. French adjectives always agree in gender (masculine or feminine) and number (singular or plural) with the nouns or pronouns they modify. In other words, all the words in a French sentence must match:

Her father is happy.	Son père est *content*.
Her mother is happy.	Sa mère est *contente*.

Adjectives Show Gender

With most adjectives, you form the feminine by simply adding an *e* to the masculine form, as shown in the following table. You will notice that a pronunciation change occurs when an *e* is added after a consonant. That consonant, which was silent in the masculine, is now pronounced in the feminine form. When the *e* is added after a vowel, there is no change in pronunciation.

Memory Enhancer

Fortunately, many adjectives follow the same, or almost the same, rules for gender and plural formation as the nouns you've studied in Chapter 6.

Forming Feminine Adjectives

Masculine		Feminine		Meaning
âgé	*ah-zhay*	âgée	*ah-zhay*	old, aged
américain	*ah-may-ree-kahN*	américaine	*ah-may-ree-kehn*	American
amusant	*ah-mew-zahN*	amusante	*ah-mew-zahNt*	amusing, fun
bleu	*bluh*	bleue	*bluh*	blue
blond	*blohN*	blonde	*blohNd*	blond
charmant	*shahr-mahN*	charmante	*shahr-mahNt*	charming
content	*kohN-tahN*	contente	*kohN-tahNt*	glad
court	*koor*	courte	*koort*	short
dévoué	*day-voo-ay*	dévouée	*day-voo-ay*	devoted
élégant	*ay-lay-gahN*	élégante	*ay-lay-gahNt*	elegant
fatigué	*fah-tee-gay*	fatiguée	*fah-tee-gay*	tired
fort	*fohr*	forte	*fohrt*	strong
français	*frahN-seh*	française	*frahN-sehz*	French
grand	*grahN*	grande	*grahNd*	big
haut	*o*	haute	*ot*	tall, big
intelligent	*aN-teh-lee-zhahN*	intelligente	*aN-teh-lee-zhahNt*	intelligent
intéressant	*aN-tay-reh-sahN*	intéressante	*aN-tay-reh-sahNt*	interesting

continues

111

Forming Feminine Adjectives (cont.)

Masculine		Feminine		Meaning
joli	*zhoh-lee*	jolie	*zhoh-lee*	pretty
lourd	*loor*	lourde	*loord*	heavy
occupé	*oh-kew-pay*	occupée	*oh-kew-pay*	busy
ouvert	*oo-vehr*	ouverte	*oo-vehrt*	open
parfait	*pahr-feh*	parfaite	*pahr-feht*	perfect
petit	*puh-tee*	petite	*puh-teet*	small
poli	*poh-lee*	polie	*poh-lee*	polite
prochain	*proh-shaN*	prochaine	*proh-shehn*	next
situé	*see-tew-ay*	située	*see-tew-ay*	situated

Attention!

Remember to make the adjective agree in gender and number—whether you are describing a person, place, thing, or idea.

Attention!

If the masculine form of the adjective ends in a silent *e*, there is no change to the adjective for the feminine form. If, however, the adjective ends in *é (which is pronounced)*, an additional *e* must be added.

Elle est triste et fatiguée.

If an adjective already ends in an *e*, it is not necessary to make any changes at all. Both the masculine and feminine forms are spelled and pronounced exactly the same (see the adjectives in Chapter 3).

aimable (*eh-mahbl*) nice

célèbre (*say-lehbr*) famous

célibataire (*say-lee-bah -tehr*) single

chauve (*shov*) bald

comique (*koh-meek*) comical

drôle (*drohl*) funny

facile (*fah-seel*) easy

faible (*fehbl*) weak

formidable (*fohr-mee- dahbl*) great

honnête (*oh-neht*) honest

maigre (*mehgr*) thin

magnifique (*mah-nyee-feek*) magnificent

malade (*mah-lahd*) sick

mince (*maNs*) thin

moderne (*moh-dehrn*) modern

pauvre (*pohvr*) poor

populaire (poh-pew-lehr) popular

propre (*prohpr*) clean

riche (*reesh*) rich

sale (*sahl*) dirty

splendide (*splahN-deed*)

sympathique (*saN-pah-teek*) nice

triste (*treest*) sad

vide (*veed*) empty

If a masculine adjective ends in *x*, the feminine is formed by changing *x* to *se,* which gives the feminine ending a *z* sound, as seen in the following table:

Adjectives Ending in *eux* and *euse*

Masculine		Feminine	
affectueux	*ah-fehk-tew-uh*	affectueuse	*ah-fehk-tew-uhz*
ambitieux	*ahN-bee-syuh*	ambitieuse	*ahN-bee-syuhz*
courageux	*koo-rah-zhuh*	courageuse	*koo-rah-zhuhz*
curieux	*kew-ryuh*	curieuse	*kew-ryuhz*
dangereux	*dahNzh-ruh*	dangereuse	*dahNzh-ruhz*
délicieux	*day-lee-syuh*	délicieuse	*day-lee-syuhz*
furieux	*few-ryuh*	furieuse	*few-ryuhz*
généreux	*zhay-nay-ruh*	généreuse	*zhay-nay-ruhz*
heureux (happy)	*uh-ruh*	heureuse	*uh-ruhz*
malheureux (unhappy)	*mahl-uh-ruh*	malheureuse	*mahl-uh-ruhz*
paresseux (lazy)	*pah-reh-suh*	paresseuse	*pah-reh-suhz*
sérieux	*say-ryuh*	sérieuse	*say-ryuhz*

If a masculine adjective ends in *f,* the feminine is formed by changing *f* to *ve.* See the following table for pronunciation changes:

Adjectives Ending in *f* and *ve*

Masculine		Feminine	
actif	*ahk-teef*	active	*ahk-teev*
attentif	*ah-tahN-teef*	attentive	*ah-tahN-teev*
imaginatif	*ee-mah-zhee-nah-teef*	imaginative	*ee-mah-zhee-nah-teev*
impulsif	*aN-pewl-seef*	impulsive	*aN-pewl-seev*
intuitif	*aN-tew-ee-teef*	intuitive	*aN-tew-ee-teev*
naïf	*nah-eef*	naïve	*nah-eev*
neuf (new)	*nuhf*	neuve	*nuhv*
sportif	*spohr-teef*	sportive	*spohr-teev*
vif (lively)	*veef*	vive	*veev*

Culture Capsule

Although French men become *âgé* or *vieux* as they mature, French women are considered *forever young*. Until her teens, a girl is *tout jeune* (very young). During adolescence and her 20s, she becomes *une jeune fille* (a young girl). In her 30s, she is *encore jeune* (still young). A middle-aged woman remains *jeune toujours* (as young as ever). And an older woman, in her 70s or 80s, she is considered *éternellement jeune* (forever young).

If a masculine adjective ends in *er*, the feminine is formed by changing *er* to *ère,* as shown in the following table:

Adjectives Ending in *er* and *ère*

Masculine		Feminine		Meaning
cher	*shehr*	chère	*shehr*	dear, expensive
dernier	*dehr-nyay*	dernière	*dehr-nyehr*	last
entier	*ahN-tyay*	entière	*ahN-tyehr*	entire
étranger	*ay-trahN-zhay*	étrangère	*ay-trahN-zhehr*	foreign
fier	*fyehr*	fière	*fyehr*	proud
léger	*lay-zhay*	légère	*lay-zhehr*	light
premier	*pruh-myay*	première	*pruh-myehr*	first

Some masculine adjectives double the final consonant and then add *e* to form the feminine, as shown in the following table.

Adjectives That Double Their Consonants

Masculine		Feminine		Meaning
ancien	*ahN-syaN*	ancienne	*ahN-syehn*	ancient, old
bas	*bah*	basse	*bahs*	low
bon	*bohN*	bonne	*bohn*	good
européen	*ew-roh-pay-aN*	européenne	*ew-roh-pay-ehn*	European
gentil	*zhahN-tee-y*	gentille	*zhahN-tee-y*	nice, kind
gros	*gro*	grosse	*gros*	fat, big
mignon	*mee-nyohN*	mignonne	*mee-noyhn*	cute

Finally, the adjectives in the following table list irregular feminine forms that must be memorized:

Irregular Adjectives

Masculine		Feminine		Meaning
beau*	*bo*	belle	*behl*	beautiful
blanc	*blahN*	blanche	*blahNsh*	white
complet	*kohN-pleh*	complète	*kohN-pleht*	complete
doux	*doo*	douce	*doos*	sweet, gentle
faux	*fo*	fausse	*fos*	false
favori	*fah-voh-ree*	favorite	*fah-voh-reet*	favorite
frais	*freh*	fraîche	*frehsh*	fresh
long	*lohN*	longue	*lohNg*	long
nouveau*	*noo-vo*	nouvelle	*noo-vehl*	new
vieux*	*vyuh*	vieille	*vyay*	old

*The French use special forms: bel, nouvel, and vieil **before** masculine nouns beginning with a vowel or vowel sound to prevent a clash between two pronounced vowel sounds. This allows the language to flow.*

un bel appartement   un nouvel appartement   un vieil appartement

If the adjective comes **after** the noun, then the regular masculine form is used:

L'appartement est beau.

L'appartement est nouveau.

L' appartement est vieux.

Un deux trois

Describe yourself using as many adjectives as possible. Then describe the members of your family.

When There's a Crowd

Perhaps you'd like to describe a physical or personality trait that is common to more than one of your family members. This is relatively simple because adjectives are often made plural in the same way as the nouns you've already studied.

The plural of most adjectives is formed by adding an unpronounced *s* to the singular form:

Singular	Plural
timide	timides
charmant(e)	charmant(e)s
joli(e)	joli(e)s
fatigué(e)	fatigué(e)s

Attention!

The masculine singular adjective *tout* (all) becomes *tous* in the plural.

If an adjective ends in *s* or *x*, it is unnecessary to add the *s*:

Singular	Plural
exquis	exquis
heureux	heureux

Most masculine singular adjectives ending in *al* change *al* to *aux* in the plural:

Singular	Plural
spécial	spéciaux

For the irregular, masculine, singular adjectives *beau, nouveau,* and *vieux,* the problem of having two conflicting vowel sounds (one at the end of the adjective and the other at the beginning of the noun that follows) is eliminated by adding an *s* or an *x* when the plural is formed. This eliminates the need for a plural form for the special masculine singular adjectives *bel, nouvel,* and *vieil* that are used only before nouns beginning with a vowel or a vowel sound. Note the plural formation for these masculine adjectives.

Singular	Plural	Example
beau	beaux	de beaux films
bel	beaux	de beaux appartements
nouveau	nouveaux	de nouveaux films
nouvel	nouveaux	de nouveaux appartements
vieux	vieux	de vieux films
vieil	vieux	de vieux appartements

Get in Position

In French, most adjectives are placed after the nouns they modify. Compare this with English, where we do the opposite:

un homme intéressant   an interesting man

Adjectives showing:

BEAUTY: beau, joli

AGE: jeune, nouveau, vieux

GOODNESS (or lack of it): bon, gentil, mauvais, vilain

SIZE: grand, petit, court, long, gros, large

generally precede the nouns they modify. Remember **BAGS**, and you'll have no trouble with these adjectives:

un beau garçon   a handsome boy

une large avenue   a wide avenue

Attention!

Des becomes *de* before an adjective.

Memory Enhancer

If more than one adjective is being used in a description, put each adjective in its proper position:
une bonne histoire intéressante

Creative Descriptions

How would you describe the Eiffel Tower, the car of your dreams, the mayor of your city? Here's an opportunity to give your opinions about certain things by using appropriate adjectives. Complete your descriptions carefully using the rules you've learned.

1. La Tour Eiffel est une _____ tour _____.
2. Les film français sont de _____ films _____.
3. Le président des États-Unis est un _____ homme _____.
4. Les boutiques parisiennes sont de _____ boutiques _____.
5. Le musée du Louvre est un _____ musée _____.

In French, adjectives must agree in gender (masculine or feminine) and number (singular or plural) with the nouns they modify. Add an *e* to the end of a masculine, singular adjective to form the feminine singular version:

Il est intelligent.   Elle est intelligente.

He is intelligent.   She is intelligent.

If the adjective ends in *e*, both the masculine and feminine forms are spelled and pronounced in exactly the same way:

Il est riche.   Elle est riche.

He is rich.   She is rich.

Note the following changes for feminine adjectives:

Masculine ending	Feminine ending
eux	euse
f	ve
er	ère

Memory Enhancer

Unlike English, adjectives are placed after the nouns they modify except for those expressing Beauty, Age, Goodness, and Size.

Un deux trois

Read the personal ads in a French newspaper. Pay special attention to the adjectives so you know if you're reading an ad seeking a male or female companion. Then pick the ad and look up every word in it that you don't know.

Some adjectives double their consonants while others are completely irregular. All irregular adjectives must be memorized.

To make most adjectives plural, add an unpronounced *s* to the singular form.

No plural ending is necessary if the adjective ends in *s* or *x*.

Most masculine singular adjectives ending in *al* change *al* to *aux* in the plural.

Perusing the Personal Ads

Read the following personal ads taken from a few French magazines and newspapers. Describe the person writing the ad and the type of person being sought.

FRANCAIS, 25 ans, plein de charme, romantique et cultivé a imerait rencontrer Jeune Francaise pour sorties sympathiques

27 ANS, excellent situation de dentiste, célibataire, BC.BG, il est dynamique et sympa, il est sentimental, il voudrait faire connaissance d'une J.F. tendre en vue de relations sérieuses et durables.

JEUNE AMERICAIN, 26 ans, séduisant sincère, intelligent, bonne situation financière, 1m79, cherche francaise pariant anglais. App. Victor

Ingénieur, Alexis, 30 ans, du charme et de l'élégance. C'est un homme sincère, courtois, généreux, qui souh. renc. une J.F. simple et naturelle pour s'investir dans une union durable. Célib.

FRANCINE, maman divorcée, simple, sage et dévouée, 35 ans, technicienne, offre son charme et sa tranquillité, à monsieur stable, courtois, aimant les enfants, la nature et la vie paisible.

Homme d'affaire, la trentaine, distingué, raffiné, aisé, généreux. Bel homme. Aimant le beau (Porsche, Cartier), désire combler belle jeune femme 20/25 ans, pour vie dorée, luxueuse et enviée.

The Least You Need to Know

➤ There are no apostrophes in the French language. To show possession you can use the following formula: thing possessed + *de* + possessor.

➤ To show possession using an adjective, the adjective must agree with the person or thing possessed, not with the possessor.

➤ *Avoir* is an important irregular verb that expresses not only physical conditions but also luck, intention, and opportunity.

➤ Adjectives agree in number and gender with the nouns they describe.

➤ Many adjectives follow the same rules for gender and plural formation as nouns.

➤ There are irregular adjectives and verbs. They follow no rules, so you'll have to memorize them.

➤ Adjectives are generally placed after the nouns they modify.

Chapter 10

Navigating the Airport

In This Chapter

➤ The ins and outs of airplanes and airports

➤ The irregular verb *aller* (to go)

➤ How to give and receive directions

➤ Getting help when you just don't understand

Congratulations! You've planned a trip, you've gotten on the plane, and you've had a very pleasant conversation with the person sitting next to you. You've gotten the names of some good restaurants, places you want to be sure to visit, and perhaps the phone number of someone to call who will show you around town.

Your plane hasn't even landed yet, but you are mentally preparing for all the things you'll have to do before you even start off for your hotel—you must get your bags, go through customs, change some money, and find a means of transportation to get to your hotel. By the end of this chapter, you'll have accomplished these things and more.

On the Plane

A plane ride is often long and tedious. Sometimes you might experience some minor inconveniences or delays. During your trip, you might want to see about changing your seat, or perhaps you have some questions for the flight crew. Maybe they've stuck you in the smoking section, and you're a militant nonsmoker; or your traveling companion is seated a few rows in front of you, and you'd like to join him or her; or perhaps you'd simply like to ask the crew about takeoff and landing. The words and phrases in the following table will help you get information and solve simple problems you may encounter on board.

Culture Capsule

When your flight finally arrives at the airport, you'll be greeted by the sign *BIENVENUE*, which means "Welcome." Then it's time to proceed with the necessary paperwork at passport control, so that you can begin your visit as soon as possible.

Inside the Plane

Airplane Term	French	Pronunciation
airplane	l'avion (m.)	*lah-vyohN*
aisle	le couloir	*luh kool-wahr*
(on the) aisle	côté couloir	*koh-tay kool-wahr*
to board, embark	embarquer	*ahN-bahr-kay*
crew	l'équipage (m.)	*lay-kee-pahzh*
to deplane, disembark, exit	débarquer	*day-bahr-kay*
emergency exit	la sortie (l'issue) de secours	*lah sohr-tee (lee-sew) duh suh-koor*
life vest	le gilet de sauvetage	*luh zhee-leh duh sohv-tahzh*
(non) smokers	(non) fumeurs	*(nohN) few-muhr*
row	le rang	*luh rahN*
seat	la place, le siège	*lah plahs, luh syehzh*
seatbelt	la ceinture de sécurité	*lah saN-tewr duh say-kew-ree-tay*
to smoke	fumer	*few-may*
(by the) window	côté fenêtre	*koh-tay fuh-nehtr*

Culture Capsule

In order to board an airplane, a passenger needs une carte d'embarquement (*ewn kahrt dahN-bahrk-mahN*)—a boarding pass, while a passenger who is about to get off a plane needs to fill out une carte de débarquement (*ewn kahrt duh day-bahrk-mahN*)—a disembarkation card. The information on this card will be reviewed by customs officers at the airport.

Airline Advice

If you've flown before, you know that airlines always have instructions about boarding, safety, and emergency procedures. Once on board, you will find an emergency card in your seat pocket, and your flight attendant will demonstrate any number of devices, from seat belts to oxygen masks. Read the following information to see if you can decipher the information the airline is trying to convey:

En cabine (In the plane)

Pour votre confort et votre sécurité, n'emportez avec vous qu'un seul bagage de cabine.

N'y placez pas d'objets considerés comme dangereux (armes, couteaux, ciseaux, etc.). Ils seront retirés lors des contrôles de sécurité.

What advice are they giving about your bags?

En soute (In the hold)

Choisissez des bagages solides, fermant à clé. Fixez à l'intérieur et à l'extérieur une étiquette d'identification. Évitez les articles suivants: médicaments, devises (securities), chèques, papiers d'affaires ou importants, bijoux et autres objets de valeur. Conservez-les avec vous en cabine.

Customs

Upon entering a country all travelers must pass through passport control, where certain paperwork is filled out and a computer verifies identity.

Customs is next. Since every nation has different rules, it is best to find out beforehand what you may and may not bring into a country. Weapons and arms of any kind are strictly prohibited, as are illegal drugs and items made from endangered animals. So if you're taking medication, don't forget to bring along a copy of your prescription. Most countries do not allow fruits, vegetables, or plants to pass their borders for fear of insect infestation, and any pet purchased abroad will be thoroughly examined and then quarantined before allowed entry. Generally, there is a limit on tobacco items, perfumes, wines and spirits, and jewelry and some items may be taxed if purchased in excess. Despite all the rules, most tourists have an easy time passing through customs. In many instances, your bags aren't even opened and your dirty laundry will remain your little secret.

The following is an example of the information required of you upon entering a foreign country. The only words that might be unfamiliar to you are: *imprimerie* (printing), *lieu* (place), and *naissance* (birth). You are now ready to fill out this card, exactly as if you were a newly arrived tourist. Note that this card is not necessary for French nationals or for subjects of the European Union:

CARTE DE DÉBARQUEMENT

ne concerne pas les voyageurs de nationalité française
ni les ressortissants des autres pays membres de la UE

1. Nom de famille: _____

   (en caractère d'imprimerie)

   Nom de jeune fille: _____

   Prénom(s): _____

2. Adresse: _____

   _____
       (numéro)   (rue)

   _____
     (ville, village)   (province état)   (code postal)

   _____
       (pays)

3. Date de naissance: _____

4. Lieu de naissance: _____

5. Profession: _____

6. Aéroport ou port d'embarquement: _____

7. Compagnie aérienne: _____

8. Numéro du vol: _____

9. Signature du voyageur: _____

At the Airport

There is a lot to do after you are inside the airport, but don't worry—there will be plenty of signs to point you in the right direction. Sometimes it's hard to judge where to go first. My first stop is usually the bathroom. After that, I slowly progress from one area to the next, taking care of all my business at a slow and steady pace. The following table gives you all the words you need to know in the airport as well as outside on the way to your first destination!

Inside the Airport

airline	la ligne aérienne	*lah lee-nyuh ahy-ryehn*
airline terminal	l'aérogare (f.), le terminal	*lahy-roh-gahr, luh tehr-mee-nahl*
airport	l'aéroport	*lahy-roh-pohr*
arrival	l'arrivée	*lah-ree-vay*
baggage claim area	la bande, les bagages (m.)	*lah bahnde, lay bah-gahzh*
bathrooms	les toilettes (f.)	*lay twah-leht*
bus stop	l'arrêt de bus (m.)	*lah-reh duh bews*
car rental	la location de voitures	*lah loh-kah-syohN duh vwah-tewr*
carry-on luggage	les bagages à main (m.)	*lay-bah-gahzh ah maN*
cart	le chariot	*luh shah-ryoh*
counter	le comptoir	*luh kohN-twahr*
customs	la douane	*lah doo-ahn*
departure	le départ	*luh day-pahr*
destination	la destination	*lah dehs-tee-nah-syohN*
elevators	les ascenseurs (m.)	*lay-zah-sahN-suhr*
entrance	l'entrée (f.)	*lahN-tray*
exit	la sortie	*lah-sohr-tee*
flight	le vol	*luh vohl*
gate	la porte	*lah pohrt*
information	les renseignements (m.)	*lay rahN-seh-nyuh-mahN*
landing	l'atterrissage (m.)	*lah-teh-ree-sahzh*
lost and found	les objets trouvés (m.)	*lay zohb-zheh troo-vay*
to miss the flight	manquer (rater) le vol	*mahN-kay (rah-tay) luh vohl*
money exchange	le bureau de change	*luh bew-ro duh shahNzh*
passport control	le contrôle des passeports	*luh kohN-trohl day pahs-pohr*
porter	le porteur	*luh pohr-tuhr*
security check	le contrôle de sécurité	*luh kohN-trohl duh say-kew-ree-tay*
stop-over	l'escale (f.)	*lehs-kahl*

continues

Inside the Airport (cont.)

suitcase	la valise	*lah vah-leez*
take-off	le décollage	*luh day-koh-lahzh*
taxis	les taxis	*lay tahk-see*
ticket	le billet, le ticket	*luh bee-yeh, luh tee-keh*
trip	le voyage	*luh vwah-yahzh*

Culture Capsule

The two airports in Paris are Charles de Gaulle, a vast international airport at Roissy, and Orly, which is for domestic flights. Charles de Gaulle is far away from town, and Orly is closer to the center of Paris. When you arrive in Paris, you'll arrive at Charles de Gaulle, so make sure that you have directions from Charles de Gaulle to the place you'll be staying.

Signs Tell It All

With airport security at a maximum due to terrorist threats and bomb scares, you can be sure that you will see many signs indicating the rules that must be followed. It is very important that you understand what you may and may not do. Even if you break a rule unintentionally, it can be scary to be approached by an armed *gendarme* speaking a language in which you have limited fluency. On the next page are the signs you can expect to see in Charles de Gaulle airport. Read them carefully and then match each sign with the information it gives you. Students traveling abroad would be well advised to inquire about the International Student Identity Card, issued by the Council on International Educational Exchange, and the Youth International Educational Exchange Card, issued by the Federation of International Youth Travel. For a very reasonable rate, these agencies offer enticing discounts to students.

AVIS AUX PASSAGERS

Il est formellement interdit par la loi de transporter une arme dissimulée à bord d'un avion.

Les règlements en vigeur imposent l'inspection des passagers et des bagages à main lors de contrôle de sécurité.

Cette inspection peut être refusé. Les passagers refusant cette inspection ne seront pas autorisés à passer le contrôle de sécurité.

A

Chariot reservé aux passagers; utilisation interdite au delà du trottoir de l'aérogare.

B

ATTENTION:
Pour des raisons de sécurité, tout objet abandonné peut être détruit par les services de police.

Les passagers sont donc instamment priés de conserver leurs bagages avec eux.

C

ATTENTION:
Ne mettez pas votre sécurité en péril: n'acceptez aucun bagage d'une autre personne.

D

Veuillez présenter tous vos bagages à l'enregistrement, y compris vos bagages à main.

E

TRANSPORT DES ARMES À FEU
Les armes à feu transportées dans les bagages enregistrés doivent être déchargés et faire l'objet d'une déclaration auprès de nos services.

Les passagers transportant des armes sans les déclarer ou chargées sont passibles d'une amende de 1000 dollars ou équivalent.

F

Which sign is telling you that:

1. If you leave something behind, it might be destroyed ___?
2. All of your baggage will be checked, even carry-ons ___?
3. You can be searched for hidden weapons ___?
4. You may carry a weapon if you declare it ___?
5. You can only use the baggage cart within the airport ___?
6. You shouldn't carry a suitcase for someone else ___?

Going Places

It's easy to get lost in sprawling international airports. To get yourself back on track, you'll need to know how to ask the right questions. One of the verbs you'll use a lot is *aller* (to go), an irregular verb that must be memorized. (See following table for conjugation.)

The Verb *aller* (to go)

je vais	*zhuh veh*	I go
tu vas	*tew vah*	you go
il, elle, on va	*eel, (ehl) (ohN) vah*	he, she, one goes
nous allons	*noo zah-lohN*	we go
vous allez	*voo zah-lay*	you go
ils, elles vont	*eel (ehl) vohN*	they go

Aller is generally, followed by the preposition *à* (to). If the location to which the subject is going is masculine, *à* contracts with *le* (the) to become *au* (to the), and with *les* (the) to become *aux* (to the), as in the following examples:

> Je vais au contrôle des passeports.
>
> I'm going to the passport control.

No changes are necessary with l' or la:

> Il va à l'aéroport.
>
> He's going to the airport.

Un deux trois

Make a list of the places to which you and your friends are going this weekend and how you are getting there.

Use *aller* + *en* to express the many different ways to go someplace:

> Je vais à Paris en voiture.
>
> I'm going to Paris by car.

The only exception is when you decide to walk:

> Nous allons au restaurant à pied.
>
> We're walking to the restaurant.

Aller is most commonly used idiomatically to express health:

> Comment allez-vous? How are you?

> Comment vas-tu?

> Je vais bien. I'm fine.

> Je vais mal.   I'm doing poorly.

Where To?

Tell where each person is going by giving the correct form of *aller*:

1. Nous _____ à Paris.
2. Marie _____ à Nice.
3. Tu _____ à Marseille.
4. Ils _____ à Grenoble.
5. Je _____ à Cannes.
6. Vous _____ à Bordeaux.

Memory Enhancer

Use the preposition *à* when you want to express going to or staying in a city.

Je vais à Lille.   I'm going to Lille.

Use the verb *aller* to express where a person is going.

Use *aller* + *à* to express going to a place:

> Il va au restaurant.

> He is going to the restaurant.

Use *aller* + *en* to express how the subject is going:

> Elle va en voiture.

> She is going by car.

Use *aller* to express health:

> Je vais bien.

> I feel fine.

Where's the...?

If the airport is unfamiliar to you, you may need to ask for directions. This is relatively easy to do. There are two different ways of asking:

Où est le comptoir?	Le comptoir, s'il vous plaît.
oo eh luh kohN-twahr?	*luh kohN-twahr seel voo pleh.*
Where is the counter?	The counter, please.
Où sont les bagages?	Les bagages, s'il vous plaît.
oo sohN lay bah-gahzh?	*lay bah-gahzh seel voo pleh.*
Where is the baggage claim?	The baggage claim, please.

Remember that you must use the verb *être* in its singular form *est* (is) if the place you are asking for is singular. If it is plural, use the plural *sont* (are).

Ask for It

Imagine that you are lost at the airport. Ask for the following places in two ways:

1. bathrooms
2. passport control
3. customs
4. elevators
5. exit
6. money exchange

Un deux trois

Imagine that you are helping someone out at the airport. Point out as many different places as you can in French.

There It Is

Sometimes, the place you are trying to find is right in front of you. For instance, suppose that you're trying to locate the ticket counter. With all the noise and confusion, you lose your bearings and don't realize that you are standing near the very place you are trying to find. When you ask the gentlemen next to you for directions, he may reply:

Voici le comptoir.	Voilà le comptoir.
vwah-see luh kohN-twahr.	*vwah-lah luh kohN-twahr.*
Here is the counter.	There is the counter.

More Complicated Directions

If the place you want to get to is not within pointing distance, you'll need other directions. The verbs in the table below will be very helpful in getting you where you want to go or perhaps in helping someone else who is lost.

Memory Enhancer

To be very polite, use *veuillez + infinitive* to say please:

Veuillez entrer. (vuh-yay ahN-tray.) Please enter.

Verbs Giving Directions

aller	*ah-lay*	to go
continuer	*kohN-tee-new-ay*	to continue
descendre	*day-sahNdr*	to go down
marcher	*mahr-shay*	to walk
monter	*mohN-tay*	to go up
passer	*pah-say*	to pass
prendre	*prahNdr*	to take
tourner	*toor-nay*	to turn
traverser	*trah-vehr-say*	to cross

When someone directs you to a location, that person is giving you a command. The subject of a command is understood to be *you* since *you* are being told where to go or what to do. Because there are two ways to say *you* in French (the familiar *tu* and the polite, and always plural, *vous*), there are two different command forms. Choose the form that best suits the situation. To form commands, simply drop the *tu* or *vous* subject pronoun:

Attention!

For *er* verbs only, drop the final *s* from the *tu* form in all commands. Example: Regarde!

Va tout droit.   Allez à gauche.
vah too drwah.   *ah-lay ah gohsh.*
Go straight ahead.   Go to the left.

Un deux trois

Pretend you have a French-speaking visitor staying at your house. Give directions, in French, to the nearest movie theater, restaurant, museum, and supermarket.

Giving Commands

You must use the command form to give directions. Use the tu or vous form (depending upon your relationship to the person and the number of people to whom you are speaking) of the present tense of the verb.

Do not use the subject tu or vous when giving a command. Imagine for a moment that, in Orly Airport, a Hungarian tourist approaches you and asks for directions. He doesn't speak English, and you don't know a word of Hungarian. Fortunately, you both bought *Complete Idiot's Guides* and know a little French. Help the poor lost Hungarian man by practicing your commands. Complete the table below by filling in the missing command forms and their meanings.

Command Forms

Verb	Tu	Vous	Meaning
aller	Va!	Allez!	Go!
continuer			
descendre			
marcher			
monter			
passer			
prendre (Chapter 11)	Prends!	Prenez!	Take!
tourner			
traverser			

Two verbs that have very irregular command forms are *être* and *avoir*. Although they are used infrequently, you should memorize them:

	être	**avoir**
Tu form	Sois	Aie!
	swah	*ay*
	Be!	Have!
Vous form	Soyez!	Ayez
	swah-yay	*ay-yay*
	Be!	Have!

Prepositions

Prepositions are used to show the relation of a noun to another word in a sentence. Refresh your memory with the idiomatic expressions for direction and location in Chapter 4 that are, in fact, prepositional phrases. Then add the simple prepositions in the following table. They are useful for giving and receiving directions.

Prepositions

à	*ah*	to, at
après	*ah-preh*	after
avant	*ah-vahN*	before
chez	*shay*	at the house (business) of
contre	*kohNtr*	against
dans	*dahN*	in
de	*duh*	from
derrière	*deh-ryehr*	behind
devant	*duh-vahN*	in front of
en	*ahN*	in
entre	*ahNtr*	between
loin (de)	*lwaN (duh)*	far (from)
par	*pahr*	by, through
pour	*poor*	for, in order to
près (de)	*preh (duh)*	near
sans	*sahN*	without
sous	*soo*	under
sur	*sewr*	on
vers	*vehr*	toward

Contractions

In certain cases, contractions form with the prepositions *à* and *de*, whether they are used alone or as part of a longer expression:

	Le	Les
à	au	aux
de	du	des

Allez à la douane.	La porte est à côté de la douane.
Allez à l'entrée.	La porte est à côté de l'entrée.

BUT

Allez **au** bureau de change.	La porte est à côté **du** bureau de change.
Allez **aux** bagages.	La porte est à côté **des** bagages.

Attention!

There are no contractions with *la* and *l'*. For example, say *de l'* or *de la*.

Are You Dazed and Confused?

What if someone gives you directions that you don't understand? Perhaps the person to whom you are speaking is mumbling, speaking too fast, has a strong accent, or uses words you don't know. Don't be embarrassed. Ask for help in a kind, polite manner. You'll find the phrases in the following table to be an invaluable aid if you need to have something repeated or if you need more information.

Expressing Confusion

Excuse me	Excusez (Excuse)-moi	*ehk-skew-zay (ehk-skewz) mwah*
Excuse me	Je m'excuse	*zhuh mehk-skewz*
Pardon me	Pardon	*pahr-dohN*
Pardon me	Pardonnez (Pardonne)-moi	*pahr-doh-nay (pah-dohn) mwah*
I don't understand	Je ne comprends pas	*zhuh nuh kohN-prahN pah*
I didn't understand	Je n'ai pas compris	*zhuh nay pah kohN-pree*
I didn't hear you	Je ne vous (t') ai pas entendu(e)	*zhuh nuh voo zay (tay) pah zahN-tahN-dew*
Please repeat it	Répétez (Répète), s'il vous (te) plaît	*ray-pay-tay (ray-peht) seel voo (tuh) pleh*
One more time (Again)	Encore une fois	*ahN-kohr ewn fwah*
Speak more slowly	Parlez (Parle) plus lentement.	*pahr-lay (pahrl) plew lahNt-mahN*
What did you say?	Qu'est-ce que vous avez (tu as) dit?	*kehs-kuh voo zah-vay (tew ah) dee?*
Did you say _____ or _____?	Vous avez (tu as) dit _____ ou _____	*voo zah-vay (tew ah) dee _____ oo_____*

Culture Capsule

Learn the word *thank you*. After getting directions, good manners dictate a simple *merci* (*mehr-see*), which means *thank you*. Are you feeling profoundly grateful? Use *merci beaucoup*, which means *thank you very much*. In either case the correct response, *Je vous en prie* (*zhuh voo zahN pree*), means *not at all*. (This phrase can also mean *Please* or *Please do*). Another possible reply is *De rien* (*duh ryaN*), which simply means *You're welcome*.

Getting from Here to There

You've been invited to spend your vacation in Canada at a friend's house. You've got all your bags and you're ready to leave the airport now. You take out the directions he gave you to his house and realize they are in French! Trace the correct route and then put an X on the map where his house should be.

The Least You Need to Know

➤ The irregular verb *aller* is used to give directions and to speak about health and well-being.

➤ A few verbs are tremendously useful in giving and taking directions: *aller* (to go), *continuer, descendre, marcher, monter, passer, prendre* (to take), *tourner*, and *traverser* (to cross).

➤ Leave out the subject (*tu* or *vous*) when you give a command.

➤ Use prepositions to show the relationship of a noun to another word in the sentence.

➤ *à* + *le* contracts to *au*. *à* + *les* contracts to *aux*.

➤ *de* + *le* contracts to *du*. *de* + *les* contracts to *des*.

➤ If you don't understand what someone is saying to you, don't be afraid to say: "Je ne comprends pas. Répétez s'il vous plaît."

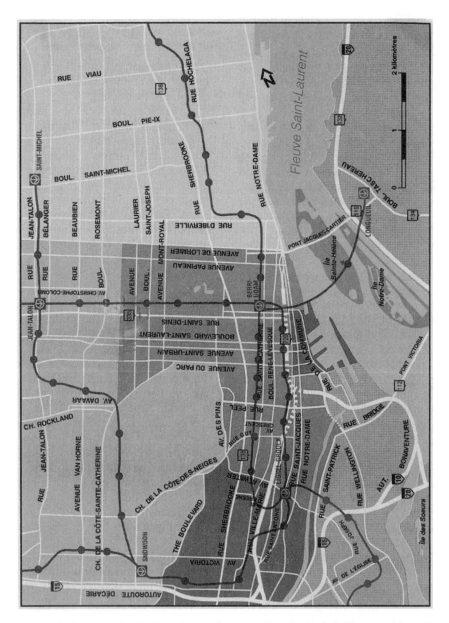

Prends le bus numéro 7. Quand tu arrives en ville, descends à l'avenue Mont-Royal. Prends l'avenue Mont-Royal et tourne à droite à la rue St.-Denis. Va tout droit. Passe par le boulevard St.-Joseph. Tu vas voir une école sur ta gauche. Puis tu vas voir une église à ta droite. Juste après l'église, tourne à gauche. Prends l'avenue Laurier. Passe près du cinéma. Juste après le cinéma, à la prochaine rue, tourne à droite. C'est l'avenue du Parc. Ma maison est là, sur la gauche, au coin de l'avenue du Parc et de l'avenue Laurier.

Getting There Without Delay

You'll probably find that it's far less painful and far more time-consuming than you thought to get through customs, find your bags, and change some money into francs. If you're lucky, you will have *transfers* (transportation provided as part of your travel package) to your hotel and someone waiting to whisk you away. If not, you must figure out on your own how you are going to get to the hotel. This chapter discusses your options.

For example, if you're visiting Paris, the Parisian R.A.T.P. (Régie Autonome des Transports Parisiens) is in charge of the user-friendly bus and subway system. Green Parisian buses post their route and destination on the outside, front of the bus and their major stops on the bus's sides. The route of each line is indicated on a sign at every stop it makes. Free bus maps (autobus Paris—Plan du Réseau) are readily available at tourist offices and some métro booths. Buy tickets ahead of time at a métro station or bureau de tabac (tobacconist), because they may not be purchased aboard the bus.

Planes, Trains, and Automobiles

Several means of transportation can get you from the airport to your hotel: bus, subway, train, taxi, or car. To make the decision that is right for you, keep the following considerations in mind: Do you really want to carry your bags on a bus or the subway? (Remember what you packed!) Although taxis are fast and efficient, they are costly. Do you feel up to renting a car in a foreign country where you are unfamiliar with the traffic laws and street signs? Think carefully before you make a choice.

A **Paris Visite** card, available through travel agencies, tourist offices, or subway and train stations, allows you to choose unlimited bus, subway, and train travel for three or five consecutive days. The **Formule 1** card is a one-day pass.

Culture Capsule

If you're going to Paris from the airport, the subway and buses are very convenient. You might also opt for a taxi, which always gives a flat rate from the airport (for other trips, it's metered) but which charges extra for handling luggage and may refuse to accept more than three passengers. Driving in Paris can be treacherous—the drivers are unpredictable, the traffic is congested, and there are very few parking spots.

If you're going farther afield, the R.A.T.P. also provides service on the R.E.R (Réseau Express Régional), the local suburban train system. The S.N.C.F. (Société Nationale des Chemins de Fer) boasts trains that are the fastest in the world. The popular T.G.V. (train à grande vitesse) travels within the entire country and links Paris to the other cities in France. It has attained the world record of 260 kilometers (162 miles) per hour.

Means of Transportation	French	Pronunciation
bus	le bus (l'autobus)	*le bews (loh-toh-bews)*
car	l'auto (f.)	*lo-to*
car	la voiture	*lah vwah-tewr*
subway	le métro	*luh may-tro*
taxi	le taxi	*le tahk-see*
train	le train	*luh traN*

Culture Capsule

The 13 numbered Parisian subway lines are indicated by different colors on maps distributed everywhere: at métro stops, hotels, department stores, tourist offices. Each station displays a *plan du quartier*, a detailed map of the surrounding area. Transfers from one subway line to another are free, and connections are indicated by orange *correspondance* signs. You may transfer as often as you like on one ticket, provided that you do not exit to the street. Exits are clearly marked by blue *Sortie* signs.

The Best Way to Go

Regardless how you decide to get where you are going, you will need to use the irregular verb *prendre* (*prahNdr*) (to take) to express which mode of transportation you have chosen. *Prendre* is a tricky verb: All singular forms end in a nasal sound, but the third person plural, *ils/elles*, is pronounced quite differently. The double *n*s eliminate the need for an initial nasal sound and give the first *e* a more open sound. Pay close attention to the table below.

Un deux trois

Say the means of transportation you would use to get to the following places: work and/or school, the supermarket, the nearest department store, downtown, a neighboring city.

The Verb *prendre* (to take)

je prends	*zhuh prahN*	I take
tu prends	*tew prahN*	you take
il, elle, on prend	*eel (ehl) (ohN) prahN*	he, she, one takes
nous prenons	*noo pruh-nohN*	we take
vous prenez	*voo pruh-nay*	you take
ils, elles prennent	*eel (ehl) prehn*	they take

Culture Capsule

Slide a Parisian métro ticket into the automatic machine and wait for it to pop up. You must keep your ticket until you reach the point where it is no longer valid—Limite de Validité des Billets—because an inspector may ask to see it and you risk a fine if you cannot furnish it, and because you may need it to transfer to the R.E.R. (French suburban train system) within Paris.

Something Different

Travelers interested in visiting France from England and Belgium may now make use of the Chunnel. Although you can't drive through these new tunnels, *Le Shuttle* carries freight and cars with passengers (up to 180 vehicles) between England and France. Just drive a car onto a train at one end and drive off at the other—in just 35 minutes. Service is available 24 hours a day, and at peak times, trains depart every 15 minutes. No reservations are accepted, so drivers will be accommodated on a first-come, first-served basis. Drivers pay a charge per car, regardless of the number of occupants.

The other Chunnel service, *Eurostar*, carries only passengers (each train carries 800 people) and provides through service from London to Paris and London to Brussels.

It's Up to You

When asking questions about the mode of transportation you've chosen, you'll use the interrogative adjective *quel* (which, what). Just like all adjectives, *which* agrees with the noun it modifies. The following table shows how easy it is to make a match between the correct form of *quel* (keeping gender and number in mind) and the noun that follows it.

The Possessive Adjective *quel*

	Masculine	Feminine
Singular	quel	quelle
Plural	quels	quelles

Be prepared for questions such as the following:

> Quel bus est-ce que vous prenez (tu prends)?
> *kehl bews ehs-kuh vous pruh-nay (tew prahN)*
> Which bus are you taking?

> Quelle marque de voiture est-ce vous louez (tu loues)?
> *kehl mahrk duh vwah-tewr ehs-kuh voo loo-ay (tew loo)*
> What make of car are you renting?

Using Quel

Did you ever have a conversation with a friend who rambles on and on about a fabulous film she's just seen but never mentions the title? You're ready to explode from frustration when she finally decides to come up for air. You grab your chance and quickly interject: Which film? Here are some typical answers that don't give enough information. Pursue your line of questioning by using *quel*:

J'aime le film. *Quel film?*

1. Je prends le train.
2. J'aime la couleur.
3. J'achète(buy) les jolies blouses.
4. Je lis (read) de bons journaux.

5. Je loue une voiture.
6. Je cherche de bonnes cassettes.
7. Je regarde le match.
8. Je prépare des plats délicieux.

The only verb that may separate *quel* from its noun is the verb *être*:

> Quel est votre (ton) nom?
>
> *kehl eh vohtr (tohN) nohN?*
>
> What's your name?

Fill 'er Up

If you are adventurous, you might want to rent a car at *une location de voitures.* Check out rates of a few car rentals before you make a decision, because rates vary from agency to agency. Keep in mind that gasoline is very expensive in most foreign countries, usually more than double the price Americans pay. Familiarize yourself with all driving and traffic laws. The following phrases are very useful when renting a car:

Un deux trois

Imagine that you are in a club in a French-speaking country. You make a new acquaintance. Ask for his name, address, phone number, and nationality.

I would like to rent a _____.
>
> Je voudrais louer une (give make of car).
>
> *zhuh voo-dreh loo-ay ewn _____.*

I prefer automatic transmission.
>
> Je préfère la transmission automatique.
>
> *zhuh pray-fehr lah tranhz-mee-syohN o-toh-mah-teek.*

How much does it cost per day (per week) (per kilometer)?
>
> Quel est le tarif à la journée (à la semaine) (au kilomètre)?
>
> *kehl eh luh tah-reef ah lah zhoor-nay (ah la suh-mehn) (o kee-lo-mehtr)?*

How much is the insurance?
>
> Quel est le montant de l'assurance?
>
> *kehl eh luh mohn-tahN duh lah-sew-rahNs?*

Is the gas included?
>
> Le carburant est compris?
>
> *luh kahr-bew-rahN eh kohN-pree?*

Do you accept credit cards? Which ones?}
>
> Acceptez-vous des cartes de crédit? Lesquelles?
>
> *ahk-sehp-tay voo day kahrt duh kray-dee? lay-kehl?*

If you've decided to rent a car, take a tip from me: Carefully inspect the car—inside and out—because you never know what might go wrong after you're on the road. Make sure there is *un cric* (*uhN kreek,* (a jack) and *un pneu de secours* (*uhN pnuh duh suh-koor,* (a spare tire) in the trunk.

Make sure to carefully inspect the outside of your rental car before driving away. You wouldn't want to be charged for damage you didn't do. The following table gives you the words you need to talk about the car's exterior:

Outside the Car

Car Part	French	Pronunciation
battery	la batterie	*lah bah-tree*
bumper	le pare-choc	*luh pahr-shohk*
carburator	le carburateur	*luh kahr-bew-rah-tuhr*
door handle	la poignée	*lah pwah-nyay*
fan	le ventilateur	*luh vahN-tee-lah-tuhr*
fender	l'aile (f.)	*lehl*

Car Part	French	Pronunciation
gas tank	le réservoir à essence	*lah ray-sehr-vwahr ah eh-sahNs*
headlight	le phare	*luh fahr*
hood	le capot	*luh kah-po*
license plate	la plaque d'immatriculation	*lah plahk dee-mah-tree-kew-lah-syohN*
motor	le moteur	*luh moh-tuhr*
radiator	le radiateur	*luh rahd-yah-tuhr*
tail light	le feu arriére	*luh fuh ah-ryehr*
tire	le pneu	*luh pnuh*
transmission	la transmission	*lah trahNz-mee-syohN*
trunk	le coffre	*luh kohfr*
wheel	la roue	*lah roo*
windshield wiper	l'essuie-glace (m.)	*leh-swee glahs*

You'll also want to verify that everything on the inside is functioning properly. The following table gives you the words you need to know to talk about the car's interior parts:

Inside the Car

Car Part	French	Pronunciation
accelerator	l'accélérateur (m.)	*lahk-say-lay-rah-tuhr*
air bag	le coussin (sac) gonflable	*luh koo-saN (sahk) gohn-flahbl*
antilock brake system	le freinage anti-blocage	*luh freh-nahzh ahn-tee bloh-kahzh*
brakes	les freins (m.)	*lay fraN*
clutch pedal	la pédale d'embrayage	*lah pay-dahl dahN-brah-yahzh*
directional signal	le clignotant	*luh klee-nyoh-tahN*
gear shift	le changement de vitesses	*luh shahNzh-mahN duh vee-tehs*
glove compartment	la boîte à gants	*lah bwaht ah gahN*
hand brake	le frein à main	*luh fraN ah maN*
horn	le klaxon	*luh klahk-sohN*
ignition	l'allumage (m.)	*lah-lew-mahzh*
radio	la radio	*lah rahd-yo*
steering wheel	le volant	*luh voh-lahN*

In Europe, distance is measured by kilometers. Refer to the following table for the approximate equivalents.

Distance Measures (Approximate)

Miles	Kilometers
.62	1
3	5
6	10
12	20
31	50
62	100

Culture Capsule

Feu (fire) refers to a traffic light. You are required to stop *au feu rouge* (at the red light), of course, and you may go *au feu vert* (at the green light). Should you get stopped for running *un feu rouge* by a *gendarme*, you could try using your foreign nationality as an excuse: *Mais, je suis américain(e)*. Perhaps a simple apology might work: *Pardon (Excusez-moi). Je le regrette.* Of course, it's best just to drive carefully. You're in unfamiliar territory; be cautious.

Un deux trois

Label the interior parts of your car. Study these vocabulary words until you have them down pat, and then remove the labels. Every time you enter your car, see whether you can name the parts. Then start on the exterior parts.

Off You Go

If you decide to rent a car, you will be required to fill out a rental agreement, which, in all probability, will be in French. Before renting a car, familiarize yourself with the terms and conditions of your rental contract. Read the fine print so that there will be no misunderstandings when you return the car. You'll want everything to go smoothly. What does this sign say?

MODALITÉS D'APPLICATION

RESERVATION: La réservation est recommandée au minimum
vingt-quatre heures à l'avance.

CONDITIONS: Le forfait PARISCAR est applicable dans toutes les agences
PARISCAR en France continentale. La durée de location facturée (minimum
un jour) se calcule par tranche de vingt-quatre heures non fractionnable. Une
tolérance de cinquante-neuf minutes est accordée. Au delà de celle-ci,
une journée supplémentaire sera facturée.

KILOMÉTRAGE: Le kilométrage inclus dans le forfait PARISCAR est illimité.

LOUEZ ICI, LAISSEZ AILLEURS: Ce service, permettant de restituer le véhicule dans une
agence différente de l'agence de départ, est compris dans ce forfait.

ASSURANCES:

En cas de dommages, seul un montant forfaitaire de 1.500 F reste à la
charge du locataire.

En cas de vol, seul un montant forfaitaire reste à la charge du locataire.

Il y a une garantie d'assistance technique et médicale vingt-quatre
heures sur vingt-quatre.

CARBURANT:

Le carburant n'est pas compris dans nos tarifs et reste à la charge du locataire.

VALIDITÉ:

Les prix indiqués sont exprimés en FF. Ils sont modifiables sans préavis.

See the Answer Key in Appendix A for translations. Remember, it is always a good idea
to purchase extra insurance.

You're Going in the Right Direction

By all means, learn those road signs—some of
them are not as obvious as they should be. It took
a one-week vacation and a near accident in Saint-
Martin for me to figure out that the sign with a
horizontal line through it meant NO ENTRY. Here
are some road signs you need to be familiar with
before you venture out on your own in a car.

Un deux trois

Look at a map of France. Find the
major cities and tell where they are
in France.

My husband and I were driving along when all of a sudden we came to a fork in the road. I screamed, "Quick, go this way!" Unfortunately, he went "that" way. Maybe next time I'll remember to tell him whether to go east or west, north or south. If you plan on driving, make sure to know your compass directions. They're all masculine.

au nord	à l'est
o nohr	*ah lehst*
to the north	to the east
au sud	à l'ouest
o sewd	*ah lwehst*
to the south	to the west

What Did You Rent?

You saw this ad in *Le Monde* and decided it was the car for you. What features does this car provide?

Renseignements et réservations: (1) 47 34 28 91

➤ L'équipement Renault 500

➤ Air conditionné

➤ Boîte automatique

➤ Systéme anti-blocage des roues ABS

➤ Volant muni d'un coussin gonflable en cas de choc

➤ Ordinateur de bord multi-fonctions

➤ Siéges à réglage électrique

➤ Autoradio avec haut-parleurs

PARISCAR

Pour vous PARISCAR a choisi **Renault** et d'autres grandes marques.

Having Trouble?

Here are some expressions you will need if you have trouble with a rental car:

Could you help me please?
Pourriez-vous m'aider, s'il vous plaît.
poo-ryay voo meh-day sel voo pleh

The car has broken down.
La voiture est en panne.
lah vwah-tewr eh tahN pahn

_____ doesn't (don't) work.
_____ ne fonctionne(nt) [marche(nt)] pas.
_____ *nuh fonNk-syohn [mahrsh] pah*

Can you fix it?
Pouvez-vous la réparer?
poo-vay voo lah ray-pah-ray

When will it be ready?
Quand sera-t-elle prête?
kahN suh-rah tehl preht

How Much Does It Cost?

In order to tell someone what flight or bus you are taking or to figure out how much a rental car is going to set you back, you'll need to learn the French numbers listed below. Believe it or not, these very same numbers will come in handy when you want to tell time, count to 10, or reveal your age.

Un deux trois

You can learn the numbers more quickly if you practice counting by 2s, 3s, 4s, 5s, and 10s. Try it. You'll see how quickly you remember all you need to know.

Cardinal Numbers

zéro	zay-ro	0
un	uhN	1
deux	duh	2
trois	trwah	3
quatre	kahtr	4
cinq	saNk	5

continues

Cardinal Numbers (cont.)

six	*sees*	6
sept	*seht*	7
huit	*weet*	8
neuf	*nuhf*	9
dix	*dees*	10
onze	*ohNz*	11
douze	*dooz*	12
treize	*trehz*	13
quatorze	*kah-tohrz*	14
quinze	*kaNz*	15
seize	*sehz*	16
dix-sept	*dee-seht*	17
dix-huit	*dee-zweet*	18
dix-neuf	*dee-znuhf*	19
vingt	*vaN*	20
vingt et un	*vaN tay uhN*	21
vingt-deux	*vaN-duh*	22
trente	*trahNt*	30
quarante	*kah-rahNt*	40
cinquante	*saN-kahNt*	50
soixante	*swah-sahNt*	60
soixante-dix	*swah-sahNt-dees*	70
soixante et onze	*swah-sahNt ay ohNz*	71
soixante-douze	*swah-sahNt-dooz*	72
soixante-treize	*swah-sahNt-trehz*	73
soixante-quatorze	*swah-sahNt-kah-tohrz*	74
soixante-quinze	*swah-sahNt-kaNz*	75
soixante-seize	*swah-sahNt-sehz*	76
soixante-dix-sept	*swah-sahNt-dee-seht*	77
soixante-dix-huit	*swah-sahNt-dee-zweet*	78
soixante-dix-neuf	*swah-sahNt-dee-znuhf*	79
quatre-vingts	*kahtr-vaN*	80
quatre-vingt-un	*kahtr-vaN-uhN*	81
quatre-vingt-deux	*kahtr-vaN-duh*	82
quatre-vingt-dix	*kahtr-vaN-dees*	90

quatre-vingt-onze	*kahtr-vaN-onze*	91
quatre-vingt-douze	*kahtr-vaN-dooz*	92
cent	*sahN*	100
cent un	*sahN uhN*	101
deux cents	*duh sahN*	200
deux cent un	*duh sahN uhN*	201
mille	*meel*	1000
deux mille	*duh meel*	2000
un million	*uhN meel-yohN*	1,000,000
deux millions	*duh meel-yohN*	2,000,000
un milliard	*uhN meel-yahr*	1,000,000,000
deux milliards	*duh meel-yahr*	2,000,000,000

When you begin, you may find the numbers from 70 to 100 take a little mathematical finesse. But you'll get the hang of it.

When numbers are used before plural nouns beginning with a vowel, the pronunciation of the numbers changes to allow for elision:

Before a Consonant	Before a Vowel Sound
deux jours (*duh zhoor*)	deux oncles (*duh zohNkl*)
trois cartes (*trwah kahrt*)	trois opinions (*trwah zoh-pee-nyohN*)
quatre valises (*kahtr vah-leez*)	quatre hôtels (*kaht ro-tehl*)
cinq dollars (*saN doh-lahr*)	cinq années (*saN kah-nay*)
six femmes (*see fahm*)	six hommes (*see zohm*)
sept francs (*seht frahN*)	sept heures (*seh tuhr*)
huit mois (*wee mwah*)	huit enfants (*wee tahN-fahN*)
neuf billets (*nuhf bee-yeh*)	neuf artistes (*nuh fahr-teest*)
dix personnes (*dee pehr-sohn*)	dix ans (*dee zahN*)

French numbers are a little tricky until you get used to them. Look carefully at the preceding table and pay special attention to the following:

Attention!

The **f** sound in *neuf* becomes a **v** sound when liaison is made with **heures** (hours, o'clock) and **ans** (years):

Il est neuf heures.	Il a neuf ans.
eel eh nuh vuhr.	*Eel ah nuh vahN*
It is nine o'clock.	He is nine years old.

➤ The conjunction *et* (and) is used only for the numbers 21, 31, 41, 51, 61, and 71. Use a hyphen in all other compound numbers through 99.

➤ *Un* becomes *une* before a feminine noun:

vingt et un hommes et vingt et une femmes

➤ To form 71–79, use 60 + 11, 12, 13, and so on.

➤ To form 91–99, use 80 (4 20s) + 11, 12, 13, and so on.

➤ 80 (quatre-vingts) and the plural of *cent* for any number over 199 drop the *s* before another number, but not before a noun:

quatre-vingts dollars	80 dollars
quatre-vingt-trois dollars	83 dollars
deux cents dollars	200 dollars
deux cent cinquante dollars	250 dollars

➤ Do not use *un* (one) before *cent* and *mille*.

➤ *Mille* doesn't change in the plural.

Culture Capsule

The French write the number one with a little hook on top. In order to distinguish a 1 from the number 7, they put a line through the 7 when they write it: 7.

In numerals and decimals, where we use commas, the French use periods and vice versa:

English	French
1,000	1.000
.25	0,25
$9.95	$9,95

Your Number's Up

Parisian phone numbers consist of eight numbers grouped in pairs of two. The regional code for Paris is (1). You must dial this number before the phone number when calling from outside the city. How would you ask the operator for these numbers?

45 67 89 77   48 21 15 51   46 16 98 13   43 11 72 94   41 34 80 61   42 85 59 02

What Time Is It?

Now that you are familiar with French numbers, it will be relatively easy to learn how to tell time, as explained in the following table. A question that you will probably ask or hear asked very often is:

What time is it?
Quelle heure est-il?
kehl uhr eh-teel?

Memory Enhancer

Instead of saying the hour minus the number of minutes, you may say the number of minutes after the hour.

It's 4:35.—Il est cinq heures moins vingt-cinq.—Il est quatre heures trente-cinq.

Telling Time

Il est une heure.	*eel eh tewn nuhr*	It is 1:00.
Il est deux heures cinq.	*eel eh duh zuhr saNk*	It is 2:05.
Il est quatre heures et quart.	*eel eh kahtr uhr ay kahr*	It is 4:15.
Il est cinq heures vingt.	*eel eh saN kuhr vaN*	It is 5:20.
Il est six heures vingt-cinq	*eel eh see zuhr vaN-saNk*	It is 6:25.
Il est sept heures et demie.	*eel eh seh tuhr ay duh-mee*	It is 7:30.
Il est neuf heures moins vingt.	*eel eh nuh vuhr mwaN vaN*	It is 8:40 (20 minutes to nine).
Il est dix heures moins le quart.	*eel eh dee zuhr mwaN luh (uhN) kahr*	It is 9:45 (a quarter to ten).
Il est onze heures moins dix.	*eel eh ohN zuhr mwaN dees*	It is 10:50 (10 minutes to eleven).
Il est midi moins cinq.	*eel eh mee-dee mwaN saNk*	It is 11:55 (5 minutes to noon).
Il est minuit.	*eel eh mee-nwee*	It is midnight.

Culture Capsule

In public announcements, such as time schedules and timetables, the official 24-hour system is commonly used. Midnight is the 0 hour:

0 h 15 = 12:15 A.M.

15 heures = 3:00 P.M.

Un deux trois

Whenever you look at a clock or your watch, say the time to yourself in French.

Keep the following in mind when you tell time:

➤ To express the time after the hour, the number of minutes is simply added; use *et* only with *quart et demi(e)*.

➤ To express time before the hour, use *moins le* (before, less, minus).

➤ To express half past noon or midnight, use the following:

> Il est midi et demi.

> Il est minuit et demi.

➤ With all other hours, *demie* is used to express half past.

It's Movie Time

You want to go to the movies while you are on vacation, so you call several theaters. Express at what time the films start, according to the recording you hear:

Ciné Beaubourg—*La leçon de piano*: 13h15, 16h20, 19h25

La leçon de piano commence à une heure et quart, à quatre heures vingt, et à sept heures vingt-cinq.

1. Ciné Georges V—*Belle du jour:* 15h10, 17h35, 20h, 22h25

2. Gaumont Opéra—*Retour vers le futur:* 14h50, 16h35, 18h20, 20h05

3. Forum Orient Express—*Mon cousin Vinnie:* 13h30, 16h15, 18h45, 2140

It's not just enough to know how to say what time it is—you might want to know *at what time* an activity is planned or whether it is taking place in the morning, afternoon, or evening. Imagine that you asked someone at what time a play was being presented, and he responded, *"Il y a deux heures."* You might mistake this as meaning "at two o'clock" or "there are two hours," which, to you, means you have two hours before the play begins. In fact, you've missed the play because it started two hours ago. The expressions in the following table will help you deal with time.

Time Expressions

a second	une seconde	*ewn suh-gohNd*
a minute	une minute	*ewn mee-newt*
an hour	une heure	*ewn nuhr*
in the morning (a.m.)	du matin	*dew mah-taN*
in the afternoon (p.m.)	de l'aprés-midi	*duh lah-preh mee-dee*
in the evening (p.m.)	du soir	*dew swahr*
at what time?	à quelle heure	*ah keh luhr*
at exactly midnight	à minuit précis	*ah mee-nwee pray-see*
at exactly 1:00	à une heure précise	*ah ewn uhr pray-seez*
at exactly 2:00	à deux heures précises	*ah duh zuhr pray-seez*
at about 2:00	vers deux heures	*vehr duh zuhr*
a quarter of an hour	un quart d'heure	*uhN kahr duhr*
a half hour	une demi-heure	*ewn duh-mee uhr*
in an hour	dans une heure	*dahN zew nuhr*
until 2:00	jusqu'à deux heures	*zhew-skah duh zuhr*
before 3:00	avant trois heures	*ah-vahN trwah zuhr*
after 3:00	après trois heures	*ah-preh trwah zuhr*
since what time?	depuis quelle heure	*duh-pwee kehl uhr*
since 6:00	depuis six heures	*duh-pwee see zuhr*
an hour ago	il y a une heure	*eel yah ewn nuhr*
per hour	par heure	*pahr uhr*
early	tôt (de bonne heure)	*to (duh boh nuhr)*
late	tard	*tahr*
late (in arriving)	en retard	*ahN ruh-tahr*

The Least You Need to Know

➤ The irregular verb *prendre* means *to take*.

➤ *Quel* is an adjective expressing *which*. It must agree in gender and number with the noun it modifies.

➤ If you plan on renting a car, you'll need to know French numbers and the metric system.

➤ Tell time easily by giving the hour and the number of minutes past the hour.

Chapter 12

A Room with a View

In This Chapter

➤ Hotel amenities

➤ Ordinal numbers

➤ "Shoe" verbs

You've successfully chosen a suitable means of transportation to get you where you want to go. Now, as you ride along, you try to get a feel for your new environment. You can hardly wait to get to the hotel so that you can unpack and start your glorious vacation. Just as your patience is wearing thin, you catch a glimpse of the hotel in the distance. Your first impression reassures you that you've chosen wisely.

Are you a traveler who is happy with the bare minimum in accommodations? Do you feel that because you won't be spending much time in your room, you'd be wasting money on something that you wouldn't truly enjoy? Perhaps you'd rather spend more money on consumables: food, drink, side trips, and souvenirs. Or, on the other hand, are you someone who prefers the creature comforts of home at the very least and, at most, outright luxury. Do you want it all and expect to be treated royally? In this chapter, you will learn how to get the room and the services you expect from your hotel.

It's a Great Hotel! But Does It Have...?

Before leaving home, you will probably want to check with your travel agent or the hotel management to be sure that the hotel you've chosen has the amenities you desire. Depending upon your requirements, you will need to know the words for everything from *bathroom* to *swimming pool*. In the 1970s, my husband and I backpacked around Europe with a copy of Arthur Frommer's *Europe on $5 a Day* under our arms. We hadn't made any reservations, so most nights we had to take whatever room we could get. In Paris, we wound up in a small room in the red-light district. The room didn't have its own bathroom, and we were not thrilled with having to share the *W.C.* down the hall; sometimes the wait was unbearable. Even with reservations, however, you may end up with some surprises; it never hurts to ask questions when you are making your arrangements. See the table below for a basic list of hotel amenities.

Hotel Services

Services	French	Pronunciation
bar	le bar	*luh bahr*
business center	le centre d'affaires	*luh sahNtr dah-fehr*
cashier	la caisse	*lah kehs*
concierge (caretaker)	le (la) concierge	*luh (lah) kohN-syehrzh*
doorman	le portier	*luh pohr-tyay*
elevator	l'ascenseur (m.)	*lah-sahN-suhr*
fitness center	le club santé	*luh klewb sahN-tay*
gift shop	la boutique	*lah boo-teek*
laundry and dry cleaning service	la blanchisserie	*lah blahN-shees-ree*
maid service	la gouvernante	*lah goo-vehr-nahNt*
restaurant	le restaurant	*luh rehs-toh-rahN*
swimming pool	la piscine	*lah pee-seen*
valet parking	l'attendance (f.) du garage	*lah-tahN-dahNs dew gah-rahzh*

Attention!

Do not use the bidet for washing your socks or your feet, as my parents did on their trip. The bidet is a marvelous accessory: straddled face-forward by the user, it allows one to wash using manually controlled jets of water.

When I was planning a trip to Martinique, my travel agent told me about a terrific hotel where the best rooms had balconies facing the ocean. She described the views as breathtaking. Unfortunately, we were not able to confirm a room with a balcony at the time of the reservation, but I figured I'd give it a shot after we arrived. As fate would have it, a travel agent and her large family arrived just as we did. She, too, was eager to trade up to a room with a view. Unfortunately, she was not able to make herself understood to the French-speaking staff. My husband and I, however, were rewarded for our fluency; we got a spectacular room overlooking the ocean! Study the following table to get a jump on the others, just as we did.

Getting What You Want Nicely Furnished

Amenities	French	Pronunciation
a single (double) room	une chambre à un (deux) lits	*ewn shahNbr ah uhN (duh) lee*
air conditioning	la climatisation	*lah klee-mah-tee-zah-syohN*
alarm clock	le réveil	*luh ray-vehy*
balcony	le balcon	*luh bahl-kohN*
bathroom (private)	la salle de bains (privée)	*lah sahl duh baN (pree-vay)*
key	la clé (clef)	*lah klay (klay)*
on the courtyard	côté cour	*koh-tay koor*
on the garden	côté jardin	*koh-tay zhahr-daN*
on the sea	côté mer	*koh-tay mehr*
safe (deposit box)	le coffre	*luh kohfr*
shower	la douche	*lah doosh*
telephone (dial-direct)	le téléphone (direct)	*luh tay-lay-fohn (dee-rehkt)*
television (color)	la télévision (en couleurs)	*lah tay-lay-vee-zyohN (ahN koo-luhr)*
toilet facilities	le *W.C.*	*luh doobl-vay say*

Culture Capsule

In French buildings, the ground floor is called *le rez-de-chaussée*, and the basement is called *le sous-sol* (literally, the "under ground"). The "first floor" is really on the second story of any building. A typical French elevator pad will look like this:

4

3

2

1

rez-de-ch.

s–s

Culture Capsule

In many foreign countries, the sink and bathtub (and/or shower) are located in what is called *the bathroom*, while the toilet and bidet are in the *W.C.* (water closet). Showers are often the hand-held type and are not affixed to the wall, which sometimes makes them rather difficult to negotiate.

Do You Need Something?

Don't you just hate it when your hotel skimps on towels? They often give four small bath towels and expect them to be enough for a couple with two kids. I alone could use three just for myself: hair, top half, and bottom half. Imagine how the rest of my family feels when they're left with my soggy remains! If you need something for your room to make your stay more enjoyable, the following phrases may help you:

I would like	Je voudrais	*zhuh voo-dreh*
I need a (some)	Il me faut un (une)(des)	*eel muh foh tuhN (tewn) (day)*
I need a (for plural use *de + noun*)	J'ai besoin d'un (d'une)	*zhay buh-zwaN duhN (ewn)*

Okay. You're all checked in, you've even unpacked, and now you're ready for a nice hot bath. But wait! The housekeeper has forgotten to provide you with any towels at all! Rather than making your sheets do double duty, call the front desk and ask for towels. The management, after all, is there to make sure that your stay is enjoyable. The following table lists a few things you might need.

Necessities

Necessity	French	Pronunciation
an ashtray	un cendrier	*uhN sahN-dree-yay*
a bar of soap	une savonnette	*ewn sah-voh-neht*
a beach towel	un drap de bain	*uhN drah dbaN*
a blanket	une couverture	*ewn koo-vehr-tewr*
hangers	des cintres (m.)	*day saNtr*
ice cubes	des glaçons (m.)	*day glah-sohN*
mineral water	de l'eau minérale	*duh lo mee-nay-rahl*
a pillow	un oreiller	*uhN noh-reh-yay*

Necessity	French	Pronunciation
tissues	des mouchoirs en papier	*day moo-shwahr ahN pah-pyay*
a roll of toilet paper	un rouleau de papier hygiénique	*uhN roo-lo duh pah-pyay ee-zhyay-neek*
a towel	une serviette	*ewn sehr-vyeht*
a transformer (an electric adaptor)	un transformateur	*uhN trahnz-fohr-mah-tuhr*

Which Hotel Offers the Most?

Imagine that your travel agent has sent you brochures for four hotels where French is spoken. Read what is available and use the chart that follows the ads to check off the services offered by each hotel. Then choose the hotel for you.

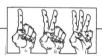

Un deux trois

Pretend you are taking a trip to a French–speaking country. Make a list in French of everything you'd expect the hotel to provide.

Hôtel
Bellevue
Monte-Carlo

Le nouveau hôtel dynamique et moderne de la Société des Bains de Mer vous offre au coeur de Monte-Carlo, à 100 m de la "place du Casino" et des plages, 100 chambres spacieuses toutes avec climatisation, salle de bains privée, balcon, télévision en couleurs, radio téléphone automatique, et mini-bar. Junior suites, appartements, et garage à votre disponibilité.

Sa piscine chauffée avec snack, son bar, et son restaurant à la cuisine française, ses salles de banquet et de réunion, son personnel spécialisé et polyglotte, ainsi que les 20 autres établissements de la S.B.M. rendront votre séjour inoubliable.

MONTRÉAL PLAZA
METRO CENTRE

100$ CAD. (+TAXE)

PAR PERSONNE/OCCUPATION DOUBLE

Hébergement dans une chambre luxueuse sur les étages standards

Transport en limousine au Casino (aller simple)

Jetons de jeux (valeur de 10$ par personne)

Petit déjeuner continental pour deux

Cadeau de bonne chance

A LIBREVILLE
LE GRAND HOTEL VOUS ATTEND

Au coeur des activités de Libreville, **le Grand Hôtel** allie la qualité de ses services à l'élegance d'un hotel moderne de luxe, 5 étoiles. Situé directement sur la plage, **le Grand Hôtel** dispose de 300 chambres dont 10 suites de très grand confort, 3 salons de conférences et réceptions, 1 restaurant ouvert 24 hr., 1 snack bar, 1 restaurant gastronomique, et d'un piano bar.

Pour vos loisirs, **le Grand Hôtel** met à votre disposition, piscine, plage, sauna, tennis, massages, galeria marchande, ainsi qu'un élégant casino. Un service de navette gratuite (hôtel- aéroport) est mis à votre disposition.

La direction et le personnel de l'hôtel **Paris Opéra** vous souhaitent la bienvenue à Paris et sont à votre service pour rendre votre séjour agréable.

A deux pas de la place de l'Opéra, découvrez cet hôtel de charme dans une ambiance accueillante et feutrée. Meubles anciens, poutres apparentes, décoration des chambres personnalisée. Toutes les chambres équipées de bains, W.C., réveil, TV en couleurs, téléphone direct.

Paris et ses boutiques de la rue de la Paix, ses restaurants, ses spectacles, ses théâtres sont à votre porte.

	Hôtel Bellevue	Montréal Plaza	Le Grand Hôtel	Paris-Opéra
bar				
TV en couleurs				
sauna				
cuisine gourmet				
téléphone direct				
petit déjeuner compris				
chambre luxueuse				
dîner spécial				
cadeau				
plage				
climatisation				
grande chambre				
casino				
garage				
massage				
transport				

Going Up

We've all had an elevator experience where we've felt like a large sardine in a small can. When you're pushed to the back or squished to the side, you have to hope that a kind and gentle soul will wiggle a hand free and ask: *Quel étage, s'il vous plaît* (*kehl ay-tahzh seel voo pleh*)? You will need the ordinal numbers in the following table to give a correct answer: *Le deuxième étage, s'il vous plaît* (*luh duh-zyehm ay-tahzh see voo pleh*).

Ordinal Numbers

premier (première)	*pruh-myay (pruh-myehr)*	1st
deuxième (second[e])	*duh-zyehm (suh-gohN[d])*	2nd
troisième	*trwah-zyehm*	3rd
quatrième	*kah-tree-yehm*	4th
cinquième	*saN-kyehm*	5th
sixième	*see-zyehm*	6th
septième	*seh-tyehm*	7th
huitième	*wee-tyehm*	8th
neuvième	*nuh-vyehm*	9th
dixième	*dee-zyehm*	10th

continues

Ordinal Numbers (cont.)

onzième	*ohN-zyehm*	11th
douzième	*doo-zyehm*	12th
vingtième	*vaN-tyehm*	20th
vingt et un (e)ième	*vaN-tay-uhN (ewn)-nyehm*	21st
soixante-douzième	*swah-sahNt doo-zyehm*	72nd
centième	*sahN-tyehm*	100th

Memory Enhancer

The French ordinal numbers are abbreviated as follows:

premier 1er (première 1re)

deuxième 2^{e}

cinquantième 50^{e}

Keep the following in mind when using ordinal numbers:

➤ *Premier* and *second* are the only ordinal numbers that must agree in gender (masculine or feminine) with the noun they describe. All other ordinal numbers must agree in number with the noun:

son premier fils	his (her) first son
sa première fille	his (her) first daughter
Les dixièmes anniversaires de mariage sont spéciaux.	Tenth wedding anniversaries are special.

➤ Except for *premier* and *second*, *ième* is added to all cardinal numbers to form the ordinal number. Drop the silent *e* before *ième*.

➤ Note that *u* is added in *cinquième,* and *v* replaces *f* in *neuvième*.

➤ *Second(e)* is generally used in a series that does not go beyond two.

➤ There is no elision with *huitième* and *onzième*. The definite article *le* or *la* does not drop its vowel:

le huitième jour	the eighth day
la onzième personne	the eleventh person

➤ In French, cardinal numbers precede ordinal numbers:

les deux premières foi	the first two times

Culture Capsule

For administrative purposes, the city of Paris is divided into arrondissements (*ah-rohN-dees-mahN*). Each one is headed by its own mayor. Addresses listed in Parisian phone books generally include the number of the arrondissement after the street address:

Bernard, S.   128 bd Charonne 20^e (01) 43 11 14 22

In the above address, 128 is the house number. 20e is the arrondissement. 01 is the area code to call Paris.

Using Ordinal Numbers

Look at the map of Paris that shows the divisions for the arrondissements. In which arrondissement would you find these famous tourist attractions?

Example: Montmartre est dans le dix-huitième arrondissement.

1. La Tour Eiffel _____ .
2. Les Invalides _____ .
3. Le Forum des Halles _____ .
4. Le Quartier Latin _____ .
5. La Bastille _____ .
6. Le Panthéon _____ .

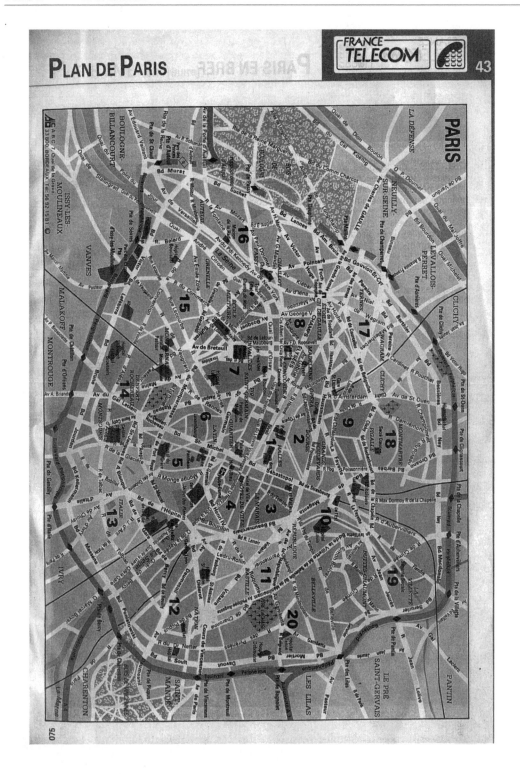

Making a Change

Imagine that you want to sample a famous French delicacy, eat in a special restaurant, pay with your credit card, or buy a special gift. Naturally, you'll want some recommendations and will probably get opinions from everyone from the concierge to the chambermaid. In the course of your conversations, you'll have to use many verbs to get the information you seek. There are a few categories of regular *er* verbs whose endings require spelling changes in certain forms. In some instances, this is necessary to maintain the proper sound of the verb. In other instances, it's just one of the idiosyncrasies of the language. You should familiarize yourself with some of these verbs in each group because they are high-frequency words that you will use and see quite often.

Attention!

"Shoe verbs" are not considered irregular since all verbs within each group follow the same rules.

These verbs are referred to as *shoe verbs* because the rules of conjugation work as if you put the subject pronouns that follow one set of rules within the shoe, and the others, outside the shoe. To make that more clear, look at the pronouns that go in and out of the shoe:

In other words, for all verbs in these categories, *je, tu, il, elle, on, ils,* and *elles* will follow one set of rules, whereas *nous* and generally, but not always, *vous* will follow a different set of rules. Now let's look at the different categories.

cer Verbs

For *cer* verbs, the *nous* form needs *ç* to maintain the soft sound of the *c* (s). This cedilla is added before the vowels *a, o,* and *u*.

Attention!

The letter *c* has a hard sound before *a, o,* and *u*.

The letter *c* has a soft sound before *e* and *i*.

A hard *c* can be made soft by attaching a cedilla under the *c*: *ç*.

Placer (To Place, Set)

je place	nous plaçons
tu places	vous placez
il, elle, on place	ils, elles placent

Other verbs conjugated like *placer* include:

annoncer	*ah-nohN-say*	to announce
avancer	*ah-vahN-say*	to advance (be fast—clocks and watches)
commencer (à)	*koh-mahN-say (ah)*	to begin
menacer	*muh-nah-say*	to threaten
remplacer	*rahN-plah-say*	to replace
renoncer à	*ruh-nohN-say ah*	to give up, renounce

Using *cer* Verbs

You should find *cer* verbs quite easy since there is really only one small change involved. Practice vocabulary and conversation by completing the sentence with the correct form of the appropriate verb from the list in the preceding section:

1. Le spectacle (commencer) _____ à neuf heures.
2. Nous (renoncer à) _____ à faire des projets.
3. Tu (remplacer) _____ ta valise?
4. Ma montre (avancer) _____.
5. Ils (annoncer) _____ le départ du train.

ger Verbs

For *ger* verbs, the *nous* form needs an extra *e* to maintain the soft sound of the *g* (zh). This extra *e* is always added after *g* before the vowels *a*, *o*, and *u*.

Manger (To Eat)

je mange	nous mangeons
tu manges	vous mangez
il, elle, on mange	ils, elles mangent

Other verbs that are conjugated like *manger* are:

arranger	*ah-rahn-zhay*	to arrange
changer	*shahN-zhay*	to change
corriger	*koh-ree-zhay*	to correct
déranger	*day-rahN-zhay*	to disturb
diriger	*dee-ree-zhay*	to direct
nager	*nah-zhay*	to swim
obliger	*oh-blee-zhay*	to oblige
partager	*pahr-tah-zhay*	to share, divide
ranger	*rahN-zhay*	to tidy

Using ger Verbs

Like *cer* verbs, *ger* verbs have only one change to memorize. Giving the correct form of the verb in each sentence should prove to be a snap:

1. La fille de chambre (ranger) _____ la chambre.
2. Tu (déranger) _____ les autres clients.
3. Nous (partager) _____ notre sandwich parce qu'il est très grand.
4. Vous (nager) _____ bien.
5. Ils (arranger) _____ tout.

yer Verbs

In *yer* verbs, the *y* is retained in the *nous* and *vous* forms. Within the shoe, an *i* is used instead of the *y*.

Employer (To Use)

j'emploie	nous employons
tu emploies	vous employez
il, elle, on emploie	ils, elles emploient

Other verbs that are conjugated like *employer* are:

Memory Enhancer

Verbs ending in *ayer* may or may not change *y* to *i* in the forms in the shoe:

essayer (de)
eh-say-yay (duh)
to try (to)

payer
peh-yay
to pay, to pay for

ennuyer	*ahN-nwee-yay*	to bother, bore
envoyer	*ahN-vwah-yay*	to send
nettoyer	*neh-twah-yay*	to clean

payer (To Pay)

je paie (paye)	nous payons
tu paies (payes)	vous payez
il, elle, on paie (paye)	ils, elles paient (payent)

essayer (To Try)

j'essaie (essaye)	nous essayons
tu essaies (essayes)	vous essayez
il, elle, on essaie (essaye)	ils, elles essaient (essayent)

Using yer Verbs

Do you feel confident with *yer* verbs? Keep the shoe image in your mind and remember that *y* changes to *i*. Now have a go at conjugating the following verbs:

1. Tu (payer) _____ trop.
2. Il (employer) _____ un plan de la ville.
3. Vous (ennuyer) _____ les autres.
4. La fille de chambre (nettoyer) _____ bien.
5. J' (essayer) _____ de parler français.

e+consonant+er Verbs

Verbs with a silent *e* in the syllable before the *er* infinitive ending (*acheter*: to buy; *peser*: to weigh) change the silent *e* to *è* for all forms in the shoe. Within the shoe, all the endings of the verbs are silent.

Acheter (To Buy)

j'achète (*ah-sheht*)	nous achetons (*ahsh-tohN*)
tu achètes (*ah-sheht*)	vous achetez (*ahsh-tay*)
il, elle, on achète (*ah-sheht*)	ils, elles achètent (*ah-sheht*)

Notice the difference in pronunciation of the verb inside and outside the shoe. Within the shoe, the first *e* has an accent grave, and *è* is pronounced. Outside the shoe, the first *e* is unpronounced.

Other verbs that are conjugated like *acheter* are:

achever	*ahsh-vay*	to finish, complete
amener	*ahm-nay*	to bring, lead to
emmener	*ahNm-nay*	to take, lead away
enlever	*ahN-lvay*	to take off, remove
peser	*puh-zay*	to weigh
promener	*prohm-nay*	to walk

Memory Enhancer

Because all the endings within the shoe are silent, adding an accent grave (*è*) to the silent *e* before the ending gives sound to that silent *e*. Two silent *es* would make the word virtually impossible to pronounce.

Appeler (to call) and *jeter* (to throw) are two verbs with a silent *e* that double the consonant before the *er* infinitive ending, instead of adding the accent grave.

Appeler (To Call)

j'appelle (*ah-pehl*)   nous appelons (*ah-plohN*)

tu appelles (*ah-pehl*)   vous appelez (*ah-play*)

il, elle, on appelle (*ah-pehl*)   ils, elles appellent (*ah-pehl*)

Jeter (To Throw)

je jette (*zheht*)   nous jetons (*zhuh-tohN*)

tu jettes (*zheht*)   vous jetez (*zhuh-tay*)

il, elle, on jette (*zheht*)   ils, elles jettent (*zheht*)

Using e+Consonant+er Verbs I

It's very important to practice the correct spelling of *e+consonant+er* verbs—and not because spelling is so important. Let's face it, you're probably not going to be writing many letters in French. Why spend time on this? Because if you understand that accents give sounds to silent letters, then you'll be much more successful at perfecting your pronunciation. Take this opportunity to read and write at the same time:

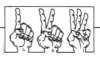

Un deux trois

Keep cards with the different "shoe" changes on your refrigerator. Pick one a day and study the change and the verbs it affects.

1. Il (walk) _____ son chien.

2. Vous (call) _____ votre ami.

3. J' (take) _____ mon chapeau.

4. On (throw) _____ les papiers dans la poubelle.

5. Nous (bring) _____ nos enfants au cinéma.

é+Consonant+er Verbs

Verbs with *é* in the syllable before the infinitive ending change *é* to *è* in the shoe, where the endings to the conjugated verb forms are all silent.

Préférer (To Prefer)

je préfère (*pray-fehr*)	nous préférons (*pray-feh-rohN*)
tu préfères (*pray-fehr*)	vous préférez (*pray-feh-ray*)
il, elle, on préfère (*pray-fehr*)	ils, elles préfèrent (*pray-fehr*)

Attention!

When conjugating a "shoe verb," you must pay attention not only to the spelling change, but also to the correct verb ending.

Other verbs that are conjugated like *préférer* are:

célébrer	*say-lay-bray*	to celebrate
espérer	*ehs-pay-ray*	to hope
posséder	*poh-say-day*	to own, possess
protéger	*proh-tay-zhay*	to protect
répéter	*ray-pay-tay*	to repeat

Using é+Consonant+er Verbs II

Once again, using accents correctly will ensure that you're speaking properly. You can practice vocabulary, spelling, and pronunciation all in one fell swoop by completing the following sentences:

1. Je (celebrate) _____ mon anniversaire demain.

2. (Repeat) _____ la phrase, s'il vous plaît.

3. Nous (protect) _____ nos amis.

4. Ils (hope) _____ voyager.

5. Elle (owns) _____ une jolie voiture.

Reviewing "Shoe" Verbs

"Shoe verbs" may have changes within or outside the shoe. The following changes occur:

Reviewing "Shoe" Verbs

Verb	Change	Subject Affected
cer	c > ç	nous
ger	g > ge	nous
yer	y > i	nous, vous
e+consonant+er	e > è	je, tu, il, elle, ils, elles
é+consonant+er	é > è	je, tu, il, elle, ils, elles

Verbs ending in *ayer* may or may not change *y* to *i*.

The verbs *appeler* and *jeter* double the consonant before the *er* ending instead of adding an accent.

Rate Your Hotel

Many hotels are curious to know whether you are happy with the services they provide. After all, they want you to return and would appreciate your recommendation to friends. How would you fill out their questionnaire?

Comment jugez-vous...?

Excellent	Bon	Moyen	Insuffisant
VOTRE ARRIVÉE			
Porteur			
Réception			
Réservation			
Sécurité			
NOS SERVICES			
Concierge			
Téléphones			
Messages			
Caissier			
Centre d'affaires			
Gouvernante			

continues

Comment jugez-vous...? (cont.)

Excellent	Bon	Moyen	Insuffisant
Blanchisserie			
Minibar			
Piscine			
Gymnase			
VOTRE CHAMBRE			
Bien equipée			
Espace de travail adapté			
Produits d'accueil en quantité suffisante			
Équipement en bon état de fonctionnement			

The Least You Need to Know

➤ To be happy in your hotel, learn the vocabulary for facilities and furnishings to facilitate asking for what you want and need.

➤ Ordinal numbers (except for *premier:* first; and second [e] used only for the second in a series of two) are formed by adding *ième* to the cardinal number.

➤ "Shoe verbs" follow a pattern of conjugation that resembles the outline of a shoe. Remember the shoe, and you'll remember how to conjugate the verbs.

Part 3
Fun Time

You want to have fun no matter where you go or what the reason, so your trip will surely include games, amusements, and diversions. This is the place to be when you're seeking a good time.

No matter what weather conditions prevail, there's always something to do. Naturally, you'll want to sightsee. Then there are other exciting activities for the most athletic and adventuresome among us: a wide gamut of sports including parasailing, scuba diving, windsurfing, and much more. Don't forget all the cultural opportunities: museums, concerts, ballets, and operas. Perhaps traveling is a shopping experience for you. Maybe it's a gastronomic feast.

The six chapters in Part 3 deal with how to get the most fun out of your vacation. You'll learn how to express what you want to do, when you want to do it, and how much you're enjoying yourself.

Chapter 13

Today's Weather Is...

In This Chapter

➤ Weather conditions

➤ Days of the week

➤ Months of the year

➤ The four seasons

➤ Expressing the date

➤ The irregular verb *faire* (to make, do)

Your hotel is fabulous. Your room suits you to a *T* and has all the creature comforts, and then some. But it is time to get up and out. Before you head to the lobby, you glance out the window and notice that the sky is overcast, and you want to be prepared in case it rains. By the way, what are you going to do if that happens?

If you were at home, you'd probably tune into the weather channel to get the latest forecast. You could give this approach a shot, but remember, in a French-speaking country, all the announcers will be speaking French—and when it comes to weather, your knowledge of cognates won't take you too far. In this chapter, you'll tackle the weather report, and you'll also learn what you need to know to find out the hours at museums, movie theatres, and other places that may beckon on a rainy day.

Attention!

The verb *faire* or the expression *il y a* is used with most weather conditions. Be careful not to use *faire* when you want to say it is raining or snowing:

Il neige.—It's snowing.

Il pleut.—It's raining.

It's 30 Degrees, but They're Wearing String Bikinis!

Let's say that you turn on the television and manage to understand the weatherman when he reports that it is 30 degrees. But it's summer—how can this be? Is it possible that *La météo* (the forecast) is wrong? Perhaps it's time to consult the friendly *concierge* (caretaker/manager) at the front desk. The phrases in the following table will help you talk about the weather.

Weather Expressions

Expression	French	Pronunciation
What's the weather?	Quel temps fait-il?	*kehl tahN feh-teel*
It's beautiful.	Il fait beau.	*eel feh bo*
It's hot.	Il fait chaud.	*eel feh sho*
It's sunny.	Il fait du soleil.	*eel feh dew soh-lehy*
It's nasty (bad).	Il fait mauvais.	*eel feh moh-veh*
It's cold.	Il fait froid.	*eel feh frwah*
It's cool.	Il fait frais.	*eel feh freh*
It's windy.	Il fait du vent.	*eel feh dew vahN*
It's lightning.	Il fait des éclairs. (m.)	*eel feh day zay-klehr*
It's thundering.	Il fait du tonnerre.	*eel feh dew toh-nehr*
It's foggy.	Il fait du brouillard.	*eel feh dew broo-yahr*
	Il y a du brouillard.	*eel yah dew broo-yahr*
It's humid.	Il fait humide.	*eel feh tew-meed*
	Il y a de l'humidité.	*eel yah duh lew-mee-dee-tay*
It's cloudy.	Il y a des nuages.	*eel yah day new-ahzh*
	Le ciel est nuageux.	*luh syehl eh new-ah-zhuh*
It's overcast.	Le ciel est couvert.	*luh syehl eh koo-vehr*
It's raining.	Il pleut.	*eel pluh*
It's pouring.	Il pleut à verse.	*eel pluh ah vehrs*
It's snowing.	Il neige.	*eel nehzh*

Expression	French	Pronunciation
There are gusts of wind.	Il y a des rafales (f.).	*eel yah day rah-fahl*
There's hail.	Il y a de la grêle.	*eel yah duh lah grehl*
There are sudden showers.	Il y a des giboulées (f.)	*eel yah day zhee-boo-lay*

So why is everyone wearing tank tops and a bikinis when it's 30 degrees outside? The answer is really quite simple. 'The French-speaking world uses Celsius (centigrade) rather than Fahrenheit to tell the temperature. This means that when it is 30 degrees Celsius, it's 86 degrees Fahrenheit.

Culture Capsule

To convert degrees Fahrenheit to degrees Celsius, subtract 32 from the Fahrenheit temperature and multiply the remaining number by five-ninths. This will give you the temperature in degrees Celsius.

To convert Celsius to Fahrenheit, multiply the Celsius temperature by nine-fifths and then add 32. This will give you the temperature in degrees Fahrenheit.

And the Temperature Is...

You never were that great in math, but you're determined to have a pretty good idea of what the temperature is. You arm yourself with a minisolar calculator and ask the concierge:

> Il fait quelle temperature?
> *eel feh kehl tahN-pay-rah-tewr?*
> What's the temperature?

If someone asks you what the temperature is (and you happen to know), respond with the phrase *il fait* followed by the number of degrees. If it is below zero, throw a *moins* (minus) before the number.

Il fait moins dix.	Il fait zéro.	Il fait soixante.
eel feh mwaN dees	*eel feh zay-ro*	*eel feh swah-sahNt*
It's 10 below.	It's zero.	It's sixty degrees.

Culture Capsule

The weather in France is much like the weather in the northeastern United States: It is temperate for much of the year and the seasons change every three months.

In the Paper It Says...

French newspapers, like American newspapers, contain weather information, complete with maps and symbols. Take a look at the following map to see if you can decipher the symbols. If you have trouble, consult the guide for help.

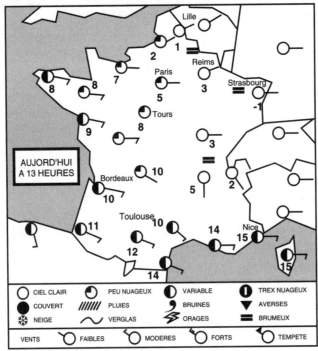

brouillards	*broo-yahr*	fog
fraîcheur	*freh-shuhr*	chilly
soleil	*soh-lehy*	sun
ciel clair	*syehl klehr*	clear sky
couvert	*koo-vehr*	cloudy
neige	*nehzh*	snow
peu nuageux	*puh new-ah-zhuh*	slightly cloudy
pluies	*plwee*	rain
verglas	*vehr-glah*	sleet
variable	*vah-ree-yahbl*	changeable
bruines	*brween*	drizzle
orages	*oh-rahzh*	storms
très nuageux	*treh new-ah-zhuh*	very cloudy
averses	*ah-vehrs*	showers (heavy rain)
brumeux	*brew-muh*	hazy, foggy
vent	*vaN*	winds
faibles	*fehbl*	weak
modérés	*moh-day-ray*	moderate
fort	*fohr*	strong
tempête	*tahN-peht*	storm

And the Forecast Is...

You're undecided about what to do today. So, you open the newspaper to the weather page to get a better idea of what plans would be appropriate. According to the headline, what weather is predicted for this day?

Un deux trois

Keep a one-week journal and record the weather for your city in French.

You're intrigued by the French weather map you see and decide to bone up on your forecast reading abilities. Give the temperature and the weather for the following cities in France at 1 P.M.:

Lille	Strasbourg	Tours
Reims	Paris	Nice

Attention!

Unlike our calendars, French calendars start with Monday. Don't let this confuse you when you give a quick glance. You want to make sure that you get to that appointment on the right day.

What Day Is It?

If you're anything like me, the day your vacation starts is the day your watch comes off. You get so involved in having a good time that you lose all track of time. Every day seems like Saturday or Sunday, and you frequently have to ask: "What day is it, anyway?" If you're on a sightseeing vacation, you really have to keep track of the days of the week so that you don't wind up at the attraction you were dying to see on the day that it's closed. That can happen very easily in Paris, where schedules differ from museum to museum. When you study the days of the week in the following table, you'll notice that they all end in *di*, except for Sunday, which begins with *di*. *Note:* The days of the week in French (which are all masculine) are not capitalized (unless they are at the beginning of a sentence).

Days of the Week

Day	French	Pronunciation
Monday	lundi	*luhN-dee*
Tuesday	mardi	*mahr-dee*
Wednesday	mercredi	*mehr-kruh-dee*
Thursday	jeudi	*zhuh-dee*
Friday	vendredi	*vahN-druh-dee*
Saturday	samedi	*sahm-dee*
Sunday	dimanche	*dee-mahNsh*

To say that something is happening "on" a certain day, the French use the definite article *le*:

Le lundi je vais en ville.
luh luhN-dee zhuh veh zahN veel.
On Monday(s) I go downtown.

The Best Month for a Trip

It's August and you want to go to Nice. Disappointment sets in when your travel agent says, "Sorry, there's nothing available." So, you book your own trip to Paris during this same time period. When you get there, the city is empty. Where *is* everyone? In France, many stores and businesses are closed during the month of August, when everyone seems to head south to La Côte d'Azur (the Riviera) for a vacation. The following table gives you the months of the year. Thus, when you glance through all those glossy vacation brochures, you can figure out the best time to take your trip.

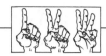

Un deux trois

Say in French the days you go to the movies; go to the supermarket; do laundry; go out with friends; eat out; work hard.

Note: Like the days of the week, all months in French are masculine and are not capitalized (unless they are used at the beginning of a sentence or are special days such as "Good Friday"—Vendredi saint).

Months of the Year

Month	French	Pronunciation
January	janvier	*zhahN-vyay*
February	février	*fay-vree-yay*
March	mars	*mahrs*
April	avril	*ah-vreel*
May	mai	*meh*
June	juin	*zhwaN*
July	juillet	*zhwee-eh*
August	août	*oo(t)*
September	septembre	*sehp-tahNbr*
October	octobre	*ohk-tohbr*
November	novembre	*noh-vahNbr*
December	décembre	*day-sahNbr*

To make clear that something is expected to happen *in* a certain month, use the preposition *en*. For example:

Je vais en France en avril.
zhuh veh zahN frahNs ahN nah-vreel
I am going to France in April.

The Four Seasons

Some seasons are better for traveling in certain countries than in others. Make sure to plan your trip when the weather will be great so that you don't have to worry about hurricanes, storms, or other adverse conditions. Maybe you're not a traveler but enjoy doing crossword puzzles where clues often call for "season (fr.)." Perhaps you'd like to know which sports and activities are performed in each season. Whatever your reason, the table below gives you the names of the seasons:

Un deux trois

Express in French in which season you go to the beach; watch a football game; go on outdoor picnics; watch the leaves turn colors.

The Seasons

l'hiver	*lee-vehr*	winter
le printemps	*luh praN-tahN*	spring
l'été	*lay-tay*	summer
l'automne	*lo-tohn*	autumn, fall

To express *in* with the seasons, the French use the preposition *en* for all the seasons, except the spring, when *au* is used:

Je vais en France en hiver (en été, en automne, **au** printemps).
zhuh veh zahN frahNs ahN nee-vehr (ahN nay-tay, ahN no-tohn, o praN-tahN)
I'm going to France in the winter (summer, fall, spring).

You Have a Date

Do you also lose track of the date while you're away from home or work? The date is something people tend to forget on a fairly regular basis, especially when they're on vacation. (I finally broke down and bought a minicomputer so that I can always have a calendar on hand.) See the following table for a few words you will need to know when making plans:

Dates

a day	un jour	*uhN zhoor*
a week	une semaine	*ewn suh-mehn*
a month	un mois	*uhN mwah*
a year	un an	*uhN nahN*
a year	une année	*ewn ah-nay*

The word for *year*, *an*, is used with cardinal numbers one, two, three, and so on, unless an adjective is used to describe the word *year*. In that case, the word *année* is used. Sometimes, either word is acceptable.

un an—one year

une année—a year

deux bonnes années—two good years

quelques années—some years

l'an dernier—last year

l'année dernière—last year

You've decided to take the plunge and get a new French coif. Perhaps you're on a business trip and have to arrange for an important meeting. Or maybe you've decided to make unexpected travel plans. Whatever the reason, you'll have to know how to express the date for your appointment.

➤ Dates in French are expressed as follows:

(le) day of week + (le) (cardinal) number + month + year

lundi onze juillet 1999

lundi le onze juillet 1999

le lundi onze juillet 1999

➤ The first day of each month is expressed by *premier*. Cardinal numbers are used for all other days:

le premier janvier   January 1st

le deux janvier   January 2nd

➤ Just as in English, years are usually expressed in hundreds. When the word for *thousand* is written in dates only, *mil* is often used instead of *mille*:

1999   dix-neuf cent quatre-vingt dix-neuf

mil neuf cent quatre-vingt dix-neuf

➤ In order to get information about the date, you need to ask the following questions:

What is today's date?	What day is today?
Quelle est la date d'aujourd'hui?	Quel jour est-ce aujourd'hui?
kehl eh lah daht doh-zhoor-dwee?	*kehl zhoor ehs oh-zhoor-dwee?*

OR

What day is today?
Quel jour sommes-nous aujourd'hui?
kehl zhoor sohm noo oh-zhoor-dwee?

183

The answer to your questions would be one of the following:

Today is
C'est aujourd'hui + (day) date
sehh toh-zhoor-dwee

Today is
Aujourd'hui nous sommes + (day) date
oh-zhoor-dwee noo sohm

Culture Capsule

When the French write the date in numbers, the sequence is day + month + year. In the United States, we tend to lead with the month, followed by the day, and then the year. Notice how different this looks:

French	English
le 22 avril 1977	April 22, 1977
22.4.77	4/22/77
le trois mai 1995	May 3, 1995
3.5.95	5/3/95

Un deux trois

Make a list in French of the important dates in your life. Read them aloud as you mark them on a calendar.

Heaven help those of us who forget important dates. It's not intentional, but it often creates problems. Practice what you've learned by giving the day and dates for these important events of the year:

Your birthday, the birthday of a friend, Thanksgiving, New Year's, Mother's Day, Valentine's Day, Father's Day, Memorial Day

When you have to make plans and schedule your time wisely, you'll need certain time-related words and expressions. Keep the expressions in the following table in mind when time is of the essence.

Time Expressions

in	dans _____	*dahN*
ago	il y a _____	*eel yah*
per	par _____	*pahr*
during	pendant _____	*pahN-dahN*

next	prochain(e)	*proh-shaN (proh-shehn)*
last	dernier (dernière)	*dehr-nyah (dehr-nyehr)*
last	passé(e)	*pah-say*
eve	la veille	*la vehy*
day before yesterday	avant-hier	*ah-vahN yehr*
yesterday	hier	*yehr*
today	aujourd'hui	*oh-zhoor-dwee*
tomorrow	demain	*duh-maN*
day after tomorrow	après-demain	*ah-preh duh-maN*
next day	le lendemain	*luh lahN-duh-maN*
from	dès _____	*deh*
a week from today	d'aujourd'hui en huit	*doh-zhoor-dwee ahN weet*
two weeks from tomorrow	de demain en quinze	*duh duh-maN ahN kaNz*

What's the Date?

Yesterday? Tomorrow? Two weeks from today? What if you don't have a calendar on you and you need the exact date? Practice your understanding of the phrases in the table above. If today were *le sept août*, give the date for the following:

Memory Enhancer

The adjectives prochain, dernier, and passé must be used in their feminine form to describe a masculine noun:

Le mois prochaine—next month

1. avant-hier _____

2. de demain en huit _____

3. d'aujourd'hui en quinze _____

4. demain _____

5. la veille _____

6. il y a sept jours _____

When Is It Open?

Read the ad for this restaurant and express when you can eat there and what special events occur on which days.

> **LA GRILLADE**
>
> à Fort-de-France
>
> Son couscous—Ses pizzas
>
> Ses viandes et poissons grillés à l'orientale
>
> Ouvert de 9 h à 23 h 30—Fermé le dimanche
>
> Salle climatisée—Ambiance musique orientale
>
> SOIRÉE ANIMÉE: MARDI, MERCREDI, VENDREDI

Say the date as follows:

(le) day of week + (le) (cardinal) number + month + year

mardi quatorze	septembre 1999
mardile quatorze	septembre 1999
le mardi quatorze	septembre 1999

The names of the days, months, and seasons are not capitalized.

Monday	lundi	January	janvier	winter	l'hiver
Tuesday	mardi	February	février	spring	le printemps
Wednesday	mercredi	March	mars	summer	l'été
Thursday	jeudi	April	avril	fall	l'automne
Friday	vendredi	May	mai		
Saturday	samedi	June	juin		
Sunday	dimanche	July	juillet		
		August	août		
		September	septembre		
		October	octobre		
		November	novembre		
		December	décembre		

What Do You Make of This?

A French friend phones and says to you, "Il fait si beau aujourd'hui. On fait du golf?" We've already seen that, in speaking about the weather, we can use the irregular verb *faire* in an impersonal way: *il fait* + the weather condition. The verb *faire*, shown in the following table, means *to make* or *to do*, and is often used to speak about household chores. *Faire* can also be used to speak about playing a sport, even though it translates poorly into English. So, will you be playing golf with your friend today?

Faire (To Make, To Do)

je fais	*zhuh feh*	I make, do
tu fais	*tew feh*	you make, do
il, elle, on fait	*eel (ehl, ohN) feh*	he (she, one) makes, does
nous faisons	*noo fuh-zohN*	we make, do
vous faites	*voo feht*	you make, do
ils, elles font	*eel (ehl) fohN*	they make, do

Expressions with *faire*

Let's say you don't want to talk about sports or the weather. How else can you use the verb *faire* to your best advantage? There are many useful idioms with the verb *faire*. If your host asked you, "*Voudriez-vous faire une partie de tennis?*," would you think he was inviting you to a tennis party? Common sense and a knowledge of cognates would trick you into thinking so. In reality, he'd only be inviting you to play in a match. Similarly, if he told you "*Je l'ai fait exprès*," would you think he did something in a rush? Again, your knowledge of English would make you think so. Actually, whatever he did, he did it on purpose. You can see why it is very important to study the idiomatic expressions with *faire* in the table below.

More Idioms with *faire*

Expression	Pronunciation	English Meaning
faire à sa tête	*fehr ah sah teht*	to do as one pleases
faire attention à	*fehr ah-tahN-syohN ah*	to pay attention to
faire de son mieux	*fehr duh sohN myuh*	to do one's best
faire des achats (emplettes)	*fehr day zah-shah (ahN-pleht)*	to go shopping
faire des courses	*fehr day koors*	to do errands (shop)
faire exprès	*fehr ehks-preh*	to do on purpose
faire la connaissance de	*fehn lah koh-neh-sahNs duh*	to meet, become acquainted with

continues

More Idioms with *faire* (cont.)

Expression	Pronunciation	English Meaning
faire la queue	*fehr lah kuh*	to stand on line
faire mal à	*fehr mahl ah*	to hurt
faire peur à	*fehr puhr ah*	to frighten
faire plaisir à	*fehr pleh-zeer ah*	to please
faire semblant de	*fehr sahN-blahN duh*	to pretend
faire ses adieux	*fehr say zah-dyuh*	to say good-bye
faire une partie de	*fehr ewn pahr-tee duh*	to play a game of
faire une promenade	*fehr ewn prohm-nahd*	to take a walk
faire un voyage	*fehr uhN vwah-yahzh*	to take a trip
faire venir	*fehr vuh-neer*	to send for

Make sure to conjugate the verb when you use it in context:

Je fais les courses le lundi.   I go on errands on Mondays.

Ils font un voyage en France.   They are taking a trip to France.

Faites venir le médecin.   Send for the doctor.

In the preceding expressions, wherever the possessive adjective *son*, *sa*, or *ses* appears, any of the equivalent possessive adjectives may be used, depending upon the subject:

Je fais à ma tête.   Nous faisons nos adieux.
zhuh feh ah mah teht   *noo fuh-zohN no zah-dyuh*
I do as I please.   We say our good-byes.

Using *faire*

Because the verb *faire* has so many different uses, it's quite important to practice it thoroughly. After you feel confident with the conjugation of *faire* and have learned its various idioms, complete the following sentences:

1. (to take a trip) Ils _____.
2. (to wait on line) Vous _____.
3. (to send for) Tu _____ le docteur.
4. (to take a walk) Nous _____.
5. (to meet) Elle _____ M. Renaud.
6. (to go shopping) Je _____.
7. (to pay attention) On _____ au directeur.
8. (to play a game of) Elles _____ golf.

188

The Least You Need to Know

➤ Use *il fait* to express weather conditions and the temperature.

➤ To express the date, use the day of the week + the number of the day + the month + the year.

➤ The irregular verb *faire* is used to discuss sports and household chores, and is in some very useful idiomatic expressions.

Chapter 14

Sightseeing

In This Chapter

➤ Typical tourist attractions

➤ Animals galore

➤ Making suggestions and plans

➤ Expressing your opinion

➤ Other countries

➤ The pronoun *y*

The weather in today's paper is calling for a mild and sunshiny day. It's perfect weather to have a café au lait at a sidewalk café, visit Notre Dame, and finally take a stroll down the Champs-Elysées. You've checked your guidebook to see what's open and at what times. Now it's time to take out your metro or bus map and plan your day so that you can leisurely enjoy the sights you long to see.

In this chapter you will be given a choice of things to do and interesting places to visit. You will become proficient in making suggestions and giving your opinions about things. And if you should decide to travel far and wide, you will be able to get there—in French.

The Sights to See

There's so much to do and so much to see in all the French-speaking countries. Are you in the mood for sightseeing or relaxing? Do you want to pack your day with activity or do you prefer to proceed at a leisurely pace? The brochures you've picked up at your hotel or at the tourist office offer many suggestions. The following table gives you the words and phrases you need to talk about your choices.

Where to Go and What to Do

Le Lieu	The Place	L'Activité	The Activity
l'aquarium (*lah-kwah-ryuhm*)	the aquarium	voir les poissons	see the fish
l'église (*lay-gleez*)	the church	voir l'architecture	see the architecture
la boîte de nuit (*lah bwaht duh nwee*)	the night club	voir un spectacle	see a show
le carnaval (*luh kahr-nah-vahl*)	the carnival	regarder le défilé	see the parade
la cathédrale (*lah kah-tay-drahl*)	the cathedral	voir les vitraux	see the stained glass windows
le château (*luh shah-to*)	the castle	voir les salles	see the rooms
le cirque (*luh seerk*)	the circus	voir les spectacles	see the shows
la foire (*lah fwahr*)	the fair	regarder les expositions	look at the exhibitions
la fontaine (*lah fohN-tehn*)	the fountain	regarder les jets d'eau	look at the spray of water
le jardin (*luh zhahr-daN*)	the garden	voir les fleurs	see the flowers
le marché aux puces (*luh mahr-shay o pews*)	the flea market	regarder la marchandise	see the merchandise
le musée (*luh mew-zay*)	the museum	voir les tableaux	see the paintings
le parc d'attractions (*luh pahrk dah-trahk-syohN*)	the amusement park	monter sur les manèges	go on the rides
la place (*lah plahs*)	the square	voir la statue	see the statue
le quai (*luh kay*)	the quay	faire une croisière	take a cruise

Culture Capsule

Euro-Disney's theme park is just 20 miles east of Paris (45 minutes by train), at Marne-La-Vallée. The 29 attractions in 5 different "lands" (Main St. USA, Fantasyland, Discoveryland, Frontierland, and Adventureland), six hotels, artificial lakes, and entertainment grounds cover an area one-fifth the size of Paris. The Disney company claims that the food in Euro-Disney is the best in all of its theme parks. It would be surprising if it weren't!

We Shall See

So will it be the exquisite painting and sculptures of a particular museum, the stained glass windows of a cathedral, the luxurious rooms of a château, or perhaps a famous monument? To express what you would like to see or are going to see, you will need the irregular verb *voir* (to see), which is presented in the table below. *Voir* is similar to a "shoe" verb in that the *nous* and *vous* forms change. These forms do not, however, look like the infinitive. In this case, the forms inside the shoe do! Consider *voir* a reverse shoe verb.

Voir (To See)

je vois	*zhuh vwah*	I see
tu vois	*tew vwah*	you see
il, elle, on voit	*eel, (ehl, ohN) vwah*	he, she, one sees
nous voyons	*noo vwah-yohN*	we see
vous voyez	*voo vwah-yay*	you see
ils, elles voient	*eel (ehl) vwah*	they see

I See...

You've visited the Tuileries Gardens and walked along the banks of the Seine. You're having a wonderful time taking in all the sights. You're so captivated by everything around you that you must express what you see: a parade, a fountain, animals, stained glass windows, a garden, flowers.

Culture Capsule

Tourists in Paris can buy a special card that allows unlimited access to more than 60 museums and monuments for 1, 3, or 5 consecutive days. You don't have to wait in line to pay for admission; just show the card and walk in.

You'd be amazed at how much time and money the card saves. It can be purchased conveniently at home through a travel agent, or in Paris at any museum or Tourist Office. Just ask for the discount museum card.

Un deux trois

Take pictures of animals out of magazines. Label them and hang them in your special French corner. Every day choose 3 different animals and say their names in French.

Are You an Animal Lover?

My friend Trudy stops to see the animals on every trip she takes. One of her biggest delights is going to a game farm to feed the baby animals. My son Michael has been partial to aquariums since his first experience years ago, at the age of 4 months. And my husband, well, he's not an animal lover at all; his male ego falls for shirts with powerful animals sewn on the pockets.

Whether you want to visit a zoo or an aquarium, to take a safari to Africa, or simply to make a purchase with an animal design or logo, the names of the animals in the following table might come in handy:

Animals and Fish

bear	l'ours (m.)	*loors*
bird	l'oiseau (m.)	*lwah-zo*
cat	le chat	*luh shah*
chicken, hen	la poule	*lah pool*
cow	la vache	*lah vahsh*
crocodile	le crocodile	*luh kroh-koh-deel*
dog	le chien	*luh shyaN*
dolphin	le dauphin	*luh do-faN*
donkey	l'âne (m.)	*lahn*
elephant	l'éléphant	*lay-lay-fahN*
fish	le poisson	*luh pwah-sohN*

fox	le renard	*luh ruh-nard*
giraffe	le girafe	*luh zhee-rahf*
goat	la chèvre	*lah shehvr*
gorilla	la gorille	*lah goh-reey*
hippopotamus	l'hippopotame (m.)	*lee-poh-poh-tahm*
horse	le cheval	*luh shuh-vahl*
kangaroo	le kangourou	*luh kahN-goo-roo*
leopard	le léopard	*luh lay-oh-pahr*
lion	le lion	*luh lee-ohN*
monkey	le singe	*luh saNzh*
panther	la panthère	*lah pahN-tehr*
pig	le cochon	*luh koh-shohN*
rabbit	le lapin	*luh lah-paN*
rhinoceros	le rhinocéros	*luh ree-noh-say-rohs*
rooster	le coq	*luh kohk*
serpent	le serpent	*luh sehr-pahN*
shark	le requin	*luh ruh-kaN*
sheep	le mouton	*luh moo-tohN*
swan	le cygne	*luh see-nyuh*
tiger	le tigre	*luh teegr*
tortoise	la tortue	*lah tohr-tew*
whale	la baleine	*lah bah-lehn*

Take Me to the Zoo

Read the ads for zoos and figure out which one is in Paris, which is closest to Paris, which is farthest from Paris, which is open all year, which are open every day, in which can you have a picnic, in which the animals roam free.

PARC ZOOLOGIQUE DU BOIS D'ATTILLY	PARC ZOOLOGIQUE DE PARIS	PARC ZOOLOGIQUE DU CHATEAU DE THOIRY
OUVERTE TOUTE L'ANNÉE GRAND PARC NATUREL PIQUE-NIQUE 25 KM DE PARIS RN4	Ouvert Tous les Jours Restaurant—Pique-Nique Autobus 46—86—325 Consultez-nous sur le 11	800 Animaux en Liberté Ouvert tous les jours 40 KM A 13 de Paris 11 -> consultez l'Annuaire Electronique

195

Making a Lot of Suggestions

You've always had your heart set on seeing the Folies Bergères. The glamorous ads, posters, and pictures you've seen have enticed you and piqued your curiosity. You don't know, however, how the others in your group feel about accompanying you. Live it up! Make the suggestion. There are two options in French that you'll find quite simple.

You can use the pronoun *on* + the conjugated form of the verb that explains what it is you want to do:

On va aux Folies Bergères?
ohN vah o foh-lee behr-zhehr
How about going to the Folies Bergères?

On fait une croisière?
ohN feh tewn krwah-zyehr
How about going on a cruise?

Another way to propose an activity is to use the command form that has **nous** as its understood subject:

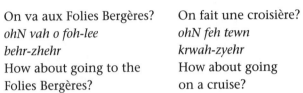

Memory Enhancer

With *on*, use the third person singular form (*il*) of the verb.

Allons aux Folies Bergères!
ah-lohN zo foh-lee behr-zhehr
Let's go to the Folies Bergères!

Faisons une croisière!
fuh-zohN zewn krwah-zyehr
Let's go on a cruise!

When using the imperative (command) form, it is unnecessary to use the subject pronoun *nous*.

Make Me an Offer

It's a gorgeous day and you're eager to go out and have a great time. Suggest five things that we can do together and express each suggestion in two different ways.

Other Useful Phrases

If you're feeling rather confident with the language at this point, you might want to take a more sophisticated approach. There are a number of phrases you can use, all of which are followed by the infinitive of the verb (The familiar forms [tu] are in parentheses.)

Ça vous (te) dit de…
sah voo (tuh) dee duh

En 10 Minutes

The irregular verb *voir* is conjugated as follows:

je vois	nous voyons
tu vois	vous voyez
il, elle, on voit	ils, elles voient

Make suggestions about what to see or do by saying:

1. *On* + third person singular form of the verb to express "How about...?"

2. The *nous* form of the verb without using the subject *nous* to express "Let's...."

Do you want to…

Ça vous (t') intéresse de…
sah voo-zaN (taN)-tay-rehs duh
Are you interested in…

Ça vous (te) plairait de…
sah voo (tuh) pleh-reh duh
Would it please you to…

Vous voulez… (Tu veux…)
voo voo-lay (tew vuh)
Do you want to…

Memory Enhancer

Remember to use *d'* instead of *de* before a vowel.

Ça vous (te) dit de (d')

Ça vous (t') intéresse de (d')   aller au cinéma?

Ça vous (te) plairait de (d')   faire une croisière?

Vous voulez (Tu veux)

Any of the preceding phrases can be made negative by using *ne…pas*:

Ça *ne* te dit *pas* de (d')
(Don't you want to…?)

Ça *ne* t'intéresse *pas* de (d')   aller au cinéma?
(Aren't you interested in…)   (going to the movies?)

Ça *ne* te plairait *pas* de (d')   faire une croisière?
(Wouldn't it please you to…)   (go on a cruise?)

Tu *ne* veux *pas*
(Don't you want to…?)

Only petulant teenagers give abrupt yes or no answers to questions. Most of the rest of us say "yes, but…" or "no, because…." If you'd like to elaborate on your answer, here's what you'll have to do: Change the pronoun *vous* or *te* (t') from the question to *me* (m') in your answer.

Memory Enhancer

When answering a negative question *yes*, *si* is used instead of *oui*. When answering in the negative, *un*, *une*, and *des* become *de*.

Oui (Si), ça me dit de (d')

Oui (Si), ça m'intéresse de (d')
aller au cinéma.

Oui (Si), ça me plairait de (d')   faire **une** croisière.

Oui (Si), je veux

Non, ça ne me dit pas de (d')

Non, ça ne m'intéresse pas de (d')   aller au cinéma.

Non ça ne me plairait pas de (d')   faire **de** croisière.

Non, je ne veux pas

Un deux trois

Look at today's weather. Make as many suggestions as you can in French for appropriate activities for the day.

What Do You Think?

How do you feel about a suggestion that was made to you? Does the activity appeal to you? If so, you would say:

J'aime la musique classique.

J'adore l'opéra.

Je suis fana de ballet.

When you do something or go somewhere new, different, exotic, out of the ordinary, you're bound to have an opinion on whether or not you liked it. Was it fun? You had a good time? You were amused? Give your positive opinion by saying the following:

C'est (*seh*)…

chouette (*shoo-eht*)! great

extra (*ehks-trah*)!

formidable (*fohr-mee-dahbl*)! great

génial (*zhay-nyahl*)!

fantastic (*fahN-tah-steek*)!

magnifique (*mah-nyee-feek*)!

merveilleux (*mehr-veh-yuh*)!

sensationnel (*sahN-sah-syoh-nehl*)!

super (*sew-pehr*)!

superbe (*sew-pehrb*)!

Memory Enhancer

Always use the masculine form of the adjective after *C'est*... (It is....

198

Perhaps you don't like the suggestion presented. Maybe the activity bores you. You might say:

Je n'aime pas	*zhuh nehm pah*	I don't like
Je déteste	*zhuh day-tehst*	I hate
Je ne suis pas fana de	*zhuh nuh swee pah fah-nah duh*	I'm not a fan of

Je n'aime pas la musique classique.

Je déteste l'opéra.

Je ne suis pas fana de ballet.

Just to be a good sport, you tried it anyway. It was just as you thought: not your cup of tea. To give your negative opinion about an activity you could say:

C'est…

affreux (*ah-fruh*)!	frightful, horrible
la barbe (*lah bahrb*)!	boring
dégoûtant (*day-goo-tahN*)!	disgusting
désagréable (*day-zah-gray-ahbl*)!	
embêtant (*ahN-beh-tahN*)!	boring
ennuyeux (*ahN-nwee-yuh*)!	boring
horrible (*oh-reebl*)!	
ridicule (*ree-dee-kewl*)!	ridiculous

Un deux trois

Look at the programs listed in the TV section of your local newspaper. What do you think of them? Do the same for current movies.

Your Sentiments Exactly

Are you one of those people who sees things as either black or white? Or do you see things in varying shades of gray? Personally, I'm a very opinionated person. I love it or I hate it. Rarely is there an in-between. I love the ballet because I like to picture myself as one of the dancers: beautiful, lean, and in the best of shape. I dislike the opera. It's just not my thing. The music is too loud and I don't understand what

Attention!

In order to talk correctly about travel **to, in,** or **from** a country, city, state, or province, it is necessary to learn the gender (masculine or feminine) of the place to which you are referring.

199

they're saying. Don't be afraid to speak up and speak your mind. Tell how you feel about visiting the following attractions:

1. (le Louvre) _____ .
2. (Notre-Dame de Paris) _____ .
3. (l'opéra) _____ .
4. (le château de Versailles) _____ .
5. (un club) _____ .
6. (un parc d'attractions) _____ .
7. (le cirque) _____ .
8. (la Bastille) _____ .
9. (un match du football) _____ .
10. (le ballet) _____ .

Memory Enhancer

If you look closely at the names of the feminine countries, you will notice that, except for Haïti (which is also the only country in the group that does not use a definite article: *la, l'*), they all end in *e*. This makes them very easy to identify.

Up, Up, and Away

Years ago, when my husband and I backpacked throughout Europe, we used our French in every single country we visited (except England, naturally). Since France borders Belgium, Luxembourg, Germany, Switzerland, Italy, and Spain, it is easily understood why French would be spoken and understood in all of those countries, and why the people in France are familiar with those languages as well. Furthermore, due to France's importance in the European Union, French is spoken in all other European countries too. Your travels may take you to many different places where French is spoken. It would prove quite helpful to learn the French names of the countries in the following tables, especially those countries in Europe.

Feminine Countries

Country	French	Pronunciation
Algeria	l'Algérie	*lahl-zhay-ree*
Austria	l'Autriche	*lo-treesh*
Belgium	la Belgique	*lah behl-zheek*

Country	French	Pronunciation
China	la Chine	*lah sheen*
Egypt	l'Égypte	*lay-zheept*
England	l'Angleterre	*lahN-gluh-tehr*
Finland	la Finlande	*lah feen-lahNd*
France	la France	*lah frahNs*
Germany	l'Allemagne	*lahl-mah-nyuh*
Greece	la Grèce	*lah grehs*
Haiti	Haïti	*ah-ee-tee*
Hungary	la Hongrie	*lah ohN-gree*
India	l'Inde	*laNd*
Italy	l'Italie	*lee-tah-lee*
Norway	la Norvège	*lah nohr-vehzh*
Poland	la Pologne	*lah poh-loh-nyuh*
Romania	la Roumanie	*lah roo-mah-nee*
Russia	la Russie	*lah rew-see*
Scotland	l'Écosse	*lay-kohs*
Spain	l'Espagne	*lehs-pah-nyuh*
Sweden	la Suède	*lah swehd*
Switzerland	la Suisse	*lah swees*
Tunisia	la Tunisie	*lah tew-nee-zee*

Masculine Countries

Country	French	Pronunciation
Canada	le Canada	*luh kah-nah-dah*
Cambodia	le Cambodge	*luh kahN-bohdzh*
Denmark	le Danemark	*luh dahn-mahrk*
Israel	Israël	*eez-rah-ehl*
Japan	le Japon	*luh zhah-pohN*
Lebanon	le Liban	*luh lee-bahN*
Morocco	le Maroc	*luh mah-rohk*
Mexico	le Mexique	*luh mehk-seek*
Netherlands	les Pays-Bas	*lay pay-ee bah*
Portugal	le Portugal	*luh pohr-tew-gahl*
United States	les États-Unis	*lay zay-tah-zew-nee*
Zaire	le Zaïre	*luh zah-eer*

Memory Enhancer

L'Antarctique (lahN–tahrk-teek, Antarctica), the seventh continent, is the only one that is masculine.

Note: Three masculine countries end in *e*. Israël does not use any definite article.

Do your travels take you far and wide? Are you fortunate enough to be able to plan a trip to another continent? The names of the seven continents in the following table are all feminine.

The Continents

Continent	French	Pronunciation
Africa	l'Afrique	*lah-freek*
Antarctica	l'Antarctique	*lahN-tahrk-teek*
Asia	l'Asie	*lah-zee*
Australia	l'Australie	*loh-strah-lee*
Europe	l'Europe	*lew-rohp*
North America	l'Amérique du Nord	*lah-may-reek dew nohr*
South America	l'Amérique du Sud	*lah-may-reek dew sewd*

Un Deux Trois

Imagine that you won the lottery—big time. Discuss the countries you are going to visit on your trip around the world.

Going

On your next trip to Europe, will you be going to Italy? Will you be staying with your relatives in Spain or Portugal? To express that you are going *to* or staying *in* another country, use the preposition *en* to express *to*. Also use *en* to express *in* before the names of feminine countries, continents, provinces, islands, and states and before masculine countries starting with a vowel:

I am going to Italy.

Je vais en Italie.
zhuh veh zahN nee-tah-lee

I'm staying in Spain.

Je reste en Espagne.
zhuh rehst ahN nehs-pah-nyuh

I am going to travel to (in) Israel.
Je vais voyager en Israël.
zhuh veh vwah-yah-zhay ahN neez-rah-ehl

The preposition *au* (*aux* for plurals) is used to express *to, in* before the names of some masculine countries, islands, provinces, and states that start with a consonant:

I am going to Japan.

Je vais au Japon.

zhuh veh zo zhah-pohN

I am staying in the United States.

Je reste aux États-Unis.

zhuh rehst o zay-tah-zew-nee

Use *dans le* to express *to, in* before geographical names that are modified by an adjective:

Je vais dans le Dakota du Nord.

J'habite dans l'État de New Jersey.

Coming

Every traveler has an accent, albeit sometimes almost imperceptible, that alerts native speakers to the fact that he (or she) is from another region or country. My French nasal sounds give me away as a New Yorker. My consultant Roger's "th" that comes out "z," is typically French. And the fact that my friend Carlos drops his final "s" is a dead give-away that he's a native Hispanic. If your accent reveals your identity and you want to say that you are from (or coming from) a country, use the preposition *de* before the names of feminine countries, continents, provinces, islands, and states and before masculine countries starting with a vowel:

Attention!

Remember that the preposition *de* (from) combines with *le* to become *du,* and *de* combines with *les* to become *des.*

I am from France.

Je suis de France.

zhuh swee duh frahNs

I am from Israel.

Je suis d'Israël.

zhuh swee deez-rah-ehl

The preposition *de* + the definite article *(le, l', les)* is used before masculine countries and geographical names that are modified by an adjective:

I am from Canada.

Je suis du Canada.

zhuh swee dew
kah-nah-dah

I am from the United States.

Je suis des États-Unis.

zhuh swee day-zay-tah-zew-nee

I am from beautiful France.

Je suis de la belle France.

zhuh swee duh lah
behl frahns

I am from North America.

Je suis de l'Amérique du Nord.

zhuh swee duh lah-may-reek
dew nohr

Exactly Where Are You Going?

Start your sentence with *Je vais* (I'm going) and tell what country you are going to if you plan to see the following:

1. (a bullfight) _____ .
2. (the Great Wall) _____ .
3. (Mexican jumping beans) _____ .
4. (the Moscow circus) _____ .
5. (the Leaning Tower of Pisa) _____ .
6. (Big Ben) _____ .
7. (the pyramids) _____ .
8. (the Eiffel Tower) _____ .
9. (Grand Canyon) _____ .
10. (home) _____ .

Y Gads!

You probably looked at this section and thought: "Oops, the author spelled the title wrong." Or perhaps you're gloating because you found a typographical mistake in the book. (Even authors and editors are human.) Everyone who looks at *Y Gads!* wants to take out a red pen and correct it. It's obvious to me that they didn't study their French well enough to see that I'm just trying to be cute. You see, *y* (*ee*) is a French pronoun that generally refers to or replaces previously mentioned places or locations, and may also refer to things or ideas. The pronoun *y* usually replaces the preposition *à (au, a l', à la, aux)* or other prepositions of location, shown in the following table, + a noun.

Prepositions of Location

Preposition	French	Pronunciation
at the house (business) of	chez	*shay*
against	contre	*kohNtr*
behind	derrière	*deh-ryehr*
between	entre	*ahNtr*
in	dans	*dahN*
in	en	*ahN*
in front of	devant	*duh-vahN*
on	sur	*sewr*
toward	vers	*vehr*
under	sous	*soo*

Culture Capsule

Use *à* to say "to" or "in" a city.

Use *en* to say "to" or "in" a feminine country, continent, province, island, or state, or a masculine state beginning with a vowel.

Use *au* to say "to" or "in" a masculine country. Use *aux* before plural names.

Use *dans le* to say "to" or "in" before geographical names that are modified by an adjective.

Use *de* to say "from" a city, a feminine country, continent, province, island, state. Use *d'* before a masculine country beginning with a vowel.

Use *de* + definite article (*du, de l', des*) to say "from" before masculine countries and geographical names that are modified by an adjective.

You received a letter today from your French friend. I, of course, would never open your mail, but I sure am curious about that letter. Is it on your desk? Are you going to answer it immediately? Are you going to go to France to visit your friend? Are you going to stay at your friend's house? Will your family say, "Go there and have a good time"? These questions can be answered in French by using the pronoun *y*.

Y means *there* when the place has already been mentioned, and can also mean *it, them, in it/them, to it/them,* or *on it/them.*

Il va à Paris.	Mon billet est dans ma poche.	Je réponds à la lettre.
Il *y* va. *eel ee vah*	Mon billet *y* est. *mohN bee-yeh ee eh*	J'*y* réponds. *zhee ray-pohN*
He goes there.	My ticket is in it (there).	I answer it.

The pronoun *y* is used to replace *de* + noun only when *de* is part of a prepositional phrase showing location:

La douane est *à côté des* bagages.

La douane *y* est.

Customs is there.

Sometimes *y* is used in French and is not translated into English:

La valise est sur la table?	Is the valise on the table?
Oui, elle *y* est.	Yes, it is.

Y is placed before the verb to which its meaning is tied. When there are two verbs, *y* is placed before the infinitive:

J'*y* vais.	I am going there.
Je n'*y* vais pas.	I'm not going there.
Je désire *y* aller.	I want to go there.
N'*y* va pas.	Don't go there.

In an affirmative command, *y* changes position and is placed immediately after the verb and is joined to it by a hyphen:

Vas-*y*! (*vah zee*)	Go (there)! (Familiar)
Allez-*y*! (*ah-lay zee*)	Go (there)! (Polite)

Use the idiomatic French expression *Allons-y* when you want to express "Let's go," or "We're off."

Using y

Word has gotten out that you'll be going to Europe this summer. Your nosey next door neighbor has heard the rumor and can't wait to pump you for information. Use *y* to efficiently answer her questions and make a rapid get-away:

1. Vous allez en France? _____
2. Vous restez à Paris? _____
3. Vous passez vos vacances chez votre famille? _____
4. Vous allez descendre en ville? _____
5. Vous allez dîner dans des restaurants élégants? _____
6. Vous allez penser à votre travail? _____

Make a Suggestion

Let's say you are planning a trip with a group of friends. Your friends are spirited and lively—and none are shy about expressing an opinion about where the group should go. It's your turn to react to the various suggestions:

> Example: aller en Italie
> Allons-y!
> N'y allons pas!

voyager en Grèce

aller à l'aquarium

rester dans un hôtel chic

passer la journée au carnaval

assister à une exposition d'art moderne

The Least You Need to Know

➤ To suggest an activity use *on* + the conjugated verb, or the *nous* form conjugated without *nous*.

➤ Simple phrases can express your likes (*C'est super!*) and dislikes (*C'est la barbe!*).

➤ Countries that end in *e* are usually feminine. The rest are masculine.

➤ The pronoun *y* can replace a preposition + a location. *Y* means *there*.

Chapter 15

I Wanna Shop Till I Drop

In This Chapter

➤ Stores and what they sell

➤ Clothing, colors, sizes, materials, and designs

➤ All about *mettre* (to put [on])

➤ Getting what you like

➤ This, that, these, and those (a.k.a. demonstrative adjectives)

You've visited just about everything on your "must see" list. For the time being you've had your fill of sightseeing. Now you would like to pick up some souvenirs of your trip, or those gifts you promised family and friends at home.

Are you particular about what you buy? Is it important to you to pick out the "perfect" gift or memento? Do you spend time agonizing over the right color, size, material, design? Or do you choose almost anything you feel will be appropriate? This chapter will help you make the shopping decisions that are best for you. Read and study all the information before you "shop till you drop."

Now That's My Kinda Store!

Today is a shopping day. Do you prefer to browse in a small boutique or are you attracted to a large, elegant mall (*un centre commercial—uhN sahNtr koh-mehr-syahl*) such as le Forum des Halles in Paris or the underground Place Bonaventure in Montreal? The following table will point you in the direction of stores that might interest you and the merchandise you can purchase in them.

Note: If you want to say that you are going to a store or that you'll be at a store, remember to use *à* (to, at) + the definite article (*au, à la, à l'*):

> au grand magasin

> à la parfumerie

Stores (les magasins—lay mah-gah-zaN)

The Store	Le Magasin	The Merchandise	La Marchandise
bookstore	la librairie *lah lee-breh-ree*	books	des livres (m.)
boutique	la boutique *lah boo-teek*	clothing	des vêtements (m.)
department store	le grand magasin *luh grahN mah-gah-zaN*	almost everything	presque tout
florist	le magasin de fleuriste *luh mah-gah-zaN duh fluh-reest*	flowers	des fleurs (f.)
jewelry store	la bijouterie *lah bee-zhoo-tree*	jewels	des bijoux (m.)
		rings	des bagues (f.)
		bracelets	des bracelets (m.)
		watches	des montres (f.)
		earrings	des boucles d'oreille (f.)
		necklaces	des colliers (m.)
leather goods store	la maroquinerie *lah mah-roh-kaN-ree*	wallets	des portefeuilles (m.)
		pocket books	des sacs (m.)
		suitcases	des valises (f.)
		briefcases	des serviettes (f.)
newsstand	le kiosk à journaux *luh kee-ohsk ah zhoor-no*	newspapers	des journaux (m.)
		magazines	des revues (f.)

The Store	Le Magasin	The Merchandise	La Marchandise
perfume store	la parfumerie *lah par-fuhN-ree*	perfume	du parfum
record store	le magasin de disques *luh mah-gah-zaN duh deesk*	records cassettes compact discs	des disques (m.) des cassettes (f.) des C.D. (m.)
souvenir shop	le magasin de souvenirs *luh mah-gah-zaN duh soo-vuh-neer*	T-shirts posters miniatures paintings	des tee-shirt (m.) des posters (m.) des monuments en miniature (m.) des tableaux (m.)
tobacconist	le bureau de tabac *luh bew-ro duh tah-bah*	tobacco cigarettes pipes cigars matches lighters	du tabac des cigarettes (f.) des pipes (f.) des cigares (f.) des allumettes (f.) des briquets (m.)

Culture Capsule

Do you want to bring home something that is inexpensive (what could be cheaper than a $20 T-shirt!), elegant, typically French, and appropriate as a gift for someone of either gender? For as little as $10 you can purchase an original watercolor painted by an artist in Montmartre, along the banks of the Seine, or in front of a wide variety of other tourist attractions.

Gems and Jewels

Some people feel, and rightfully so, that they can get a very good bargain when they purchase jewelry in a foreign country because they can avoid certain taxes and duties. Here's the living proof of that. In honor of our wedding anniversary, my husband purchased a beautiful watch for me during a trip to Saint Martin (French side, of course). The watch, a well-known brand name, was double the price in a popular stateside store reputed far and wide to give the best deals on jewelry. He really got an incredible deal. If you know your prices and are a good shopper, or if you're simply in the mood to buy some jewelry, you can use the following table to get exactly what you want.

Jewels (les bijoux—lay bee-zhoo)

Jewel	French	Pronunciation
amethyst	une améthyste	*ewn ah-may-teest*
aquamarine	une aige-marine	*ewn ehg mah-reen*
diamond	un diamant	*uhN dee-ah-mahN*
emerald	une émeraude	*ewn aym-rod*
ivory	un ivoire	*uhN nee-vwahr*
jade	un jade	*uhN zhahd*
onyx	un onyx	*uhN noh-neeks*
pearls	des perles (f.)	*day pehrl*
ruby	un rubis	*uhN rew-bee*
sapphire	un saphir	*uhN sah-feer*
topaz	une topaze	*ewn toh-pahz*
turquoise	une turquoise	*ewn tewr-kwahz*

When buying jewelry, you might want to ask:

Est-ce en or?	*ehs ahN nohr*	Is it gold?
Est-ce en argent?	*ehs ahN nahr-zhahN*	Is it silver?

Un deux trois

Write a list of the different items of jewelry you own; be very specific about the gems and jewels that each piece contains.

Clothing

It's simply impossible to take a trip to France, the fashion capital of the world, and not come home with at least one article of clothing. You want to have one French label so that you can brag that you are *dans le vent* (*dahN luh vahN*) in fashion. The following table will help you in your quest for something *au courant*.

Clothing (les vêtements—lay veht-mahN)

Clothing	French	Pronunciation
bathing suit	le maillot	*luh mah-yo*
belt	la ceinture	*lah saN-tewr*
bikini	le bikini	*luh bee-kee-nee*
string bikini	la ficelle	*lah fee-sehl*
bikini briefs	le slip	*luh sleep*
boots	les bottes (f.)	*lay boht*
blouse	le chemisier	*luh shuh-meez-yay*
	la blouse	*lah blooz*
brassière	le soutien-gorge	*luh soo-tyaN gohrzh*
coat	le manteau	*luh mahN-to*
dress	la robe	*lah rohb*
evening gown	la robe du soir	*lah rohb dew swahr*
fur coat	le manteau de fourrure	*luh mahN-to duh foo-rewr*
gloves	les gants (m.)	*lay gahN*
handkerchief	le mouchoir	*luh moo-shwahr*
hat	le chapeau	*luh shah-po*
jacket	la veste	*lah vehst*
jeans	le jean	*luh zheen*
jogging suit	le survêt	*luh sewr-veh,*
	le jogging	*luh zhoh-geeng*
negligée	le peignoir	*luh peh-nywahr*
overcoat	le manteau	*luh mahN-to*
pajamas	le pyjama	*luh pee-zhah-mah*
panties	la culotte	*lah kew-loht*
pants	le pantalon	*luh pahN-tah-lohN*
pantyhose (tights)	le collant	*luh koh-lahN*
pocketbook	le sac	*luh sahk*
pullover	le pull	*luh pewl*
raincoat	l'imperméable (m.)	*laN-pehr-may-ahbl*
robe	la robe de chambre	*lah rohb duh shahNbr*
sandals (f.)	les sandales	*lay sahN-dahl*
scarf	l'écharpe (f.)	*lay-shahrp,*
	le foulard	*luh foo-lahr*
shirt (man-tailored)	la chemise	*lah shuh-meez*
shoes	les chaussures (f.),	*lay sho-sewr,*
	les souliers (m.)	*lay soo-lyay*

continues

Clothing (les vêtements—lay veht-mahN) (cont.)

Clothing	French	Pronunciation
shorts	le short	*luh shohrt*
skirt	la jupe	*lah zhewp*
slip (half)	le jupon	*luh zhew-pohN*
(full)	la combinaison	*lah kohN-bee-neh-zohN*
sneakers	les tennis	*lay tuh-nees*
socks	les chaussettes (f.)	*lay sho-seht*
stockings	les bas (m.)	*lay bah*
suit (men)	le complet	*luh kohN-pleh*
	le costume	*luh kohs-tewm*
suit (women)	le tailleur	*luh tah-yuhr*
T-shirt	le tee-shirt	*luh tee-shehrt*
tie	la cravate	*lah krah-vaht*
umbrella	le parapluie	*luh pah-rah-plwee*
undershirt	le maillot de corps	*luh mah-yo duh kohr*
undershorts	le slip	*luh sleep*
underwear	les sous-vêtements (m.)	*lay soo-veht-mahN*
vest	le gilet	*luh zhee-leh*
windbreaker	le blouson	*luh bloo-zohN*

Because Europeans use the metric system, their sizes are different from ours. Look at the following conversion chart to determine the sizes you would wear:

Women

Shoes

American	4	4¹/₂	5	5¹/₂	6	6¹/₂	7	7¹/₂	8	8¹/₂	9	9¹/₂	10
Continental	35	35	36	36	37	37	38	38	39	39	40	40	41

Dresses, suits

American	8	10	12	14	16	18
Continental	36	38	40	42	44	46

Blouses, sweaters

American	32	34	36	38	40	42
Continental	40	42	44	46	48	50

Men

Shoes

American	7	7¹/₂	8	8¹/₂	9	9¹/₂	10	10¹/₂	11	11¹/₂
Continental	39	40	41	42	43	43	44	44	45	45

Suits, coats

American	34	36	38	40	42	44	46	48
Continental	44	46	48	50	52	54	56	58

Shirts

American	14	14¹/₂	15	15¹/₂	16	16¹/₂	17	17¹/₂
Continental	36	37	38	39	40	41	42	43

You want to make sure that you get your right size. Tell the salesperson:

Je porte du...	petit	moyen	grand
zhuh pohrt dew	*puh-tee*	*mwah-yaN*	*grahN*
I wear...	small	medium	large

Ma taille est...	petite	moyenne	grande
Ma tahy eh	*puh-teet*	*mwah-yehn*	*grahNd*
My size is...	small	medium	large

For shoes you would say:

Je chausse du... + size
zhuh shohs dew
I wear shoe size...

Un deux trois

Look in your clothes closet. Give the sizes for all your clothes and shoes in French.

Culture Capsule

A value-added tax (T.V.A.—taxe à la valeur ajoutée) is added to the price of all products in France (except medicine, food, and books). This tax varies according to the purchase. Visitors from outside the European Community can receive a reimbursement of their T.V.A. payments if they spend above a certain amount (often 13 percent on a minimum purchase of 2,000F). So always save your sales receipts and present them at the T.V.A. desk at the airport.

Colors

My sister Susan, an *artiste*, has taught her seven-year-old son to describe things as chartreuse, teal, aubergine, and tangerine. I, on the other hand, see the world in primary colors. Whether you go for the *exotique* or the *ordinaire*, the following table will help you with the basic colors.

Note: colors are adjectives and, therefore, must agree with the noun they are describing. For example, say:

un chemisier blanc
a white blouse

une chemise blanche
a white shirt

Memory Enhancer

To describe a color as *light*, add the word *clair*; to describe a color as *dark*, add the word *foncé*. For example, *light blue* is *bleu clair*, and *dark green* is *vert foncé*.

Colors (les couleurs—lay koo-luhr)

beige	beige	*behzh*	gray	gris(e)	*gree(z)*
black	noir(e)	*nwahr*	green	vert(e)	*vehr(t)*
blue	bleu(e)	*bluh*	orange	orange	*oh-rahNzh*
brown	brun(e)	*bruhN (brewn)*	pink	rose	*roz*
purple	mauve	*mov*	white	blanc(he)	*blahN(sh)*
red	rouge	*roozh*	yellow	jaune	*zhon*

Materials

While traveling, you might be tempted to make a clothing purchase. Do you find linen sexy? Do you love the feel of silk? Do you crave the coolness of cotton? Is leather a turn-on? Are you into wrinkle-free? We choose or reject different fabrics for a wide variety of reasons. The following table will help you pick the material you prefer for your special purchases:

Materials (les tissus—lay tee-sew)

Material	French	Pronunciation
cashmere	cachemire	*kahsh-meer*
corduroy	velours côtelée	*vuh-loor koht-lay*
cotton	coton	*koh-tohN*
denim	jean	*zheen*
felt	feutre	*fuhtr*
flannel	flanelle	*flah-nehl*
gabardine	gabardine	*gah-bahr-deen*
knit	tricot	*tree-ko*
leather	cuir	*kweer*
linen	lin	*laN*
nylon	nylon	*nee-lohN*
polyester	polyester	*poh-lee-ehs-tehr*
silk	soie	*swah*
suede	daim	*daN*
terry cloth	tissu éponge	*tee-sew ah-pohnzh*
wool	laine	*lehn*

To express that an item of clothing is made out of a certain material, use the preposition *en* (*ahN*).

It's a silk shirt.   Ç'est une chemise en soie.

Read the Labels

Have you ever accidentally washed a "dry clean only" shirt? Or have you ever washed a 100 percent cotton pair of jeans only to find that they've shrunk and can never be worn again? Make sure to read all labels carefully for the following information:

non-rétrécissable	lavable	en tissu infroissable
nohN-ray-tray-see-sahbl	*lah-vahbl*	*ahN tee-sew aN-frwah-sahbl*
non-shrinkable	washable	wrinkle-resistant

Un deux trois

Describe the favorite items in your wardrobe. Be sure to include the color, material, and design of what you select.

Designs

Designs are very important when selecting a garment. Horizontal stripes make a person appear heavier, whereas vertical stripes do the opposite. Plaids and polka dots also change the way we look. The following table will enable you to pick what's right for you.

Designs (le dessin—luh deh–saN)

checked	à carreaux	*ah kah-ro*
in herringbone	à chevrons	*ah shuh-vrohN*
in plaid	en tartan	*ahN tahr-tahN*
with polka dots	à pois	*ah pwah*
in a solid color	uni(e)	*ew-nee*
with stripes	à rayures	*ah rah-yewr*

Memory enhancer

The regular *er* verb *porter* means to wear.

You're Putting Me On

Now that your wardrobe is full, you will have to decide what to put on. The verb *mettre* in the following table will help you say this. Because it is an irregular verb, you should probably memorize it.

mettre (to put [on])

je mets	*zhuh meh*	I put (on)
tu mets	*tew meh*	you put (on)
il, elle, on met	*eel (ehl, ohN) meh*	he, she, one puts (on)
nous mettons	*noo meh-tohN*	we put (on)
vous mettez	*voo meh-tay*	you put (on)
ils, elles mettent	*eel (ehl) meht*	they put (on)

Put It On

Does your lifestyle demand an extensive wardrobe or are you strictly a jeans and T-shirt kind of person? Imagine that you've found yourself in the following situations. Describe in detail (including jewelry) what you put on to go:

1. (to work) _____ .
2. (to the beach) _____ .
3. (to a formal dinner party) _____ .
4. (to a friend's house) _____ .
5. (skiing) _____ .

What Are You Looking For?

You're on a shopping spree, and everything looks so enticing. Say what you could buy in each of the following stores:

Madame Paris

Prestige de la France
Parfums, produits de beauté, bijoux,
foulards, accessoires, maroquinerie.

Georges Figaro

"Le maître de la chemise"

Premier couturier français de la chemise
pour hommes et femmes, GEORGES FIGARO
préfère le mariage de l'élégance et de la qualité.

Une sélection de plus de six cents tissus, neuf tailles, deux longueurs de manche,
deux formes de poignets, de la couleur en uni, en rayures… tout existe. Il ne vous reste
qu'à choisir.

Vivianne

VIVIANNE est la spécialiste de la grande taille (du 38 au 58). Elle vous propose les
plus grandes marques du prêt-à-porter féminin et accessoires assortis (sacs, ceintures,
chapeaux) pour vous séduire. Elle assure des retouches gratuites.

PARFUMERIES PÉPIN

Une chaîne de parfumeries qui vous offre un large éventail des plus grandes marques.
L'acceuil y est vraiment chaleureux et les prix forts intéressants: 20% de remise sur la
plupart des articles.

VARIATIONS

100% pure mode, 100% pur charme, tout VARIATION en une boutique moderne pour
l'homme et la femme. Pulls, polos, chemisiers, jupes, ensembles, dans une sélection des
matières naturelles douces et chaudes vous permettront de créer des coordonnés aux
couleurs de la mode; 100% laine vierge, angoras, mélanges, 100% coton. Alliez la mode
avec le charme des choses qui durent.

Vanessa

Paris

De pull en pull...

Des pulls de toutes les couleurs, de tous les styles, travaillés façon main, fantaisie, en laine mélangée, coton, de quoi varier et se changer tous les jours de l'année.

CHAUSSURES DE PARIS

La recherche de la différence

Exclusif! Une sélection exhaustive des dernières créations dans une atmosphère relaxante. Pour hommes et femmes.

CHANTAL

Un nom de renommée légendaire. Les sacs luxueux, les serviettes et valises de la manufacture de cuir la plus célèbre d'Allemagne sont faits aujourd'hui, exactement comme il y a 130 ans—en cuir de premier choix et cousu main. CHANTAL présente les derniers modèles de la marque, riche en traditions.

The Object of My Affection

I have an absolutely fabulous red dress. Imagine that I was telling you about it and said: "I put on my red dress to go to parties. I love my red dress. I wear my red dress very often." How tedious and boring! It sounds much better to say: "I put on my red dress to go to parties. I love it and wear it often."

What did I do to improve my conversation? I stopped repeating **my red dress** (a direct object noun) and replaced it with **it** (a direct object pronoun). Just what exactly are direct objects? Let's take a closer look.

En 10 Minutes

Learn the irregular verb *mettre* (to put on):

je mets	nous mettons
tu mets	vous mettez
il/elle/on met	ils/elles mettent

Direct objects (which can be nouns or pronouns) answer the question **whom** or **what** the subject is acting upon, and may refer to people, places, things, or ideas:

I see **the boy.**	I see **him.**
I like **the dress.**	I like **it.**
He pays **John and me.**	He pays **us.**

Memory Enhancer

Read the following two sentences:

I write (**to**) him love letters.

I buy (**for**) him presents.

Notice that the **to** and **for** are often understood but not used in English. So be careful in French when choosing a direct or indirect object pronoun. If the words **to** or **for** make sense in the sentence (even though they do not actually appear), use an indirect object pronoun.

How do indirect objects differ from direct objects? We'll need a closer look.

Indirect object nouns can be replaced by indirect object pronouns. Take the story of my friend Georgette who is crazy about her new boyfriend, Paul. This is what she told me: "I write to Paul. Then I read my love letters to Paul. I buy presents for Paul. I make cakes for Paul. I cook dinners for Paul." To get to the point more efficiently, all she had to say was: "I write to Paul and then I read him (to him) my love letters. I buy him (for him) presents. I make him (for him) cakes and I cook him (for him) dinners."

Indirect objects answer the question **to whom** the subject is doing something or **for whom** the subject is acting. Indirect objects refer only to people or domesticated animals:

I speak **to the boys.**	I speak **to them.**
I buy a gift **for Mary.**	I buy a gift **for her.** (I buy her a gift.)
	He gives (**to**) **me** a tie every Christmas.

We use direct and indirect pronouns automatically in English all the time to prevent the constant, monotonous repetition of a word and to allow our conversation to flow naturally. Direct and indirect object nouns in French may be replaced by the pronouns in the following table:

Object Pronouns

Direct Object Pronoun	Pronunciation	Meaning	Indirect Object Pronoun	Pronunciation	Meaning
me (m')	*muh*	me	me (m')	*muh*	(to) me
te (t')	*tuh*	you (familiar)	te (t')	*tuh*	(to) you (familiar)
le (l')	*luh*	he, it	lui	*lwee*	(to) him
la (l')	*lah*	her, it	lui	*lwee*	(to) her
nous	*noo*	us	nous	*noo*	(to) us
vous	*voo*	you (polite)	vous	*voo*	(to) you
les	*lay*	them	leur	*luhr*	(to) them

The clue to the correct usage of an indirect object is the French preposition *à (au, à la, à l', aux)* followed by the name of or reference to a person. Some verbs, such as *répondre (à), téléphoner (à),* and *ressembler (à),* are always followed by *à* + person and will, therefore, always take an indirect object pronoun.

As you can see, you should have little problem using the direct or indirect object pronouns for me (to me), you, (to you), or us (to us), because these pronouns are all exactly the same. You must be careful, however, when expressing him, her, or to/for him, her, and them, or to/for them because there are now two sets of pronouns. Sometimes this does get a bit tricky. Remember to choose the pronoun that reflects the number and gender of the noun to which you are referring:

Attention!

Be careful! Some verbs, such as *écouter* (to listen to), *chercher* (to look for), *payer* (to pay for), and *regarder* (to look at), take direct objects in French.

Elle met le pantalon noir.	Elle le met.
Il met la chemise blanche.	Il la met.
Je mets mes gants bruns.	Je les mets.
Il téléphone *à Marie.*	Il *lui* téléphone.
Il téléphone *à Marie et à Luc.*	Il *leur* téléphone.

Position of Object Pronouns

Although we can automatically put object pronouns in their proper place in English, their correct placement in French does not follow English rules and requires some practice. Let's take a closer look.

Object pronouns are placed before the verb to which their meaning is tied (usually the conjugated verb). When there are two verbs, object pronouns are placed before the infinitive:

Je *la* mets.	Je *lui* parle.
Je ne *la* mets pas.	Je ne *lui* parle pas.
Je vais *la* mettre.	Je ne vais pas *lui* parler.
Ne *la* mets pas!	Ne *lui* parle pas!

In an affirmative command, object pronouns change position and are placed immediately after the verb and are joined to it by a hyphen. *Me* becomes *moi* when it follows the verb:

Mets-*la*!	Parle-*lui*!
Mettez-*la*!	Parlez-*lui*!
	Donnez-*moi* la robe!

Direct objects tell you *whom* or *what* the subject is acting on, and can refer to people, places, things, or ideas.

Indirect objects tell you *to whom* or *for whom* the subject is doing something. Indirect objects only refer to people.

Using Direct Object Pronouns

Imagine that you are on a shopping spree in the Samaritaine department store in Paris and your arms are loaded with all your "finds." A friend joins you and questions your choices. Answer his questions efficiently by using a direct object pronoun:

1. Aimez-vous le pantalon bleu?
2. Prenez-vous les gants noirs?
3. Choisissez-vous la cravate rouge?
4. Regardez-vous les chaussuers brunes?
5. Achetez-vous la chemise blanche?
6. Adorez-vous le blouson beige?

Using Indirect Object Pronouns

Your friend doesn't know what gifts to buy her friends and family members. Offer suggestions, following the examples:

Paul/une radio	ses frères/une chemise
Offre-lui une radio.	Offre-leur une chemise.

1. Robert/une montre

2. ses parents/un tableau

3. Luc et Michel/des cravates

4. ses soeurs/des robes

5. son amie/un bracelet

6. sa grand-mère/un pull

You Want It? Ask for It!

Sometimes you just want to browse and resent having a salesperson hover over you waiting to make a sale. At other times, you have specific wants and needs and require assistance. Here are some phrases to help you deal with most common situations.

When you enter a store an employee might ask you:

May I help you?

Est-ce que je peux vous aider?	Puis-je vous aider?	Vous désirez?
ehs-kuh zhuh puh voo zeh-day	*pweezh voo zeh-day*	*voo day-zee-ray*

If you are just browsing, you would answer:

No, thank you, I am (just) looking.

Non, merci, je regarde (tout simplement).
nohN mehr-see zhuh ruh-gahrd (too saN-pluh-mahN)

If you want to see or buy something, you would answer:

Yes, I would like to see…please.	I'm looking for…
Oui, je voudrais voir…s'il vous plât.	Je cherche…
wee zhuh voo-dreh vwahr…seel voo pleh	*zhuh shehrsh*

And, of course, if you're a shopper like I am, you'd want to know:

Are there any sales?	Have you slashed your prices?
Y a-t-il des soldes?	Avez-vous cassé les prix?
ee ah teel day sohld	*ah-vay-voo kah-say lay pree*

Expressing Preferences

If the salesperson is going to help you, she or he has to understand your preferences:

Which pullover do you prefer?
Quel pull est-ce que vous préférez?
kehl pewl esh-kuh voo pray-fay-ray

If you are deciding among different items, the salesperson would ask **which one(s)** you prefer by using one of the interrogative pronouns in the following table:

Interrogative Pronouns

	Masculine	Feminine
Singular	lequel (*luh-kehl*)	laquelle (*lah-kehl*)
Plural	lesquels (*lay-kehl*)	lesquelles (*lay-kehl*)

These interrogative pronouns must agree with the nouns to which they refer:

Lequel de ces pulls est-ce que vous préférez?
luh-kehl duh say pewl ehs-kuh voo pray-fay-ray
Which one of these pullovers do you prefer?

Lesquelles de ces robes est-ce que vous prenez?
lay-kehl duh say rohb ehs-kuh voo pruh-nay
Which ones of these dresses are you taking?

To express your preference (that is, to say *the...one* or *the...ones*), simply use the appropriate definite article plus an adjective that agrees. When speaking about the pullover, you might say:

Je préfère le bleu clair.
zhuh pray-fehr luh bluh klehr
I prefer the light blue one.

Je préfère le grand.
zhuh pray-fehr luh grahN
I prefer the big one.

When speaking about the dresses, you might say:

Je prends les petites.
zhuh prahN lay puh-teet
I am taking the small ones.

Je prends la rouge et la bleue.
zhuh prahN lah roozh ay lah bluh
I am taking the red one and the blue one.

Expressing Opinions

That shirt is you. You just love those pants. What a perfect jacket! When you are happy with an item, you will want to express your pleasure by saying one of the following phrases:

Ça me plaît.	*sah muh pleh*	I like it.
Ça me va.	*sah muh vah*	It suits (fits) me.
C'est agréable.	*seh tah-gray-ahbl*	It's nice.
C'est élégant(e).	*seh tay-lay-gahN*	It's elegant.
C'est pratique.	*seh prah-teek*	It's practical.

If you are unhappy with what you see, you might use the following:

Ça ne me plaît pas.	*sah nuh muh pleh pah*	I don't like it.
Ça ne me va pas.	*sah nuh muh vah pah*	It doesn't suit (fit) me.
Il (elle) est abominable.	*eel (ehl) eh tah-boh-mee-nahbl*	It's horrible.
Il (elle) est trop petit(e).	*eel (ehl) eh tro puh-tee(t)*	It's too small.
Il (elle) est trop serré(e).	*eel (ehl) eh tro suh-ray*	It's too tight.
Il (elle) est trop court(e).	*eel (ehl) eh tro koor(t)*	It's too short.
Il (elle) est trop long(ue).	*eel (ehl) eh tro lohN(g)*	It's too long.
Il (Elle) est trop criard(e).	*eel (ehl) eh tro kree-ahr*	It's too loud.
Il (Elle) est trop étroit(e).	*eel (ehl) eh tro pay-trwaht*	It's too narrow.

If you're not satisfied and want something else, try saying:

I'm looking for something more (less)…
Je cherche quelque chose de plus (moins) + adjective
zhuh shehrsh kehl-kuh shooz duh plew (mwaN)

I'll Take This, That, One of These, and Some of Those

While considering a purchase, it's not uncommon to ask a friend or salesperson for an opinion of this suit, that shirt, these shoes, or those ties. A *demonstrative adjective* points out

Attention!

Remember to change verbs and adjectives to accommodate plural subjects:

Ils sont trop étroits.
Elles sont trop étroites.

someone or thing being referred to and allows you to be specific by expressing *this*, *that*, *these*, and *those*, as shown in the following table.

Demonstrative Adjectives: This, That, These, Those

used before masculine singular nouns beginning with a consonant	used before masculine singular nouns beginning with a vowel	used before all feminine singular nouns	used before all plural nouns
ce (*suh*)	cet (*seht*)	cette (*seht*)	ces (*say*)
ce sac	cet imperméable	cette écharpe	ces sacs
		cette robe	ces écharpes

➤ Demonstrative adjectives precede the nouns they modify and agree with them in number and gender. The special masculine form *cet* is used to prevent a clash of two vowel sounds together.

➤ Demonstrative adjectives are repeated before each noun:

Ce pantalon et cette chemise sont formdables.

➤ The tags *-ci* (this, these) and *-là* (that, those) may be added to make further distinctions:

Je préfère ce chemisier-ci.
zhuh pray-fehr suh shuh-meez-yay see
I prefer *this* blouse.

Ce pantalon-là est trop grand.
suh pahN-tah-lohN lah eh tro grahN
That pair of pants is too big.

What Do You Think?

Look at the following articles of clothing and say how you feel about them. Give as much detail as possible.

_____
_____

_____
_____

_____
_____

_____
_____

The Least You Need to Know

➤ To shop successfully in a French-speaking country, you must use the metric system.

➤ To make your conversation more fluid, use object pronouns to replace object nouns.

➤ Object pronouns are usually placed before the conjugated verb.

➤ When there are two verbs, the pronoun is placed before the infinitive.

➤ Object pronouns come after the verb in affirmative commands only.

➤ If you know how to ask for what you want, you'll probably get it.

➤ Demonstrative adjectives (ce, cet, cette, ces) agree in number and gender with the nouns they describe.

Chapter 16

An Old-Fashioned, Home-Cooked Meal

In This Chapter

➤ Specialty food stores

➤ Selecting the right wine

➤ Quantities and amounts

➤ Using irregular *ir* verbs

➤ A chocolate delight

In the preceding chapter you learned to shop for souvenirs, gifts, and some everyday odds and ends. You also picked out some fabulous French fashions and even managed, despite the metric system, to get the right size. Shopping is hard work and you've really worked up an appetite. It's a bit early for dinner. What should you do next?

Your best bet is to stop in one of the local food stores to pick up a snack to tide you over until your next meal. You can grab a sandwich (*un sandwich—uhN sahNd-weesh*) made on a long loaf of French bread (*une baguette—ewn bah-geht*), a pastry (*une pâtisserie—ewn pah-tees-ree*), or just a large chunk of cheese (*du fromage—dew froh-mahzh*). This chapter provides you with many alternatives, and assures that you get the right quantities. And at the end there's a special treat.

Memory Enhancer

Many of the types of stores that you will frequent end in *erie*. Drop this ending and add *ier* (*ière*) to get the name of the male (female) person who works in the store:

l'épicier—the (male) grocer

l'épicière—the (female) grocer

You'd Better Shop Around

I loved going on a class trip to Paris in 1990 with my youngest son, Michael. Like his mother, he's an incorrigible junk food addict and truly appreciates the sweet things in life. It seems that there are pastry shops on every corner in Paris, and he and I enjoyed many an *éclair* together. Are you like us? Do you like to keep snacks in your hotel room just in case you get the midnight munchies? Or have you rented a condo or an apartment and prefer to do your own cooking? In any French-speaking country you will be able to enjoy the culinary delights in the shops listed in the following table.

Culture Capsule

Bread and rolls are generally sold in a *boulangerie*. You can choose from *croissants*, crescent rolls made from a puff-pastry dough; *pains au chocolat*, croissants filled with bittersweet chocolate; *brioches*, soft, sweet rolls made of butter, eggs, flour, and yeast; and *baguettes*, French loaves. Pastries, such as *éclairs, charlottes russes,* and *napoléons,* are sold in a *pâtisserie*.

Food Shops

The Store	Le magasin	Pronunciation
bakery	la boulangerie	*lah boo-lahNzh-ree*
butcher shop	la boucherie	*lah boosh-ree*
candy store	la confiserie	*lah kohN-feez-ree*
dairy store	la crémerie	*lah kraym-ree*
delicatessen	la charcuterie	*lah shahr-keww-tree*
fish store	la poissonnerie	*lah pwah-sohn-ree*
fruit store	la fruiterie	*la frwee-tree*
grocery (vegetable) store	l'épicerie	*lay-pees-ree*

The Store	Le magasin	Pronunciation
liquor store	le magasin de vins	*luh mah-gah-zaN duh vaN*
pastry shop	la pâtisserie	*lah pah-tees-ree*
supermarket	le supermarché	*luh sew-pehr-mahr-shay*

Going Here and There

You've scouted out the shops in the area where you are staying and now you're ready to venture out on your own and do some serious shopping. When it's time to stock up and you're ready to leave, use the verb *aller* and the preposition *à* + the appropriate definite article (*au, à la, à l'*) to indicate the store to which you are going:

Je vais à l'épicerie.   I'm going to the grocery store.

Je vais à la boulangerie.   I'm going to the bakery.

It is very common to use the preposition *chez* (to [at] the house [business] of) + *the person* to express where you are going:

Je vais chez l' épicier (épicière).

Je vais chez le (la) boulanger (boulangère).

Try it. Tell your traveling companion where you are going to buy the following:

1. vegetables _____ .
2. pastry _____ .
3. meat _____ .
4. fruit _____ .
5. fish _____ .
6. candy _____ .
7. milk _____ .

Culture Capsule

Many French shoppers still do most of their shopping at small neighborhood shops, despite the convenience of the larger *supermarchés* or *hypermarchés*. Favoring quality over convenience, many French people would rather make numerous stops—at their favorite bread shop, cheese shop, butcher, and so forth—than settle for supermarket brands.

The delectable displays of food in the windows of various food stores across France just beckon you to enter and try something new and exotic. What foods (*aliments* m.) are among your favorites: fruits? vegetables? pastries? cheeses? Are you interested in trying different meat, poultry, game, or fish? Perhaps there's a wine that has caught your fancy? The following tables will help you enjoy the culinary experience of your choice.

At the Grocery Store

Vegetables	Les Légumes	Pronunciation
artichokes	les artichauts (m.)	*lay zahr-tee-sho*
asparagus	les asperges (f.)	*lay zahs-pehrzh*
beans (green)	les haricots verts (m.)	*lay zah-ree-ko vehr*
beets	les betteraves (m.)	*lay beht-rahv*
broccoli	le brocoli	*luh broh-koh-lee*
cabbage	le chou	*luh shoo*
carrot	la carotte	*lah kah-roht*
cauliflower	le chou-fleur	*luh shoo-fluhr*
corn	le maïs	*luh mah-ees*
cucumber	le concombre	*luh kohN-kohNbr*
eggplant	l'aubergine (f.)	*lo-behr-zheen*
leeks	les poireaux (m.)	*lay pwah-ro*
lettuce	la laitue	*lah leh-tew*
mushroom	le champignon	*luh shahN-pee-nyohN*
onion	l'oignon (m.)	*loh-nyohN*
peas	les petits pois (m.)	*lay puh-tee pwah*
pepper	le piment, le poivron	*luh pee-mahN, luh pwah-vrohN*
potato	la pomme de terre	*lah pohm duh tehr*
rice	le riz	*luh ree*
sauerkraut	la chocroute	*lah shoo-kroot*

Vegetables	Les Légumes	Pronunciation
shallot	l'échalote (f.)	*lay-shah-loht*
spinach	les épinards (m.)	*lay zay-pee-nahr*
sweet potato	la patate douce	*lah pah-taht doos*
tomato	la tomate	*lah toh-maht*
turnip	le navet	*luh nah-veh*
zucchini	la courgette	*lah koor-zheht*

Fruit and Nuts

Fruits	Les Fruits	Pronunciation
apple	la pomme	*lah pohm*
apricot	l'abricot (m.)	*lah-bree-ko*
avocado	l'avocat (m.)	*lah-voh-kah*
banana	la banane	*lah bah-nahn*
blueberry	la myrtille	*lah meer-tee-y*
cherry	la cerise	*lah suh-reez*
date	la datte	*lah daht*
fig	la figue	*lah feeg*
grape	le raisin	*luh reh-zahN*
grapefruit	le pamplemousse	*luh pahNpl-moos*
lemon	le citron	*luh see-trohN*
lime	la limette	*lah lee-meht*
orange	l'orange (f.)	*loh-rahNzh*
peach	la pêche	*lah pehsh*
pear	la poire	*lah pwahr*
pineapple	l'ananas (m.)	*lah-nah-nah*
plum	la prune	*lah prewn*
prune	le pruneau	*luh prew-no*
raisin	le raisin sec	*luh reh-zaN sehk*
raspberry	la framboise	*lah frahN-bwahz*
strawberry	la fraise	*lah frehz*

Nuts	Les Noix	Pronunciation
almond	l'amande (f.)	*lah-mahNd*
chestnut	le marron	*luh mah-rohN*
hazelnut	la noisette	*lah nwah-zeht*
walnut	la noix	*lah nwah*

Culture Capsule

Would you love to snack on a peanut-butter-and-jelly sandwich? You're out of luck. Peanut butter (*le beurre de cacahouètes—luh buhr duh kah-kah-weht*) is not sold in France!

At the Butcher or Delicatessen

Meats	Les Viandes	Pronounciation
bacon	le lard, le bacon	*luh lahr, luh bah-kohN*
beef	le boeuf	*luh buhf*
blood pudding	le boudin	*luh boo-daN*
bologna	la mortadelle	*lah mohr-tah-dehl*
brains	les cervelles (f.)	*lay sehr-vehl*
chopped meat	la viande hachée	*lah vyahNd ah-shay*
goat	la chèvre	*lah sheh-vruh*
ham	le jambon	*luh zhahN-bohN*
kidneys	les rognons (m.)	*lay roh-nyohN*
lamb	l'agneau (m.)	*lah-nyo*
liver	le foie	*luh fwah*
pâté	le pâté	*luh pah-tay*
pork	le porc	*luh pohr*
roast beef	le rosbif	*luh rohs-beef*
sausage	les saucisses (f.)	*lay so-sees*
sweetbreads	les ris de veau (m.)	*lay ree dvo*
tongue	la langue	*lah lahNg*
veal	le veau	*luh vo*

Fowl and Game	La Volaille et le Gibier	Pronounciation
chicken	le poulet	*luh poo-leh*
duck	le canard	*luh kah-nard*
goose	l'oie (f.)	*lwah*
hare	la lièvre	*lah lyehvr*
pheasant	le faisan	*luh feh-zahN*

Fowl and Game	La Volaille et le Gibier	Pronounciation
quail	la caille	*lah kahy*
rabbit	le lapin	*luh lah-paN*
turkey	la dinde	*lah daNd*
venison	le chevreuil	*luh sheh-vruhy*

Culture Capsule

Pâté is a paste (thicker than our traditional meat loaf), usually made with goose liver, but it may also be prepared with duck, pork, or chicken. Wine is added to the ground meat mixture and then it is baked in a loaf. The pâté is then allowed to cool and is served cold, often with bread or crackers. At times, pâté is baked in a decorated pastry crust (en croûte—*ahN kroot*), making it even more flavorful.

At the Fish Store

Fish and Seafood	Le Poisson et les Fruits de Mer	Pronunciation
anchovy	l'anchois (m.)	*lahN-shwah*
bass	la perche	*lah pehrsh*
clam	la palourde	*lah pah-loord*
codfish	la cabillaud	*lah kah-bee-yo*
crab	le crabe	*luh krahb*
crawfish	les écrivisses	*lay zay-kruh-vees*
eel	l'anguille(f.)	*lahN-gee*
flounder	le carrelet	*luh kahr-leh*
frogs' legs	les cuisses de grenouille (f.)	*lay kwees duh gruh-nuhy*
grouper	le mérou	*luh may-roo*
halibut	le flétan	*luh flay-tahN*
herring	le hareng	*luh ah-rahN*
lobster	le homard	*luh oh-mahr*
mackerel	le maquereau	*luh mahk-roh*

continues

At the Fish Store (cont.)

Fish and Seafood	Le Poisson et les Fruits de Mer	Pronunciation
monkfish	la lotte	*lah loht*
mussels	les moules (f.)	*lay mool*
oyster	l'huître (f.)	*lwee-truh*
red snapper	la perche rouge	*lah pehrsh roozh*
salmon	le saumon	*luh so-mohN*
sardines	les sardines (f.)	*lay sahr-deen*
scallops	les coquilles	*lay koh-kee*
sea bass	le bar	*luh bahr*
shrimp	la crevette	*lah kruh-veht*
snail	l'escargot (m.)	*lehs-kahr-go*
sole	la sole	*lah sohl*
squid	le calmar	*luh kahl-mahr*
swordfish	l'espadon (m.)	*lehs-pah-dohN*
trout	la truite	*lah trweet*
tuna	le thon	*luh tohN*

At the Dairy

Dairy Products	Les Produits Laitiers	Pronunciation
butter	le beurre	*luh buhr*
cheese	le fromage	*luh froh-mahzh*
cream	la crème	*lah krehm*
eggs	des oeufs (m.)	*day zuh*
yogurt	le yaourt	*luh yah-oort*

At the Bakery and Pastry Shop

Breads and Desserts	Les Pains et Les Desserts	Pronunciation
apple turnover	le chausson aux pommes	*luh sho-sohN o pohm*
bread	le pain	*luh paN*
brioche	la brioche	*lah bree-ohsh*
cake	le gâteau	*luh gah-to*
chocolate croissant	le pain au chocolat	*luh paN o shoh-koh-lah*
cookie	le biscuit	*luh bees-kwee*

Breads and Desserts	Les Pains et Les Desserts	Pronunciation
cream puffs	les choux à la crème (m.)	*lay shoo ah lah krehm*
crescent roll	le croissant	*luh krwah-sahN*
danish	la danoise	*lah dah-nwahz*
doughnut	le beignet	*luh beh-nyeh*
loaf of French bread	la baguette	*lah bah-geht*
pie	la tarte	*lah tahrt*
roll	le petit pain	*luh puh-tee paN*

Culture Capsule

To maintain a nutritious, healthy diet, look for *une maison de régime* (*ewn meh-zohN duh ray-zheem*) or *une diététique* (*ewn dee-ay-tay-teek*)—a health-food store. Product advertising is not widespread in France, so the French rely on the professional advice of the store owner when it comes to purchasing products. Teas (especially herbal teas), vitamins, and breads are the most popular items sold in these stores.

At the Candy Store

Sweets	Les Sucreries	Pronunciation
candy	les bonbons (m.)	*lay bohN-bohN*
chocolate	le chocolat	*luh shoh-koh-lah*
gum	le chewing-gum	*luh shween-guhm*

At the Supermarket

Drinks	Les Boissons	Pronunciation
beer	la bière	*lah byehr*
champagne	le champagne	*luh shahN-pah-nyuh*
cider	le cidre	*luh seedr*
coffee	le café	*luh kah-fay*

continues

At the Supermarket (cont.)

Drinks	Les Boissons	Pronunciation
juice	le jus	*luh zhew*
hot chocolate (cocoa)	le chocolat	*luh shoh-koh-laht*
lemonade	le citron pressé	*lun see-trohN preh-say*
milk	le lait	*luh leh*
mineral water	l'eau minérale (f.)	*lo mee-nay-rahl*
carbonated	gazeuse	* gah-zuhz*
non-carbonated	plate	* plaht*
orangeade	l'orangeade (f.)	*loh-rahN-zhahd*
soda	le soda	*luh soh-dah*
tea	le thé	*luh tay*
wine	le vin	*luh vaN*

If you want to be specific about a type of juice, use *de* + the name of the fruit:

le jus d'orange   orange juice

Serious Shopping

Tell what items you would purchase in the following stores. Begin your answers with: *J'achèterais* (I would buy).

1. à la boucherie _____ .
2. à la pâtisserie _____ .
3. à la boulangerie _____ .
4. à l'épicerie _____ .
5. à la fruiterie _____ .
6. à la charcuterie _____ .

What's That Wine?

Have you ever looked at a wine label and wondered what all the information meant? We've come to the rescue with a convenient key that will help you make sense of wine labels. Both French and American governments have strict rules concerning wine and labeling, but in a nutshell, this is what you should know:

➤ The region where the wine was produced, such as Bourgogne (Burgundy), Bordeaux, Champagne.

➤ Product of France.

➤ The *appellation* of the wine (trademark) indicates the region in which the wine was produced and affirms that the grapes were grown, picked, fermented, and bottled according to strict government controls. Only better quality wines are marked with an *appellation.* Table wine is clearly marked as such and has no *appellation* since it is of a lesser quality. A champagne label merely states: "Champagne."

Culture Capsule

There are many great wine buying guides, including Hugh Johnson's book, which is published annually.

➤ The quality of the wine (from the lowest to the highest):

vin de table: ordinary table wine that has no vintage.

village wine: No vineyard is mentioned, probably meaning that the wine is made from a variety of grapes from different vineyards.

premier cru and grand cru: Premier and grand cru indicate that the grapes used to produce the wine were of a superior quality because they were grown on the most fertile land, under the best climatic conditions. Although premier cru is considered the ultimate wine, many *connaisseurs* prefer the taste of grand cru. The ordinary palate would not be able to distinguish between the two.

➤ The town where the wine was bottled.

➤ The name and origin of the shipper. (For champagne, the champagne house is usually the shipper.)

➤ The net contents.

➤ The percentage of alcohol by volume.

➤ The name and address of the importer.

The following information may or may not be included on a wine label:

➤ The vintage (the year the wine was bottled)

➤ The brand or château name

➤ Whether the wine was "estate" or "château" bottled

Culture Capsule

The only true champagne comes from the Champagne province in northwest France. All others are imitation sparkling wines. French wine growers work all year to grow and harvest the most perfect grapes, which are then separated by type, village of origin, and harvest date. They are then pressed, and their juice is fermented in different vats. In the spring, the wine is bottled. According to French law and tradition, the wine then ferments a second time in the bottle (creating the bubbles) and ages in cellars from three to five years to reach perfect maturity.

Your Likes and Dislikes

Do you cringe at the sight of broccoli but start to drool when you pick up the scent of ribs cooking on a grill? Are you a picky eater or will you eat just about anything to stop your stomach from growling? For each of the following groups, tell what you love (*J'adore*), like (*J'aime*), and dislike (*Je déteste*).

1. fruits _____ .

2. vegetables _____ .

3. meat _____ .

4. fish _____ .

5. bread _____ .

6. cake _____ .

Quantity Counts

You've decided to go on a picnic with a friend in the French countryside and stop by a *charcuterie* to purchase some sandwich meat. You figure that half a pound ought to be sufficient. But when you get to the counter to order, you find that no one understands how much you want. Why are you having this problem and how will you get the right amount of meat? In France the metric system is used for measuring quantities of food: Liquids are measured in *liters* and solids are measured in *kilograms* or fractions thereof. Since most of us are used to dealing with ounces, pounds, pints, quarts, and gallons, I've included a conversion chart to help you out until the metric system becomes second nature.

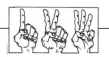

Un deux trois

For an entire week, keep a log in French of everything you eat.

Measuring Quantities of Food

Approximate Solid Measures	
1 oz. = 28 grams	3/4 lb. = 375 grams
1/4 lb. = 125 grams	1.1 lb. = 500 grams
1/2 lb. = 250 grams	2.2 lb. = 1000 grams (1 kilogram)

Approximate Liquid Measures	
1 oz. = 30 milliliters	16 oz. (1 pint) = 475 milliliters
32 oz. (1 quart) = 950 milliliters (approximately 1 liter)	1 gallon = 3.75 liters

Not having been brought up on the metric system myself, I can understand that you might still be a bit confused. So I've made it even easier for you. Sometimes it's just easier to ask for a box, bag, jar, etc., and to commit to memory the amounts we're accustomed to: a pound, a quart, etc. Consult the following table to easily get the amount you want or need.

Getting the Right Amount

2 pounds of	un kilo de	*uhN kee-lo duh*
a bag of	un sac de	*uhN sahk duh*
a bar of	une tablette de	*ewn tah-bleht duh*
a bottle of	une bouteille de	*ewn boo-tehy duh*
a box of	une boîte de	*ewn bwaht duh*
a can of	une boîte de	*ewn bwaht duh*
a dozen	une douzaine de	*ewn doo-zehn duh*
a half pound of	deux cent cinquante grammes de	*duh sahN saN-kahNt grahm duh*
a jar of	un bocal de	*uhN boh-kahl duh*
a package of	un paquet de	*uhN pah-keh duh*
a pound of	un demi-kilo de, cinq cents grammes de	*uhN duh-mee kee-lo duh, saNk sahN grahm duh*
a quart of	un litre de	*uhN lee-truh duh*
a slice of	une tranche de	*ewn trahNsh duh*

You're on a diet but you must have "just a taste" of the chocolate mousse that your French host spent hours preparing for you. He starts filling your bowl and you try to motion "enough." Too bad, he just keeps heaping it on. Now there's really a lot of mousse on your plate. Finally, there's just too much. Don't allow yourself to get into this bind. Here are some expressions that will help you limit the quantity you receive:

Amounts

a little	un peu de	*uhN puh duh*
a lot of	beaucoup de	*bo-koo duh*
enough	assez de	*ah-say duh*
too much	trop de	*tro duh*

All of these expressions of quantity include the word *de* (of). Before a vowel *de* becomes *d'*. In all other instances, *de* never changes:

> beaucoup de bonbons   a lot of candies
>
> une douzaine d'oeufs   a dozen eggs

Is the Fridge Bare?

When you arrive at the check-in desk at your hotel in Saint Martin, you are delighted to find that your room has been upgraded and there's a refrigerator at your disposal. You look out the window and there's a convenience store in walking distance. What snacks would you purchase for that occasional craving? Write your shopping list in French and include the amounts you need.

Culture Capsule

Be advised: It is not customary to receive a shopping bag in individual neighborhood stores. French shoppers usually bring along *un filet* (*uhN fee-leh*), a net bag, in which to stow their purchases. This bag is reusable and is, therefore, environment-friendly. You can purchase one at a supermarket, drugstore, or variety store.

I'd Like...

Someone will always be eager to help you in a small neighborhood store. Be prepared for the questions that you might be asked and the proper way to give an answer that will get you what you want:

What would you like?
Vous désirez?
voo day-zee-ray

May I help you?
Est-ce que je peux vous aider?
ehs-kuh zhuh puh voo zeh-day

Your answer might begin:

I would like...
Je voudrais...
zhuh voo-dreh

Could you give me...?
Pourriez-vous me donner...?
poo-ryay voo muh doh-nay

Please
S'il vous plaît
seel voo pleh

Un deux trois

You're on your own. Tell a shop-keeper that you would like the following: a pound of ham, a liter of soda, a chocolate bar, a box of cookies, a bag of candy, and a half pound of turkey.

You might then be asked:

And with that?	Is that all?
Et avec ça?	C'est tout?
ay ah-vehk sah	*seh too*

An appropriate response would be to either give additional items that you want or to answer:

Yes, that's all, thank you.
Oui, c'est tout, merci.
wee seh too mehr-see

ir Verb Irregularities

Snacking is fine, but now you're in the mood for a good dinner. Imagine walking along the port in Martinique and **smelling** the aromas emanating from the various restaurants. Of course you want to know what type of cuisine is being **served**. Let's take a closer look at these verbs and some other similar ones. The verb *servir* (to serve) and a few others that end in *ir* (*dormir*—to sleep, *partir*—to leave, *sentir*—to feel, smell, and *sortir*—to go out) do not follow the pattern of present tense conjugation for *ir* verbs that has already been studied. They drop the consonant before the *ir* of the infinitive in the singular forms and retain that consonant in the plural forms:

dormir (to sleep)		
je dors	*zhuh dohr*	I sleep
tu dors	*tew dohr*	you sleep
il, elle, on dort	*eel (ehl, ohN) dohr*	he (she, one) sleeps
nous dormons	*noo dohr-mohN*	we sleep
vous dormez	*voo dohr-may*	you sleep
ils, elles dorment	*eel (ehl) dohrm*	they sleep

partir (to leave)		
je pars	*zhuh pahr*	I leave
tu pars	*tew pahr*	you leave
il, elle, on part	*eel (ehl, ohN) pahr*	he (she, one) leaves
nous partons	*noo pahr-tohN*	we leave
vous partez	*voo pahr-tay*	you leave
ils, elles partent	*eel (ehl) pahrt*	they leave

246

sentir (to smell, feel)

je sens	*zhuh sahN*	I smell, feel
tu sens	*tew sahN*	you smell, feel
il, elle, on sent	*eel (ehl, ohN) sahN*	he (she, one) smells, feels
nous sentons	*noo sahN-tohN*	we smell, feel
vous sentez	*voo sahN-tay*	you smell, feel
ils, elles sentent	*eel (ehl) sahNt*	they smell, feel

servir (to serve)

je sers	*zhuh sehr*	I serve
tu sers	*tew sehr*	you serve
il, elle, on sert	*eel (ehl, ohN) sehr*	he (she, one) serves
nous servons	*noo sehr-vohN*	we serve
vous servez	*voo sehr-vay*	you serve
ils, elles servent	*eel (ehl) sehrv*	they serve

sortir (to go out)

je sors	*zhuh sohr*	I go out
tu sors	*tew sohr*	you go out
il, elle, on sort	*eel (ehl, ohN) sohr*	he (she, one) goes out
nous sortons	*noo sohr-tohN*	we go out
vous sortez	*voo sohr-tay*	you go out
ils, elles sortent	*eel (ehl) sohrt*	they go out

It's a Puzzle to Me

Do you want to make sure that you have all those verb forms down pat? Practice can make perfect in a fun way. Complete the crossword puzzle with the correct forms of all the verbs.

Horizontalement

1. (leave) je
3. (sleep) you
7. (serve) ils
8. (server) nous
10. (sleep) elles
12. (go out) nous
14. (feel) ils
15. (leave) nous
17. (serve) il
18. (feel) vous
19. (serve) tu
20. (sleep) vous

Verticalement

1. (leave) elles
2. (go out) vous
3. (sleep) nous
4. (feel) il
5. (feel) nous
6. (serve) vous
9. (go out) ils
11. (sleep) il
13. (leave) elle
15. (leave) vous
16. (feel) je
17. (go out) tu
18. (go out) elle

The Treat's on Me

Why not impress your friends with this treat from *Bon Appétit*: frozen chocolate mousse? It's delicious, easy to prepare, and freezes beautifully. You will need:

8 oz. semi-sweet chocolate bits

1 square unsweetened chocolate

2 TB. butter

1 TB. very strong black instant coffee

2 eggs, separated

1 TB. Grand Marnier

1 pint heavy cream

In a microwave oven set on medium heat, melt the semi-sweet chocolate, the unsweetened chocolate, and the butter. Stir. Let the mixture cool slightly. While the mixture is cooling, beat the egg whites until stiff and the cream until whipped but not stiff.

Add the coffee, Grand Marnier, and egg yolks to the chocolate mixture. Stir.

Then slowly fold in the egg whites. Add the whipped cream. Mix slowly so that the cream remains fluffy.

Spoon into individual dessert cups and let chill for at least 4 hours. Serve with additional whipped cream.

Serves 12

The Least You Need to Know

➤ Use the verb *aller* + *à* + the definite article to express where you are going.

➤ Purchasing the correct amount of food in France requires a knowlege of the metric system.

➤ Ask for a box or a jar of something if you are not familiar with the metric system.

➤ Certain *ir* verbs follow a different pattern of conjugation and should be memorized.

Chapter 17

Eating Out

> ## In This Chapter
>
> ➤ How to order in a restaurant
>
> ➤ Getting exactly what you want
>
> ➤ Special diets
>
> ➤ Exclamations

Let's say you're in Paris, the city of lights. Alas, it is neither lunch nor dinner time, but using the lessons from the last chapter, you've managed to grab a snack to tide you over until your next real meal. Or maybe you've stocked your hotel room refrigerator and are lying around your room snacking on *biscuits, fromage,* and *citronnade;* your new knowledge of the metric system helped you when ordering the right amount of cheese.

But now you are really hungry; it's time to head out and find a place for dinner. The French are fanatical about food, and their haute cuisine is considered the finest and most sophisticated in the world. Indeed, when Americans started taking food more seriously, they turned to France for guidance and inspiration. (Remember, Boston's own Julia Child built her reputation around teaching French cooking.) With all the French cooking terms that have crept into our culture, there are plenty of places at home to practice gastromic French—from menus to cookbooks and magazines. By the end of this chapter, you will be a pro at ordering from a French menu, even if you have certain dietary needs or restrictions. And if, perchance, you are dissatisfied with your meal, you will be able to send it back and get what you want.

Select a Place You'd Like

Wherever you decide to eat, France offers a wide variety of eating establishments to suit your hunger and your pocketbook. Are you going out for breakfast (le petit déjeuner, *luh puh-tee day-zhuh-nay*), lunch (le déjeuner, *luh day-zhuh-nay*), dinner (le dîner, *luh dee-nay*), or an early afternoon snack (le goûter, *luh goo-tay*)? If you're not in the mood for a formal restaurant, why not try:

➤ une auberge (*ewn o-behrzh*), an inn

➤ un bistro (*uhN bees-tro*), a small informal neighborhood pub or tavern

➤ une brasserie (*ewn brahs-ree*), a large café serving quick meals

➤ une cabaret (*ewn kah-bah-reh*), a nightclub

➤ un café (*uhN kah-fay*), a small neighborhood restaurant where residents socialize

➤ un cafétéria (*uhN kah-fay-tay-ryah*), a self-service restaurant

➤ une casse-croûte (*ewn kahs-kroot*), a restaurant serving sandwiches

➤ une crêperie (*ewn krehp-ree*), a stand or restaurant serving *crêpes* (filled pancakes)

➤ un fast-food (*uhN fahst-food*), a fast-food chain restaurant

➤ un self (*uhN sehlf*), a self-service restaurant

Culture Capsule

What's the typical French breakfast, lunch, or dinner? For breakfast, *un croissant* (uhN krwah-sahN), *une brioche* (ewn bree-ohsh), or *une tartine* (ewn tahr-teen—a piece of bread with butter or jam) is served with a bowl of hot chocolate (*un bol de chocolat,* uhN bohl duh shoh-koh-lah) or coffee. Eggs are eaten at dinnertime, as omelettes.

Which Restaurant Do You Prefer?

You've opened a tourist magazine and found ads for restaurants. Now you have to decide what you feel in the mood for this evening. Explore the ads and determine what you would expect to get in each of these restaurants:

NOTRE SELECTIONS DE RESTAURANTS

Noms	Spécialités	N°P
LE SAINT-NICOLAS	CUISINE FINE TRADITONNELLE	4
LES QUATRES SAISONS (Abela Hôtel Monaco)	CUISINE FRANÇAISE SPECIALITES LIBANAISES	5
LE SAINT-BENOIT	CUISINE DE LA MER	6
TIP TOP BAR	SPECIALITES ITALIENNES	7
FLASHMAN'S	RESTAURATION ANGLAISE	13
STARS'N'BARS	CUISINE AMERICAINE MUSIQUE TOUS LES SOIRS	13
LE METROPOLE PALACE	CUISINE FRANÇAISE	15
LES AMBASSADEURS (Hôtel Métropole)	SPECIALITES LIBANAISES ET FRANÇAISE	15
LA PORTE D'OR	SPECIALITES VIETNAMIENNES ET CHINOISES	16
LE CHINA TOWN	SPECIALITES VIETNAMIENNES ET CHINOISES	16
CAFE MOZART	BUFFET CHAUD & FROID, GLACES, PATISSERIES	82
RESTAURANT DU PORT	POISSONS, SPECIALITES ITALIENNES	24
LA CANTINELLA	SPECIALITES ITALIENNES	Plan
SASS' CAFE	PIANO BAR	Plan
LE PARADISE	RESTAURANT GLACIER	56
L'ESCALE	SPECIALITES DE POISSONS	55
HARRY'S BAR	MENU HOMMES D'AFFAIRES	12

If you've chosen to dine in a restaurant, it might be necessary to reserve a table. When you call, make sure to include all the pertinent information:

Culture Capsule

Lunch, in many parts of the country, still remains the main meal of the day and is served in many courses: appetizer, soup, entrée (main course), salad, cheese, and dessert. Note that the French eat their salad after the main course.

Je voudrais réserver une table...
zhuh voo-dreh ray-sehr-vay ewn tahbl
I would like to reserve a table...

pour ce soir	pour demain soir	pour samedi soir
poor suh swahr	*poor duh-maN swahr*	*poor sahm-dee swahr*
for this evening	for tomorrow evening	for Saturday night

pour deux personnes
poor duh pehr-sohn
for two people

à huit heures et demie
ah wee tuhr ay duh-mee
at 8:30 p.m.

sur (à) la terrasse, s'il vous plaît.
sewr (ah) lah teh-rahs seel voo pleh
on the terrace, please (outdoors)

Un deux trois

Practice what you've learned by reserving a table for Friday evening, at 9:00 p.m., for six people. Also request a table outdoors.

We're Dining Out

Let's say that you did not reserve a table and show up at a restaurant unannounced. The maître d' will most certainly ask:

Une table pour combien de personnes?
ewn tahbl poor kohN-byaN duh pehr-sohn?
A table for how many?

Your response should contain all the necessary information:

Une table pour quatre personnes, s'il vous plaît.
ewn tahbl poor kahtr pehr-sohn seel voo pleh
A table for four, please.

Un deux trois

Label all the different things you put on your dinner table. Study the names carefully for a few days. When you feel confident, remove the labels and name as many items as you can.

You've now been seated, and you look around and are delighted with the fine china, the crystal, the linen napkins, and the crisp white tablecloth. But wait! Madam's place has not been properly set. The following table gives you the vocabulary you need when asking the waiter for cutlery, as well as other terms that will come in handy.

A Table Setting

Item	French	Pronunciation
bowl	le bol	*luh bohl*
carafe	la carafe	*lah kah-rahf*
cup	la tasse	*lah tahss*
dinner plate	l'assiette (f.)	*lah-syeht*
fork	la fourchette	*lah foor-sheht*
glass	le verre	*luh vehr*
knife	le couteau	*luh koo-to*
menu	le menu, la carte	*luh muh-new, lah kahrt*
napkin	la serviette	*lah sehr-vyeht*
pepper shaker	le poivrier	*leh pwah-vree-yeh*
place setting	le couvert	*luh koo-vehr*
salt shaker	la salière	*lah sahl-yehr*
saucer	la soucoupe	*lah soo-koop*
soup dish	l'assiette à soupe (f.)	*lah-syeht ah soop*
tablecloth	la nappe	*lah nahp*
teaspoon	la cuillère	*lah kwee-yehr*
tablespoon	la cuillère à service	*lah kwee-yehr ah sehr-vees*
waiter	le garçon	*luh gahr-sohN*
waitress	la serveuse	*lah sehr-vuhz*
wine glass	le verre à vin	*luh vehr ah vaN*

Culture Capsule

In France, most restaurants offer a *prix fixe* (price fixed) menu or *menu touristique*, which consists of an appetizer, soup, main course, salad, dessert, and drink for a pre–determined price. Although your choices of dishes might be restricted, this still offers an excellent value for the money. Ordering *à la carte* is, without exception, a more expensive option.

If you find that something is missing from your table, or if you need to make a request of the staff, the following phrases will help you get want you want:

➤ Use an indirect object pronoun:

Il me faut...	*eel muh foh*	I need
Il te faut...	*eel tuh foh*	You need
Il lui faut...	*eel lui foh*	He/She needs
Il nous faut...	*eel noo foh*	We need
Il vous faut...	*eel voo foh*	You need
Il leur faut...	*eel leur foh*	They need

➤ Use the expression *avoir besoin de* (to need):

J'ai besoin de...	*zhay buh-zwaN duh*	I need
Tu as besoin de...	*tew ah buh-zwaN duh*	You need
Il a besoin de...	*eel ah buh-zwaN duh*	He needs
Elle a besoin de...	*ehl ah buh-zwaN duh*	She needs
Nous avons besoin de...	*noo zah-vohN buh-zwaN duh*	We need
Vous avex besoin de...	*voo sah-vay buh-zwaN duh*	You need
Ils ont besoin de...	*eel zohN buh-zwaN duh*	They need
Elles ont besoin de...	*ehl zohN buh-zwaN duh*	They need

Oh, Waiter!

Now, use what you've learned to tell your server that you need:

1. a salt shaker _____ .
2. a napkin _____ .
3. a fork _____ .
4. a knife _____ .
5. a plate _____ .
6. a spoon _____ .

Garçon, What Do You Recommend?

It's time to order. It's always a good idea to get the server's recommendations before ordering:

What is today's specialty?
Quel est le plat du jour?
kehl eh luh plah dew zhoor

What is the house specialty?
Quelle est la spécialité de la maison?
kehl eh lah spay-see-ah-lee-tay duh lah meh-zohN

What do you recommend?
Qu'est-ce que vous recommandez?
kehs-kuh voo ruh-koh-mahN-day

Culture Capsule

Two popular French lunches are *un croque-monsieur* (uhN krohk muh-syuh), a toasted ham and cheese sandwich, and *un croque-madame* (uhN krohk mah-dahm), the same sandwich with an egg on top. You can pick them up at a restaurant or on the run, along with *une crêpe* (ewn krehp), a pancake filled with cheese, seafood, meat, or a dessert, or *une mini-quiche,* (ewn mee-nee keesh), an egg and cheese pie filled with vegetables, bacon, or ham.

The waiter has come to give you a menu and see if you'd like a drink before dinner. You may use the following to order both drinks and food:

I would like...	I'll have...	Please bring me...
Je voudrais...	Je prendrai...	Apportez-moi, s'il vous plaît...
zhuh voo-dreh	*zhuh prahN-dray*	*ah-pohr-tay mwah seel voo pleh*
a before-dinner drink	a cocktail	Nothing for me
un apéritif	un cocktail	Rien pour moi
uhN nah-pay-ree-teef	*uhN kohk-tehl*	*ryaN poor mwah*

Culture Capsule

It is customary for the French to enjoy *un apéritif* before dinner. Although these drinks are touted as being an appetite stimulant, a real Frenchman will tell you that having an apéritif is just an excuse for enjoying a before-dinner drink. Among the more popular varieties are: Vermouth (a wine made from red or white grapes—Martini and Cinzano are the all-time favorites), Pernod and Ricard (licorice-flavored drinks made from anise), Cynar (made from artichoke hearts), and Dubonnet et Byrrh (wine and brandy flavored with herbs and bitters).

Attention!

In some areas, business establishments still close for two hours at lunchtime to allow for a long, leisurely meal. This custom is dying, however, especially with the infiltration of *le fast-food*.

This Menu Is Greek to Me

A French menu can be confusing and overwhelming unless you know certain culinary terms. And if you are a novice to the French language, you might feel that it is too embarrassing or pointless to ask about a dish because you know that you probably won't understand the waiter's explanation! The following table gives you the terms you need to interpret sauce names and other items on a French menu.

What's on the Menu?

Dishes Served	Pronunciation	Contain
aïoli	*ah-yoh-lee*	mayonnaise flavored with garlic
à la bonne femme	*ah lah bohn fahm*	a white wine sauce with vegetables
béarnaise	*bay-ahr-nehz*	a butter-egg sauce flavored with wine, shallots, and tarragon
bercy	*behr-see*	a meat or fish sauce
blanquette	*blahN-keht*	a creamy egg and white wine sauce usually served with stew
crécy	*kray-see*	carrots
daube	*dohb*	a stew, usually beef, with red wine, onions, and garlic

Dishes Served	Pronunciation	Contain
farci(e)	*fahr-see*	a stuffing
florentine	*floh-rahN-teen*	spinach
forestière	*foh-rehs-tyehr*	wild mushrooms
hollandaise	*oh-lahN-dehz*	an egg yolk butter sauce with lemon juice or vinegar
jardinière	*zhahr-dee-nyehr*	vegetables
maÎtre d'hôtel	*mehtr do-tehl*	a butter sauce with parsley and lemon juice
mornay	*mohr-nay*	a white sauce with cheese
parmentier	*pahr-mahN-tyay*	potatoes
périgourdine	*pay-ree-goor-deen*	mushrooms (truffles)
provençale	*proh-vahN-sahl*	a vegetable garnish
rémoulade	*ray-moo-lahd*	mayonnaise flavored with mustard
véronique	*vay-rohN-neek*	grapes
vol-au-vent	*vohl-o-vahN*	puff pastry with creamed meat

Now you should feel somewhat confident to order. The following tables will help you get from the appetizer through the main course. If you have any problems with the names of various types of meat or fish, refer back to Chapter 16.

(Dinner in France is a light meal and is generally served after 7 p.m. Don't be surprised to see eggs or pizza on a dinner menu.)

Appetizers (les hors-d'oeuvres—lay zohr-duhvr)

Appetizer	Pronunciation	Description
crudités variées	*krew-dee-tay vah-ryay*	sliced raw vegetable usually in a vinaigrette sauce
escargots	*ehs-kahr-go*	snails
foie gras	*fwah grah*	fresh, sometimes uncooked, goose liver, served with toasted French bread
pâté	*pah-tay*	pureed liver or other meat served in a loaf
quiche lorraine	*keesh loh-rehn*	egg custard tart served with meat (bacon or ham)
quenelles	*kuh-nehl*	dumpling.
rillettes	*ree-yeht*	pork mixture served as a spread

Soups (les soupes—lay soop)

Soup	Pronunciation	Description
la bisque	*lah beesk*	creamy soup made with crayfish
la bouillabaise	*lah boo-yah-behs*	seafood stew
le consommé	*luh kohN-soh-may*	clear broth
la petite marmite	*lah puh-teet mahr-meet*	rich consommé served with vegetables and meat
le potage	*luh poh-tahzh*	thick soup made of pureed vegetables
la soupe à l'oignon	*lah soop ah loh-nyohN*	onion soup served with bread and cheese
velouté	*vuh-loo-tay*	creamy soup

Meats (les viandes—lay vyahnd)

Meat	Pronunciation	Description
le bifteck	*luh beef-tehk*	steak
l'entrecôte (f.)	*lahNtr-koht*	sirloin steak
l'escalope (f.)	*leh-skah-lohp*	scallopine, cutlet
la côte de boeuf	*lah koht duh buhf*	prime rib
la poitrine de...	*lah pwah-treen duh*	breast of...
le carré d'agneau	*luh kah-ray dah-nyo*	rack of lamb
le chateaubriand	*luh shah-to-bree-yahN*	a porterhouse steak
le foie	*luh foie*	liver
le gigot d'agneau	*luh zhee-go dah-nyo*	leg of lamb
le pot-au-feu	*luh poh-to-fuh*	boiled beef
le rosbif	*luh rohs-beef*	roastbeef
le tournedos	*luh toor-nuh-do*	small fillets of beef
les côtes de porc (f.)	*lay koht duh pohr*	pork chops
les côtes de veau (f.)	*lay koht duh vo*	veal chops
les médaillons de... (m.)	*lay may-dah-yohN duh*	small rounds of
les saucisses (f.)	*lay so-sees*	sausages
le hamburger	*luh ahm-bewr-gehr*	hamburger

I'm Hungry. Let's Eat!

Even if you know how to order your hamburger or veal chops, you want to be certain that your entree is cooked to your specifications. The waiter might ask:

> Vous le (la, les) voulez comment?
> *voo luh (lah, lay) voo-lay koh-mahN*
> How do you want it (them)?

Remember to use the appropriate direct object pronoun to refer to the noun you are using:

> Vous recommandez *le gigot*?
> Vous *le* recommandez?

The following table will help you to express your wants and needs.

How Would You Like It Prepared?

Meats and Vegetables		*viandes et légumes*		*vee-yahNd ay lay-gewm*
baked	cuit au four	*kwee to foor*	broiled	rôti	*ro-tee*
boiled	bouilli	*boo-yee*	browned	gratiné	*grah-tee-nay*
fried	frit	*free*	sautéed	sauté	*so-tay*
grilled	grillé	*gree-yay*	steamed	à la vapeur	*ah lah vah-puhr*
in its natural juices	au jus	*o zhew*	stewed	en cocotte	*ahN koh-koht*
mashed	en purée	*ahN pew-ray*	very rare	bleu	*bluh*
poached	poché	*poh-shay*	rare	saignant	*seh-nyahN*
pureed	en pureé	*ahN pew-ray*	medium	à point	*ah pwaN*
roasted	rôti	*ro-tee*	well-done	bien cuit	*byaN kwee*
with sauce	en sauce	*ahN sos*			

Eggs	*des oeufs*	*day zuh*
fried	au plat	*o plah*
hard-boiled	durs	*dewr*
medium-boiled	mollets	*moh-leh*
omelette	une omelette	*ewn nohm-leht*
plain omelette	une omelette nature	*ewn nohm-leht nah-tewr*
poached	pochés	*poh-shay*
scrambled	brouillés	*broo-yay*
soft-boiled	à la coque	*ah lah kohk*

Culture Capsule

Keep in mind that a French chef has a different interpretation of the terms *rare, medium,* and *well-done* than an American chef. In French cooking, *rare* means almost alive, *medium* is a tiny bit more cooked than our rare, and *well-done* is a bit more than our medium. What the chef thinks is burned is what we mean by well-done. He may prepare it well-done, but don't expect a smile when it is served.

Hot and Spicy

The French use a lot of herbs, spices, seasonings, and condiments to flavor their foods. Knowing the words in the following table will help you determine the ingredients of your dish or enable you to ask for a seasoning you prefer:

Herbs, Spices, and Condiments

basil	le basilic	*luh bah-zee-leek*
bay leaf	la feuille de laurier	*lah fuhy duh loh-ryay*
butter	le beurre	*luh buhr*
capers	les câpres (m.)	*lay kahpr*
chives	la ciboulette	*lah see-boo-leht*
dill	l'aneth (m.)	*lah-neht*
garlic	l'ail (m.)	*lahy*
ginger	le gingembre	*luh zhaN-zhahNbr*
honey	le miel	*luh myehl*
horseradish	le raifort	*luh reh-fohr*
jam, jelly	la confiture	*lah kohN-fee-tewr*
ketchup	le ketchup	*luh keht-chuhp*
lemon	le citron	*luh see-trohN*
maple syrup	le sirop d'érable	*luh see-roh day-rahbl*
mayonnaise	la mayonnaise	*lah mah-yoh-nehz*
mint	la menthe	*lah mahNt*
mustard	la moutarde	*lah moo-tahrd*
oil	l'huile (f.)	*lweel*
oregano	l'origan (m.)	*loh-ree-gahN*

parsley	le persil	*luh pehr-seel*
pepper	le poivre	*luh pwahvr*
salt	le sel	*luh sehl*
sugar	le sucre	*luh sewkr*
tarragon	l'estragon (m.)	*lehs-trah-gohN*
vinegar	le vinaigre	*luh vee-nehgr*

Culture Capsule

It is unnecessary to specify that you do not want m.s.g. in your food, since this flavor enhancer is not used in France. The acronym *m.s.g.* is completely foreign to the average French person and to those who prepare other types of cuisine in French-speaking countries.

Diet Do's and Don'ts

If you have specific likes, dislikes, or dietary restrictions that you would like to make known, keep the following phrases handy:

I am on a diet.	Je suis au régime.	*zhuh swee zo ray-zheem*
I'm a vegetarian.	Je suis végétarien(ne).	*zhuh swee vay-zhay-tah-ryaN (ryen)*
I can't have...	Je ne tolére...	*zhuh nuh toh-lehr*
any dairy products	aucun produit laitier	*o-kuhN proh-dwee leh-tyay*
any alcohol	aucun produit alcoolique	*o-kuhN proh-dwee ahl-koh-leek*
any saturated fats	aucune matière grasse animale	*o-kewn mah-tyehr grahs ah-nee-mahl*
any shellfish	aucun fruit de mer	*o-kuhN frweed mehr*
I'm looking for a dish...	Je cherche un plat...	*zhuh shehrsh uhN plah*
high in fiber	riche en fibre	*reesh ahN feebr*
low in cholesterol	léger en cholestérol	*lay-zhay ahN koh-lehs-tay-rohl*

low in fat	léger en matières grasses	*lay-zhay ahN mah-tyehr grahs*
low in sodium	léger en sodium	*lay-zhay ahN sohd-yuhm*
non-dairy	non-laitier	*nohN-leh-tyay*
salt-free	sans sel	*sahN sehl*
sugar-free	sans sucre	*sahN sewkr*
without artificial coloring	sans colorant	*sahN koh-loh-rahN*
without preservatives	sans conservateurs	*sahN kohN-sehr-vah-tuhr*

Culture Capsule

When your meal arrives, good manners dictate that you should wish your fellow diners *bon appétit* (bohN nah–pat–tee), a hearty appetite.

Back to the Kitchen

Certainly there are times, even in France, when the cooking or table setting is just not up to your standards. The following table presents some problems you might run into:

Possible Problems

...is cold	...est froid(e)	*eh frwah(d)*
...is too rare	...n'est pas assez cuit(e)	*neh pah zah-say kwee(t)*
...is over-cooked	...est trop cuit(e)	*eh tro kwee(t)*
...is tough	...est dur(e)	*eh dewr*
...is burned	...est brûlé(e)	*eh brew-lay*
...is too salty	...est trop salé(e)	*eh tro sah-lay*
...is too sweet	...est trop sucré(e)	*eh tro sew-kray*
...is too spicy	...est trop épicé(e)	*eh tro ay-pee-say*
...is spoiled	...est tourné(e)	*eh toor-nay*
...is bitter	...est aigre	*eh tehgr*
...tastes like...	...a le goût de...	*ah luh goo duh*
...is dirty	...est sale	*eh sahl*

Fancy Finales

In France, it is traditional to have *une salade* (ewn sah-lahd) followed by *des fromages variés* (day froh-mahzh vah-ryay—cheeses). Popular cheeses include: boursin, brie, camembert, chèvre, munster, port-salut, and roquefort. When choosing a cheese you might want to ask:

Attention!

It is quite customary in France to serve a plate of cheese as dessert. But feel free to ask for something else.

Is it...	Est-il...	eh-teel
mild	maigre	*mehgr*
sharp	piquant	*pee-kahN*
hard	fermenté	*fehr-mahN-tay*
soft	à pâte molle	*ah paht mohl*

Finally, it's time for dessert. But there are so many French specialties from which to choose. The following table will help you make a decision.

Divine Desserts

Dessert	Pronunciation	Description
une bavaroise	*ewn bah-vahr-wahz*	bavarian cream
des beignets	*day beh-nyeh*	fruit doughnuts
une bombe	*ewn bohNb*	ice cream with many flavors
une charlotte	*ewn shahr-loht*	sponge cake and pudding
une crème caramel sauce	*ewn krehm kah-rah-mehl*	egg custard served with caramel
une gaufre	*ewn gohfr*	waffle
des oeufs à la neige	*day zuh ah lah nehzh*	meringues in a custard sauce
une omelette norvégienne	*ewn nohm-leht nohr-vay-zhyehn*	baked Alaska
des poires belle hélène	*day pwahr behl ay-lehn*	poached pears with vanilla ice cream and chocolate sauce
des profiteroles	*day proh-fee-trohl*	cream puffs with chocolate sauce

Culture Capsule

Champagne is considered a dessert wine and is consumed after the meal. Some popular French after-dinner drinks include: Cognac (brandy), Armagnac (unblended brandy), Bénédictine (a blend of 150 plants and herbs), Chambord (raspberry–flavored liqueur), Cointreau (cognac blended with sweet and bitter orange peels), and Grand Marnier (orange-flavored liqueur).

If you are ordering ice cream, the following terms will help you get the type and flavor (le parfum luh pahr-fuhN) you prefer:

an ice cream	une glace	*ewn glahs*
a yogurt	un yaourt	*uhN yah-oort*
a cone	un cornet	*uhN kohr-neh*
a cup	une coupe	*ewn koop*
chocolate	au chocolat	*o shoh-koh-lah*
vanilla	à la vanille	*ah lah vah-nee-y*
strawberry	aux fraises	*o frehz*

Drink to Me Only

The French usually drink wine with dinner. The wines you might order include the following:

red wine	le vin rouge	*luh vaN roozh*
rosé wine	le vin rosé	*luh vaN ro-zay*
white wine	le vin blanc	*luh vaN blahN*
sparkling wine	le vin mousseux	*luh vaN moo-suh*
champagne	le champagne	*luh shahN-pah-nyuh*

Perhaps you do not indulge in alcohol or prefer something else to drink with your meal. During the course of a meal, you might even wish to have several different drinks: juice, water, soda, coffee, or tea. Other beverages you might enjoy during or after dinner are presented in the following table.

Beverages

coffee	un café	*uhN kah-fay*
with milk (morning)	au lait	*o leh*
espresso	express	*ehks-prehs*
with cream	crème	*krehm*
black	noir	*nwahr*
iced	glacé	*glah-say*
decaffeinated	décaféiné	*day-kah-fay-ee-nay*
tea	un thé	*uhN tay*
with lemon	au citron	*o see-trohN*
with sugar	sucré	*sew-kray*
herbal	une tisane	*ewn tee-zahn*
mineral water	de l'eau minérale	*duh lo mee-nay-rahl*
carbonated	gazeuse	*gah-zuhz*
non-carbonated	plate	*plaht*

Culture Capsule

The French do not load their drinks with ice cubes (*des glaçons*—day glah–sohN) the way many Americans do. In fact, "on the rocks" is not even an option in some places. You might even have to pay extra for ice since it's a rare commodity.

I'm Dying of Thirst

You've spent a long and tiring day sightseeing and you feel that it's time to stop and pause for a moment. You'd like to rest your weary feet and you need a quick pick-me-up. You see a French café and realize that it's the perfect place to stop, grab a nice cool drink, and people-watch. If you're thirsty, learning the irregular verb *boire* (to drink) in the following table will help you order what you like. *Boire* is similar to a "shoe verb" in that the nous and vous forms change. They do not, however, look like the infinitive. The forms for the other subject pronouns do.

Culture Capsule

Generally, French men prefer brandies (which are made by distilling wine or fermented fruit mash that has been aged in wooden casks), while French women opt for the sweeter tasting liqueurs (which are made by combining a spirit, such as brandy, with sugar and fruit or mint and other plant extracts).

Boire (To Drink)

je bois	*zhuh bwah*	I drink
tu bois	*tew bwah*	you drink
il, elle, on boit	*eel (ehl, ohN) bwah*	he, she, one drinks
nous buvons	*noo bew-vohN*	we drink
vous buvez	*voo bew-vay*	you drink
ils, elles boivent	*eel (ehl) bwahv*	they drink

The cost of a drink or meal in a French café depends upon where it is consumed. The same soft drink is cheapest if purchased at the indoor counter (because you have to stand), more expensive at an indoor table (because the scenery isn't terribly exciting), and most expensive at a table on the outside terrace (where you can take in everything that is going on). Don't be surprised to pay $3 for a 6 oz. bottle of Coke!

Un deux trois

Look at a menu from your favorite restaurant. Try ordering the meal you prefer in French.

You Can't Have It All

The food is delicious, even better than you expected. *Pâtisseries* beckon on every corner. Temptations lurk everywhere. You do not, however, want to return from vacation 20 pounds heavier. Don't eat it all, share some with a companion.

The partitive is used in French to express part of a whole, or an indefinite quantity, and is equivalent to the English *some* or *any*.

Partitive	Used Before
du (de + le)	masculine singular nouns beginning with a consonant
de la	feminine singular nouns beginning with a consonant
de l'	any singular noun beginning with a vowel
des (de + les)	all plural nouns

In a negative sentence, or before an adjective preceding a plural noun, the partitive is expressed by *de*. (No definite article is used.)

> Nous n'avons pas de ragout.
> *noo nah-vohN pah duh rah-goo*
> We don't have (any) stew.

> Je ne mange pas de fruits.
> *zhuh nuh mahNzh pah duh frwee*
> I don't eat fruit.

> Elle prépare de bons gâteaux.
> *ehl pray-pahr duh bohN gah-to*
> She prepares good cakes.

Did you ever just feel like lounging around your hotel room and being lazy, perhaps after several days of intensive sightseeing? Order the breakfast of your choice.

N° de Chambre ☐ Nombre de personnes ☐

Heure de service désirée entre 7 h et 11 h ☐

PETIT-DÉJEUNER CONTINENTAL

Corbeille de notre boulanger :
Petit pain, croissant, pain au chocolat, beurre et confiture

☐ Café au lait   ☐ Café noir   ☐ Chocolat

☐ Thé au lait   ☐ Thé nature   ☐ Thé citron

☐ Lait chaud   ☐ Lait froid   ☐ Verveine Tilleul

SUPPLEMENTS

☐ Œuf coque	15 F		☐ Œufs brouillés	20 F	
☐ Œufs au plat	20 F		☐ Œufs au plat jambon	25 F	
☐ Omelette	20 F		☐ Omelette au jambon	25 F	
☐ Jus d'Orange Pamplemousse	15 F		☐ Perrier, Evian, Vittel	10 F	

Taxes et service compris

The Pronoun *en*

Imagine that you've spent the whole day out on the town with a friend and now you'd like to go eat. You reach into your pocket and lo and behold you find that you've exhausted your cash supply. You turn to your companion and ask the logical question: "Do you have any money?" He wants to answer you in French and say: "Yes, I do." He can't use the verb *faire* (to do), however, because *faire* cannot stand alone. If he said: "Je fais de l'argent." that would mean he is making money—not something he'd want to admit. The way around this predicament is to use the pronoun *en*, a handy word, that, when used properly, will prove to be extremely helpful.

The pronoun *en* refers to previously mentioned things or places. *En* usually replaces *de* + noun and may mean some or any (of it/them), of it/them, about it/them, from it/them, or from there:

Il veut *des biscuits*.	Je ne veux pas *de salade*.
Il *en* veut.	Je n'*en* veux pas.
eel ahN vuh	*zhuh nahN vuh pah*
He wants some (of them).	I don't want any (of it).
Nous parlons *du restaurant*.	Elles sortent *du café*.
Nous *en* parlons.	Elles *en* sortent.
noo zahN pahr-lohN	*ehl zahN sohrt*
We speak about it.	They leave (it) from there.

En is always expressed in French even though it may have no English equivalent or is not expressed in English:

As-tu *de l'argent*?	Do you have any money?
Oui, j'*en* ai.	Yes, I do.

Attention!

En never refers to people.

En is used with idiomatic expressions requiring *de*:

J'ai besoin *d'un couteau*.	I need a knife.
J'*en* ai besoin.	I need one.

En is used to replace a noun (*de* + noun) after a number or a noun or adverb of quantity:

Il prépare *dix sandwiches*.	He is preparing ten sandwiches.
Il *en* prépare dix.	He is preparing ten (of them).

Il prépare une tasse *de thé*.	He is preparing a cup of tea.
Il *en* prépare une tasse.	He is preparing a cup of it.

Il prépare beaucoup *de tartes*.	He is preparing a lot of pies.
Il *en* prépare beaucoup.	He is preparing a lot (of them).

En is placed before the verb to which its meaning is tied, usually before the conjugated verb. When there are two verbs, *en* is placed before the infinitive:

J'*en* prends.	I take (eat) some.
Je n'*en* prends pas.	I don't take (eat) any.

In an affirmative command, *en* changes position and is placed immediately after the verb and is joined to it by a hyphen. The familiar command forms of *er* verbs (regular and irregular) retain their final *s* before *en*. This is to prevent the clash of two vowel sounds together. Remember to put a liaison (linking) between the final consonant and *en*:

Manges-*en*! (*mahNzh zahN*)	Eat some! (Familiar)
Mangez-*en*! (*mahN-zhay zahN*)	Eat some! (Polite)

Yes or No?

You've returned from a fabulous trip only to discover that you can't buckle your belt and you ripped your jeans as you bent over. You want to lose weight, but temptations abound everywhere. What does your conscience dictate?

Je mange du chocolat? des fruits?

Du chocolat? N'en mange pas. Des fruits? Manges-en.

1. Je mange des bonbons? des légumes?
2. Je prépare de la salade? de la mousse?
3. Je prends du poisson? des saucisses?
4. Je choisis de la glace? du yaourt?
5. J'achète de l'eau minérale? du soda?

Memory Enhancer

Quel must agree with the noun it is modifying.

Délicieux!

I'm interested in your opinion. What did you think of your meal? Was it just average, or did you give it a rave review? If you thought it was truly exceptional, you might want to exclaim your pleasure by using the adjective *quel* in the following table to express *what a...!*

Quel and Quelle

	Masculine	Feminine
Singular	quel	quelle
Plural	quels	quelles

Memory Enhancer

Adjectives describing Beauty, Age, Goodness, and Size (BAGS) usually precede the noun they modify. All other adjectives generally are placed after the nouns they modify.

Make sure to put the adjective in its proper position:

Quel repas formidable!
kehl ruh-pah fohr-mee-dahbl
What a great meal!

Quels desserts délicieux!
kehl deh-sehr day-lee-syuh
What delicious desserts!

Quelle mousse excellente!
kehl moos ehk-seh-lahNt
What an excellent mousse!

Quelles bonnes omelettes!
kehl bohn zohm-leht
What good omelettes!

Un deux trois

Comment in French about all the foods you eat in one day.

Merci Beaucoup

I knew you'd love French food. Now you want to tell me just how much you enjoyed it. Use the correct form of *quel* to express how you felt about what you ate and drank: soup, steak, wine, salad, cheese, and mousse.

Don't forget to ask for the check at the end of your meal:

L'addition, s'il vous plaît.
lah-dee-syohN seel voo pleh
The check, please.

The Least You Need to Know

➤ To get what you want in a restaurant, learn the terms for the foods you like to eat and the way you like them prepared.

➤ Use the partitive (*de, du, de la, de l', des*) to express *some*.

➤ The pronoun *en* expresses *some* and may replace the partitive.

➤ To make an exclamation, use *quel + noun*. When using an adjective, make sure to put it in its proper place.

Chapter 18

Fun and Games

In This Chapter

➤ Fun things to do

➤ The irregular verbs *vouloir* (to want) and *pouvoir* (to be able to)

➤ Extending, accepting, and refusing invitations

➤ Using adverbs to describe abilities

You've seen the sights, collected mementos, and purchased souvenirs and designer clothing. You feel much better, too, now that you have eaten. It's time to have fun and enjoy yourself, or simply to take a pause and relax.

Are you off to the sea to engage in water sports, up to the mountains for skiing or hiking, onto the links for a round of golf, or onto the courts for a brisk tennis match? Are you a film buff or a theater-goer? Do you enjoy a lively opera or an elegant ballet? Perhaps the game's the thing and you'll spend some time with a one-armed bandit in a luxurious casino. This chapter will help you do it all, invite someone to accompany you, and describe your abilities.

Sports Are My Life

My husband loves to golf; his clubs have seen nearly as many countries as we have! I adore the beach and like nothing better than to feel the sand between my toes as I gaze out at the ocean. Whether you're a sports fanatic or a beach lover, you'll need some specific phrases and terms to make your preferences known. The following table provides a list of sports and outdoor activities.

Use the verb *faire* when talking about engaging in a sport:

Je fais du volley-ball.
(I play volleyball.)

Sports

One Plays	On fait	OhN feh
aerobics	de l'aérobic (m.)	*duh lahy-roh-beek*
baseball	du base-ball	*dew bays-bohl*
basketball	du basket-ball	*dew bahs-keht bohl*
bicycling	du vélo	*dew vay-lo*
boating	du canotage	*dew kah-noh-tahzh*
bodybuilding	de la musculation	*duh lah mew-skew-lah-syohN*
canoeing	du canoë	*dew kah-noh-ay*
cycling	du cyclisme	*dew see-kleez-muh*
deep-sea fishing	de la pêche sous-marine	*duh la pehsh soo-mah-reen*
diving	du plongeon	*dew plohN-zhohN*
fishing	de la pêche	*duh lah pehsh*
football	du football américain	*dew foot-bohl ah-may-ree-kaN*
golf	du golf	*dew gohlf*
hockey	du hockey	*dew oh-kee*
horseback riding	de l'équitation (f.)	*duh lay-kee-tah-syohN*
hunting	de la chasse	*duh lah shahs*
jogging	du jogging	*dew zhoh-geeng*
mountain climbing	de l'alpinisme (m.), de l'escalade (f.)	*duh lahl-pee-neez-muh, duh lehs-kah-lahd*
parasailing	du parachutisme	*dew pah-rah-shew-teez-muh*
ping-pong	du ping-pong	*dew peeng-pohNg*
roller skating	du patin à roulettes	*dew pah-taN ah roo-leht*
sailing	du bateau à voiles	*dew bah-to ah vwahl*
scuba diving	de la plongée sous-marine	*duh lah plohN-zhay soo-mah-reen*
skating	du patin	*dew pah-taN*
skiing	du ski	*dew skee*
soccer	du football	*dew foot-bohl*

One Plays	On fait	OhN feh
surfing	du surf	*dew sewrf*
swimming	de la natation	*duh lah nah-tah-syohN*
tennis	du tennis	*dew tuh-nees*
volleyball	du volley-ball	*dew voh-lee bohl*
waterskiing	du ski nautique	*dew skee no-teek*
windsurfing	de la planche à voile	*duh lah plahNsh ah vwahl*

Use *du* (*de + le*) before the name of a masculine, singular sport that begins with a consonant.

Use *de l'* before the name of any sport that begins with a vowel.

Use *de la* before the name of any feminine, singular sport.

Want to Join Me?

It really isn't much fun to play alone. Why not ask someone to join you? To extend an invitation, you may use the irregular verbs *vouloir* (to want) and *pouvoir* (to be able to) in the following tables. Both verbs have similar conjugations. They are similar to "shoe verbs" in that their nous and vous forms begin like the infinitive, while their other forms undergo a change.

Vouloir (To Want)

je veux	*zhuh vuh*	I want
tu veux	*tew vuh*	you want
il, elle, on veut	*eel, (ehl, ohN) vuh*	he (she, one) wants
nous voulons	*noo voo-lohN*	we want
vous voulez	*voo voo-lay*	you want
ils, elles veulent	*eel (ehl) vuhl*	they want

Pouvoir (To Be Able to [Can])

je peux	*zhuh puh*	I am able to (can)
tu peux	*tew puh*	you are able to (can)
il, elle, on peut	*eel, ehl, ohN puh*	he, she, one is able to (can)
nous pouvons	*noo poo-vohN*	we can
vous pouvez	*voo poo-vay*	you can
ils, elles peuvent	*eel, (ehl) puhv*	they can

To invite someone to do something, you would ask:

Vous voulez (Tu veux) + infinitive of the verb
(Do you want to...?)

Vous voulez (Tu veux) faire du ski? Do you want
to go skiing?

or

Vous pouvez (Tu peux) + infinitive of the verb
(Can you...?)

Vous pouvez (Tu peux) aller à la pêche?
Can you go fishing?

Un deux trois

In French, write a list of all the sports
that you can play and the seasons in
which you play them. For example:
Je peux faire de la natation en été.

Each sport has its own particular playing field or milieu. When you're ready for some
exercise refer to the following table to choose the place where you would go to participate in the sport or activity:

Where to Go

Place	French	Pronunciation
beach	la plage	*lah plahzh*
course (golf)	le parcours	*luh pahr-koor*
court	le court	*luh koort*
court (jai alai)	le fronton	*luh frohN-tohN*
field	le terrain	*luh teh-raN*
gymnasium	le gymnase	*luh zheem-nahz*
mountain	la montagne	*lah mohN-tah-nyuh*
ocean	l'océan (m.)	*loh-see-ahN*
park	le parc	*luh pahrk*
path	le sentier	*luh sahN-tyay*
pool	la piscine	*lah pee-seen*
rink	la patinoire	*lah pah-tee-nwahr*
sea	la mer	*lah mehr*
slope	la piste	*lah peest*
stadium	le stade	*luh stahd*
track	la piste	*lah peest*

I'll Meet You There

Various traveling companions have been invited for a day of sports. Say that the given subjects can engage in the following sports and say where they want to go.

Example:

> je (swimming)
> Je peux faire de la natation.
> Je veux aller à la plage.

1. tu (tennis) _____ .
2. nous (golf) _____ .
3. vous (fishing) _____ .
4. elle (baseball) _____ .
5. ils (skating) _____ .

The Necessary Equipment

You probably don't want to lug your sports equipment with you on vacation. You certainly wouldn't want it to get lost in the shuffle. So if you are interested in borrowing or renting equipment you would say:

I need	I need	Could you lend (rent) me
Il me faut	J'ai besoin de	Pourriez-vous me prêter (louer)
eel muh foh	*zhay buh-zwaN duh*	*poor-yay voo muh preh-tay (loo-ay)*

s'il vous plaît
please
seel voo pleh

Refer to the following table for more examples.

Sports Equipment (l'équipement sportif [lay-keep mahN spohr-teef])

Equipment	French	Pronunciation
ball		
football, soccer	un ballon	*uhN bah-lohN*
jai alai	une pelote	*ewn puh-loht*
baseball, tennis	une balle	*ewn bahl*

continues

Sports Equipment (l'équipement sportif [lay-keep mahN spohr-teef]) (cont.)

Equipment	French	Pronunciation
bat	une batte	*ewn baht*
bicycle	un vélo	*uhN vay-lo*
	une bicyclette	*ewn bee-see-kleht*
boat	un bateau	*uhN bah-to*
boots (ski)	des chaussures de ski (f.)	*day sho-sewr duh skee*
canoe	un canoë	*uhN kah-noh-ay*
diving suit	un scaphandre	*uhN skah-fahNdr*
fishing rod	une canne à pêche	*ewn kahn ah pehsh*
flippers	des nageoires (f.)	*day nahzh-wahr*
goggles	des lunettes protectrices (f.)	*day lew-neht proh-tehk-trees*
golf clubs	des club de golf (m.)	*day klewb duh gohlf*
helmet (diver's)	un casque de scaphandre	*uhN kahsk duh skah-phahNdr*
jogging shoes	des joggers	*day zhohg-gehr*
jogging suit	un survêt	*uhN sewr-veh*
knee pads	des genouillères	*day zhuh-noo-yehr*
mitt	un gant	*uhN gahN*
net	un filet	*uhN fee-leh*
poles (ski)	des bâtons (m.)	*day bah-tohN*
puck	une rondelle (Canada)	*ewn rohN-dehl*
	un palet (France)	*uhn pah-leh*
racket	une raquette	*ewn rah-keht*
sailboard	une planche à voile	*ewn plahNsh ah vwahl*
skateboard	une planche à roulettes	*ewn plahNsh ah roo-leht*
skates	des patins (m.)	*day pah-taN*
ice	à glace	*ah glahs*
roller	à roulettes	*ah roo-leht*
ski bindings	des fixations de ski	*day feek-sah-syohN duh skee*
skis	des skis (m.)	*day skee*
stick (hockey)	une crosse	*ewn krohs*
waterskis	des skis nautiques (m.)	*day skee no-teek*
surfboard	une planche de surf	*ewn plahNsh duh sewrf*
weights	des haltères (m.)	*day zahl-tehr*
wet suit	une combinaison	*ewn kohN-bee-neh-zohN*
	de plongée	*duh plohN-zhay*

Doing the Inviting

Tomorrow's forecast is perfect for the sports-minded. Pick up the phone and invite someone to go with you to the proper place so that you can go: hiking, skiing, jogging, skating, mountain-climbing, or diving.

Memorize the irregular verbs *vouloir* (to want) and *pouvoir* (to be able to) so that you can easily extend an invitation.

Un deux trois

Express in French the equipment you need to play all the sports you love.

A Polite Yes

Whether you've been invited to participate in a sport or an outing, visit a museum, or just stay at someone's home, the phrases in the following table will allow you to graciously accept any invitation extended to you:

Acceptance

Phrase	French	Pronunciation
With pleasure.	Avec plaisir.	*ah-vehk pleh-zeer*
Of course.	Bien entendu.	*byaN nahN-tahN-dew*
Of course.	Bien sûr.	*byaN sewr*
That's a good idea.	C'est une bonne idée.	*seh tewn bohn ee-day*
Great!	Chouette!	*shoo-eht*
O.K. (I agree)	D'accord.	*dah-kohr*
And how! You bet!	Et comment!	*ay koh-mahN*
There's no doubt about it.	Il n'y a pas d'erreur.	*eel nyah pah deh-ruhr*
Why not?	Pourquoi pas?	*poor-kwah pah*
If you want to.	Si tu veux (vous voulez)	*see tew vuh (voo voo-lay)*
Gladly.	Volontiers!	*voh-lohN-tyay*

A Polite Refusal and an Excuse

What if you really can't go to an event because of some prior engagement or commitment? Or, perhaps you just feel like being alone. You can cordially refuse any invitation without hurting anyone's feelings by expressing your regrets or giving an excuse.

You might use an expression from the table below:

Regrets and Excuses

Phrase	French	Pronunciation
It's impossible.	C'est impossible.	*seh taN-poh-seebl*
Not again!	Encore!	*ahN-kohr*
I don't feel like it.	Je n'ai pas envie.	*zhuh nay pah zahN-vee*
I can't.	Je ne peux pas.	*zhuh nuh puh pah*
I'm not free.	Je ne suis pas libre.	*zhuh nuh swee pah leebr*
I don't want to.	Je ne veux pas.	*zhuh nuh vuh pah*
I'm sorry.	Je regrette.	*zhuh ruh-greht*
I'm sorry.	Je suis désolé(e).	*zhuh swee day-zoh-lay*
I'm tired.	Je suis fatigué(e).	*zhuh swee fah-tee-gay*
I'm busy.	Je suis occupé(e).	*zhuh swee zoh-kew-pay*

Un deux trois

Whenever a friend invites you to do something or go somewhere, think of as many suitable responses as you can in French.

I Really Don't Care

We all have days when we're very wishy-washy. One minute we're gung-ho about an idea, and the next we don't even contemplate it. If you can't make up your mind, or if you are indifferent to an idea, you might use one of the phrases from the following table:

Expressing Indifference and Indecision

Phrase	French	Pronunciation
It depends.	Ça dépend.	*sah day-pahN*
It's all the same to me.	Ça m'est égal.	*sah meh tay-gahl*
Whatever you want.	Comme tu veux (vous voulez).	*kohm tew vuh (voo voo-lay)*
I really don't know.	Je ne sais pas trop.	*zhuh nuh seh pah tro*
Perhaps. Maybe.	Peut-être.	*puh-tehtr*

Other Things to Do

Perhaps sports aren't part of your agenda. There are plenty of other activities you can pursue to have a good time. The phrases in the following table will give you the tools to make many other intriguing suggestions:

Places to Go and Things to Do

The Place	Le Lieu	The Activity	L'Activité
ballet	aller au ballet	see the dancers	voir les danseurs
beach	aller à la plage	swim sunbathe	nager prendre un bain de soleil
casino	aller au casino	gamble	jouer
concert	aller au concert	listen to the orchestra	écouter l'orchestre
disco	aller à une discothèque	dance	danser
hike	faire une randonnée	see the sights	voir les sites pittoresques
mall	aller au centre commercial	go window shopping	faire du lèche-vitrines
movies	aller au cinéma	see a film	voir un film
opera	aller à l'opéra	listen to the singers	écouter les chanteurs
stay in one's room	rester dans sa chambre	play cards	jouer aux cartes

Will You Be Joining Us?

Let's say you've received a ton of invitations; one friend would like you to go window shopping, while another is urging you to go surfing. You also have conflicting plans for the evening: Your husband wants to go to the movies, but your daughter is eager to go to a disco. And, if that isn't enough, business colleagues have even asked you to spend the evening at the opera! Fashion a reply to all these invitations using the phrases you've learned so far.

Attention!

Should you delight in going to the opera, ballet, theater, or a concert, don't forget to bring along les jumelles (*lay zhew-mehl*) (f.)— binoculars.

1. shopping _____ .
2. surfing _____ .
3. movies _____ .
4. discotheque _____ .
5. opera _____ .

At the Shore

Did you ever arrive at the pool or beach only to realize that you forgot to bring your suntan lotion or some other essential item? Your day could be ruined unnecessarily. Remember to pack the items in the following table for a pleasant day in the sun:

Beach Stuff

beach ball	un ballon de plage	*uhN bah-lohN duh plahzh*
beach chair	une chaise longue	*ewn shehz lohNg*
beach towel	un drap de bain	*uhN drah dbaN*
sunglasses	des lunettes de soleil (f.)	*day lew-neht duh soh-lehy*
suntan lotion	la lotion solaire	*lah loh-syohN soh-lehr*
	la crème solaire	*lah krehm soh-lehr*
suntan oil	l'huile solaire	*lweel soh-lehr*

Culture Capsule

In France and on some of the French islands of the Caribbean, it is not uncommon to see women sunbathing topless, or to see men (and women) in very thin string (*ficelle*) and thong bikinis. Don't gawk! The French attitude toward sunbathing is much more relaxed than the American; to blend in, you might have to join in.

At the Movies and on T.V.

Do you crave some quiet relaxation? Is the weather bad? Do you feel like getting away from everyone and everything? There's always a movie or T.V. It seems that cable has invaded the planet and can accommodate anyone who needs a few carefree hours in the room. So if you want to be entertained, consult the following table for the possibilities.

What kind of film are they showing?	What's on T.V.?
On passe quel genre de film?	Qu'est-ce qu'il y a à la télé?
ohN pahs kehl zhahNr duh feelm	*kehs keel yah ah lah tay-lay*

Movies and Television Programs

adventure film	un film d'aventure	*uhN feelm dah-vahN-tewr*
cartoon	un dessin animé	*uhN deh-saN ah-nee-may*
comedy	un film comique	*uhN feelm koh-meek*
documentary	un documentaire	*uhN doh-kew-mahN-tehr*
drama	un drame	*uhN drahm*
game show	un jeu	*uhN zhuh*
horror movie	un film d'horreur	*uhN feelm doh-ruhr*
love story	un film d'amour	*uhN feelm dah-moor*
mystery	un mystère	*uhN mees-tehr*
news	les informations (f.)	*lay zaN-fohr-mah-syohN*
police story	un film policier	*uhN feelm poh-lee-syay*
science-fiction film	un film de science-fiction	*uhN feelm duh see-ahNs-feek-syohN*
soap opera	un feuilleton (mélodramatique)	*uhN fuhy-tohN (may-loh-drah-mah-teek)*
spy movie	un film d'espionnage	*uhN feelm dehs-pee-yoh-nazh*
talk show	une causerie	*ewn koz-ree*
weather	la météo	*lay may-tay-o*
western	un western	*uhN wehs-tehrn*

The abbreviations in the following table will help you when choosing a movie or theater:

Movie Abbreviations

INT-18 ans	Interdit aux moins de 18 ans	Forbidden for those under 18
V.O.	Version originale	Original version, subtitled
V.F.	Version française	Dubbed in French
T.R.	Tarif réduit	Reduced rate
C.V.	Carte vermeille	"Red" senior citizens' card

Culture Capsule

In French movie theaters, an usher, usually a young woman (une ouvreuse—*ewn noo-vruhz*), will show you to your seat and expect a tip (un pourboire—*uhN poor-bwahr*). Commercials are often shown for at least 15 minutes before the main feature. During that time the usher comes around with a selection of candy and ice cream. Do you crave popcorn? Sorry, it's not sold!

What Did You Think?

Use the following phrases to express your enjoyment of a film or program.

I love it!	J'adore!	*zhah-dohr*
It's a good movie.	C'est un bon film.	*seh tuhN bohN feelm*
It's amusing!	C'est amusant!	*seh tah-mew-zahN*
It's great!	C'est génial!	*seh zhay-nyahl*
It's moving!	C'est émouvant!	*seh tay-moo-vahN*
It's original!	C'est original!	*seh toh-ree-zhee-nahl*

If you are less than thrilled with the show, try these phrases:

I hate it!	Je déteste!	*zhuh day-tehst*
It's a bad movie!	C'est un mauvais film.	*seh tuhN mo-veh feelm*
It's a loser!	C'est un navet!	*seh tuhN nah-veh*
It's garbage!	C'est bidon!	*seh bee-dohN*

| It's the same old thing! | C'est toujours la même chose! | *seh too-zhoor lah mehm shohz* |
| It's too violent! | C'est trop violent! | *seh tro vee-oh-lahN* |

I Think...

Using the phrases you've learned, give your opinion of the following types of movies:

1. a love story _____ .
2. a science-fiction film _____ .
3. a horror film _____ .
4. a police film _____ .
5. a mystery _____ .
6. a cartoon _____ .

Take a Hike

With so much emphasis today on physical fitness and staying in shape, many people find it rewarding to go for a long walk. The following table will help you identify the things you see along the way, whether you take a leisurely hike, a stroll in the country, or a tour of the city:

Un deux trois

Look at the T.V. and movie sections of your newspaper. Express in French your opinions of the programs you watch and the movies you've seen.

Nature calls

bridge	le pont	*luh pohN*
farm	la ferme	*lah fehrm*
fields	les champs (m.)	*lay shahN*
flowers	les fleurs (f.)	*lay fluhr*
forest	la forêt	*lah foh-reh*
lake	le lac	*luh lahk*
landscape	le paysage	*luh pay-ee-sahzh*
moon	la lune	*lah lewn*
mountains	les montagnes (f.)	*lay mohN-tah-nyuh*
ocean	l'océan (m.)	*loh-say-ahN*
pond	l'étang (m.)	*lay-tahN*

continues

Nature Calls (cont.)

river	la rivière	*lah reev-yehr*
sky	le ciel	*luh syehl*
stars	les étoiles (f.)	*lay zay-twahl*
stream	le ruisseau	*luh rwee-so*
trees	les arbres (m.)	*lay zahrbr*
valley	la vallée	*lah vah-lay*
view	la vue	*lah vew*
village	le village	*luh vee-lahzh*
waterfall	la cascade	*lah kahs-kahd*
woods	les bois (m.)	*lay bwah*

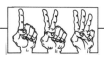

Un deux trois

Look at the CD boxes of your favorite musical groups or bands. In French, name the instruments they use.

At a Concert

A friend has invited you to the Opéra in Paris, but you feel a little hesistant about going. Although you're familiar with some French composers and their works (*Carmen,* by Bizet, is your personal favorite), you're afraid you won't be able to hold up your end of the conversation. The names of the instruments in the following table should assist you in expressing your ideas:

Musical Instruments

accordion	l'accordéon (m.)	*lah-kohr-day-ohN*
cello	le violoncelle	*luh vee-oh-lohN-sehl*
clarinet	la clarinette	*lah klah-ree-neht*
drum	le tambour	*luh tahN-boor*
drums	la batterie	*lah bah-tree*
flute	la flûte	*lah flewt*
guitar	la guitare	*lah gee-tahr*
harp	la harpe	*lah ahrp*
horn	le cor	*luh kohr*
oboe	le hautbois	*luh o-bwah*
piano	le piano	*luh pyah-no*
piccolo	le piccolo	*luh pee-koh-lo*
saxophone	le saxophone	*luh sahk-soh-fohn*

trombone	le trombone	*luh trohN-bohn*
trumpet	la trompette	*lah trohN-peht*
violin	le violon	*luh vee-oh-lohN*

Jouer à vs. Jouer de

In English, we use the verb *to play* whether we are referring to the playing of an instrument or the playing of a sport. The French, however, make a distinction. The verb *jouer* means to play. When followed by the preposition *de* + definite article (*du, de la, de l', des*) *jouer* refers to the playing of musical instruments:

Memory Enhancer

Remember your contractions:

à + le = au   de + le = du

à + les = aux   de + les = des

Il joue du piano.	Elle joue de la
eel zhoo dew pyah-no	clarinette.
	ehl zhoo duh lah
	klah-ree-neht
He plays the piano.	She plays the clarinet.

When referring to sports or to games (such as card or board games) *jouer* is followed by *à* + definite article (*au, à la, à l', aux*):

Ils jouent au tennis.	Elles jouent aux cartes.
eel zhoo o teh-nees	*ehl zhoo o kahrt*
They play tennis.	They play cards.

Let's Play

Would you use *jouer à* or *jouer de* to complete the following sentences?

1. Nous _____ football.
2. Vous _____ flûte.
3. Tu _____ guitare.
4. Ils _____ tennis.
5. Je _____ piano.
6. Elle _____ cartes.

Memory Enhancer

If the masculine form of the adjective ends in a consonant, first change it to the feminine form and then add *ment.*

Just How Good Are You?

Adverbs are often used to describe how well you do something, such as "he plays the cello *beautifully.*" (In English, most adverbs end in *ly.*) In French, adverbs are used for the same purpose, and they generally end in *ment.*

Adverbs are formed by adding *ment* to the masculine, singular form of adjectives that end in a vowel. If the masculine form of the adjective ends in a consonant, first change it to the feminine form and then add *ment.* This works quite well as long as you look for the proper letter at the end of the adjective and remember the feminine forms. The following tables show you just how easy this is:

Adverbs Formed from Masculine Adjectives

Masculine Adjective	Adverb	Meaning
facile (*fah-seel*)	facilement (*fah-seel-mahN*)	easily
passionné (*pah-syoh-nay*)	passionnément (*pah-syoh-nay-mahN*)	enthusiastically
probable (*proh-bahbl*)	probablement (*proh-bahbl-mahN*)	probably
rapide (*rah-peed*)	rapidement (*rah-peed-mahN*)	rapidly, quickly
sincère (*saN-sehr*)	sincèrement (*saN-sehr-mahN*)	sincerely
vrai (*vreh*)	vraiment (*vreh-mahN*)	truly, really

Adverbs Formed from Feminine Adjectives

Masculine Adjective	Feminine Adjective	Adverb	Meaning
lent (*lahN*)	lente (*lahNt*)	lentement (*lahNt-mahN*)	slowly
certain (*sehr-taN*)	certaine (*sehr-tehn*)	certainement (*sehr-tehn-mahN*)	certainly
seul (*suhl*)	seule (*suhl*)	seulement (*suhl-mahN*)	only

Masculine Adjective	Feminine Adjective	Adverb	Meaning
actif (*ahk-teef*)	active (*ahk-teev*)	activement (*ahk-teev-mahN*)	actively
complet (*kohN-pleh*)	complète (*kohN-pleht*)	complètement (*kohN-pleht-mahN*)	completely
continuel (*kohN-tee-new-ehl*)	continuelle (*kohN-tee-new-ehl*)	continuellement (*kohN-tee-new-ehl-mahN*)	continuously
doux (*doo*)	douce (*doos*)	doucement (*doos-mahN*)	gently
fier (*fyehr*)	fière (*fyehr*)	fièrement (*fyehr-mahN*)	proudly
franc (*frahN*)	franche (*frahNsh*)	franchement (*frahNsh-mahN*)	frankly
sérieux (*say-ree-yuh*)	sérieuse (*say-ree-uhz*)	sérieusement (*say-ree-uhz-mahN*)	seriously

The following table lists two irregular adverb formations:

Irregular Adverbs

Masculine Adjective	Feminine Adjective	Adverb	Meaning
bref (*brehf*)	brève (*brehv*)	brièvement (*bree-ehv-mahN*)	briefly
gentil (*zhahN-tee*)	gentille (*zhahN-tee*)	gentiment (*zhahN-tee-mahN*)	gently

Exceptions to the Rule

Life would be so easy if there were no exceptions to the rules. This, however, is not the case with French adverbs. Fortunately, the irregularities are easy to understand and should present no difficulties in adverb formation.

As shown in the following table, some adverbs are formed by changing a silent *e* from the adjective to *é* before the adverbial *ment* ending.

When forming adverbs, watch out for irregular adjectives:

Elle travaille *intensément.*

More Irregular Adverbs

Adjective	Adverb	Meaning
énorme (*ay-nohrm*)	énormément (*ay-nohr-may-mahN*)	enormously
intense (*aN-tahNs*)	intensément (*aN-tahN-say-mahN*)	intensely
précis (*pray-see*)	précisément (*pray-see-zay-mahN*)	precisely
profond (*proh-fohN*)	profondément (*proh-fohN-day-mahN*)	profoundly

Adjectives ending in *ant* and *ent* have adverbs ending in *amment* and *emment*, respectively, as shown in the following table:

Even More Irregular Adverbs

Adjective	Adverb	Meaning
constant (*kohN-stahN*)	constamment (*kohN-stah-mahN*)	constantly
courant (*koo-rahN*)	couramment (*koo-rah-mahN*)	fluently
différent (*dee-fay-rahN*)	différemment (*dee-fay-reh-mahN*)	differently
évident (*ay-vee-dahN*)	évidemment (*ay-vee-deh-mahN*)	evidently
récent (*ray-sahN*)	récemment (*ray-seh-mahN*)	recently

Be careful with the adverbs in the following table; they have distinct forms from adjectives:

Very Irregular Adverbs

Adjective	Adverb
bon (*bohN*)/good	bien (*byaN*)/well
mauvais (*moh-veh*)/bad	mal (*mahl*)/badly
meilleur (*meh-yuhr*)/better	mieux (*myuh*)/better
petit (*puh-tee*)/little	peu (*puh*)/little

Elle est petite et elle mange peu.
ehl eh puh-teet ay ehl mahNzh puh
She is little and she eats little.

Ils sont de bons musiciens et ils jouent bien
de la guitare.
*eel sohN duh bohN mew-zee-syaN ay eel zhoo
byaN duh lah gee-tahr*
They are good musicians and they play the
guitar well.

Some adverbs and adverbial expressions are not
formed from adjectives at all and, therefore, do
not end in *ment.* The following table gives the
most common adverbs that follow this rule. These
familiar, high-frequency words are extremely
useful in everyday conversation.

Memory Enhancer

If you can't think of the adverb, or if
one does not exist, use the phrases
d'une façon (dewn fah-sohN) or
d'une manière (dewn mah-nyehr),
both of which express *in a way, in a
manner,* or *in a fashion.*

Adverbs and Adverbial Expressions Not Formed from Adjectives

Adverb	Pronunciation	Meaning
alors	*ah-lohrs*	then
après	*ah-preh*	afterward
aussi	*o-see*	also, too
beaucoup	*bo-koo*	much
bientôt	*byaN-to*	soon
comme	*kohm*	as
d'habitude	*dah-bee-tewd*	usually, generally
déjà	*day-zhah*	already
encore	*ahN-kohr*	still, yet, again
enfin	*ahN-faN*	finally, at last
ensemble	*ahN-sahNbl*	together
ensuite	*ahN-sweet*	then, afterwards
ici	*ee-see*	here
là	*lah*	there
loin	*lwaN*	far
longtemps	*lohN-tahN*	a long time
maintenant	*maNt-nahN*	now
même	*mehm*	even
moins	*mwaN*	less
parfois	*pahr-fwah*	sometimes
plus	*plew*	more
près	*preh*	near

continues

Adverbs and Adverbial Expressions Not Formed from Adjectives (cont.)

Adverb	Pronunciation	Meaning
presque	*prehsk*	almost
puis	*pwee*	then
quelquefois	*kehl-kuh-fwah*	sometimes
si	*see*	so
souvent	*soo-vahN*	often
tard	*tahr*	late
tôt	*to*	soon, early
toujours	*too-zhoor*	always, still
tout	*too*	quite, entirely
tout à coup	*too tah koo*	suddenly
tout à fait	*too tah feh*	entirely
tout de suite	*toot sweet*	immediately
très	*treh*	very
trop	*tro*	too much
vite	*veet*	quickly

En 10 Minutes

Adverbs modify verbs and tell how well you do something. To form most adverbs in French, add *ment* (the equivalent of the English *ly*) to the masculine form of an adjective ending in a vowel.

There are many irregular adverbs to memorize.

Position of Adverbs

Adverbs are generally placed after the verb they modify. Sometimes, however, the position of the adverb varies and the adverb is placed where we would logically put an English adverb.

D'habitude il joue bien au football.
dah-bee-tewd eel zhoo byaN o foot-bohl.
Usually he plays soccer well.

Il joue très bien au football.
eel zhoo treh byaN o foot-ball
He plays soccer very well.

What Do You Do Well?

How's your cooking? Can you carry a tune? Are you light on your feet or do you stomp on your partner's toes on the dance floor? We each perform according to our own individual abilities. Express how you fare at the following activities by using adverbs:

Example: parler anglais   Je parle anglais couramment.

1. parler français _____ .
2. jouer du piano _____ .
3. jouer au golf _____ .
4. cuisiner (cook) _____ .
5. penser (think) _____ .
6. travailler _____ .
7. voyager _____ .
8. chanter _____ .
9. danser _____ .
10. nager _____ .

The Least You Need to Know

➤ The verb *faire* is used to express participation in a sport.

➤ *Vouloir* (to want) and *pouvoir* (to be able) + a verb infinitive can be used to propose, accept, and refuse invitations.

➤ *Jouer* + *à* + definite article (*au, à la, à l', aux*) is used to discuss playing a sport or game. *Jouer* + *de* + definite article is used to discuss playing a musical instrument.

➤ Many adverbs are formed by adding *ment* to adjectives ending in a vowel.

Part 4
Time Out: Problems

No one likes to encounter problems, especially when traveling in a foreign country. Unfortunately, life's little annoyances tend to crop up at the most inopportune times. In Part 4, you'll learn how to deal with those bothersome inconveniences that interfere with your daily routine and threaten to ruin the best of times.

The minor problems—forgetting your toothbrush, tearing an item of clothing, running out of film, wearing down the soles of your shoes, making a phone call, or sending a letter or package—are easy to deal with. Other situations are more serious and require a more extensive knowledge of the language and fast attention: an illness, a torn contact lens, broken glasses, or a forgotten prescription.

Part 4 covers a multitude of possible problems and the phrases you'll need to deal with them as effortlessly and quickly as possible.

Chapter 19

Bad Hair? Torn Jacket? Broken Glasses? Personal Services

In This Chapter

➤ Personal services

➤ Problems and solutions

➤ Using stress pronouns

➤ Making comparisons

You've been traveling and having a wonderful time. All of a sudden there is a problem that just can't wait: your roots have surfaced in record time, you've spilled mustard on your new white silk shirt, your contact lens has torn, you've broken a heel on your shoe, or your five-year-old has dropped your camera, smashing the lens. You're not home, and you're very hesitant about what to do. Ask the concierge of your hotel or consult *les pages jaunes* (*lay pahzh zhon*), the yellow pages. Don't worry, the French have competent, expert technicians; all you have to do is know what to say to get the job done. This chapter will make that task easy.

I'm Having a Bad Hair Day

You're on vacation and feeling quite carefree; the sky's the limit. You pass by a salon and are struck by a sudden whim to return home with a brand new look. Why not be daring? You're in Paris, the world-famous center of *haute couture* (high style and fashion). You want a more tantalizing "you," and this is the place to get it.

Memory Enhancer

If you're very particular and think you'll have trouble explaining exactly what you want to say in French, simply use: *Je voudrais* (zhuh voo–dreh) and then show the stylist a picture from a newspaper or magazine.

In the past, men went *chez le coiffeur* (to the barber's) while women were accustomed to going *au salon de beauté* (to the beauty parlor). Today, these establishments have become more or less unisex with men and women demanding more or less the same services. To get what you want, simply ask:

Could you give me...
Pourriez-vous me donner...
poo-ryay voo muh doh-nay

I would like...
Je voudrais...
zhuh voo-dreh

Please
S'il vous plaît
seel voo pleh

Today's salons provide the services listed in the following table:

Hair Care

Phrase	French	Pronunciation
a blunt cut	une coupe en carré	*ewn koop ahN kah-ray*
a coloring (vegetable)	une teinture (végétale)	*ewn taN-tewr (vay-zhay-tahl)*
a facial	un massage facial	*uhN mah-sahzh fah-syahl*
a haircut	une coupe de cheveux	*ewn koop duh shuh-vuh*
highlights	des reflets (m.)	*day ruh-fleh*
layers	une coupe dégradée	*ewn koop day-grah-day*
a manicure	une manucure	*ewn mah-new-kewr*
a pedicure	une pédicurie	*ewn pay-dee-kew-ree*
a permanent	une permanente	*ewn pehr-mah-nahNt*
a rinse	un rinçage colorant	*uhN raN-sahzh koh-loh-rahN*
a set	une mise en plis	*ewn mee-zohN plee*
a shampoo	un shampooing	*uhN shahN-pwaN*
a trim	une coupe	*ewn koop*
a waxing	une épilation	*ewn ay-pee-lah-syohN*

The following table gives you the phrases you need to get other services. Use the following phrase to preface your request:

Could you please...?
Pourriez-vous...s'il vous plaît?
poo-ryay voo...seel voo pleh

Other Services

Service	French	Pronunciation
blow dry my hair	me donner un brushing	*muh doh-nay uhN bruh-sheeng*
curl my hair	me friser les cheveux	*muh free-zay lay shuh-vuh*
shave my beard	me raser la barbe	*muh rah-zay lah bahrb*
my mustache	la moustache	*lah moo-stahsh*
straighten my hair	me défriser les cheveux	*muh day-free-zay lay shuh-vuh*
trim my bangs	me rafraîchir la frange	*muh rah-freh-sheer lah frahNzh*
trim my beard	me rafraîchir la barbe	*muh rah-freh-sheer*
sideburns	les pattes	*lay paht*

Culture Capsule

If you're interested in a new look, why not pick up a copy of *La Coiffure de Paris,* a technical magazine that has become the professional hairdresser's bible in Europe?

Just a Trim, Please

It is hard enough getting the haircut and style you want when there is no language barrier; imagine the disasters that could befall your poor head in a foreign country? The following phrases will help you make your styling and coloring preferences clear:

I prefer my hair...
Je préfère mes cheveux...
zhuh pray-fehr may shuh-vuh

long	longs	*lohN*
medium	mi-longs	*mee-lohN*
short	courts	*koor*
curly	bouclés	*boo-klay*
straight	raides (lissés)	*rehd (lee-say)*
wavy	frisés	*free-zay*
auburn	auburn, châtain clair	*oh-bewrn, shah-taN klehr*

black	noir	*nwahr*
blond	blond	*blohN*
brunette	brun	*bruhN*
chestnut brown	châtain	*shah-taN*
red	roux	*roo*
a darker color	une teinte plus foncée	*ewn taNt plew fohN-say*
a lighter color	une teinte plus claire	*ewn taNt plew klehr*
the same color	la même couleur	*lah mehm koo-luhr*

Culture Capsule

Cover that gray with a natural-looking color! Let a student at L'Oréal headquarters in Clichy, a suburb of Paris, work miracles on you. In the early 1900s, Eugène Schueller, a Parisian hairdresser, developed the first permanent hair color using an oxidation process. Elated with his success, Mr. Schueller continued to do extensive research in the hair care field, created many new products (shampoos, setting lotions, conditioners, mousse) and launched the company that is today L'Oréal.

Are you allergic to any products or specific chemicals? Are you sensitive to smells? Do you hate it when your hair feels like cardboard? If you don't like certain hair care products, don't be shy. Tell the hairdresser:

Ne mettez pas de (d')...s'il vous plaît.
nuh meh-tay pah duh ...seel voo pleh
Don't put any...please

conditioner	après-shampooing	*ah-preh shahN-pwaN*
	shampooing démelant	*shahN-pwaN day-muh-lahN*
gel	gel coiffant (m.)	*zhehl kwah-fahN*
hairspray	laque (f.)	*lahk*
lotion	lotion (f.)	*loh-syohN*
mousse	mousse coiffante (f.)	*moos kwah-fahN*
shampoo	shampooing (m.)	*shahN-pwaN*

Problems and Then Some

There are phrases that will come in handy when you are seeking certain services or are trying to have something repaired. Use the following phrases at the dry-cleaner, the shoemaker, the optometrist, the jeweler, or the camera store:

At what time do you open?
Vous êtes ouvert à quelle heure?
voo zeh too-vehr ah kehl uhr

At what time do you close?
Vous fermez à quelle heure?
voo fehr-may ah kehl uhr

What days are you open? Closed?
Vous êtes ouvert (vous fermez) quels jours?
voo zeht oo-vehr (voo fehr-may) kehl zhoor

Can you fix it (them) today?
Pouvez-vous le (la, l', les)
réparer aujourd'hui?
*poo-vay voo luh (lah, lay)
ray-pah-ray o-zhoor-dwee*

Can you fix... for me?
Pouvez-vous me réparer...?
poo-vay voo muh ray-pah-ray

May I have a receipt?
Puis-je avoir un reçu?
pweezh ah-vwahr uhN ruh-sew

Can you fix it (them) temporarily (while I wait)?
Pouvez-vous le (la, l', les) réparer provisoirement (pendant que j'attends)?
poo-vay voo luh (lah, lay) ray-pah-ray proh-vee-zwahr-mahN (pahN-dahN kuh zhah-tahN)

At the Dry-Cleaner's— à la Teinturerie

You've unpacked. Your blue pants look like you slept in them and your tan jacket has an ugly stain on the sleeve that you hadn't noticed when you packed it. Don't fret; your stains, spots, tears, and wrinkles can be taken care of if you know how to explain your problem and ask for the necessary service:

What's the problem? There is (are)...
Quel est le problème?*Il y a*...
kehl eh luh proh-blehm eel yah

Attention!

Your best bet is to travel with as many permanent press clothes as possible. You can do your wash in the sink. Enjoy the bidet, but it's definitely not for washing your clothes.

301

a hole	un trou	*uhN troo*
a missing button	un bouton qui manque	*uhN boo-tohN kee mahNk*
a spot	une tache	*ewn tahsh*
a tear	une déchirure	*ewn day-shee-rewr*

Culture Capsule

Don't expect to find as many laundromats in France as in the United States. And don't expect the quick same-day service that has spoiled so many of us. Although French laundries are very good, they are slow. Plan on waiting a few days to get your stains removed and your clothes cleaned. If you're lucky, in big cities you might find a dry-cleaner who can have your laundry ready in a day.

Now that you've explained the problem, state what you'd like done about it:

Can you (dry) clean this (these)...for me?
Vous pouvez me nettoyer (à sec) ce (cette, cet, ces)...?
voo poo-vay muh neh-twah-yay ah sehk suh (seht, seht, say)

Can you mend this (these)...for me?
Vous pouvez me faire recoudre ce (cette, cet, ces)...?
voo poo-vay muh fehr ruh-koodr suh (seht, seht, say)

Can you press this (these)...for me?
Vous pouvez me repasser (réparer) ce (cette, cet, ces)...?
voo poo-vay muh ruh-pah-say (ray-pah-ray) suh (seht, seht, say)

Can you starch this (these)...for me?
Vous pouvez m'amidonner ce (cette, cet, ces)...?
voo poo-vay mah-mee-doh-nay suh (seht, seht, say)

Can you weave this (these)...for me?
Vous pouvez me tisser ce (cette, cet, ces)...?
voo poo-vay muh tee-say suh (seht, seht, say)

Do you do invisible mending?
Vous faites le stoppage?
voo feht luh stoh-pahzh

If you'd like a service performed for someone else, use the appropriate indirect object: *te* (you), *lui* (him, her), *nous* (us), *vous* (you), *leur* (them):

Can you please weave this coat for him (her)? Vous pouvez *lui* tisser ce manteau?

Use the verb *faire* (to make, do) before an infinitive to say that you want something done for yourself:

I would like to have my suit dry cleaned.
Je voudrais faire nettoyer à sec mon costume.

At the Laundry—à la Blanchisserie or à la Laverie Automatique

If your laundry has piled up and you don't mind doing it yourself, you might try to seek out a laundromat. Use the following phrases to get the information you need:

Un deux trois

Supply the English for the laundry slip from your hotel. Then fill it out as if you had dirty clothes to have laundered and dry-cleaned.

I have a lot of dirty laundry.
J'ai beaucoup de lessive.
zhay bo-koo duh leh-seev

I'd like to wash my clothes.
Je voudrais laver mes vêtements.
zhuh voo-dreh lah-vay may veht-mahN

I'd like to have my clothes washed.
Je voudrais faire laver mes vêtements.
zhuh voo-dreh fehr lah-vay may veht-mahN

So you're embarrassed to have anyone see your dirty laundry. Or perhaps you're afraid that your beautiful new silk shirt will get ruined by an amateur. If you want to do the job yourself, the following phrases might serve you well:

Is there a free washing machine (dryer)?
Y a-t-il une machine à laver (un séchoir) libre?
ee ah-tee ewn mah-sheen ah lah-vay
(uhN saysh-wahr) leebr

Where can I buy soap powder?
Où puis-je acheter de la lessive en poudre?
oo pweezh ahsh-tay duh lah leh-seev ahN poodr

At the Shoemaker's—Chez le Cordonnier

Let's say that you've walked so much that you've worn your soles down, or you've broken a shoelace on your dress shoes, or perhaps you would just like a shine. The following phrases will help you describe your problem:

Can you repair… for me?
Pouvez-vous me réparer…?
poo-vay voo muh ray-pah-ray

these shoes	these boots
ces chaussures	ces bottes
say sho-sewr	*say boht*
this heel	this sole
ce talon	cette semelle
suh tah-lohN	*seht suh-mehl*

Do you sell shoelaces?
Vendez-vous des lacets?
vahN-day-voo day lah-seh?

I'd like a shoe shine.
Je voudrais un cirage.
zhuh voo-dreh zuhN see-rage

These Boots Were Made for Walking

You've got an unexpected, important business meeting to attend, and your walking shoes are inappropriate attire. Your dress shoes are in need of repair, and you need them in a hurry. What service does this shoemaker provide?

```
CV, CORDONNERIE, VARTAN
Prend et Livre à domicile
83, r. de Longchamp
765016 PARIS
```

At the Optometrist's—Chez l'Opticien

What could be more annoying than losing or tearing a contact lens, or breaking or losing a pair of glasses while away from home? For those of us who depend on these optical necessities, the following phrases could one day prove useful:

The lens (the frame) is broken.
Le verre (la monture) est cassé(e).
Luh vehr (lah mohN-tewr) eh kah-say

Can you repair these glasses for me?
Pouvez-vous me réparer ces lunettes?
poo-vay voo muh ray-pah-ray say lew-neht

Can you replace this contact lens?
Pouvez-vous remplacer cette lentille (ce verre) de contact?
poo-vay voo rahN-plah-say seht lahN-tee-y (suh vehr) duh kohN-tahkt

Do you have progressive lenses?
Avez-vous des verres progressifs?
ah-vay-voo day vehr proh-greh-seef

Do you sell sunglasses?
Vendez-vous des lunettes de soleil?
vahN-day voo day lew-neht duh soh-lehy

Culture Capsule

Varilux, or progressive eyeglass lenses, are now being used by many individuals to replace bifocals. These lenses, developed and perfected in France, contain several different increasing or decreasing strength presciptions in just one lens. They allow the near-sighted and far-sighted alike to have excellent near, mid-range, and distant vision without having to look through annoying lines that cut across the visual field.

I Can't See Without Them

Individuals with very poor vision may have eyeglasses with lenses as thick as coke bottles that distort the size and shape of their eyes. Because of the strength of their prescription, these same people may have trouble finding replacement lenses in an emergency. What two services does the following optometrist offer?

OPTIQUE, **ANTOINE**

S.O.S. LUNETTES, EN 1 HEURE, RENSEIGNEZ-VOUS, SPÉCIAL MYOPES
verres de fortes correction, ne déformant plus le visage
37 bd St Germain, 75005 PARIS

Un deux trois

You have to meet a friend at a specific time. You look at your watch and realize that it isn't working properly. You pass by a jewelry store and decide to stop in for a quick repair. Explain your problem and the service you want.

At the Jeweler's—*Chez le Bijoutier*

If your watch has stopped or isn't working as it should, you might find it necessary to have it repaired before returning home:

Can you repair this watch?
Pouvez-vous réparer cette montre?
poo-vay voo ray-pah-ray seht mohNtr

My watch doesn't work.
Ma montre ne marche pas.
mah mohNtr nuh mahrsh pah

My watch is fast (slow).
Ma montre avance (retarde).
ma mohNtr ah-vahNs (ruh-tahrd)

Do you sell bands (batteries)?
Vendez-vous des bandes (des piles)?
vahN-day voo day bahnd (day peel)

At the Camera Shop—*au Magasin de Photographie*

For many people, a vacation is not a vacation unless they capture it on film. If you need to visit a camera shop or film store in a French-speaking country, the following words will come in handy:

a camera	un appareil-photo	*uhN nah-pah-rahy foh-to*
a video camera	un appareil vidéo	*uhN nah-pah-rahy vee-day-o*

If you have special needs, you might ask:

Do you sell rolls of 20 (36) exposure film in color (black and white)?
Vendez-vous des pellicules de vingt (trente-six) en couleur (noir et blanc)?
vahN-day voo day peh-lee-kewl duh vaN (trahNt-sees) ahN koo-luhr (nwahr ay blahN)

Do you sell film for slides?
Vendez-vous des pellicules pour diapositives?
vahN-day voo day peh-lee-kewl poor dee-ah-poh-zee-teev

I would like to have this film developed.
Je voudrais faire développer ce film.
zhuh voo-dreh fehr day-vloh-pay suh feelm

Do You Get the Picture?

Are you dissatisfied with the pictures you've been taking? Perhaps you just want something a bit more modern that's easier to use. What services would you expect to receive at this photo store supply?

> **PHOTO-EXPERT, TOUTES LES GRANDES MARQUES**
>
> Vente-Achat-Échange, Réparation
>
> Vente au plus bas prix, Achat au plus haut cours

Other Services

In addition to the shoemaker, the camera store, and the hairdresser, you may need other special services from time to time. For instance, you may need to find your consulate to report a lost passport. Or perhaps your handbag has been stolen and you'd like to file a police report. You may even want a translator to make sure you don't get into deeper trouble. The following phrases should help:

Where is…	the police station?
Où est…	le commissariat de police?
oo eh	*luh koh-mee-sah-ryah duh poh-lees*
the American consulate?	the American embassy?
le consulat américain?	l'ambassade américaine?
luh kohN-sew-lah ah-may-ree-kaN	*lahN-bah-sahd ah-may-ree-kehn*
I lost…	my passport.
J'ai perdu…	mon passeport.
zhay pehr-dew	*mohN pahs-pohr*
my wallet.	Help me, please.
mon portefeuille.	Aidez-moi, s'il vous plaît.
mohN pohr-tuh-fuhy	*eh-day mwah seel voo pleh*

I need an interpreter.
Il me faut un interprète.
eel muh fo tuhN naN-tehr-preht

Does anyone here speak English?
Y a-t-il quelqu'un qui parle anglais?
ee ah teel kehl kuhN kee pahrl ahN-gleh

Under Stress

Stress pronouns are so named because you use them to emphasize a certain fact. Stress pronouns may highlight or replace certain nouns or pronouns or they are used after prepositions. Whereas in English we tend to add stress with our voices: **I'm** leaving, the French tend to add stress by adding a pronoun: **Moi**, je pars. This concept sounds more confusing than it is. The following table shows subject pronouns with their corresponding stress pronouns.

Memory Enhancer

To get the services you need, you'll have to use **prepositions**. What are prepositions? They are words that are used to show the relation of a noun to another word in the sentence.

Stress Pronouns

subject	Singular stress pronoun	meaning	subject	Plural stress pronoun	meaning
(je)	moi (*mwah*)	I, me	(nous)	nous (*noo*)	we, us
(tu)	toi (*twah*)	you (fam.)	(vous)	vous (*voo*)	you (pl. pol.)
(il)	lui (*lwee*)	he, him	(ils)	eux (*uh*)	they, them
(elle)	elle (*ehl*)	she, her	(elles)	elles (*ehl*)	they, them
(on)	soi (*swah*)	oneself			

Memory Enhancer

Stress pronouns are used in comparisons:

Elle est plus riche que moi.

Stress Pronouns at Work

Stress pronouns can be used in situations where you want to emphasize the subject:

Moi, je veux parler au propriétaire.
mwah zhuh vuh pahr-lay o proh-pree-ay-tehr
Me, I want to speak to the owner.

Lui, il a fait une faute.
lwee eel ah feh tewn foht
He made a mistake.

Stress pronouns are used after *ce + être* (it is):

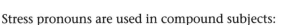

Qui est-ce? C'est moi.	C'est lui qui répare les montres.
kee ehs? seh mwah	*seh lwee kee ray-pahr lay mohNtr*
Who is it? It is I.	He (It is he who) repairs watches.

Stress pronouns are used when the pronoun has no verb:

Qui est la propriétaire? Elle.
kee eh lah proh-pree-ay-tehr ehl
Who is the owner? She (is).

En 10 Minutes

The stress pronouns in French are as follows:

moi	nous
toi	vous
lui	eux
elle	elles

Stress pronouns are used in compound subjects:

Anne et eux vont chez le coiffeur.
ahn ay uh vohN shay luh kwah-fuhr
Anne and they are going to the hairdresser.

If one of the stress pronouns is *moi*, the subject pronoun *nous* is used in summary (because *someone + me* = we) but does not have to appear in the sentence:

Henri et moi, nous allons chez l'opticien.
Henri et moi allons chez l'opticien.
Henry and I go to the optometrist.

If one of the stress pronouns is *toi*, the subject *vous* is used in summary (because *someone + you* [singular] = you [plural]) but does not have to appear in the sentence:

Guy et toi, vous allez chez le cordonnier?
Guy et toi allez chez le cordonnier?
Guy and you go to the shoemaker.

Stress pronouns are used after a preposition when referring to a person or persons:

Je vais chez toi.	Ne pars pas sans lui.
zhuh veh shay twah	*nuh pahr pah sahN lwee*
I'm going to your house.	Don't leave without him.

Stress pronouns are used after certain verbs that do not use a direct object:

avoir affaire à	*ah-vwahr ah-fehr ah*	to have business with
être à	*ehtr ah*	to belong to
penser à	*pahN-say ah*	to think about (of)
se fier à	*suh fee-ay ah*	to trust
s'intéresser à	*saN-tay-reh-say ah*	to be interested in

J'ai affaire à lui.   Cette montre est à moi.
zhay ah-fehr ah lwee   *seht mohNtr eh tah mwah*
I have business with him.   That watch is mine.

Stress Relief

If you want to speak like a native, make sure that you use stress pronouns correctly. Here are some examples of the different types of sentences that require them. Fill in the appropriate pronoun:

1. (us) Il a affaire à _____.
2. (he, I) _____ et _____ allons à l'ambassade.
3. (you fam.) _____, tu vas chez le coiffeur?
4. (she) _____, elle répare bien les vêtements.
5. (they, masc.) Je ne peux pas partir sans _____.
6. (you, pol.) C'est _____ qui allez m'accompagner.

Comparison Shopping

Which shop offers the least expensive merchandise? Which merchant is the most honest? Who is the most reliable? When shopping for goods or services, we often compare cost, reputation, and the goods or services themselves before making a choice. The following table gives you the phrases and adjectives you need when making comparisons:

Comparison of Adjectives—Inequality

	Adjective	Pronunciation	Meaning
Positive	honnête	*oh-neht*	honest
Comparative	plus honnête	*plew zoh-neht*	more honest
	moins honnête	*mwaN zoh-neht*	less honest
Superlative	le (la, les) plus honnête(s)	*luh (lah) (lay) plew zoh-neht*	the most honest
	le (la, les) moins honnête(s)	*luh (lah) (lay) mwaN zoh-neht*	the least honest

Que may or may not be used after the comparative. When used, *que* expresses *than*. *Que* becomes *qu'* before a vowel or vowel sound:

> Qui est plus charmant(e)?

> Roger est plus charmant (que Lucien).

> Sylvie est plus chamante (qu'Anne).

The preposition *de* + definite article *(du, de la, de l', des)* may be used to express *in (of) the*:

> Ce cordonnier est honnète.

> Ce cordonnier est plus honnète que lui.

> Ce cordonnier est le plus honnète (de la ville).

> Ces coiffeuses sont aimables.

> Ces coiffeuses sont les plus aimables.

> Ces coiffeuses sont les moins aimables (du salon).

When I prepare my special recipe for French pot roast, everyone gathers around the table in eager anticipation. My son Eric eats the slowest and savors every morsel. My husband eats with gusto. But my son Michael eats the fastest of all. His reasoning is: "More for me!" Whether it's eating, working, or running, the different ways in which people do things may be compared. The following table shows how to make comparisons using adverbs:

Memory Enhancer

The comparative and superlative forms of the adjectives used must agree in gender and number with the nouns they describe:

Jeanne est moins *grande* que son frère.

311

Comparison of Adverbs—Inequality

	Adjective	Pronunciation	Meaning
Positive	rapidement	*rah-peed-mahN*	rapidly
Comparative	plus rapidement	*plew rah-peed-mahN*	more rapidly
	moins rapidement	*mwaN rah-peed-mahN*	less rapidly
Superlative	le plus rapidement	*luh plew rah-peed-mahN*	the most rapidly
	le moins rapidement	*luh mwaN rah-peed-mahN*	the least rapidly

That's Highly Irregular

Beware of irregular comparisons. Never use *plus* or *mauvais* with the adjective *bon.* There are special comparative forms that express *better* and *best*:

bon(ne)(s)/good   meilleur(e)(s)/better
le (la, les) meilleur(e)(s)/the best

Comparisons of Equality

You've spent the day visiting museums in Paris. The Louvre is vast and contains treasures from antiquity, while the Picasso museum is very modern. Did you find these museums equally appealing, or did you prefer one over the other? Did you spend equal amounts of time in each, or did one visit last longer than the other? If everything were equal, you can express this equality by using:

aussi + adjective or adverb + *que*
(as…as)

Il est aussi charmant qu'eux.
eel eh to-see shahr-mahN kuh
He is as charming as they.

Elle travaille aussi dur que nous.
ehl trah-vahy o-see dewr kuh noo
She works as hard as we do.

Memory Enhancer

The tags *-ci* (this, these) and *-là* (that, those) can be joined to nouns to help differentiate between two things or actions being compared:

Ce coiffeur-*ci* est plus sympathique que ce coiffeur-*là*.
This hairdresser is nicer than that hairdresser.

You Compare

How do you compare to those you know? Are you shorter? Thinner? More charming? Do you dance better? Work more seriously? Listen more patiently? Use what you've learned to compare yourself to friends or family members.

_____

_____

_____

_____

_____

_____

_____

_____

The Least You Need to Know

➤ You can solve your problems and get the services you need in a foreign country with a few simple key phrases.

➤ Stress pronouns are used for emphasis after *c'est* and *ce sont,* in compound subjects, after prepositions and certain verbs, alone when there is no verb, or in comparisons.

➤ Use *plus* (more) or *moins* (less) before adjectives or adverbs to make comparions or to state the superlative.

➤ Use *aussi...que* (as...as) before adjectives and adverbs to express that things are equal.

I Need a Doctor...Now!

In the preceding chapter, you learned how to take care of minor problems and repairs. With just a few simple sentences, you can readily deal with life's petty annoyances. In this chapter, you'll learn the key words and phrases you'll need should you become sick while abroad.

Falling ill while you're away from home is hard enough, but the situation is even tougher if you can't communicate what is wrong. In this chapter, you will learn how to explain your ailments and how long you've been experiencing the symptoms.

It Hurts Right Here

I feel especially well-suited to writing this chapter, since our family seems to have spent an inordinate amount of time in foreign hospitals while we were supposed to be on vacation! For instance, one year my uncle arrived in France for a holiday only to be hit with a gall bladder attack. He spent the rest of his vacation flat on his back

Attention!

Jet lag is an annoying disturbace that upsets the body's biological clock. To minimize it: wear loose clothing, drink 8 oz. of water for every hour in flight, eat lightly, and get plenty of exercise.

recovering from surgery for gallstones. Or take my son, who, while vacationing in the Dominican Republic, was rushed to a hospital after he smashed his tooth against a toilet bowl. And then there was the year that my husband and I were nearly leveled by *jet lag* while backpacking through Europe. After going without sleep for 10 days, we finally got sleeping medication from a Parisian doctor. But by the end of our trip, I wound up in a hospital in Leeds, England, with severe gastroenteritis.

While I hope your luck isn't like ours, it pays to be prepared if illness strikes. To begin with, familiarize yourself with the parts of the body in the following table.

Parts of the Body

Body Part	French	Pronunciation
ankle	la cheville	*lah shuh-vee-y*
arm	le bras	*luh brah*
back	le dos	*luh do*
body	le corps	*luh koor*
brain	le cerveau, la cervelle	*luh sehr-vo, lah sehr-vehl*
chest	la poitrine	*lah pwah-treen*
chin	le menton	*luh mahN-tohN*
ear	l'oreille (f.)	*loh-rehy*
elbow	le coude	*luh kood*
eye	l'oeil (m.)	*luhy*
eyes	les yeux	*lay zyuh*
face	la figure, le visage	*lah fee-gewr, luh vee-zahzh*
finger	le doigt	*luh dwah*
foot	le pied	*luh pyay*
hand	la main	*lah maN*
head	la tête	*lah teht*
heart	le coeur	*luh kuhr*
knee	le genou	*luh zhuh-noo*
leg	la jambe	*lah zhahNb*
lip	la lèvre	*lah lehvr*
liver	le foie	*luh fwah*
lung	le poumon	*luh poo-mohN*
mouth	la bouche	*lah boosh*

Body Part	French	Pronunciation
nail	l'ongle (m.)	*lohNgl*
neck	le cou	*luh koo*
nose	le nez	*luh nay*
shoulder	l'épaule (f.)	*lay-pohl*
skin	la peau	*lah po*
spine	l'épine dorsale (f.), la colonne vertébrale	*lay-peen dohr-sahl, lah koh-lohn vehr-tay-brahl*
stomach	l'estomac (m.), le ventre	*leh-stoh-mah, luh vahNtr*
throat	la gorge	*lah gohrzh*
toe	l'orteil (m.)	*lohr-tehy*
tongue	la langue	*lah lahNg*
tooth	la dent	*lah dahN*
wrist	le poignet	*luh pwah-nyeh*

You Give Me a Pain in the...

Do you want to avoid a trip to the doctor while on vacation? The soundest piece of advice anyone can give you is: If you don't have a cast-iron stomach, don't drink the tap water when you travel. But let's say you forgot this warning and ate salad greens that were washed with tap water. Or, you ordered a drink on the rocks, ignorant of the future gastrointestinal effects of the ice cubes. You've spent too much time in *les toilettes* and now find it necessary to go to the doctor. The obvious first question will be: "What's the matter with you? (Qu'est-ce que vous avez?—*kehs-kuh voo zah-vay*)" To say what hurts or bothers you, the expression *avoir mal à* + definite article is used:

Un deux trois

Keep a full length picture of someone in your special French corner. Point to the different parts of the body and practice naming them in French.

I have a stomach ache.
J'ai mal au ventre.
zhay mahl o vahNtr

Their feet hurt.
Ils ont mal aux pieds.
eel zohN mahl o pyay

Another way of talking about your symptoms is to use the expression *faire mal à*—to hurt (which requires an indirect object for *à* + person). Use the appropriate indirect object pronoun to refer to those who might be in pain (*me* [to me], *te* [to you], *lui* [to him/her], *nous* [to us], *vous* [to you], *leur* [to them]). Remember, too, to use the correct form of the possessive adjective that refers to the person in question (*mon, ma, mes; ton, ta, tes; son, sa, ses; notre, nos; votre, vos; leur, leurs*).

> My stomach hurts (me).
> Mon ventre me fait mal.
> *mohN vahNtr muh feh mahl*
>
> His (Her) feet hurt (him, her).
> Ses pieds lui font mal.
> *say pyay lwee fohN mahl*

Attention!

The verb *faire* must agree with the subject. If you are talking about symptoms, *faire* must agree with the body part that is ailing you.

Ouch! That Hurts!

Let's say that your symptoms are more specific than a vague ache or pain. The following table gives a list of symptoms that will come in handy if you need to describe a problem. Use the phrase *J'ai* (zhay)—I have—to preface your complaint.

Remember to conjugate the verb *avoir* so that it agrees with the subject. Although the French use *avoir* to express what's bothering them, our English may not include the word *have*:

> Elle a mal aux yeux.
> Her eyes hurt.

Other Symptoms

abscess	un abscès	*uhN nahb-seh*
blister	une ampoule	*ewn nahN-pool*
broken bone	une fracture	*ewn frahk-tewr*
bruise	une contusion	*ewn kohN-tew-zyohN*
bump	une bosse	*ewn bohs*
burn	une brûlure	*ewn brew-lewr*
chills	des frissons	*day free-sohN*
cough	une toux	*ewn too*
cramps	des crampes	*day krahNp*
cut	une coupure	*ewn koo-pewr*
diarrhea	de la diarrhée	*dun lah dee-ah-ray*
fever	de la fièvre	*duh lah fyehvr*

fracture	une fracture	*ewn frahk-tewr*
indigestion	une indigestion	*ewn naN-dee-zhehs-tyohN*
infection	une infection	*ewn aN-fehk-syohN*
lump	une grosseur	*ewn groh-sewr*
migraine	une migraine	*ewn mee-grehn*
pain	une douleur	*ewn doo-luhr*
rash	une éruption	*ewn nay-rewp-syohN*
sprain	une foulure	*ewn foo-lewr*
swelling	une enflure	*ewn nahN-flewr*
wound	une blessure	*ewn bleh-sewr*

Other useful phrases include:

I'm coughing.
Je tousse.
zhuh toos

I'm sneezing.
J'éternue.
zay-tehr-new

I'm bleeding.
Je saigne.
zhuh seh-nyuh

I'm constipated.
Je suis constipé(e).
zhuh swee kohN-stee-pay

I'm nauseous.
J'ai des nausées.
zhay day no-zay

I have trouble sleeping.
J'ai du mal à dormir.
zhay dew mahl ah dohr-meer

I feel bad.
Je me sens mal.
zhuh muh sahN mahl

I hurt everywhere.
J'ai mal partout.
zhay mahl pahr-too

I'm exhausted.
Je n'en peux plus.
zhuh nahN puh plew

Attention!

If you have to go to the dentist, use the expression *avoir mal aux dents* (to have a toothache) or *avoir une rage* (ewn rahzh) *de dents* (to have a very bad toothache):

J'ai mal aux dents.
I've got a toothache.

What's Wrong?

Now use all that you've learned so far to describe your symptoms and complaints to a doctor. Pretend you have the following health problems:

1. flu-like symptoms _____ .
2. an allergy _____ .
3. a sprained ankle _____ .
4. a migraine _____ .

Memory Enhancer

Remember that *de* contracts with *le* to become *du* and with *les* to become *des*, and that *de* becomes *d'* before a vowel or vowel sound (*h, y*).

And the Diagnosis Is...

Obviously, you won't be the only one doing the talking when you visit the doctor. You will also be asked to fill out forms, tell about any medications you are taking, and answer other questions about your symptoms and general health. The doctor or nurse may ask you about the medical problems listed in the following table:

Avez-vous subi (eu)...?   Souffrez-vous de (d')...?
ah-vay voo sew-bee (ew)   *soo-fray voo duh*
Have you had...?   Do you suffer from...?

Medical Problems

Problem	French	Pronunciation
allergic reaction	une réaction allergique	*ewn ray-ahk-syohN ah-lehr-zheek*
angina	une angine	*ewn nahN-zheen*
appendicitis	l'appendicite (f.)	*lah-pahN-dee-seet*
asthma	l'asthme (m.)	*lahz-muh*
bronchitis	la bronchite	*lah brohN-sheet*
cancer	le cancer	*luh kahN-sehr*
cold	un rhume	*uhN rewm*
diabetes	le diabète	*luh dee-ah-beht*
dizziness	le vertige	*luh vehr-teezh*
dysentery	la dysenterie	*lah dee-sahN-tree*
exhaustion	l'épuisement (m.)	*lay-pweez-mahN*
flu	la grippe	*lah greep*
German measles	la rubéole	*lah rew-bay-ohl*
gout	la goutte	*lah goot*
hay fever	le rhume des foins	*luh rewm day fwaN*
heart attack	une crise cardiaque	*ewn kreez kahr-dyahk*
hepatitis	l'hépatite (f.)	*lay-pah-teet*

320

Problem	French	Pronunciation
measles	la rougeole	*lah roo-zhohl*
mumps	les oreillons (m.)	*lay zoh-reh-yohN*
pneumonia	la pneumonie	*lah pnuh-moh-nee*
polio	la poliomyélite	*lah poh-lyoh-myay-leet*
smallpox	la variole	*lah vah-ryohl*
stroke	une attaque d'apoplexie	*ewn nah-tahk dah-poh-plehk-see*
sunstroke	une insolation	*ewn naN-soh-lah-syohN*
tetanus	le tétanos	*luh tay-tah-no*
tuberculosis	la tuberculose	*lah tew-behr-kew-lohz*
whooping cough	la coqueluche	*lah kohk-lewsh*

How Long Have You Felt This Way?

Your doctor will probably ask how long you've been experiencing your symptoms. The phrases in the following table suggest the number of ways you may hear the question posed and the ways in which to answer the question. The phrases vary in difficulty but all mean the same thing. If you need to ask *how long*, the first expression is the easiest one to use.

Un deux trois

Keep a diary for a week in which you write how you feel each day. Include all your symptoms.

How Long Have Your Symptoms Lasted?

Question		Answer	
Depuis quand… (*duh-pwee kahN*)	Since when…	Depuis… (*duh-pwee*)	since…
Depuis combien de temps… (*duh-pwee kohN-byaN duh tahN*)	How long has (have)…been	Depuis… (*duh-pwee*)	for…
Combien de temps y a-t-il que… (*kohN-byaN duh tahN ee ah-teel kuh*)	How long has (have)…been	Il y a + time + que… (*eel yah + time + kuh*)	for…

continues

How Long Have Your Symptoms Lasted? (cont.)

Question		Answer	
Ça fait combien de temps que... (*sah feh kohN-byaN duh tahN kuh*)	How long has (have)...been	Ça fait + time + que... (*sah feh + time + kuh*), Voilà + time + que (*vwah-lah + time + kuh*)	for...
Depuis combien de temps souffrez-vous? *duh-pwee kohN-byaN duh tahN soo-fray voo*	How long have you been suffering?	Depuis deux jours. *duh-pwee duh zhoor*	For two days.
Depuis quand souffrez-vous? *duh-pwee kahN soo-fray voo*	Since when have you been suffering?	Depuis hier. *duh-pwee yehr*	Since yesterday.
Combien de temps y a-t-il que vous souffrez? *kohN-byaN duh tahN ee ah-teel kuh voo soo-fray*	How long have you been suffering?	Il y a un jour. *eel yah uhN zhoor*	For one day.
Ça fait combien de temps que vous souffrez? *sah feh kohN-byaN duh tahN kuh voo soo-fray*	How long have you been suffering?	Ça fait une semaine./Voilà une semaine. *sah feh tewn suh-mehn/vwah-lah ewn suh-mehn*	It's been a week./For a week.

Un deux trois

Think of five things you like to do and tell how long you've been doing them.

Tell It to the Doctor

Look at the following example of a medical form you might have to fill out. Practice what you've learned by giving the most up-to-date information about yourself.

FRÉDÉRICK A. PEREIRA
68 Rue Napoléon
Paris, France
Tél: 47 35 19 56
Fax: 47 22 80 04

FICHE MÉDICALE

Date: _____

Nom: _____   Prénoms: _____

Adresse: _____

N° de téléphone: _____

Date de naissance: _____   âge: _____

Profession: _____

Situation de famille: célibataire   _____

                         marié(e)   _____

                         divorcé(e)   _____

                         veuf (veuve)   _____

Symptômes

_____

_____

_____

_____

Antécédants Médicaux

Maladies subies

❏ angine
❏ appendicite
❏ asthme
❏ attaque d'apoplexie
❏ bronchite
❏ cancer
❏ coqueluche
❏ crise cardiaque
❏ diabète
❏ dysenterie
❏ goutte
❏ grippe
❏ hépatite
❏ oreillons
❏ pneumonie
❏ poliomyélite
❏ réaction allergique
❏ rhume des foins
❏ rougeole
❏ tétanos

❏ tuberculose
❏ variole
❏ vertige

Allergies

❏ à la penicilline
❏ aux antibiotiques
❏ autres

Vaccinations

❏ coqueluche
❏ oreillons
❏ poliomyélite
❏ rougeole
❏ rubéole
❏ tétanos
❏ tuberculose
❏ variole

Me? A Hypochondriac?

Now use all the variations to explain how long you've been suffering. Talk about a cough you've had for two weeks, a headache that has hung on for three days, or the stomachache that has been bugging you for nearly a month.

1. couch _____ .

2. headache _____ .

3. stomachache _____ .

Tell It Like It Is

What do you say when someone asks how you are? Do you say that you are fine, or do you describe every little ache and pain you've been experiencing? When you want to express what you say or tell someone, use the irregular verb *dire* (to tell, say), as shown in the following table:

Dire (To Say, Tell)

je dis	*zhuh dee*	I say, tell
tu dis	*tew dee*	you say, tell
il, elle, on dit	*eel (ehl, ohN) dee*	he (she, one) says, tells
nous disons	*noo dee-zohN*	we say, tell
vous dites	*voo deet*	you say, tell
ils, elles disent	*eel (ehl) deez*	they say, tell

Memory Enhancer

To say *that* after *dire* use *que*:

On dit que je ne suis pas gravement malade.

They say that I'm not very sick.

What Are You Doing to Yourself?

If you want to express how you feel, you can use the irregular verb *se sentir*. As you can see, *se sentir* is not just an ordinary verb because it has a special pronoun before it. This pronoun, which can act as either a direct or indirect object pronoun, is called a *reflexive pronoun*. A reflexive pronoun shows that the subject is performing an action upon itself. The subject and the reflexive pronoun refer to the same person(s) or thing(s): *She* hurt *herself. They* enjoy *themselves.* Sometimes, as with the verb *se sentir*, it is unclear from the English that the verb is reflexive. The following table demonstrates how to conjugate a reflexive verb using the correct reflexive pronouns:

Se Sentir (To Feel)

je **me** sens	*zhuh muh sahN*	I feel
tu **te** sens	*tew tuh sahN*	you feel
il, elle, on **se** sent	*eel (ehl, ohN) suh sahN*	he, (she, one) feels
nous **nous** sentons	*noo noo sahN-tohN*	we feel
vous **vous** sentez	*voo voo sahN-tay*	you feel
ils, elles **se** sentent	*eel (ehl) suh sahNt*	they feel

Now you can express how you feel:

I feel well.	I feel bad.
Je me sens bien.	Je me sens mal.
zhuh muh sahN byaN	*zhuh muh sahN mahl*

I feel better.	I feel worse.
Je me sens mieux.	Je me sens pire.
zhuh muh sahN myuh	*zhuh muh sahN peer*

You're on your way out the door, but not before paying the bill (*sa note*—sah noht) and asking the following question:

> May I please have a receipt for my medical insurance?
> Puis-je avoir une quittance pour mon assurance maladie, s'il vous plaît?
> *pweezh ah-vwahr ewn kee-tahNs poor mohN nah-sew-rahNs mah-lah-dee seel voo pleh*

Memory Enhancer

The reflexive pronouns are the same as direct and indirect object pronouns except for the third person singular *se* (to himself/herself) and the third person plural *se* (to themselves).

Is It Reflexive?

Of course you know the feeling of returning home from a trip with a suitcase packed with gifts for family members and friends. But do you treat yourself right, too? Do you cast aside all financial concerns and treat yourself to that special souvenir you wanted? In French, when you perfom an action *upon* or *for* yourself, that action (verb) is reflexive and requires a reflexive pronoun. In many instances, you can use the same verb, without the reflexive pronoun and perform the action *upon* or *for* someone else. In these cases, an object pronoun (direct or indirect) is used.

Je *me* lave.	Je lave mon chien.	Je *le* lave.
I wash myself.	I wash my dog.	I wash him.

Memory Enhancer

You can tell a verb is reflexive if the infinitive is preceded by *se*.

In the last example, the direct object pronoun *le* expresses *him*.

> Je *m'*achète un sac.
> I buy myself a bag.

> J'achète un sac à Anne.
> I buy a bag for Anne.

> Je *lui* achète un sac.
> I buy (for) her a bag.

In the last example, the indirect object pronoun *lui* expresses *for her*.

There are some verbs that are usually or always used reflexively. The following table provides a list of the most common reflexive verbs:

Common Reflexive Verbs

s'appeler *	*sah-play*	to be named, called
s'approcher de	*sah-proh-shay duh*	to approach
s'arrêter de	*sah-ruh-tay duh*	to stop
se baigner	*suh beh-nyay*	to bathe
se blesser	*suh bleh-say*	to hurt oneself
se brosser	*suh broh-say*	to brush
se casser	*suh kah-say*	to break
se coiffer	*suh kwah-fay*	to do one's hair
se coucher	*suh koo-shay*	to go to bed
se demander	*suh duh-mahN-day*	to wonder
se dépêcher	*suh day-peh-shay*	to hurry
se déshabiller	*suh day-zah-bee-yay*	to undress
se détendre	*suh day-tahNdr*	to relax
s'endormir	*sahN-dohr-meer*	to go to sleep
s'évanouir	*say-vah-nweer*	to faint
se fâcher (contre)	*suh fah-shay (kohNtr)*	to get angry (with)
s'habiller	*sah-bee-yay*	to dress
s'inquiéter de *	*saN-kee-ay-tay duh*	to worry about
se laver	*suh lah-vay*	to wash
se lever *	*suh luh-vay*	to get up
se maquiller	*suh mah-kee-yay*	to apply make-up
se mettre à	*suh mehtr ah*	to begin
s'occuper de	*soh-kew-pay duh*	to take care of
se peigner	*suh peh-nyay*	to comb

se promener *	*suh proh-mnay*	to take a walk
se rappeler *	*suh rah-play*	to recall
se raser	*suh rah-zay*	to shave
se reposer	*suh ruh-poh-zay*	to rest
se réunir	*suh ray-ew-neer*	to meet
se réveiller	*suh ray-veh-yay*	to wake up
se servir de	*suh sehr-veer duh*	to use
se tromper	*suh trohN-pay*	to make a mistake

* Remember that these verbs are "shoe verbs." They all have spelling changes and must be conjugated accordingly. Refer to Chapter 12 to refresh your memory. Here are some examples:

| *Je me lève.* | *I get up.* |
| *Je m'appelle Jean.* | *My name is John.* |

Suppose you are telling someone all the things you do in the morning to prepare yourself for work or school. You might say: "I brush my teeth. I shave my mustache. I wash my hair." Since you use the word *my*, you don't have to finish the sentence with "for myself." It's understood. In French, however, the opposite is done. The reflexive pronoun *me* (for myself) is used. It then becomes unnecessary to use the possessive adjective *my* (*mon, ma, mes*) when referring to parts of the body, since the action is obviously being performed on the subject. And so, the definite article is used instead.

Je me brosse les dents.	Il se rase la barbe.
zhuh muh brohs lay dahN	*eel suh rahz lah bahrb*
I brush my teeth.	He shaves his beard.

Un deux trois

Practice the reflexive verbs with spelling changes. Every day select two from the list and use them in complete French sentences.

Memory Enhancer

Verbs that are not ordinarily reflexive can be made reflexive by simply adding a reflexive pronoun providing the sentence makes sense:

Je parle.
I speak.

Je me parle.
I talk to myself.

Position of Reflexive Pronouns

No matter what language you study, it is not uncommon to find that word orders differ from one language to the next. In English, we generally put reflexive pronouns after verbs. You might tell a friend: "I always look *at myself* in the mirror before I go out." In French, this is not the case. The reflexive pronoun is placed in the same position as the other pronouns you have studied (direct, indirect, *y* and *en*)—that is, before the verb to which their meaning is tied (usually the conjugated verb). When there are two verbs, the pronoun is placed before the infinitive.

Je *me* lave.	I wash (myself).
Je ne *me lave* pas.	I don't wash (myself).
Je vais *me* laver.	I'm going to wash (myself).
Ne *te* lave pas!	Don't wash (yourself).

Attention!

Te becomes *toi* in an affirmative command.

In an affirmative command, reflexive pronouns change position and are placed immediately after the verb and are joined to it by a hyphen. *Te* becomes *toi* when it follows the verb:

Lave-*toi!*   Lavez-*vous!*

Using Reflexive Verbs

Use what you've learned so far to describe all the things you do before leaving the house in the morning. *(Je me lave.)* Then, talk about the things you are going to do before going to bed at night. *(Je vais me laver.)*

1. _____ .
   _____ .
2. _____ .
   _____ .

You're In Command

You're traveling in a group and sharing a room with a few friends. You're all getting ready to go out on the town. Practice using reflexive verbs by telling a friend (and then a group of friends) to do and not to do the following:

Example: brush your hair
                 Brosse-toi les cheveux!
                 Ne te brosse pas les cheveux!
                 Brossez-vous les cheveux!
                 Ne vous brossez pas les cheveux!

1. take a bath _____.
2. hurry up _____.
3. shave _____.
4. get dressed _____.
5. brush your teeth _____.
6. have fun _____.

The Least You Need to Know

➤ If you fall ill in another country, know how to name the different parts of the body as well as your symptoms and feelings.

➤ To ask *how long* something has lasted, use *depuis quand..., depuis combien de temps..., combien de temps y a-t-il que...,* or *ça fait combien de temps que....*

➤ Reflexive verbs, identified by the reflexive pronouns that accompany them, are used to show that the subject is acting upon itself.

Chapter 21

Oops, I Forgot to Pack My Toothbrush!

> **In This Chapter**
>
> ➤ Large and small drugstore and medical items
>
> ➤ The irregular verb *venir* (to come)
>
> ➤ Speaking in the past

Chapter 20 helped you express how you feel. You learned to communicate good health as well as aches and pains. Whether you just need a few aspirins or a prescription drug, you'll want to take a trip to the drugstore. When you get there, you'll be amazed at all the other things you can purchase.

On the last trip we took, both my husband and I forgot to pack our toothbrushes, toothpaste, and a hair brush. Imagine our dismay when we realized our blunder. We laughed it off, however, and simply went to the nearest drugstore. In France, we had the choice of going to *une pharmacie* (*ewn fahr-mah-see*), *une droguerie* (*ewn drohg-ree*), or *un drugstore* (*uhN druhg-stohr*). Confused? Don't worry, this chapter will guide you to the correct spot where you can find all your toiletry needs as well as any medication. In addition, you'll learn how to express yourself in the past tense.

I Need an Aspirin

Whether you are trying to obtain medication or a bottle of shampoo, you want to be sure you're in the right place in France.

Attention!

You can buy prescription medicine only in **une pharmacie**, which is easily identifiable by its green cross. **Une droguerie** sells personal hygiene and household items only.

Un deux trois

Put French labels on all the items in your medicine cabinet. Memorize their names, and then remove the labels and try to name everything you have on hand. Or look for products, aimed at the Canadian market, with labels in both French and English.

Une pharmacie, which is easily identified by a green cross above the door, sells prescription drugs, over-the-counter medications, items intended for personal hygiene, and some cosmetics. If the pharmacy is closed, there will usually be a sign on the door telling customers where they can locate a neighboring pharmacy that is open all night (*une pharmacie de garde*).

Une droguerie sells chemical products, paints, household cleansers and accessories (mops, brooms, buckets), and some hygiene and beauty products, but does not dispense prescriptions.

Un drugstore resembles a small department store. You would expect to find varied sections selling personal hygiene items, books, magazines, newspapers, records, maps, guides, gifts and souvenirs, but no prescription medicine. Additionally, you may find fast-food restaurants, a bar, and even a movie theater.

If you are indeed trying to fill a prescription, you can say to the druggist:

> I need medication.
> Il me faut des médicaments.
> *eel muh fo day may-dee-kah-mahN*

> Could you please fill this prescription (immediately)?
> Pourriez-vous exécuter (tout de suite) cette ordonnance, s'il vous plaît?
> *poo-ryay voo ehg-zay-kew-tay (toot sweet) seht ohr-doh-nahNs seel voo pleh*

If you're simply looking for something over-the-counter, the following table will help you find it. Begin by saying to a clerk:

> Je cherche...
> *zhuh shersh*
> I'm looking for...

Drugstore Items

For Men and Women

| alcohol | de l'alcool (m.) | *duh lahl-kohl* |
| antacid | un anti-acide | *uhN nahN-tee ah-seed* |

For Men and Women

antihistamine	un antihistaminique	*uhN nahn-tee-ees-tah-mee-neek*
antiseptic	un antiseptique	*uhN nahN-tee-sehp-teek*
aspirins	des aspirines	*day zah-spee-reen*
bandages (wound)	des pansements (m.)	*day pahNs-mahN*
bobby pins	des épingles à cheveux (f.)	*day zay-paNgl ah shuh-vuh*
brush	une brosse	*ewn brohs*
cleansing cream	de la crème démaquillante	*duh lah krehm day-mah-kee-yahNt*
condoms	des préservatifs (m.)	*day pray-zehr-vah-teef*
cotton (absorbent)	du coton de l'ouate	*dew koh-tohN duh lwaht*
cough drops	des pastilles (f.)	*day pah-stee-y*
cough syrup	le sirop contre la toux	*luh see-roh kohNtr lah too*
deodorant	du déodorant	*dew day-oh-doh-rahN*
depilatory	un dépilatoire	*uhN day-pee-lah-twahr*
eye drops	les gouttes pour les yeux (f.), du collyre	*lay goot poor lay zyuh, dew koh-leer*
eye liner	du traceur à paupièères	*dew trah-suhr ah po-pyehr*
eye shadow	du fard à paupières	*dew fahr ah po-pyehr*
eyebrow pencil	un crayon pour les yeux	*uhN kreh-yohN poor lay zyuh*
first-aid kit	un paquet de pansement	*uhN pah-keh duh pahNs-mahN*
gauze pads	des bandes de gaze(f.)	*day bahnd duh gahz*
heating pad	un thermoplasme	*uhN tehr-moh-plahz-muh*
ice pack	une vessie de glace	*ewn veh-see duh glahs*
laxative (mild)	un laxatif (léger)	*uhN lahk-sah-teef (lay-zhay)*
lipstick	du rouge à lèvres	*dew roozh ah lehvr*
make-up	du maquillage	*dew mah-kee-yahzh*
mascara	du mascara	*dew mahs-kah-rah*
mirror	un miroir	*uhN meer-whahr*
moisturizer	de la crème hydratante	*duh lah krehm ee-drah-tahNt*
mouthwash	un dentifrice	*uhN dahN-tee-frees*
nail file	une lime à ongles	*ewn leem ah ohNgl*
nail polish	du vernis à ongles	*dew vehr-nee ah ohNgl*
nail polish remover	du dissolvant	*dew dee-sohl-vahN*
nose drops	des gouttes nasales (f.)	*day goot nah-zahl*
perfume	du parfum	*dew pahr-fuhN*
powder	de la poudre	*duh lah poodr*
razor (electric)	un rasoir (électrique)	*uhN rah-zwahr (ay-lehk-treek)*
razor blades	des lames de rasoir (f.)	*day lahm duh rah-zwahr*

continues

333

Drugstore Items (cont.)

For Men and Women

safety pins	des épingles de süreté (f.)	*day zay-paNgl duh sewr-tay*
sanitary napkins	des serviettes hygiéniques (f.)	*day sehr-vyeht ee-zhyay-neek*
scissors	des ciseaux (m.)	*day see-zo*
shampoo (anti-dandruff)	du shampooing (anti-pellicules)	*dew shahN-pwaN (ahN-tee peh-lee-kewl)*
shaving cream	de la crème à raser	*duh lah krehm ah rah-zay*
sleeping pills	des somnifères (m.)	*day sohm-nee-fehr*
soap (bar)	une savonette	*ewn sah-voh-neht*
suntan lotion	de la lotion solaire	*duh lah loh-syohN soh-lehr*
talcum powder	du talc	*dew tahlk*
tampons	des tampons périodiques (m.)	*day tahN-pohN pay-ree-oh-deek*
thermometer	un thermomètre	*uhN tehr-mo-mehtr*
tissues	des mouchoirs en papier (m.)	*day moosh-wahr ahN pah-pyay*
toothbrush	une brosse à dents	*ewn brohs ah dahN*
toothpaste	de la pâte dentifrice	*duh lah paht dahN-tee-frees*
tweezers	une pince à épiler	*ewn paNs ah ay-pee-lay*
vitamins	des vitamines (f.)	*day vee-tah-meen*

For Babies

bottle	un biberon	*uhN beeb-rohN*
diapers (disposable)	des couches (disponibles) (m.)	*day koosh dees-poh-neebl*
pacifier	une sucette	*ewn sew-seht*

What Do You Need?

You're away on vacation and are not feeling quite up to par. Ask the clerk for everything that you need for the following situations. Begin each sentence with *Il me faut...*—I need...

1. you have a cold _____ .
2. you have a headache _____ .
3. you got a cut _____ .
4. your stomach is upset _____ .
5. you forget shaving equipment/make-up _____ .
6. your baby is crying a lot _____ .

Special People, Special Needs

A pharmacy that specializes in *la location d'appareils médiaux* (lah loh-kah-syohn dah-pah-rehy may-dee-ko)—the rental of medical appliances—would either sell or have information concerning the items for the physically challenged featured in the following table.

> Where can I get...
> Où puis-je obtenir...
> *oo pweezh ohb-tuh-neer*

Special Needs

cane	une canne	*ewn kahn*
crutches	des béquilles	*day bay-kee*
hearing aid	un audiophone	*uhN no-dyoh-fohn*
seeing-eye dog	un chien d'aveugle	*uhN shyaN dah-vuhgl*
walker	un déambulateur	*uhN day-ahN-bew-lah-tuhr*
wheelchair	un fauteuil roulant	*uhN fo-tuhy roo-lahN*

Come Along

If you called a pharmacy to locate a certain product, you would use the verb *venir* to inform the pharmacist of when you would be *coming* to pick it up. The following table provides the forms of this irregular verb, which is similar to a shoe verb in that the *nous* and *vous* forms look like the infinitive, whereas the forms for the other subject pronouns do not.

Use *venir* + *de* (*d'* before a vowel or vowel sound) + infinitive for something that has just happened:

> Je viens d'arriver. (I just arrived.)

Venir (To Come)

je viens	*zhuh vyaN*	I come
tu viens	*tew vyaN*	you come
il, elle, on vient	*eel (ehl, ohN) vyaN*	he, she, one comes
nous venons	*noo vuh-nohN*	we come
vous venez	*voo vuh-nay*	you come
ils, elles viennent	*eel (ehl) vyehn*	they come

You Must Be Living in the Past

"Oh, no!" you exclaim to yourself. It seems you've misplaced your eye drops or you can't find your shaving cream. One reason you might go to a *pharmacie* or a *droguerie* is because you forgot something at home that you really need. In order to express what you did or did not do, you must use the past tense. In French, this tense is called the *passé composé*—the compound past. The word *compound* is a key word because it implies that the past tense is made up of more than one part. Two elements are needed to form the *passé composé*: a helping verb, which expresses that something **has** taken place, and a past participle, which expresses exactly what the action was. In English, we most often use only the past participle and not the helping verb, although it is implied. We'd say: "Oh, no! I forgot my toothbrush." (not, "Oh no! I have forgotten my toothbrush.") In French, the helping verb must be used: "Zut! J'ai oublié ma brosse à dents."

Memory Enhancer

The passé composé is formed as follows:

subject (noun or pronoun) + helping verb + past participle

The Helping Verb Avoir

Since *avoir* means "to have," it is quite logical that it would serve as a helping verb. Because it is the first verb to follow the subject, the verb *avoir* must be conjugated. Then you must add a past participle.

Forming the Past Participle of Regular Verbs

All regular *er*, *ir*, and *re* verbs form their past participles differently, as shown in the following table. There are no changes made to the past participles of shoe verbs

(*-cer, -ger, -yer, e* + consonant + *er*, and *é* + consonant + *er* verbs). The past participle remains the same for every subject: J'ai dansé, Tu as dansé, etc.

Past Participle Formation

er Verbs	*ir* Verbs	*re* Verbs
voya**ger** voya**gé**	choi**sir** choi**si**	répon**dre** répon**du**

Tu as oublié les aspirines.
tew ah oo-blee-yay lay zah-spee-reen
You forgot the aspirins.

Ils ont rendu le rasoir.
eel zohN rahN-dew luh rah-zwahr.
They returned the razor.

Le docteur a réfléchi avant d'agir.
luh dohk-tuhr ah ray-flay-shee ah-vahN dah-zheer
The doctor thought before acting.

Memory Enhancer

Some short adverbs may be placed before the past participle:

Elle a trop mangé.
She ate too much.

It Didn't Happen That Way

Since the helping verb is conjugated, it is the verb that is used to form the negative and questions. *Ne* and *pas* are placed around it:

Tu *n'*as *pas* oublié les aspirines.
tew nah pah zoo-bee-yay lay zah-spee-reen
You didn't forget (You haven't forgotten) the aspirins.

Le docteur *n'*a *pas* réfléchi avant d'agir.
luh dohk-tuhr nah pas ray-flay-shee ah-vahN dah-zheer
The doctor didn't think before acting.

Ils *n'*ont *pas* rendu le rasoir.
eel nohN pah rahN-dew luh rah-zwahr
They didn't return (They haven't returned) the razor.

Memory Enhancer

All negatives are placed around the helping verb.

Il n'a pas agi. (He didn't act.)
Je n'ai jamais joué au golf. (I never played golf.)

You Didn't, Did You?

A trip to the doctor is often necessary and rarely pleasant when one isn't feeling up to par. In order to get well, one should cooperate. Some patients, as we all know, are very stubborn. Tell what each person did and didn't do in the past:

Example:

> je/parler à l'infirmière
> J'ai parlé à l'infirmière.
> Je n'ai pas parlé à l'infirmière.

1. je/remplir le formulaire

2. tu/répondre franchement

3. tu/obéir au docteur

4. nous/acheter nos médicaments

5. elle/chercher ses pilules

6. ils/attendre le pharmacien

Asking About the Past

You can make a question by using *intonation, est-ce que,* or *n'est-ce pas*:

> Ils ont rendu le rasoir?
> *eel zohN rahN-dew luh rah-zwahr*
>
> Est-ce qu'ils ont rendu le rasoir?
> *ehs-keel zohN rahN-dew luh rah-zwahr*
>
> Ils ont rendu le rasoir, n'est-ce pas?
> *eel zohn rahN-dew luh rah-zwahr nehs pah*

To use inversion, simply invert the *subject pronoun* and the conjugated helping verb.

> As-tu oublié les aspirines?
> *ah-tew oo-blee-yay lay zah-spee-reen*
> Did you forget (Have you forgotten) the aspirins?
>
> Le docteur, a-t-il réfléchi avant d'agir?
> *luh dohk-tuhr ah-teel ray-flay-shee ah-vahN dah-zheer*
> Did the doctor think before acting?
>
> A-t-il rendu le rasoir?
> *ah-teel rahN-dew luh rah-zwahr*
> Did he return (Has he returned) the razor?

Asking About the Past Negatively

This is relatively easy without inversion:

> Ils *n'ont pas* rendu le rasoir?
> *eel nohN pah rahN-dew luh rah-zwahr*

338

Est-ce qu'ils n'ont pas rendu le rasoir?
ehs-keel nohN pah rahN-dew luh rah-zwahr
Haven't they returned (Didn't they return) the razor?

Forming a negative question with inversion is a bit trickier. *Ne* and *pas* are placed around the inverted pronoun and verb:

N'as-tu pas oublié les aspirines?
nah-tew pah zoo-blee-yay lay zah-spee-reen
Did*n't* you forget (Have*n't* you forgotten) the aspirins?

Le docteur, n'a-t-il pas réfléchi avant d'agir?
luh dohk-turh nah-teel pah ray-flay-shee ay-vahN dah-zheer
Did*n't* the doctor think before acting?

N'ont-ils pas rendu le rasoir?
nohN-teel pah rahN-dew luh rah-zwahr
Did*n't* they return (Have*n't* they returned) the razor?

Your Past Is in Question

What makes a person get sick? Eating too much? Working too hard? Not following the doctor's orders? Ask both affirmative and negative questions in the past about each of these subjects:

Example:

il/trop crier
A-t-il trop crié?
N'a-t-il pas trop crié?

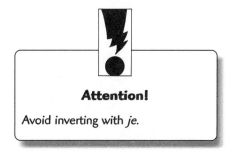

Attention!

Avoid inverting with *je.*

1. nous/travailler trop dur _____ .
2. elle/obéir au docteur _____ .
3. ils/perdre conscience _____ .
4. vous/trop maigrir _____ .
5. tu/trop manger _____ .
6. il/attendre dehors longtemps _____ .

Past Participles of Irregular Verbs

Those verbs not belonging to the *er, ir,* or *re* family have irregular past participles shown in the following table. We have studied some of these verbs in depth in previous chapters; others will appear in subsequent chapters as noted.

To make a sentence in the past negative, put the negative phrase around the conjugated helping verb:

> Il n'a jamais fumé.

Irregular Past Participles

Infinitive	Past Participle	
avoir (to have)	eu	*ew*
boire (to drink)	bu	*bew*
connaître (to be acquainted with, *Chap.23)	connu	*koh-new*
devoir (to have to, *Chap. 22)	dû	*dew*
dire (to say, tell)	dit	*dee*
écrire (to write, *Chap. 23)	écrit	*ay-kree*
être (to be)	été	*ay-tay*
faire (to make, do)	fait	*feh*
lire (to read, *Chap. 23)	lu	*lew*
mettre (to put [on])	mis	*mee*
pouvoir (to be able to)	pu	*pew*
prendre (to take)	pris	*pree*
recevoir (to receive)	reçu	*ruh-sew*
savoir (to know, *Chap. 23)	su	*sew*
voir (to see)	vu	*vew*
vouloir (to want)	voulu	*voo-lew*

Un deux trois

Make flashcards to memorize the past participles of irregular verbs. Write the infinitive of the verb on one side and the past participle on the flip side. Practice five verbs a day until you have them all down pat.

These verbs form the *passé composé* in the same way as regular verbs:

> Il a été au cinéma.
>
> Il n'a pas été au cinéma.
>
> A-t-il été au cinéma?
>
> N'a-t-il pas été au cinéma?

The Helping Verb *être*

A few common verbs use *être* instead of *avoir* as the helping verb. Most of these verbs show some kind of motion either involving going up, down, in, out, or staying at rest.

	Infinitive	Past Participle	
D	devenir (to become)	devenu*	*duh-vuh-new*
R	revenir (to come back)	revenu*	*ruh-vuh-new*
M	mourir (to die)	mort*	*mohr*
R	retourner (to return)	retourné	*ruh-toor-nay*
S	sortir (to go out)	sorti	*sohr-tee*
V	venir (to come)	venu*	*vuh-new*
A	arriver (to arrive)	arrivé	*ah-ree-vay*
N	naître (to be born)	né*	*nay*
D	descendre (to descend, go down)	descendu	*deh-sahN-dew*
E	entrer (to enter)	entré	*ahN-tray*
R	rentrer (to return)	rentré	*rahN-tray*
T	tomber (to fall)	tombé	*tohN-bay*
R	rester (to remain, stay)	resté	*rehs-tay*
A	aller (to go)	allé	*ah-lay*
M	monter (to go up, mount)	monté	*mohN-tay*
P	partir (to leave)	parti	*pahr-tee*
P	passer (to pass by [without a direct object])	passé	*pah-say*

*All * past participles are irregular and must be memorized. All reflexive verbs use être as their helping verb. They will be discussed in the next chapter.*

Notice what happens, however, when we add the past participle in the following table. (The * indicates that the subject may be singular or plural.)

The Past Tense with *être*

Masculine Subjects	Feminine Subjects
je suis allé	je suis allée
tu es allé	tu es allée
il est allé	elle est allée
nous sommes allés	nous sommes allées
vous êtes allé(s)*	vous êtes allée(s)*
ils sont allés	elles sont allées

As you can see, the past participles of all verbs conjugated with *être* agree in gender (masculine or feminine [add *e*]) and number (singular or plural [add *s*]) with the subject. For a mixed group, always use the masculine forms. If the masculine past participle ends in an unpronounced consonant, the consonant will be pronounced for the feminine singular and plural forms.

Il est resté.	Elle est restée.	Ils sont restés.
eel eh reh-stay	*ehl eh reh-stay*	*eel sohN reh-stay*
He stayed.	She stayed.	They stayed.
Il est venu tôt.	Elle est venue tôt.	Ils sont venus tôt.
eel eh vuh-new to	*ehl eh vun-new to*	*eel sohN vuh-new to*
He came early.	She came early.	They came early.
Il est mort.	Elle est morte.	Elles sont mortes.
eel eh mohr	*ehl eh mohrt*	*ehl sohN mohrt*
He died.	She died.	They died.

Attention

Some French verbs use *être* as their helping verb.

Negatives and questions are formed in the same way with *être* as the helping verb as with *avoir*:

Elle est arrivée.

Elle *n'*est *pas* arrivée.

Est-elle arrivée?

*N'*est-elle *pas* arrivée?

Who Did What?

Yesterday was Saturday, and most people were free to do as they wished. Did they go out or hang out around the house? Tell what each person did using the correct helping verb (*avoir* or *être*) and the past participle:

1. il/faire du football _____ .
2. nous/être en ville _____ .
3. tu/voir ce film _____ .
4. je/pouvoir finir le travail _____ .
5. elles/prendre une grande décision _____ .
6. vous/lire un livre _____ .
7. ils/avoir un rendez-vous _____ .

8. elle/faire des courses _____ .

9. je (f.)/arriver chez un ami _____ .

10. nous (m.)/revenir du Canada _____ .

11. ils/rester à la maison _____ .

12. tu (f.)/partir à la campagne _____ .

13. vous (m. pl.)/aller _____ .

14. elle/sortir avec des amies à la plage _____ .

15. ils/descendre en ville _____ .

16. elles/rentrer tard_____ .

The Least You Need to Know

➤ To get prescription drugs you must go to *une pharmacie* not *un drugstore*.

➤ Use the irregular verb *venir* to express "to come." *Venir* + *de* + the infinitive means "to have just."

➤ The past tense in French is made up of two parts: a helping verb (*avoir* or *être*) and a past participle.

Chapter 22

Phone Home...or Anywhere Else

In This Chapter

➤ Making a phone call

➤ Proper telephone etiquette

➤ When there's a problem

➤ The irregular verb devoir (to have to)

➤ Using reflexive verbs in the past tense

Your medicinal problems and toiletry needs were taken care of in the last chapter. You feel great and would like to let your family and friends know that everything is all right; it's time to phone home.

Placing a long-distance telephone call from a foreign country is always a bit of a challenge. It is often necessary to speak with an operator, and most people don't realize how difficult it is to communicate by telephone with someone who speaks a different language. The luxury of relying on reading someone's body language or watching his lips for clues disappears once a telephone is introduced. This chapter will help you place a call within or outside the country you are visiting; prepare you for dealing with busy signals, wrong numbers, and other phone mishaps; and teach you how to use reflexive verbs in the past tense.

Making a Call

If you plan to call long distance from a foreign country, expect that someone will have to explain to you how to use the phone system. It is also likely that the procedures for making local calls will be different from the ones you are used to back home. One thing you will want to make sure to do is correctly express the type of call you wish to make. The following table provides some options.

Types of Phone Calls

collect call	la communication en P.C.V.	*lah koh-mew-nee-kah-syohN ahN pay-say-vay*
credit-card call	la communication par carte de crédit	*lah koh-mew-nee-kah-syohN pahr kahrt duh kray-dee*
local call	la communication locale	*lah koh-mew-nee-kah-syohN loh-kahl*
long-distance call	la communication interurbaine	*lah koh-mew-nee-kah-syohN aN-tehr-ewr-behn*
out-of-the-country call	la communication à l'étranger	*lah koh-mew-nee-kah-syohN ah lay-trahN-zhay*
person-to-person call	la communication avec préavis	*lah koh-mew-nee-kah-syohN ah-vehk pray-ah-vee*

In case you have problems using a telephone, you should familiarize yourself with the different parts of the phone featured in the following table:

The Telephone

booth	la cabine téléphonique	*lah kah-been tay-lay-foh-neek*
button	le bouton	*luh boo-tohN*
coin return button	le bouton de remboursement	*luh boo-tohN duh rahN-boors-mahN*
cordless phone	le poste sans cordon	*luh pohst sahN kohr-dohN*
portable phone	le téléphone portatif	*luh tay-lay-fohn pohr-tah-teef*
dial	le cadran	*luh kah-drahN*
keypad	le clavier à touches	*luh klah-vyay ah toosh*
phone card	la télécarte	*lah tay-lay-kahrt*

public phone	le téléphone public	*luh tay-lay-fohn pew-bleek*
receiver	le combiné, le récepteur	*luh kohN-bee-nay, luh ray-sehp-tuhr*
slot	la fente	*lah fahNt*
speaker telephone	le poste mains libres	*luh pohst maN leebr*
telephone	le téléphone	*luh tay-lay-fohn*
telephone book	l'annuaire (m.)	*lahn-wehr*
telephone number	le numéro de téléphone	*luh new-may-ro duh tay-lay-fohn*
token	le jeton	*luh zheh-tohN*
touch-tone phone	le poste à clavier (à touches)	*luh pohst ah klah-vyay (ah toosh)*

You are now ready to place a call. Be prepared for your hotel to charge exorbitant rates; that's usually the case. In France, it's an excellent idea to purchase a *Télécarte* (available at post offices, cafés, and convenience stores) which enables you to buy 50 or 120 message units of calls. The number of message units required for the call depends on the total speaking time and the area phoned. More message units are necessary to call a farther distance or to speak for a longer period of time. A magnetic strip on the Télécarte, similar to the one on a credit card, allows you to use French phones. Because the pictures on these cards vary and change over time, some of the Télécartes will one day be collector's items. The following table explains how to complete your call using a Télécarte.

Keep track of your Télécarte. If you lose it, anyone can use it, since there is no means of identifying the owner.

Un deux trois

Label the parts of your telephone. Look at the labels every time you use the phone. Study the vocabulary words until you know them well, and then remove the labels and see if you can name the parts of your phone.

Culture Capsule

The telephone system in France, France Télécom, is controlled by the government agency P. T. T. (postes, télégraphes et téléphones) and provides many services to its *abonné(e)s* (*ah-boh-nay*—subscribers). Generally, you don't need operator assistance to place local or long-distance calls. Public pay phones are available in post offices, cafés, some convenience stores, and on the streets of larger cities.

How to Make a Phone Call

to call back	rappeler, retéléphoner	*rah-play (ruh-tay-lay-fohn-nay)*
to dial	composer (faire) le numéro	*kohN-po-zay (fehr) luh new-may-ro*
to hang up (the receiver)	raccrocher, quitter	*rah-kroh-shay (kee-tay)*
to insert the card	introduire la carte	*aN-troh-dweer lah kahrt*
to know the area code	savoir l'indicatif, du pays (country), de la ville (city)	*sah-vwahr laN-dee-kah-teef dew pay-ee duh lah veel*
to leave a message	laisser un message	*leh-say uhN meh-sahzh*
to listen for the dial tone	attendre la tonalité	*ah-tahNdr lah toh-nah-lee-tay*
to pick up (the receiver)	décrocher	*day-kroh-shay*
to telephone	téléphoner, donner un coup de fil	*tay-lay-foh-nay, doh-nay uhN koo duh feel*

Calling from Your Hotel Room

POUR TÉLÉPHONER

Pour vos communications locales	Faites le 1
Pour vos communications interurbaines	Faites le 1 + 16
Pour vos communications à l'étranger	Faites le 1 + 19
Pour parler à une autre chambre	Faites le 2 suivi par le n° de la chambre
Pour commander un repas	Faites le 3
Réception	Faites le 4
Concierge (bagages, réveil, restaurant)	Faites le 5
Bar (à partir de 16 h.)	Faites le 6
Service de blanchissage	Faites le 7

This card was by the phone in your hotel room. What number would you call for the following:

1. to get something to drink? _____

2. to get your laundry done? _____

3. to make a long-distance call? _____

4. to make a local call? _____

5. to make a call abroad? _____

6. to speak to a friend in another room? _____

7. to place a wake-up call? _____

8. to speak to the front desk? _____

In English, to say that someone is going to do something again, we use the prefix *re-*, as in *redial* or *recall*. The French add the same prefix: *recomposer*—to redial. Drop the *e* from *re* before a vowel: *rappeler*—to call back.

Using a Public Phone

Translate the following directions explaining how to use a *Télécarte* to place a call. Use your dictionary for help if you need it.

Comment utiliser la Télécarte:

1. Décrocher.

2. Introduire la carte.

3. Attendre la tonalité.

4. Composer votre numéro.

5. Communiquer.

Culture Capsule

From older telephones, out in the countryside, it might be necessary to purchase *un jeton* (*uhN zheh-tohN*—a slug) at a café or post office. To make a call from one of these phones:

1. Insert the *jeton* in the slot.

2. Lift the receiver.

3. Wait for the dial tone.

4. Dial the number.

5. After someone answers, press the button on the front of the phone. (Pressing the button allows your call to be completed.)

Please Phone Home

The front of the French yellow pages (*les pages jaunes—lay pahzh zhon*) provides a tremendous amount of information. What choices are given if you want to phone home?

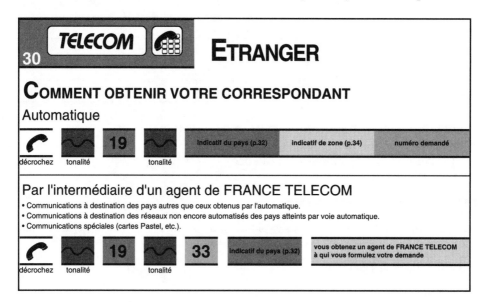

Special Needs

Many telephone products are available for those with limited visual, auditory, and motor skills. Read the following description of items available to the physically challenged. Can you figure out what kinds of products can be obtained? (Answers below.)

> Pour aider les personnes handicapées qui ont des difficultés à utiliser le téléphone, cinq produits de base concernant les déficients auditifs, visuels et moteurs, sont proposés:
>
> —le combiné téléphonique à écoute amplifiée réglable
>
> —l'avertisseur lumineux d'appel téléphonique
>
> —le poste téléphonique simplifié à 2 numéros préenregistrés
>
> —la bobine (reel) magnétique pour capsule téléphonique
>
> —les couronnes (rings, rims) à gros chiffres, à repères (with marks) ou en braille adaptables sur un poste téléphonique à cadran

Did you say an adjustable, amplified receiver? A special light informing the user that a call was made? A simplified phone with two preregistered numbers? A close-captioned telephone? An outer ring with large numbers? A telephone dial written in braille? Good for you!

Culture Capsule

The grey, open public phone booths in France use the 50 or 120 "Unités Télécom" telecards. These cards are on sale at tobacconists, post offices, and in any location with a sign that reads "Télécarte en vente ici."

To call the United States or Canada, dial 19 + 1 + area code + number.

Hello? Who's Calling?

Telephone dialogues are a lot more difficult to conduct than face-to-face conversations, since you're not able to observe a person's facial expressions and gestures. In addition, telephones tend to distort voices and sounds. Familiarize yourself with the words used to make and answer a phone call. The following table shows you how to begin a telephone conversation.

Making a Phone Call

Calling		Answering	
allô (*ah-lo*)	hello	allô (*ah-lo*)	hello
Je suis bien chez ...? (*zhuh swee byaN shay*)	Is this the... residence?	Qui est à l'appareil? (*kee eh tah lah-pah-rehy*)	Who's calling?
C'est... (*seh*)	It's...	Ici... (*ee-see*)	This is...
...est là? (*... eh lah?*)	Is... in (*there*)?		
Je voudrais parler à... (*zhuh voo-dreh pahr-lay ah*)	I would like to speak to...	Ne quittez (quitte) pas. (*nuh kee-tay (keet) pah*),	Hold on,
		Un moment (*uhN moh-mahN*),	Just a moment,
		Il (Elle) n'est pas là (*eel [ehl] neh pah lah*)	He (She) is not in.
Quand sera-t-il (elle) de retour? (*kahN suh-rah-teel [tehl] duh ruh-toor*)	When will he (she) be back?	Voulez-vous (veux-tu) laisser un message? (*voo-lay voo [vuh-tew] leh-say uhN meh-sahzh*)	Do you want to leave a message?

continues

Making a Phone Call (cont.)

Calling	Answering
Je vais rappeler plus tard. (*zhuh veh rah-play plew tahr*)	I'll call back later.

Attention!

Allô is used only on the telephone in France. To greet someone in person, use *bonjour*, *bonsoir* (in the evening only), or *salut* (to be more friendly).

Sorry, Wrong Number

You can run into many problems when making a phone call: a wrong number, a busy signal, a hang up. Here are some examples of phrases you might say or hear should you run into any difficulties:

Vous demandez quel numéro?
voo duh-mahN-day kehl new-may-ro?
What number are you calling?

C'est une erreur. (J'ai) Vous avez le mauvais numéro.
seh tewn eh-ruhr (zhay) voo zah-vay luh moh-veh new-may-ro
It's a mistake. (I have) You have the wrong number.

On nous a coupés.
ohN noo zah koo-pay.
We got cut off (disconnected).

Recomposez le numéro, s'il vous plaît.
ruh-kohN-poh-zay luh new-may-ro seel voo pleh
Please redial the number.

Le téléphone est en panne (hors de service).
luh tay-lay-fohn eh tahN pahn (tohr dsehr-vees)
The telephone is out of order.

J'entends mal.	Je ne peux pas vous (t') entendre.
zhahN-tahN mahl	*zhuh nuh puh pah voo zahN-tahNdr (tahN tahNdr)*
I can't hear you.	I can't hear you.

Rappelez-moi (Rappelle-moi) plus tard.
rah-play (rah-pehl)-mwah plew tahr
Call me back later.

Minitel

Minitel is France's telephone-database network that allows you to accomplish many tasks easily: find out the weather, make reservations at hotels and restaurants, choose television programs to watch, purchase tickets to events, do your banking—just to name a few. If your hotel subscribes to Minitel, you are in luck. Read the following ad and see if you can determine what other important benefit this service provides to the telephone user.

Le Minitel est un petit terminal de fonctionnement simple qui se branche sur la ligne téléphonique. Il se compose d'un écran et d'un clavier et permet de communiquer avec de nombreux services (informations, renseignements, dialogues, etc.). Ainsi, de partout en France, vous pouvez obtenir le service de l'annuaire électronique.

L'annuaire électronique vous permet d'obtenir le numéro de téléphone et l'adresse de tous les abonnés de France.

What Are Your Obligations?

Perhaps you are very busy and do not have the time to talk on the phone today. The irregular verb *devoir*, shown in the following table, enables you to express what you have to do instead. This verb resembles a shoe verb in that the *nous* and *vous* forms look like the infinitive, while the other forms do not.

Devoir (To Have to)

je dois	*zhuh dwah*	I have to
tu dois	*tew dwah*	you have to
il, elle, on doit	*eel (ehl, ohN) dwah*	he (she, one) has to
nous devons	*noo duh-vohN*	we have to
vous devez	*voo duh-vay*	you have to
ils, elles doivent	*eel (ehl) dwahv*	they have to

Since the verb *devoir* is followed by another verb, *devoir* is conjugated while the second verb remains in the infinitive:

Je dois raccrocher.　　　　　　　　Ils doivent se reposer.
zhuh dwah rah-kroh-shay　　　　　*eel dwahv suh ruh-po-zay*
I have to hang up.　　　　　　　　　They have to rest.

Nous devons téléphoner à notre famille.
noo duh-vohN tay-lay-foh-nay ah nohtr fah-mee-y
We have to call our family.

353

Un deux trois

Write a list, in French, of five things that you and your family members have to do today.

I Can't Talk Now

We've all had experiences where the phone has started ringing just as we've gotten one foot out the door, or when we're up to our elbows in grease. Sometimes we're in too much of a hurry to turn around and pick it up. Tell why each of these people can't speak on the phone right now by using *devoir* (conjugated) + infinitive:

1. elle/réparer sa voiture _____ .
2. nous/aller en ville _____ .
3. tu/sortir _____ .
4. vous/faire des courses _____ .
5. ils/travailler _____ .
6. je/partir tout de suite _____ .

Attention!

The past participle of reflexive verbs agrees in gender and number with the preceding direct object pronoun. If the direct object follows the noun, there is no agreement. All reflexive verbs use *être* as a helping verb in the *passé composé*.

What Did You Do to Yourself?

Other reasons why you can't talk on the phone may involve a reflexive verb in the past tense. All reflexive verbs use *être* as a helping verb in the *passé composé*:

Je me suis endormi(e).	Nous nous sommes endormi(e)s.
Tu t'es endormi(e).	Vous vous êtes endormi(e)(s).
Il s'est endormi.	Ils se sont endormis.
Elle s'est endormie.	Elles se sont endormies.

In the negative and in questions the reflexive pronoun stays before the conjugated helping verb:

> Elle ne *s'est* pas réveillée à temps.
> *S'est*-elle réveillée à temps?
> Ne *s'est*-elle pas réveillée à temps?

There is no agreement of the past participle if the reflexive pronoun is used as an indirect object. This happens only rarely:

> Elle *s'*est lavée.
> She washed *herself.*

Herself is the direct object. Since *s'* is a preceding direct object, the past participle *lavée* must agree with the preceding feminine direct object pronoun *s'*.

> Elle *s'*est lavé les cheveux.
> She washed her hair *herself.*

The implied *(for) herself* is the indirect object. *Hair* is the direct object. Since *s'* is a preceding indirect object and the direct object (*les cheveux*) comes after the verb, there is no agreement of the past participle *lavé* with the preceding indirect object pronoun *s'*.

Making Excuses

Tell why each person didn't get to make the phone call he or she was supposed to make:

1. je (f.)/se casser le bras _____ .
2. elle/se réveiller tard _____ .
3. nous (m.)/s'occuper d'autre chose _____ .
4. ils/se mettre à travailler _____ .
5. vous (f. pl.)/se lever _____ .
6. tu (f.)/se coucher tôt à midi _____ .

The Least You Need to Know

➤ Use the information in the front of the French yellow pages to help you make the most of your phone calls.

➤ A *Télécarte* allows you to use most French telephones.

➤ Reflexive verbs use *être* as their helping verb in the past tense.

Chapter 23

Please, Mr. Postman

In This Chapter

➤ Sending and receiving your mail

➤ The irregular verbs *écrire* (to write) and *lire* (to read)

➤ The difference between *savoir* and *connaître*

➤ Comparing the *passé composé* and the imperfect

In the previous chapter you learned how to make a phone call, begin a telephone conversation, explain any difficulties with the line, and use proper phone etiquette. You also learned that public telephones are readily available in French post offices—and that's where we are off to next.

Chances are that you won't go to a post office to make a phone call, but you will visit one to send letters, postcards, and packages to family and friends. You'll learn how to send registered and special delivery letters as well as letters via air mail so that you can be assured your mail gets to its destination—and gets there fast. In your correspondence you'll be able to express facts you learned and people you became acquainted with as well as describe all the activities you participated in from the time of your arrival.

Sending Your Mail

You've just visited the Musée du Louvre, dined at La Tour d'Argent, and shopped at Chanel, and now you can't wait to share your experiences with your friends and family. Usually, any letter sent through the mail arrives at its destination. The real question is how soon it will get there. If it's speed you want, postage rates will be higher. It costs 2.80F to send a first-class, local letter in France. At an exchange rate of 5F=$1, American postage is a bargain. You cannot mail a letter or package, of course, without a few mail essentials, such as envelopes and stamps. The following table provides the vocabulary you need to send your mail:

Mail and Post Office Terms

address	l'addresse (f.)	*lah-drehs*
addressee	le destinataire	*luh dehs-tee-nah-tehr*
air letter	l'aérogramme (m.)	*lahy-roh-grahm*
commemorative stamp	le timbre commémoratif	*luh taNbr koh-may-moh-rah-teef*
envelope	l'enveloppe (f.)	*lahN-vlohp*
letter	la lettre	*lah lehtr*
mailbox	la boîte aux lettres	*lah bwaht o lehtr*
money order	le mandat-poste	*luh mahN-dah pohst*
package	le paquet	*luh pah-keh*
parcel	le colis	*luh koh-lee*
postcard	la carte postale	*lah kahrt pohs-tahl*
postage	l'affranchissement (m.)	*lah-frahN-shees-mahN*
postal code	le code postal (régional)	*luh kohd pohs-tahl (ray-zhoh-nahl)*
postal meter	la machine à affranchir	*lah mah-sheen ah ah-frahN-sheer*
postal worker	le facteur (m.), la factrice (f.)	*luh fahk-tuhr, lah fahk-trees*
postmark	le cachet de la poste	*luh kah-sheh duh lah pohst*
rate	le tarif	*luh tah-reef*
sender	l'expéditeur (m.), l'expéditrice (f.)	*lehks-pay-dee-tuhr, lehks-pay-dee-trees*
sheet of stamps	la feuille de timbres	*lah fuhy duh taNbr*
slot	la fente	*lah fahNt*
stamp	le timbre	*luh taNbr*
window	le guichet	*luh gee-sheh*

Culture Capsule

In France, the P. T. T. regulates the post office, as well as the telephone system. Many post offices open as early as 8:00 A.M. and close as late as 7:00 P.M., but may take a two hour lunch break! The main branch in Paris is always open. You can purchace stamps at some cafés, bureaux de tabac, and hotels. If you don't want to take a trip to the post office, look for a yellow mailbox.

Service with a Smile

So you've written your letter, folded it, and sealed it in an envelope. Now all you need to do is find a post office or a mailbox. If you don't know where one is located, simply ask:

> Where is the nearest post office (mailbox)?
> Où se trouve (est) le bureau de poste le plus proche (la boîte aux lettres) la plus proche?
> *oo suh troov (eh) luh bew-ro duh pohst luh plew prohsh (lah bwaht o lehtr) lah plew prohsh*

Different types of letters and packages require special forms, paperwork, and special postage rates. It is important to know how to ask for the type of service you need:

> What is the postage rate…?
> Quel est le tarif de l'affranchissement…?
> *kehl eh luh tah-reef duh lah-frahN-shees-mahN*

Foreign Country

pour l'étranger (for overseas)	*poor lay-trahN-zhay*	
for the United States	pour les États-Unis	*poor lay zay-tah zew-nee*
for an air mail letter	pour une lettre envoyée par avion	*poor ewn lehtr ahN-vwah-yay pahr ah-vyohN*

continues

Foreign Country (cont.)

pour l'étranger (for overseas)		*poor lay-trahN-zhay*
for a registered letter	pour une lettre recommandée	*poor ewn lehtr ruh-koh-mahN-day*
for a special delivery letter	pour une lettre par exprès	*poor ewn lehtr pahr ehks-preh*

Memory Enhancer

Remember to put the correct form of the demonstrative adjective (*ce, cet, cette,* or *ces*) before the noun you are using:

Combien coûtent *ces* cartes postales?

How much do these post cards cost?

I would like to send this letter (this package) by regular mail (by air mail, special delivery).
Je voudrais envoyer cette lettre (ce paquet) par courrier régulier (par avion, par exprès).
zhuh voo-dreh zahN-vwah-yay seht lehtr (suh pah-keh) pahr koo-ryay ray-gew-lyay (pahr ah-vyohN, pahr ehks-preh)

I would like to send this package C.O.D.
Je voudrais envoyer ce paquet livrable contre remboursement (payable à l'arrivée).
zhuh voo-dreh zahN-vwah-yay suh pah-keh lee-vrahbl kohNtr rahN-boors-mahN (peh-yahbl ah lah-ree-vay)

How much does this letter (package) weigh?
Combien pèse cette lettre (ce paquet)?
kohN-byaN pehz seht lehtr (suh pah-keh)

When will it arrive? When will they arrive?
Quand arrivera-t-il (elle)? Quand arriveront-ils (elles)?
kahN tah-ree-vrah teel (tehl) kahN tah-ree-vrohN teel (tehl)

At the Post Office

So you finally found a post office. You walk in and immediately notice the following sign:

Les P. T. T. annonce une nouvelle série de timbres du Chunnel pour commémorer son premier anniversaire. La série sera émise en timbres de 5F et de 10F. Les timbres seront disponible dès le 3 mai dans les bureaux de poste.

You can't help it; you're an incorrigible collector. What is the post office offering? What is it celebrating? When is it available?

Sending a Telegram

There's wonderful news—your daughter just had a bouncing baby boy. There's a great business deal—a prestigious French firm wants to market your line of clothing. There's a reason to celebrate—your book of poems has been published. There's a surprise—you're getting married after a whirlwind courtship. You can't wait to share the good news and decide to send a telegram. The following will get you started:

I would like to send a telegram (collect).
Je voudrais envoyer un télégramme (en P.C.V.)
zhuh voo-dreh zahN-vwah-yay uhN tay-lay-grahm (ahN pay-say-vay)

What is the rate per word?
Quel est le tarif par mot?
kehl eh luh tah-reef pahr mo

May I please have a form?
Puis-je avoir un formulaire, s'il vous plaît?
pweezh ah-vwahr uhN fohr-mew-lehr seel voo pleh

Attention!

Invert with *je only* with the following verbs:

puis-je (may I)   suis-je (am I)
ai-je (have I)   dois-je (must I)

What Should I Write?

As you fill out different kinds of paperwork, you will be asked to write down a variety of information. Familiarize yourself with the irregular verb *écrire* (to write) in the following table. Notice that it is necessary to add a *v* before the ending in all the plural forms. The past participle of *écrire* is *écrit* (ay-kree).

Attention!

Remember to use a *v* in all the plural forms of *écrire*.

Écrire (To Write)

j'écris	*zhay-kree*	I write
tu écris	*tew ay-kree*	you write
il, elle, on écrit	*eel (ehl, ohN) nay-kree*	he (she, one) writes
nous écrivons	*noo zay-kree-vohN*	we write
vous écrivez	*voo zay-kree-vay*	you write
ils, elles écrivent	*eel (ehl) zay-kreev*	they write

I Love to Read

You will be doing a lot of reading in French, whether it be forms, signs, menus, magazines, or newspapers. The irregular verb *lire* (to read) is presented in the following table. It is necessary to add an *s* before the ending in all the plural forms. The past participle of *lire* is *lu* (lew).

Lire (To Read)

je lis	*zhuh lee*	I read
tu lis	*tew lee*	you read
il , elle, on lit	*eel (ehl, ohN) lee*	he (she, one) reads
nous lisons	*noo lee-zohN*	we read
vous lisez	*voo lee-zay*	you read
ils, elles lisent	*eel (ehl) leez*	they read

Un deux trois

Make a list in French of all the things you read in one day.

Do French magazines intrigue you? Are you interested in catching up on the news? Is there a sign you don't understand? I'll never forget the time I saw a sign that read: EAU NON-POTOBLE. Although I was a French major, I had never come across this phrase; "potable" was an unfamiliar English cognate to me. I knew that *eau* was water, but that was all I understood. It's a good thing I didn't take a drink. When I later looked up the phrase, I found that it meant that the water was unfit to drink. The following table features items that you may read while in France:

Things to Read

ad	une annonce publicitaire	*ewn nah-nohNs pew-blee-see-tehr*
book	un livre	*uhN leevr*
magazine	un magazine, une revue	*uhN mah-gah-zeen, ewn ruh-vew*
menu	la carte, le menu	*lah kahrt, luh muh-new*
newspaper	un journal	*uhN zhoor-nahl*
novel	un roman	*uhN roh-mahN*
pamphlet	une brochure	*ewn broh-shewr*
receipt	le reçu	*luh ruh-sew*
sign	un écriteau	*uhN nay-kree-to*
warning	un avertissement	*uhN nah-vehr-tees-mahN*

Do You Know Anything About This?

Do you know the name of a great French restaurant? You do? Do you know where it's located? How about the phone number? You know the owner too? He's your second cousin and he really knows how to prepare a mean bouillabaisse? That's great. To express certain facts, information, relationships, and abilities, you will need the two French verbs that express *to know*: *savoir* in the table below and *connaître* in the table that follows it:

Memory Enhancer

The circumflex accent (ˆ) is used over the *i* in *connaitre* when it is followed by a *t*. The past participle of *connaître* is *connu*.

Savoir (To Know) (past participle: su)

je sais	*zhuh seh*	I know
tu sais	*tew seh*	you know
il, elle, on sait	*eel (ehl, ohN) seh*	he (she, one) knows
nous savons	*noo sah-vohN*	we know
vous savez	*voo sah-vez*	you know
ils, elles savent	*eel (ehl) sahv*	they know

Connaître (To Know) (past participle: connu)

je connais	*zhuh koh-neh*	I know
tu connais	*tew koh-neh*	you know
il, elle, on connaît	*eel (ehl, ohN) koh-neh*	he (she, one) knows
nous connaissons	*noo koh-neh-sohN*	we know
vous connaissez	*voo koh-neh-say*	you know
ils connaissent	*eel koh-nehs*	they know

Know the Difference?

If there are two ways to express *to know*, how are you supposed to know when to use each one? The important thing to remember is that the French differentiate between knowing facts and how to do things (*savoir*) and knowing (being acquainted with) people, places, things, and ideas (*connaître*).

363

Memory Enhancer

Use *savoir* to show knowledge gained through learning and experience, to state a fact, and to express knowing how to do something.

Use *connaître* to show familiarity with a person, place, or thing. You should be able to substitute the words "to be acquainted with" for "to know."

Savez-vous l'adresse?
sah-vay voo lah-drehs
Do you know the address?

Sait-il faire du ski?
seh-teel fehr dew skee
Does he know how to ski?

The verb *connaître* shows familiarity with a person, place, or thing. If you can replace *to know* with *to be acquainted with*, use the verb *connaître*.

Connaissez-vous Marie?

koh-neh-say-voo mah-ree

Do you know Marie?

(Are you acquainted with her?)

Connais-tu cette chanson?

koh-neh-tew seht shahN-sohN

Do you know that song?

(Have you heard it? But you don't know the words?)

Notice the difference between:

Je sais ce poème.

Je connais ce poème.

I know this poem (by heart).

I know this poem. (I'm familiar with it.)

Using Savoir and Connaître

Keep the differences between the two verbs in mind and you will quickly learn to use them properly. Show that you've gotten the hang of it by filling in the blanks with the correct form of *savoir* or *connaître*.

1. Ils _____ où se trouve le bureau de poste.

2. Je ne _____ pas son nom.

3. _____-vous les Dupont?

4. Nous _____ parler français.

5. _____-tu cet homme?

6. Elle _____ Paris.

7. _____-vous que je suis de Nice?

8. Nous _____ ce monument.

What Was Going On?

I **was sitting** idly at a club on the boulevard St. Germain, sipping a Cointreau and watching everyone else have a good time. **I didn't know** anyone and **I was getting bored.** All of a sudden, the music *started up* and I *became* intrigued by a sexy Frenchman who **could dance** up a storm. I'm not shy so I *went over* to him and *asked* him for the next dance. **I couldn't** believe he *said* yes. We *danced* and *talked* all night and I *wound up* having a very pleasant evening. He even *asked me* for my number.

Un deux trois

Write two separate lists in French: one of the most important people you know, and one of the special things you know how to do.

It happened recently but, nonetheless, in the past. In English, we speak or write easily in the past. In French, however, it's not that simple because there are two different past tenses: the *passé composé* and the *imperfect (l'imparfait)*, as shown in the preceding paragraph. This tends to make speaking in the past a bit confusing. If you mistake one for the other, you'll still be understood. Sometimes either tense is correct. What's the difference? The *passé composé* expresses specific actions or events that were completed in the past, whereas the *imperfect* expresses an uncompleted action or a continuing state in the past.

Formation of the Imperfect

Before going into a more detailed explanation, let's see how the imperfect is formed. For regular and irregular verbs, the imperfect tense is formed by dropping the *ons* ending from the *nous* form of the present tense and adding the following endings:

je	*ais*	nous	*ions*
tu	*ais*	vous	*iez*
il, elle, on	*ait*	ils, elles	*aient*

Memory Enhancer

The imperfect is different from the passé composé in that the imperfect doesn't require a helping verb.

The following table shows how easy this is:

The Imperfect

er Verbs	*ir* Verbs	*re* Verbs
nous parl**ons**	nous finiss**ons**	nous répond**ons**
je parlais *(zhuh pahr-leh)*	je finissais *(zhuh fee-nee-seh)*	je répondais *(zhuh ray-pohN-deh)*

continues

The Imperfect (cont.)

er Verbs	*ir* Verbs	*re* Verbs
tu parlais *(tew pahr-leh)*	tu finissais *(tew fee-nee-seh)*	tu répondais *(tew ray-pohN-deh)*
il, elle, on parlait *(eel [ehl,ohN] pahr-leh)*	il, elle, on finissait *(eel [ehl, ohN] fee-nee-seh)*	il, elle, on répondait *(eel [ehl, ohN] ray-pohN-deh)*
nous parlions *(noo pahr-lyohN)*	nous finissions *(noo fee-nee-syohN)*	nous répondions *(noo ray-pohN-dyohN)*
vous parliez *(voo pahr-lyay)*	vous finissiez *(voo fee-nee-syay)*	vous répondiez *(voo ray-pohN-dyay)*
ils, elles parlaient *(eel [ehl] pahr-leh)*	ils, elles finissaient *(eel [ehl] fee-nee-seh)*	ils, elles répondaient *(eel [ehl] ray-pohN-deh)*

Memory Enhancer

Verbs ending in *ions* in the present tense have an *i* before the *ions* and *iez* imperfect tense endings:

nous vérif*ions*   nous vérif*iions*

The only verb that is irregular in the imperfect is *être*:

j'étais *(zay-teh)* — nous étions *(noo zay-tyohN)*

tu étais *(tew ay-teh)* — vous étiez *(voo zay-tyay)*

il, elle, on était
(eel [ehl, ohN] ay-teh) — ils, elles étaient
(eel [ehl] zay-teh)

For all other irregular verbs in the present tense, you must know the correct *nous* form in order to form the imperfect. How good is your memory? Fill in the *nous* form for the irregular verbs in the following table and then supply the correct form of the imperfect for the subject given:

The Imperfect of Irregular Verbs

avoir (to have)	nous _____	elle _____
boire (to drink)	nous _____	je _____
connaître (to be acquainted with)	nous _____	vous _____
devoir (to have to)	nous _____	tu _____
dire (to say, tell)	nous _____	ils _____
dormir (to sleep)	nous _____	nous _____
écrire (to write)	nous _____	elles _____
faire (to make, do)	nous _____	vous _____
lire (to read)	nous _____	je _____
mettre (to put [on])	nous _____	nous _____
partir (to leave)	nous _____	tu _____

366

pouvoir (to be able to)	nous _____	elle _____
prendre (to take)	nous _____	ils _____
recevoir (to receive)	nous _____	vous _____
savoir (to know)	nous _____	elles _____
sentir (to feel, smell)	nous _____	il _____
servir (to serve)	nous _____	elle _____
sortir (to go out)	nous _____	tu _____
voir (to see)	nous _____	elles _____
vouloir (to want)	nous _____	je _____

Certain shoe verbs have spelling changes:

➤ *cer* verbs

Verbs ending in *cer* change *c* to *ç* before *a* or *o* to maintain the soft *c* sound. These changes occur within the shoe:

j'avançais	nous avancions
tu avançais	vous avanciez
il, elle, on avançait	ils, elles avançaient

➤ *ger* verbs

Verbs ending in *ger* insert a silent *e* between *g* and *a* or *o* to keep the soft *g* sound. These changes occur within the shoe:

je mangeais	nous mangions
tu mangeais	vous mangiez
il, elle, on mangeait	ils, elles mangeaient

Memory Enhancer

The imperfect is for past events that occurred over a period of time (a wavy line) and the passé composé is for past events that occurred in an instant (a dot).

The Passé Composé vs. the Imperfect

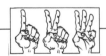

Un deux trois

Write a list of things you used to do as a child.

Which should you use? And when? The *passé composé* expresses an action that was completed at a specific time in the past. Think of a camera. The *passé composé* represents an action that could be captured by an instamatic; the action happened and was completed.

The *imperfect* expresses an action that continued in the past over an indefinite period of time. Think again of a camera. The *imperfect* represents an action that could be captured by a video camera; the action continued to flow, it *was* happening, *used to* happen, or *would* (meaning *used to*) happen. The *imperfect* is a descriptive tense. The following table provides a more in-depth look at the differences between the two tenses:

Comparison of the Passé Composé and the Imperfect

Passé Composé	Imperfect
1. Events that were started and completed at a definite time in the past (even if the time isn't mentioned): *J'ai parlé au directeur.* (I spoke to the director.)	1. Continuous events in the past (which may or may not have been completed): *Je parlais au directeur.* (I was speaking to the director.)
2. A specific event that occurred at a specific point in time: *Hier il est sorti à midi.* (Yesterday he went out at noon.)	2. Repeated events that took place in the past: *D'habitude il sortait à midi.* (He usually went out at noon.)
3. A specific event that was repeated a stated number of times: *Ils sont allés au cinéma six fois.* (They went to the movies six times.)	3. Describing a person, place, thing, or state of mind: *Nous étions contents.* (We were happy.) *La mer était calme.* (The sea was calm.) *La porte était ouverte.* (The door was open.) *Je voulais partir.* (I wanted to leave.)

Un deux trois

Speak about what happened yesterday. Use the *passé composé* and the imperfect to talk about your day.

Passé Composé or Imparfait?

The weather was beautiful and I went on a picnic with a friend. Something unforeseen happened that almost ruined our day. Complete our story with the correct form of the verb in the *passé composé* or in the imperfect:

C'(être) _____ une belle journeé de printemps. Le ciel (être) _____ bleu et les oiseaux (chanter) _____. Je ne (faire) _____ pas grand chose quand tout à coup le téléphone (sonner) _____. C'(être) _____ mon amie Barbara. Elle me (m') (demander) _____ si je (vouloir) _____ faire un pique-nique dans les bois. Je (J') (dire) _____ "Oui, volontiers!" Alors je (partir) _____ la chercher à 10 h chez elle et nous (aller) _____ au parc en voiture. En route, nous (s'arrêter) _____ à la charcuterie pour acheter des sandwiches et des boissons. À 11 h nous (arriver) _____ au parc. Le soleil (briller) _____ et il (faire) _____ si beau. Nous (trouver) _____ vite un endroit pour nous installer. Nous (commencer) _____ à manger nos sandwiches quand tout à coup une abeille (attaquer) _____ Barbara. Elle (crier) _____ mais elle (s'échapper) _____. Nous (passer) _____ le reste de la journée à parler de nos amis et à nous amuser. L'après-midi (être) _____ magnifique.

The Least You Need to Know

➤ *Savoir* means to know a fact or how to do something. *Connaître* means to be acquainted with a person, place, or thing.

➤ The imperfect is used to describe what the subject *was* doing. The *passé composé* states what the subject *did*.

➤ The imperfect is usually formed by adding appropriate endings to the *nous* form (minus the *ons* ending) of the verb.

Part 5
It's Time for Business

Today, more than ever, businesses seek bilingual personnel who can communicate effectively in our ever-expanding, multilingual world. Knowing a foreign language can be the key to a very successful career.

Part 5 is for readers whose jobs and businesses require more than a cursory knowledge of French. Our modern, high-tech society demands a knowledge of current computer terms and phrases, as well as the vocabulary necessary to fax and photocopy important documents. Business and banking expressions are also a must. And for travelers who are constantly on the go, or who like to combine business with pleasure, alternatives to the traditional hotel stay are presented.

By the time you've completed Part 5, if you've worked diligently, ambitiously, and conscientiously, you'll be ready to face any situation that you might encounter in French. I know you can do it on your own!

Chapter 24

For the Businessperson

In This Chapter

➤ Stationery store supplies

➤ Photocopies, faxes, and computers

➤ Business talk

➤ The future tense

Chapter 23 helped you find a mailbox and a post office, purchase stamps, envelopes, and other mail essentials, and inquire about postal rates. You also learned how to express in French what you wish to read or write, facts and people you know, and activities you carried out in the past.

Now that you're a pro at letter writing, you might make an attempt to conduct some business in French. To do so, you'll need office supplies and a knowledge of the fax, photocopy, and computer phrases presented in this chapter. You'll learn some key phrases that all good businesspeople use and how to express your future business plans.

I Need Supplies

To carry out any kind of business, you'll need to purchase some necessary tools of the trade. One important stop would be *à la papeterie* (ah lah pah-puh-tree—at the stationery store), where you'll find the business items listed in the following table. Begin your transaction by saying:

I would like to buy...
Je voudrais acheter...
zhuh voo-dreh zahsh-tay

Culture Capsule

Because it is a world economic leader, France offers a wealth of business opportunities. France has the fourth largest economy, is the European leader in the aerospace industry, and is the world leader in tourism, with over 60 million visitors a year.

At the Stationery Store

Item	French	Pronunciation
ball-point pen	un stylo (à bille)	*uhN stee-lo (ah beey)*
calculator (solar)	une calculette (solaire)	*ewn kahl-kew-leht (soh-lehr)*
envelopes	des envelopes (f.)	*day zahN-vlohp*
eraser	une gomme	*ewn gohm*
glue	de la colle	*duh lah kohl*
notebook	un cahier	*uhN kah-yay*
paper	du papier	*dew pah-pyay*
paper clips	des agrafes (f.), des pinces (f.)	*day ah-grahf day paNs*
pencil sharpener	un taille-crayon	*uhN tahy-kreh-yohN*
pencils	des crayons (m.)	*day kreh-yohN*
post-its	des billets (m.)	*day bee-yeh*
ruler	une règle	*ewn rehgl*
scotch tape	une bande adhésive un scotch	*ewn bahNd ah-ay-seev uhN skohtch*
stapler	une agrafeuse	*ewn ah-grah-fuhz*
stationery	du papier à lettres	*dew pah-pyay ah lehtr*
string	de la ficelle	*duh lah fee-sehl*
wrapping paper	du papier d'emballage	*dew pah-pyay dahN-bah-lahzh*
writing pad	un bloc	*uhN blohk*

Photocopies, Faxes, and Computers

Today, most businesses require three essential items to help facilitate and expedite business projects: faxes, photocopy machines, and computers.

Photocopying

Imagine that your firm has sent you to France on a business trip. You have a generous expense account for which you must submit receipts. Your wallet is quite full of them and you'd like a back-up copy in case one or two get lost in your travels. A wise idea would be to have photocopies made as soon as possible. Here's what you might have to say:

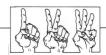

Un deux trois

Write French labels for all the stationery items you keep on your desk. Don't remove the labels until you have all the names down pat. Then test yourself.

I would like to make a photocopy of this paper (this document).
Je voudrais faire une photocopie de ce papier (ce document).
zhuh voo-dreh fehr ewn foh-to-koh-pee duh suh pah-pyay (suh doh-kew-mahN)

I would like to have a photocopy made of this document.
Je voudrais faire faire une photocopie de ce papier (ce document).
zhuh voo-dreh fehr fehr ewn foh-to-koh-pee duh suh pah-pyay (suh doh-kew-mahN)

What is the cost per page?
Quel est le prix par page?
kehl eh luh pree pahr pahzh

Can you enlarge it (by 50 percent)?
Pouvez-vous l'élargir (de cinquante pour cent)?
poo-vay voo lay-lahr-zheer (duh saN-kahNt poor sahN)

Can you reduce it (by 25 percent)?
Pouvez-vous le réduire (de vingt-cinq pour cent)?
poo-vay vous luh ray-dweer (duh vaN-saNk poor sahN)

Can you make a color copy?
Pouvez-vous en faire une copie en couleurs?
poo-vay voo ahN fehr ewn koh-pee ahN koo-luhr

Attention!

Although the verb *faxer* is often used informally, it's use is frowned upon by purists, who regard it as nothing more than *franglais*.

Faxing

Businesses have come to realize that faxing information and documents is an extremely convenient service. Being able to transmit and receive information in a matter of seconds or minutes speeds up the time it takes to transact business. And that translates into extra dollars and francs. If you are conducting business in France, you will want to be fax-literate:

Do you have a fax machine?
Avez-vous un télécopieur?
ah-vay voo uhN tay-lay-kohp-yuhr

What is your fax number?
Quel est le numéro de votre télécopieur?
kehl eh luh new-may-ro duh vohtr tay-lay-kohp-yuhr

I'd like to send a fax.
Je voudrais transmettre une télécopie.
zhuh voo-dreh trahNz-mehtr ewn tay-lay-koh-pee

May I fax this, please?
Puis-je transmettre cette télécopie, s'il vous plaît?
pweezh trahNz-mehtr seht tay-lay-koh-pee seel voo pleh

May I fax this letter (document) to you?
Puis-je vous transmettre une télécopie de cette lettre (de ce document)?
pweezh voo trahNz-mehtr ewn tay-lay-koh-pee duh seht lehtr (duh suh doh-kew-mahN)

Fax it to me.
Envoyez-m'en (Envoie-m'en) une télécopie.
ahN-vwah-yay mahN (ahN-vwah mahN) ewn tay-lay-koh-pee

I didn't get your fax.
Je n'ai pas reçu votre télécopie.
zhuh nay pah ruh-sew vohtr tay-lay-koh-pee

Did you receive my fax?
Avez-vous reçu ma télécopie?
ah-vay voo ruh-sew mah tay-lay-koh-pee

Your fax is illegible.
Votre télécopie n'est pas lisible.
vohtr tay-lay-koh-pee neh pah lee-zeebl

Please send it again.
Veuillez la transmettre de nouveau.
vuh-yay lah trahNz-mehtr duh noo-vo

Culture Capsule

The main products that the United States imports from France are: aircraft and spacecraft (engines, motors and parts); alcoholic beverages (Chambord, Cointreau, Pernod, wines, champagnes); motor vehicle parts and accessories; perfumes and cosmetics (Chanel, Dior, Yves Saint-Laurent, Guerlain, Lancôme); and works of art, antiques, and glassware (Baccarat, Lalique). Due to the French T.V.A. (value added tax), some products made in France are less expensive to buy in the United States.

Computing

In today's fast-paced world, you must have some computer knowledge to conduct business. It's important to know what system, programs, and peripherals other businesses are using. Will your word processors and spreadsheets be compatible? Can you network? The following phrases will help you, even if you're not a computer geek. Don't worry, you'll be able to get by using the terms in the following table.

What kind of computer do you have?
Quel système (type, genre) d'ordinateur avez-vous?
kehl sees-tehm (teep, zhahNr) dohr-dee-nah-tuhr ah-vay voo

What operating system are you using?
Quel système opérant employez-vous?
kehl sees-tehm oh-pay-rahN ahN-plwah-yay-voo

What word processing program are you using?
Quel système de traitement de texte employez-vous?
kehl sees-tehm duh treht-mahN duh tehkst ahN-plwah-yay-voo

What spreadsheet program are you using?
Quel tableur employez-vous?
kehl tah-bluhr ahN-plwah-yay-voo

What peripherals do you have?
Quels périphériques avez-vous?
kehl pay-ree-fay-reek ah-vay voo

Are our systems compatible?
Nos systèmes, sont-ils compatibles?
no sees-tehm sohN teel kohN-pah-teebl

Do you have...?	Do you use...?
Avez-vous...?	Employez-vous...?
ah-vay voo	*ahN-plwah-yay-voo*

Culture Capsule

The main products that the United States exports to France are: engines, motors, aircraft and spacecraft, measuring and analysis equipment, parts for office machines, gold, medicinal products, medical and dental instruments, appliances, and telecommunication equipment.

Mini–Dictionary for Computer Users

Word	French	Pronunciation
access	l'accès (m.)	*lahk-seh*
(to) access	accéder	*ahk-say-day*
accessibility	l'accessibilité (f.)	*lahk-seh-see-bee-lee-tay*
bar graph	l'histogramme (m.)	*lees-toh-grahm*
(to) boot	démarrer	*day-mah-ray*
brand name	la marque	*lah mahrk*
bug	la bogue	*lah bohg*
byte	le byte	*luh beet*
cable	le câble	*luh kahbl*
cartridge (laser) (ink jet)	la cartouche (laser) (jet d'encre)	*lah kahr-toosh (lah-zehr) (zheh dahNkr)*
CD-ROM disc	le disque optique numérique	*luh deesk ohp-teek new-may-reek*
chip	la puce	*lah pews*
(to) click	cliquer	*klee-kay*
clipboard	le presse-papiers	*luh prehs-pah-pyay*
clone	le clone	*luh klon*
compatible	compatible	*kohN-pah-teeble*
computer	l'ordinateur (m.)	*lohr-dee-nah-tuhr*
computer science	l'informatique (f.)	*laN-fohr-mah-teek*
connection	le raccordement	*luh rah-kohrd-mahN*

Word	French	Pronunciation
connector	le connecteur	*luh koh-nehk-tuhr*
CPU	l'unité centrale (f.)	*lew-nee-tay sahN-trahl*
cursor	le curseur	*luh kuhr-suhr*
database	la base de données	*lah bahz duh doh-nay*
(to) debug	déboguer	*day-boh-gay*
debugger (software)	le débogueur	*luh day-boh-guhr*
desktop computer	l'ordinateur (m.)	*lohr-dee-nah-tuhr*
diskette (3 1/2 in.) (5 1/4 in.)	la disquette (de trois pouces et demi) (de cinq pouces et quart)	*lah dees-keht (duh trwah poos ay duh-mee) (duh saNk poos ay kahr)*
disk drive	le lecteur de disques	*luh lehk-tuhr duh deesk*
DOS	le disque système opérant	*luh deesk sees-tehm oh-pay-rahN*
(to) download	décharger	*day-shahr-zhay*
drop-down menu	le menu-déroulant	*luh muh-new day-roo-lahN*
e-mail	la messagerie électronique le courrier électronique	*lah meh-sahzh-ree ay-lehk-troh-neek* *luh koor-yay ay-lehk-troh-neek*
field	la zone	*lah zon*
filter	le filtre écran	*luh feeltr ay-krahN*
floppy disk	le disque souple	*luh deesk soopl*
freeware	le graciel	*luh grah-syehl*
function key	la touche de fonction	*lah toosh duh fohNk-syohN*
furniture	le mobilier	*luh moh-bee-lyay*
graphics card (high resolution)	la carte graphique (haute résolution)	*lah kahrt grah-feek (ot ray-soh-lew-syohN)*
hacker	le pirate	*luh pee-raht*
hard disk	le disque dur	*luh deesk dewr*
hardware	le matériel	*luh mah-tay-ryehl*
home computer use	le domotique	*luh doh-moh-teek*
(to) insert	introduire, insérer	*aN-troh-dweer, aN-say-ray*
Internet	l'Internet	*laN-tehr-neh*
joystick	la manette de jeux	*lah mah-neht duh zhuh*
key	la touche	*lah toosh*
keyboard	le clavier	*luh klah-vyay*
laptop computer	l'ordinateur portable (m.)	*lohr-dee-nah-tuhr pohr-tahbl*
mail merge	le mailing le publipostage	*luh meh-leeng* *luh pew-blee-pohs-tahzh*

continues

Mini-Dictionary for Computer Users (cont.)

Word	French	Pronunciation
mainframe	le grand système le gros ordinateur	*luh grahN sees-tehm* *luh gro zohr-dee-nah-tuhr*
memory	la mémoire	*lah may-mwahr*
memory card	la carte d'extension de mémoire	*lah kahrt dehk-stahN-syohN* *duh may-mwahr*
microcomputer	le micro-ordinateur	*luh mee-kro ohr-dee-nah-tuhr*
modem	le modem	*luh moh-dehm*
monitor (black and white) (color)	le moniteur (noir et blanc) (couleur)	*luh moh-nee-tuhr (nwahr ay* *blahN) (koo-luhr)*
motherboard	la carte-mère	*lah kahrt mehr*
mouse	la souris	*lah soo-ree*
network	le réseau	*luh ray-zo*
online service	les serveurs en ligne (m.)	*lay sehr-vuhr ahN lee-nyuh*
operating system	le système opérant le système d'exploitation	*luh sees-tehm oh-pay-rahN* *luh sees-tehm dehks-plwah-* *tah-syohN*
pairing telephone and computer	la télématique	*lah tay-lay-mah-teek*
peripherals	les périphériques (m.)	*lay pay-ree-fay-reek*
pie graph	le camembert le fromage le graphe circulaire	*luh kah-mahN-behr* *luh froh-mahzh* *luh grahf seer-kew-lehr*
power surge	le parasite violent	*luh pah-rah-seet vee-oh-lahN*
public domain	le domaine publique	*luh doh-mehn pew-bleek*
(to) reboot	redémarrer	*ruh-day-mah-ray*
(to) scan	scanner digitaliser	*skah-nay* *dee-zhee-tah-lee-zay*
scanner	le scanneur le numériseur	*luh skah-nuhr* *luh new-may-ree-zuhr*
scanning	le balayage	*luh bah-lah-yahzh*
screen	l'écran (m.)	*lay-krahN*
software	le logiciel	*luh loh-zhee-syehl*
speed	la vitesse	*lah vee-tehs*
spell checker	le correcteur orthographique	*luh koh-rehk-tuhr* *ohr-toh-grah-feek*
spreadsheet	le tableur	*luh tah-bluhr*
system	le système	*luh sees-tehm*
terminal	le terminal	*luh tehr-mee-nahl*

Word	French	Pronunciation
thesaurus	le thesaurus la recherche de synonymes	*luh tuh-so-rews* *lah ruh-shehrsh duh* *see-noh-neem*
training	la formation	*lah fohr-mah-syohN*
user	l'utilisateur (m.)	*lew-tee-lee-zah-tuhr*
word processer	le système de traitement de texte	*luh sees-tehm duh treht-mahN* *duh tehkst*
worksheet	la feuille de calcul	*lah fuhy duh kahl-kewl*
workstation	la station de travail	*lah stah-syohN duh trah-vahy*

Surfing the Net

Whenever I need some help and can't seem to find anyone around, I just go down to the den. Chances are my husband or one of my sons is there, face glued to the computer screen, eyes fixed on the monitor, fingers poised on the keyboard. Everyone's passion these days seems to be surfing the Net. You can spend hours traveling to different countries and collecting information about every subject imaginable for a minimal fee. If you would like, you can do so in French! It's so simple that I did it myself in a matter of minutes. Here's what you do:

1. Go to the location box on your Web browser.
2. Type http://www.altavista.digital.com or www.hotbot.com.
3. Click Enter.
4. You will see a search screen. Click on "any language."
5. Select French.
6. You can search for any subject you like and practice everything you've learned so far.

Memory Enhancer

To say "Internet" in French, use *l' Internet* and pronounce it with your best French accent. To say "e-mail," use *la messagerie* or *le courrier électronique*.

Un deux trois

Can't find your dictionary? Need a word in French? Try http:// www.olf.gouv.qc.ca/service/pages/ p10c.html, the *Office de la Langue Française*.

Do You Know Your Computer?

Let's say you want to communicate via computer with a business associate in France. You will have to be able to give certain facts about your system in order to facilitate the transmission. Can you answer these questions about your computer?

1. Quel système d'ordinateur employez-vous?
2. Quels périphériques employez-vous?
3. Votre système a combien de megabytes de mémoire?
4. Quelle est la vitesse de votre système?
5. Quels logiciels employez-vous?

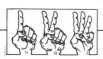

Un deux trois

If you need tourist or cultural information about France, go to http://paris.org/OTP/, the *Office de Tourisme de Paris*. This Web site offers valuable information in French, English, German, Italian, and Spanish.

Un deux trois

You can contact the French embassy in Washington, D.C. at the following site to get information on economic, political, scientific, and linguistic matters:

http://www.info-france-usa.org

Being a Good Businessperson

If you are planning to export or ship goods to a French firm, the following shipping phrases ought to help you expedite matters:

You (We) pay the shipping.
Les frais de transport sont à votre (notre) charge.
lay freh duh tranz-pohr sohN tah vohtr (nohtr) shahrzh.

We give you the choice of (having the merchandise shipped) by truck or by plane.
Nous vous donnons le choix soit par camionneur soit par avion.
noo voo doh-nohN luh shwah swah pahr kah-myoh-nuhr swah pahr ah-vyohN

We send a delivery slip as well as a copy of the invoice with each delivery.
Nous adressons un bon de livraison ainsi qu'une copie de la facture dans chaque livraison.
noo zah-dreh-sohN uhN bohN duh lee-vreh-zohN aN-see kewn koh-pee duh lah fahk-tewr dahN shahk lee-vreh-zohN.

What a Deal!

Everybody loves a good price, or better yet, a discount. When you want to seal a deal, try these phrases:

Our prices are very competitive.
Nos prix sont très compétitifs.
noo pree sohN treh kohN-pay-tee-teef

We can reduce the cost (sell you the merchandise at a better price).
Nous pouvons vous vendre la marchandise à meilleur prix.
noo poo-vohN voo vahNdr lah mahr-shahN-deez ah meh-yuhr pree

We can give you a 1 percent discount on the merchandise.
Nous pouvons vous faire une exonération d'un pour cent sur la marchandise.
noo poo-vohN voo fehr ewn ehk-zoh-nay-rah-syohN duhN poor sahN sewr lah mahr-shahN-deez

Culture Capsule

It is very rare to receive what Americans might consider a large discount. The price is usually the price. In fact, a real discount is referred to as an "American discount!" However, as retail markets are deregulated, allowing more stores to open in any one area, the kinds of discounts Americans are accustomed to are becoming more common.

If you pay within 30 days, we can give you a discount of 5 percent.
Si vous réglez la facture dans les trente jours, nous pouvons vous faire une réduction de 5 pour cent.
see voo ray-glay lah fahk-tewr dahN lay trahNt zhoor noo poo-vohN voo fehr ewn ray-dewk-syohN duh saNk poor sahN

A Job Well Done

No one likes to feel that he is being taken for a ride, especially if there's a language barrier. Instill confidence in your customers with the following phrases:

You will find our merchandise to be high quality.
Vous trouverez notre marchandise de très bonne qualité.
voo troo-vray nohtr mahr-shahN-deez duh treh bohn kah-lee-tay

Is there anything else I can do for you?
Il y a quelque chose d'autre que je peux faire pour vous?
eel yah kehl-uh shoz dohtr kuh zhuh puh fehr poor voo

You can return the merchandise if you are not completely satified.
Vous pouvez nous rendre la marchandise au cas où vous n'êtes pas complètement satisfait.
voo poo-vay noo rahNdr lah mahr-shahN-deez o kah zoo voo neht pah koh-pleht-mahN sah-tees-feh

It's a pleasure doing business with you.
C'est un plaisir travailler avec vous.
seh tuhN play-zeer trah-vah-yay ah-vehk voo

It's a pleasure to serve you.
C'est un plaisir vous servir.
seh tuhN play-zeer voo sehr-veer

Culture Capsule

France is the world's fourth largest exporter and importer, leads the world in wine production, and produces almost 8 percent of the world's automobiles.

The preceding phrases were just to give you a taste of what you might need to say. If
you're really serious about doing business, the mini-dictionary in the following table
gives you all the necessary terms that the average businessperson might need:

Mini-Dictionary for Businesspeople

accountant	le comptable	*luh kohN-tahbl*
activity	le mouvement d'affaires	*luh moov-mahN dah-fehr*
amount	le montant	*luh mohN-tahN*
(to) appraise	évaluer	*ay-vah-lew-ay*
assets	l'actif (m.)	*lahk-teef*
(to) authorize	autoriser	*o-to-ree-zay*
balance sheet	le bilan	*luh bee-lahN*
bankruptcy	la faillite	*lah fah-yeet*
bill	la facture de paiement	*lah fahk-tewr duh peh-mahN*
bill of exchange	la lettre de change	*lah lehtr duh shahNzh*
bill of lading	le connaissement	*luh koh-nehs-mahN*
bill of sale	la lettre de vente	*lah lehtr duh vahNt*
bookkeeping	la comptabilité	*lah kohN-tah-bee-lee-tay*
business	l'affaire (f.)	*lah-fehr*
(to) buy	acheter	*ahsh-tay*
(to) buy for cash	payer comptant	*peh-yay kohN-tahN*
cash	l'argent (m.)	*lahr-zhahN*
(to) cash a check	toucher un chèque	*too-shay uhN shehk*

compensation for damage	le dédommagement	*luh day-doh-mahzh-mahN*
competitive price	le prix de concurrence	*luh pree duh kohN-kew-rahNs*
consignee	le destinataire	*luh dehs-tee-nah-tehr*
consumer	le consommateur	*lun kohN-soh-mah-tuhr*
contract	le contrat	*luh kohN-trah*
contractual obligations	les obligations du contrat (f.)	*lay zohb-lee-gah-syohN dew kohN-tah*
cost price	le prix de revient	*luh pree duh ruh-vyaN*
credit	le crédit	*luh kray-dee*
date of maturity	l'écheance (f.)	*lay-shay-ahNs*
debit	le débit	*luh day-bee*
(to) deliver	livrer	*lee-vray*
discount	l'exonération (f.)	*lehk-zoh-nay-rah-syohN*
	la réduction	*lah ray-dewk-syohN*
	le rabais	*luh rah-beh*
due	échu	*ay-shew*
expenditures	les dépenses (f.)	*lay day-pahNs*
expenses	les frais (m.)	*lay freh*
(to) export	exporter	*ehks-pohr-tay*
foreign trade	le commerce extérieur	*luh koh-mehrs ehks-tay-ryuhr*
goods	les produits (m.)	*lay proh-dwee*
	les biens (m.)	*lay byaN*
home trade	le commerce intérieur	*luh koh-mehrs aN-tay-ryuhr*
(to) import	importer	*aN-pohr-tay*
interest rates	les intérêts (m.)	*lay zaN-tay-reh*
invoice	la facture	*lah fahk-tewr*
lawsuit	le procès	*luh proh-seh*
lawyer	l'avocat (m.)	*lah-voh-kah*
liabilities	le passif	*luh pah-seef*
mail-order business	l'établissement de vente par correspondance (m.)	*lay-tah-blees-mahN duh vahNt pahr koh-rehs-pohN-dahNs*
maintenance expenses	les frais d'entretien (m.)	*lay freh dahNtr-tyaN*
management	la gestion	*lah zhehs-tyohN*
manager	le gérant	*luh zhay-rahN*
merchandise	la marchandise	*lah mahr-shahN-deez*
middleman	l'intermédiaire (m.)	*laN-tehr-mayd-yehr*

continues

Mini-Dictionary for Businesspeople (cont.)

money	l'argent (m.)	*lahr-zhahN*
office	le bureau	*luh bew-ro*
outlay	la mise de fonds	*lah meez duh fohN*
overhead expenses	les frais généraux (m.)	*lay freh zhay-nay-ro*
owner	le propriétaire	*luh proh-pree-yay-tehr*
(to) package	emballer	*ahN-bah-lay*
partner	l'associé (m.)	*lah-soh-syay*
past due	arriéré/en retard	*ah-ryay-ray/ahN ruh-tahr*
(to) pay	payer/régler	*peh-yay/ray-glay*
payment	le versement	*luh vehrs-mahN*
percent	pour cent	*poor sahN*
producer	le producteur	*luh proh-dewk-tuhr*
property	la propriété	*lah proh-pree-yay-tay*
purchase	l'achat (m.)	*lah-shah*
recession	la crise	*lah kreez*
retailer	le détaillant	*luh day-tah-yahN*
running expenses	les frais d'exploitation (m.)	*lay freh dehks-plwah-tah-syohN*
sale	la vente	*lah vahNt*
sample	l'échantillon (m.)	*lay-shahN-tee-yohN*
(to) sell	vendre	*vahNdr*
(to) sell for cash	vendre au comptant	*vahNdr o kohN-tahN*
selling price	le prix de vente	*luh pree duh vahNt*
(to) send	envoyer adresser	*ahN-vwah-yay ah-dreh-say*
(to) send back	renvoyer	*rahN-vwah-yay*
(to) send C.O.D.	envoyer payable à l'arrivée	*ahN-vwah-yay peh-yahbl ah lah-ree-vay*
(to) settle	régler	*ray-glay*
shipment	l'expédition (f.)	*lehks-pay-dee-syohN*
shipper	l'expéditeur (m.)	*lehks-pay-dee-tuhr*
slump	la baisse	*lah behs*
supply and demand	l'offre (m.) et la demande	*lohfr ay lah duh-mahNd*
tax	l'impôt (m.)	*laN-po*
tax-exempt	exempt d'impôts	*ehg-zahN daN-po*
trade	le commerce	*luh koh-mehrs*
transact business	faire des affaires	*fehr day zah-fehr*
(to) transfer	transférer	*trahNz-fay-ray*

transportation charges	les frais de transport (m.)	*lay freh duh trahNz-pohrt*
value added tax	la taxe sur la valeur ajoutée	*lah tahks sewr lah vah-luhr ah-zhoo-tay*
wholesaler	le grossiste	*luh groh-seest*
(to) wrap	emballer	*ahN-bah-lay*
(to) yield a profit	rendre un bénéfice	*rahNdr uhN bay-nay-fees*

There's Hope for the Future

An optimistic businessperson tends to look to the future and prepare wisely for it. In French, the future may be expressed in one of two ways: by using *aller* (to go) + an infinitive or by using the future tense.

Memory Enhancer

Refresh your memory. Here's the irregular verb *aller* (to go):

je vais	nous allons
tu vas	vous allez
il/elle/on va	ils/elles vont

Aller + Infinitive

Since the verb *aller* means *to go*, it is understandable that it is used to express what the speaker *is going to do*. Since *to go* will be the first verb used, it will have to be conjugated.

> I'm going to go into the city.
> Je vais aller en ville.
> *zhuh veh zah-lay ahN veel*

> They are going to send the letter.
> Ils vont envoyer la lettre.
> *eel vohN tahN-vwah-yay lah lehtr*

The Future Tense

The future can also be expressed by changing the verb to the future tense. The future tense tells what the subject *will* do or what action *will* take place in future time. The future of regular verbs is formed by adding endings to the infinitive of the verb, as shown in the following table. Notice that the endings for the future resemble the conjugation of the verb *avoir*, except for the *nous* and *vous* forms, where the *av* (*nous avons, vous avez*) beginning is dropped.

Un deux trois

Imagine that you are staying with a French family. Everyone is asleep and you want to go out and take care of some personal matters. Write a note of five things you are going to do.

387

For *re* verbs, drop the final *e* from the infinitive before adding the appropriate ending:

> Il m'attendra à midi.
> He will wait for me at noon.

The Future

er Verbs	*ir* Verbs	*re* Verbs
travailler—to work	choisir—to choose	vendre—to sell
will work	will choose	will sell
je travaille**rai** *zhuh tra-vahy-ray*	je choisi**rai** *zhuh shwah-zee-ray*	je vend**rai** *zhuh vahN-dray*
tu travaille**ras** *tew trah-vahy-rah*	tu choisi**ras** *tew shwah-zee-rah*	tu vend**ras** *tew vahN-drah*
il, elle, on travaille**ra** *eel (ehl, ohN)trah-vahy-rah*	il, elle, on choisi**ra** *eel (ehl, ohN) shwah-zee-rah*	il, elle, on vend**ra** *eel (ehl, ohN) vahN-drah*
nous travaille**rons** *noo trah-vahy-rohN*	nous choisi**rons** *noo shwah-zee-rohN*	nous vend**rons** *noo vahN-drohN*
vous travaille**rez** *voo trah-vahy-ray*	vous choisi**rez** *voo shwah-zee-ray*	vous vend**rez** *vous vahN-dray*
ils, elles travaille**ront** *eel (ehl) trah-vahy-rohN*	ils, elles choisi**ront** *eel (ehl) shwah-zee-rohN*	ils, elles vend**ront** *eel (ehl) vahN-drohN*

The Future Tense of Shoe Verbs

Only certain shoe verbs use the changes within the shoe to form *every* form of the future tense. The other shoe verbs form the future tense as described in the preceding section.

➤ Verbs ending in *yer* change *y* to *i* in all forms of the future. There is no more shoe, since all verb forms are using *i* instead of *y*. Verbs ending in *ayer* may or may not change *y* to *i*. Both *je paierai* and *je payerai* are acceptable:

Attention!

Note that the *e* of the *er* infinitive remains silent in the future tense:

Je lui parlerai.
*zhuh lwee **pahrl**-ray*
I'll speak to him (her).

j'emploierai *zhahN-plwah-ray*	nous emploierons *noo zahN-plwah-rohN*
tu emploieras *tew ahN-plwah-rah*	vous emploierez *voo zahN-plwah-ray*

il, elle, on emploiera	ils, elles emploieront
eel (ehl, ohN) ahN-plwah-rah	*eel (ehl) ahN-plwah-rohN*

➤ Verbs ending in *e* + consonant + *er* (but not (*é* + consonant + *er*) change silent *e* to è in the future. Once again, there will be no more shoe, since changes are made in all forms:

j'achèterai	nous achèterons
zhah-sheht-ray	*noo zah-sheht-rohN*
tu achèteras	vous achèterez
tew ah-sheht-rah	*voo zah-sheht-ray*
il, elle, on achètera	ils, elles achèteront
eel (ehl, ohN) ah-sheht-rah	*eel (ehl) zah-sheht-rohN*

➤ The verbs *appeler* and *jeter*, double their consonants in the shoe in the present tense; they do the same in all forms of the future tense:

j'appellerai	nous appellerons
zhah-pehl-ray	*noo zah-pehl-rohN*
tu appelleras	vous appellerez
tew ah-pehl-rah	*voo zah-pehl-ray*
il, elle, on appellera	ils, elles appelleront
eel (ehl, ohN) ah-pehl-rah	*eel (ehl) zah-pehl-rohN*
je jetterai	nous jetterons
zhuh zheht-ray	*noo zheht-rohN*
tu jetteras	vous jetterez
tew zheht-rah	*voo zheht-ray*
il, elle, on jettera	ils, elles jetteront
eel (ehl, ohN) zheht-rah	*eel (ehl) zheht-rohN*

Verbs Irregular in the Future

The verbs in the following table have irregular stems in the future tense. Simply add the future endings to these stems to get the correct future form. Complete the chart with the correct form of the future tense:

Verbs Irregular in the Future

Infinitive	Stem	
avoir (to have)	aur- (*ohr*)	tu _____
devoir (to have to)	devr- (*duhv*)	nous _____
envoyer (to send)	enverr- (*ahN-vuhr*)	il _____
être (to be)	ser- (*sehr*)	elles _____
faire (to make, do)	fer- (*fuhr*)	je _____
pouvoir (to be able to)	pourr- (*poor*)	vous _____
recevoir (to receive)	recevr- (*ruh-suhv*)	nous _____
savoir (to know)	saur- (*sohr*)	ils _____
venir (to come)	viendr- (*vyaNdr*)	tu _____
voir (to see)	verr- (*vuhr*)	je _____
vouloir (to want)	voudr- (*voodr*)	elle _____

Memory Enhancer

The future endings are the same for all verbs, whether regular or irregular: *-ai, -as, -a, -ons, -ez, -ont*. For regular verbs, attach the endings to the infinitive. For irregular verbs, attach them to the correct future stem.

Un deux trois

Write, in French, your plans for the future.

Predicting the Future

Do you wish you had a crystal ball to look into the future, or would you rather not know? If you're curious, consult your horoscope to see what's in store for you. What does the horoscope predict for each sign?

Bélier (21 mars–20 avril)
Des opportunités financières exceptionnelles se présenteront.

Taureau (21 avril–20 mai)
Vous passerez un mois très agréable.

Gémeaux (21 mai–20 juin)
Vous aurez des tensions et des disputes avec des collègues.

Cancer (21 juin–22 juillet)
Vous serez en très bonne forme.

Lion (23 juillet–21 août)
Vous vous concentrerez sur vos affaires financières.

Vierge (22 août–22 septembre)
Vous prendrez une décision importante concernant votre avenir professionnel.

Balance (23 septembre–22 octobre)
Vous serez en harmonie avec vos amis.

Scorpion (23 octobre–22 novembre)
Votre ambition vous servira.

Sagittaire (23 novembre–20 décembre)
Vous aurez des discussions importantes avec
des membres de votre famille.

Capricorne (21 décembre–20 janvier)
Tout ira bien pour vous.

Verseau (21 janvier–19 février)
Vous ferez la connaissance d'une personne importante.

Poissons (20 février–20 mars)
Votre agenda sera tous les soirs plein et les propositions de week-end afflueront.

En 10 Minutes

The future may be implied by using
the present tense.

J'arrive dans dix minutes.
I'll arrive in 10 minutes.

The Least You Need to Know

➤ To conduct business abroad, it is essential to become familiar with certain
technological terms for items such as photocopiers, fax machines, and
computers.

➤ To express that an action will take place in the near future, use the correct
conjugated form of the verb *aller* + the infinitive of the action that is going to
take place.

➤ The future tense usually is formed by adding the following endings to the
infinitive: *-ai, -as, -a, -ons, -ez, -ont.* A few irregular verbs must be memorized.

WELL, THE REALTOR DID SAY IT NEEDED A LITTLE WORK...

Chapter 25

Buying and Renting Property

> ### In This Chapter
>
> ➤ Apartments and houses
>
> ➤ Rooms, furniture, appliances, and amenities
>
> ➤ The conditional

Although you love the luxury of a well-appointed hotel, this might not prove to be cost-efficient in the long run. You could be better off purchasing or renting an apartment, a house, a condominium, or even buying time in a time-sharing property. This chapter will teach you how to get the facilities you want and need and how to express what you *would* do in certain circumstances.

Rent a Château

Renting a château might be a stretch to the pocketbook, but renting or buying a piece of property in a French-speaking country is not at all uncommon today. If you're even considering such a move, read Peter Mayle's *A Year in Provence*. Not only is the book an enjoyable, light read, but it may convince you to live in the south of France. So if you've decided that it's time to get daring and buy a home of your own, you will want to be able to read and understand the ads in the papers and to ask an agent or seller what is being offered. Whether it be a fireplace, huge closets, or central heating, the following table will help you decipher what features a house or apartment contains. Use *Il me faut* (*eel muh fo*—I need) to express your needs.

The House, the Apartment, the Rooms

air conditioning (central)	la climatisation (centrale)	*lah klee-mah-tee-zah-syohN (sahN-trahl)*
apartment	l'appartement (m.)	*lah-par-tuh-mahN*
apartment building	l'immeuble (m.)	*lee-muhbl*
attic	le grenier	*luh gruh-nyay*
backyard	le jardin	*luh zhahr-daN*
balcony	le balcon	*luh bahl-kohN*
basement	le sous-sol	*luh soo-sohl*
bathroom	la salle de bains le W.C.	*lah sahl duh baN luh doobl vay say*
bedroom	la chambre (à coucher)	*lah shahNbr (ah koo-shay)*
cathedral ceiling	le vide cathédrale	*luh veed kah-tay-drahl*
ceiling	le plafond	*luh plah-fohN*
closet	la penderie la garde-robe	*lah pahN-dree lah gahrd-rohb*
courtyard	la cour	*lah koor*
cupboard	le placard	*luh plah-kahr*
den	la salle de séjour le living	*lah sahl duh say-zhoor luh lee-veeng*
dining room	la salle à manger	*lah sahl ah mahN-zhay*
door	la porte	*lah pohrt*
elevator	l'ascenseur (m.)	*lah-sahN-suhr*
entrance	l'entrée (f.)	*lahN-tray*
fireplace	la cheminée	*lah shuh-mee-nay*
fixtures	les aménagements (m.)	*lay zah-may-nahzh-mahN*
floor	le plancher	*luh plahN-shay*
floor (story)	l'étage (m.)	*lay-tahzh*
garage	le garage	*luh gah-rahzh*
ground floor	le rez-de-chaussée	*luh rayd-sho-say*
hallway	le couloir le vestibule	*luh koo-lwahr luh vehs-tee-bewl*
heating electric gas	le chauffage électrique au gaz	*luh sho-fahzh ay-lehk-treek o gahz*
house	la maison	*lah meh-zohN*
key	la clef	*lah klay*
kitchen	la cuisine	*lah kwee-zeen*
laundry room	la buanderie	*lah bwahN-dree*
lawn	la pelouse	*lah pluh-looz*

lease	le bail	*luh bahy*
living room	le salon	*luh sah-lohN*
maintenance	l'entretien (m.)	*lahNtr-tyaN*
owner	le propriétaire	*luh proh-pree-yay-tehr*
private road	l'allée privée (f.)	*lah-lay pree-vay*
rent	le loyer	*luh lwah-yay*
roof	le toit	*luh twah*
room	la pièce	*lah pyehs*
	la salle	*lah sahl*
security deposit	la caution	*lah ko-syohN*
shower	la douche	*lah doosh*
stairs	l'escalier (m.)	*lehs-kah-lyay*
storage room	le débarras	*luh day-bah-rah*
tenant	le locataire	*luh loh-kah-tehr*
terrace	la terrasse	*lah teh-rahs*
wall	le mur	*luh mewr*
water-heater	le chauffe-eau	*luh shof o*
window	la fenêtre	*lah fuh-nehtr*

Culture Capsule

France has always enjoyed a renowned gastronomical reputation. Surprisingly, older French kitchens were somber, dark rooms hidden away in the rear of the house, almost as if they were an embarrassment. In today's French home, however, the kitchen, with its sleek, ultra-modern and dynamic design, holds a place of honor.

Home Sweet Home

You simply must have a double oven so that you can impress your French business associates with your repertoire of *nouvelle cuisine*. A microwave oven is a must. How about a dishwasher? What about furniture, a television, and washer and dryer? What furniture and appliances come with the property you have purchased or rented? Consult the following table for a complete list of just about everything there is. Use *Y a-t-il...?* (*ee ah-teel*—Is [Are] there...?) to ask your questions.

Furniture and Accessories

armchair	un fauteuil	*uhN fo-tuhy*
bed	un lit	*uhN lee*
bookcase	une étagère	*ewn nay-tah-zhehr*
carpet	un tapis	*uhN tah-pee*
chair	une chaise	*ewn shehz*
	un siège	*uhN syehzh*
clock	une pendule	*ewn pahN-dewl*
curtains	des rideaux (m.)	*day ree-do*
dishwasher	un lave-vaisselle	*uhN lahv veh-sehl*
dresser	une commode	*ewn koh-mohd*
dryer	un séchoir	*uhN say-shwahr*
	un sèche-linge	*uhN sehsh-laNzh*
food processor	un robot multifunctions (m.)	*uhN roh-bo mewl-tee-fuhNk-syohN*
freezer	un congélateur	*uhN kohN-zhay-lah-tuhr*
furniture	des meubles (m.)	*day muhbl*
home appliances	des appareils-électro-ménagers (m.)	*day zah-pah-rehy ay-lehk-tro-may-nah-zhay*
lamp	une lampe	*ewn lahNp*
microwave oven	un four à micro-ondes	*uhN foor ah mee-kro ohNd*
mirror	un miroir	*uhN meer-wahr*
oven	un four	*uhN foor*
picture	un tableau	*uhN tah-blo*
refrigerator	un réfrigérateur	*uhN ray-free-zhay-rah-tuhr*
rug	un tapis	*uhN tah-pee*
shades	des stores (m.)	*day stohr*
sofa	un canapé	*uhN kah-nah-pay*
	un divan	*uhN dee-vahN*
stereo	une chaîne stéréo	*ewn shehn stay-ray-o*
stove	une cuisinière	*ewn kwee-zee-nyehr*
table	une table	*ewn tahbl*
night	de nuit	*duh nwee*
television	une télévision	*ewn tay-lay-vee-zyohN*
large screen	à grand écran	*ah grahN day-krahN*
VCR	un magnétoscope	*uhN mah-nyay-toh-skohp*
wardrobe	une armoire (f.)	*ewn nahr-mwahr*
washing machine	une machine à laver	*ewn mah-sheen ah lah-vay*

Purchasing Furniture

Suppose you've rented or purchased an unfurnished place. What are some services you'd expect
a furniture store to provide?

Read the following ad to find out what attractive
offers you could expect from the company.

Un deux trois

Imagine that you are looking for a
house or apartment in a French-
speaking country. Tell the real-estate
agent what you want.

MOBILIER DE CANNES
UNE VALUER SÛRE

Nous vous garantissons gratuitement (free) vos meubles pendant 5 ans et le
revêtement de sièges pendant 2 ans contre tout défaut de fabrication.

Nous nous déplaçons gratuitement chez vous pour prendre des mesures, établir
des devis (estimates), et vous conseiller.

Nous vous offrons une garantie tous risques, gratuitement, pendant un an.

Nous reprenons vos vieux meubles lors de l'achat de meubles neufs.

Nous assurons ces services et garanties, sans supplément de prix, dans tous nos
magasins, partout en France continentale.

Should You Buy or Rent?

Whether you buy or rent there are bound to be certain preferences you'd like to
express or particular questions you have. Use the following phrases and expressions to
help you get exactly what you want:

I'm looking for…
Je cherche…
zhuh shersh

the classified ads
les petites annonces
lay puh-tee tah-nohNs

a real estate agency
une agence immobilière
ewn nah-zhahNs ee-moh-bee-lyehr

the real-estate advertising section
la publicité immobilière
lah pew-blee-see-tay ee-moh-bee lyehr

I would like to rent (buy)…
Je voudrais louer (acheter)…
zhuh voo-dreh loo-ay (ahsh-tay)

an apartment	a condominium	a house
un appartement	un condominium	une maison
uhN nah-pahr-tuh-mahN	*uhN kohN-doh-mee-nyuhm*	*ewn meh-zohN*

Is it luxurious?	Are there break-ins?
Est-ce de haute prestation?	Y a-t-il des cambriolages?
ehs duh ot prehs-tah-syohN	*ee ah-teel day kahN-bree-oh-lahzh*

Is there time-sharing?	What is the rent?
Y a-t-il le partage du temps?	Quel est le loyer?
ee ah-teel luh pahr-tahzh dew tahN	*kehl eh luh lwah-yay*

How much is the maintenance of the apartment (house)?
Ça coûte combien l'entretien de l'appartement (de la maison)?
sah koot kohN-byaN lahNtr-tyan duh lah-pahr-tuh-mahN (duh lah meh-zohN)

Is… included?	the electricity	the heat
… est compris(e)?	l'électricité (f.)	le chauffage
…eh kohN-pree(z)	*lay-lehk tree-see-tay*	*luh sho-fahzh*

the gas	the air conditioning
le gaz	la climatisation
luh gahz	*lah klee-mah-tee-zah-syohN*

How much are the monthly payments?
À combien sont les paiements mensuels?
ah kohN-byaN sohN lay peh-mahN mahN-swehl

Do I have to leave a deposit?	I'd like to take out a mortgage.
Dois-je payer une caution?	Je voudrais prendre une hypothèque.
dwahzh peh-yay ewn ko-syohN	*zhuh voo-dreh prahNdr ewn nee-poh-tehk*

I'm going to the bank.
Je vais à la banque.
zhuh veh zah lah bahnk

Cracking the Code

Armed with a pencil and cup of coffee, you've decided to begin reading the real estate ads. Instantly, you frown and become exasperated at all the unfamiliar jargon. The following table will help you decode the abbreviations so that you can determine what is really being offered.

How to Read a Real Estate Ad

1. À vendre—for sale.

2. maison de caractère—a house with character.

3. 2 kms mer—2 kilometers from the sea.

4. 8 kms Montpellier—8 kilometers from the city of Montpellier.

5. 150m2 habitable—living space of 150.2 meters.

6. 20m2 patio—a patio that measures 20.2 meters.

7. grand séjour avec cheminée—a large living room with a fireplace.

8. 4 chambres—4 bedrooms.

9. mezzanine—a landing between the ground and first floors.

10. chauffage électrique—electric heat.

11. the price of the house 850.000 francs—in new French currency:

    85 million—in old French currency

    $140,000—in American dollars

12. 19 bis—This street has a #19 and then a second #19 called *19 bis*. This is the equivalent of an address that reads 19, followed by a second address that reads 19A.

13. allée du bas Vaupereux Verrière le Buisson—the street on which the house is located.

14. 91370—a regional code.

15. Villeneuve-les-Maguelonne France—the city or village in which the house is located.

16. tél—the telephone number to call if you are interested.

Here Are the Conditions

Would you like a big or small house? Would you like it furnished or unfurnished? How about a swimming pool? The *conditional* is a mood in French that expresses what the speaker *would* do or what *would happen* under certain cirumstances. The conditional of the verb *vouloir* or *aimer* is frequently used to express what the speaker *would like*:

> Je voudrais (J'aimerais) louer un appartement.
> *zhuh voo-dreh (zhehm-ray) loo-ay uhN*
> *nah-pahr-tuh-mahN*
> I would like to rent an apartment.

Attention!

Since they look so much alike, you will have to look carefully at the endings tacked onto the infinitive stems of verbs to differentiate between the future (what the subject *will* do) and the conditional (what the subject *would* do).

Formation of the Conditional

The conditional is formed with the same stem that is used to form the future, whether you are using a regular, irregular, or shoe verb. The endings for the conditional, however, are different. They are exactly the same as the endings for the imperfect. In other words, to form the conditional, start with the future stem and add the imperfect endings shown in the following table. For *re* verbs, drop the final *e* from the infinitive before adding the appropriate ending.

The Conditional of Regular Verbs

er Verbs	*ir* Verbs	*re* Verbs
travailler (to work)	choisir (to choose)	vendre (to sell)
would work	would choose	would sell
je travaillerais	je choisirais	je vendrais
zhuh tra-vahy-reh	*zhuh shwah-zee-reh*	*zhuh vahN-dreh*
tu travaillerais	tu choisirais	tu vendrais
tew trah-vahy-reh	*tew shwah-zee-reh*	*tew vahN dreh*
il, elle, on travaillerait	il, elle, on choisirait	il, elle, on vendrait
eel, ehl, ohN trah-vahy-reh	*eel, ehl, ohN shwah-zee-reh*	*eel, ehl, ohN vahN-dreh*
nous travaillerions	nous choisirions	nous vendrions
trah-vahy-ryohN	*noo shwah-zee-ryohN*	*noo vahN-dryohN*
vous travailleriez	vous choisiriez	vous vendriez
voo trah-vahy-ryay	*voo shwah-zee-ryay*	*voo vahN-dryay*
ils, elles travailleraient	ils, elles choisiraient	ils, elles vendraient
eel, ehl trah-vahy-reh	*eel, ehl shwah-zee-reh*	*eel, ehl vahN-dreh*

The Conditional of Shoe Verbs

Only certain shoe verbs use the changes within the shoe to form all forms of the conditional. All other shoe verbs follow the rules for conditional formation previously listed.

➤ Verbs ending in *yer* change *y* to *i* in all forms of the conditional. There is no more shoe since all verb forms are using *i* instead of *y*. Verbs ending in *ayer* may or may not change *y* to *i*. Both *je paierais* and *je payerais* are acceptable:

j'emploierais	nous emploierions
zhahN-plwah-reh	*noo zahN-plwah-ryohN*
tu emploierais	vous emploieriez
tew ahN-plwah-reh	*voo zahN-plwah-ryay*
il, elle, on emploierait	ils, elles emploieraient
eel (ehl, ohN) ahN-plwah-reh	*eel (ehl) ahN-plwah-reh*

➤ Verbs ending in *e + consonant + er* (but not (*é + consonant + er*)) change silent *e* to *è* in the conditional. Once again, there will be no more shoe, since changes are made in all forms:

j'achèterais	nous achèterions
zhah-sheh-treh	*noo zah-sheht-ryohN*
tu achèterais	vous achèteriez
tew ah-sheh-treh	*voo zah-sheht-ryay*
il, elle, on achèterait	ils, elles achèteraient
eel (ehl, ohN) ah-sheh-treh	*eel (ehl) ah-sheh-treh*

➤ The verbs *appeler* and *jeter* double their consonants in the shoe in the present, and do the same in all forms of the conditional:

j'appellerais	nous appellerions
zhah-pehl-reh	*noo zah-pehl-ryohN*
tu appellerais	vous appelleriez
tew ah-pehl-reh	*voo zah-pehl-ryay*
il, elle, on appellerait	ils, elles appelleraient
eel (ehl, ohN) ah-pehl-reh	*eel (ehl) ah-pehl-reh*
je jetterais	nous jetterions
zhuh zheh-treh	*noo zheht-ryohN*

tu jetterai
tew zheh-treh

vous jetteriez
voo zheht-ryay

il, elle, on jetterait
eel (ehl, ohN) zheh-treh

ils, elles jetteraient
eel (ehl) zheh-treh

Un deux trois

Dreams are wonderful. Write a list of everything you would do if you won the lottery tomorrow.

Irregular Verbs in the Conditional

The verbs in the following table have irregular stems in the conditional. To complete the chart, simply add the conditional endings to these stems to get the correct conditional form.

The Conditional of Irregular Verbs

Infinitive	Stem	
avoir (to have)	aur- (*ohr*)	tu _____
devoir (to have to)	devr- (*duhv*)	nous _____
envoyer (to send)	enverr- (*ahN-vuhr*)	il _____
être (to be)	ser- (*sehr*)	elles _____
faire (to make, do)	fer- (*fuhr*)	je _____
pouvoir (to be able to)	pourr- (*poor*)	vous _____
recevoir (to receive)	recevr- (*ruh-suhvr*)	nous _____
savoir (to know)	saur- (*sohr*)	ils _____
venir (to come)	viendr- (*vyaNdr*)	tu _____
voir (to see)	verr- (*vuhr*)	je _____
vouloir (to want)	voudr- (*voodr*)	elle _____

The Least You Need to Know

➤ Learning the correct vocabulary will help you get the living accommodations you want and need.

➤ The conditional is formed by using the future stem (usually the infinitive) and the imperfect endings: *–ais, –ais, –ait, –ions, –iez, –aient.*

➤ As always, a few irregular verbs must be memorized.

Chapter 26

Money Is the Issue

In This Chapter

➤ Banking terms

➤ The subjunctive

Chapter 25 prepared you for an extended stay in a French-speaking country. You learned the words and phrases you would need if you wanted to rent an apartment or condominium or even buy a house. You know how to describe the features you need to live comfortably, whether it includes a gourmet kitchen with a breakfast nook or a living room with cathedral ceilings.

This final chapter is for anyone who must make a trip to the bank: a tourist who wants to change money, a businessperson with financial obligations, an investor with monetary concerns, or someone who is interested in purchasing real estate or a business. You will also learn how to express your specific, personal needs by using the subjunctive.

At the Bank

There are many reasons for a person to stop into a bank in a foreign country. The most common reason is to exchange money. (Banks do give a very favorable rate of exchange.) But perhaps you have greater goals: Maybe you want to purchase real estate, set up a business, make investments, dabble in the stock market, or stay a while and open a savings and checking account. If so, you will need to familiarize yourself with the phrases in the following table.

Culture capsule

French banks open anywhere between 8 A.M. and 9 A.M. and close between 3 P.M. and 5 P.M. Some banks close during the lunch break, which can last as long as two hours.

Mini-Dictionary of Banking Terms

automatic teller machine	un distributeur automatique de billets	*uhN dee-stree-bew-tuhr o-to-mah-teek duh bee-yeh*
	un guichet automatique de banque	*uhN gee-sheh o-to- mah-teek duh bahNk*
balance	le solde	*luh sohld*
bank	la banque	*lah bahNk*
bank book	le livret d'épargne	*luh lee-vreh day-pahr-nyuh*
bill	le billet/la coupure	*luh bee-yeh/lah koo-pewr*
(to) borrow	emprunter	*ahN-pruhN-tay*
branch	la succursale	*lah sew-kewr-sahl*
cash	l'argent liquide (m.)	*lahr-zhahN lee-keed*
(to) cash	toucher/encaisser	*too-shay/ahN-keh-say*
cash flow	la marge brute	*lah mahrzh brewt*
cashier	la caisse	*lah kehs*
change (coins)	la monnaie	*lah moh-neh*
change (transaction)	le change	*luh shahnzh*
check	le chèque	*luh shehk*
checkbook	le carnet de chèques	*luh kahr-neh duh shehk*
	le chéquier	*luh shay-kyay*
checking account	le compte-chèques	*luh kohNt shehk, luh*
	le compte-courant	*kohNt koo-rahN*
coin	la pièce	*lah pyehs*
credit	le crédit	*luh kray-dee*
currency	la monnaie	*lah moh-neh*
customer	le (la) client(e)	*luh (lah) klee-yahN(t)*
debt	la dette	*lah deht*
deposit	le dépôt	*luh day-po*
	le versement	*luh vehrs-mahN*
(to) deposit	déposer	*day-po-zay*
	verser	*vehr-say*

down payment	l'acompte (m.)	*lah-kohNt*
	les arrhes (f.)	*lay zahr*
due date	la date d'échéance	*lah daht day-shay-ahNs*
employee	l'employé(e)	*lahN-plwah-yay*
(to) endorse	endosser	*ahN-doh-say*
(to exchange)	échanger	*ay-shahN-zhay*
exchange rate	le cours du change	*luh koor dew shahNzh*
final payment	le versement de	*luh vehrs-mahN duh*
	libération	*lee-bay-rah-syohN*
	le versement final	*luh vehrs-mahN fee-nahl*
guarantee	la caution	*lah ko-syohN*
holder	le titulaire	*luh tee-tew-lehr*
installment payment	le versement échelonné	*luh verhs-mahN aysh-loh-nay*
interest (compound)	l'intérêt (m.) (composé)	*laN-tay-reh (kohN-po-zay)*
interest rate	le taux d'intérêt	*luh to daN-tay-reh*
(to) invest	placer	*plah-say*
investment	le placement	*luh plahs-mahN*
loan	l'emprunt (m.)	*lahN-pruhN*
	le prêt	*luh preh*
(to) take out a loan	faire un emprunt	*fehr uhN nahN-pruhN*
long term	à long terme	*ah lohN tehrm*
(to) manage	gérer	*zhay-ray*
money exchange bureau	le bureau de change	*luh bew-ro duh shahNzh*
monthly statement	le relevé mensuel	*luh ruh-lvay mahN-swehl*
mortgage	l'hypothèque (f.)	*lee-poh-tehk*
open account	le compte courant	*luh kohNt koo-rahN*
overdraft	le découvert	*luh day-koo-vehr*
overdrawn check	le chèque sans provision	*luh shehk sahN proh-vee-zyohN*
(to) pay cash	payer comptant	*peh-yay kohN-tahN*
payment	le versement	*luh vehrs-mahN*
	le paiement	*luh peh-mahN*
percentage	le pourcentage	*luh poor-sahN-tahzh*
promissory note	le billet à ordre	*luh bee-yeh ah ohrdr*
purchase	l'achat (m.)	*lah-shah*
quarter	le trimestre	*luh tree-mehstr*
receipt	le reçu	*luh vehrs-mahN*
	la quittance	*lah kee-tahNs*

continues

405

Mini-Dictionary of Banking Terms (cont.)

revenue	le revenu	*luh ruhv-new*
safe	le coffre-fort	*luh kohfr-fohr*
sale	la vente	*lah vahNt*
(to) save	économiser	*ay-koh-noh-mee-zay*
	épargner	*ay-pahr-nyay*
savings account	le compte d'épargne	*luh kohNt day-pahr-nyuh*
short term	à court terme	*ah koor tehrm*
(to) sign	signer	*see-nyay*
signature	la signatue	*lah see-nyah-tewr*
sum	la somme	*lah sohm*
teller	le caisser	*luh keh-syay*
	la caissière	*lah keh-syehr*
total	le montant	*luh mohN-tahN*
transfer	le virement	*luh veer-mahN*
traveler's check	le chèque de voyage	*luh shehk duh vwah-yahzh*
void	annulé	*ah-new-lay*
window	le guichet	*luh gee-sheh*
(to) withdraw	retirer	*ruh-tee-ray*
withdrawal	le retrait	*luh ruh-treh*

Attention!

Before you take a trip, it's a wise idea to change at least $50 into foreign currency. Generally, the exchange rate at airports is not to your advantage.

Money can also be exchanged at *un bureau de change*. These money exchanges can be found all over the streets of Paris, and all over the world. Some offer excellent rates, while others charge exorbitant commissions. It is always wise to investigate a few first.

You will notice that this receipt, from the airport where rates are not very good, shows a 15FF commission (about $2.50) for an exchange of $45. The worst exchange rates are given by hotels, so avoid them whenever possible.

```
           C  C  F   CHANGE
                08/04/90

                           08:42 VG

     Siege Social 39 Rue Bassano
     Paris 8      47 23 43 99
     AEROPORT PARIS ORLY

          OPERATION DE CHANGE No 004080096
          SUR CAISSE No 004

     ACHAT DEVISES BILLETS

            45.00 USD
     x       5.4500 /    1 =    245.30 FRF

     COMMISSION FIXE              15.00 FRF

                           --------
                        =    230.30 FRF
```

Services I Need

If you're planning on a trip to the bank, the following phrases will be most helpful in common, everyday banking situations: making deposits and withdrawals, opening a checking account, or taking out a loan:

Attention!

The Minitel computer system enables you to easily perform all your banking transactions.

What are the banking hours?
Quelles sont les heures d'ouverture et de fermeture?
kehl sohN lay zuhr doo-vehr-tewr ay duh fehr-muh-tewr

I would like...	to make a deposit.
Je voudrais...	faire un dépôt (un versement).
zhuh voo-dreh	*fehr un day-po (uhN vehrs-mahN)*
to make a withdrawal.	to make a payment.
faire un retrait.	faire un paiement (un versement).
fehr uhN ruh-treh	*fehr un peh-mahN (uhN vehrs-mahN)*
to take out a loan.	to cash a check.
faire un emprunt.	toucher un chèque.
fehr uhN nahN-pruhN	*too-shay uhN shehk*

to open an account.
ouvrir un compte.
oo-vreer uhN kohNt

to close an account.
fermer un compte.
fehr-may uhN kohNt

to change some money.
changer de l'argent.
shahN-zhay duh lahr-zhahN

Will I get a monthly statement?
Est-ce que je recevrai un relevé mensuel?
ehs-kuh zhuh ruh-sehv-ray uhN ruh-lvay mahN-swehl

What is today's exchange rate?
Quel est le cours du change aujourd'hui?
kehl eh luh koor dew shahNzh o-zhoor-dwee

Do you have an automatic teller machine?
Avez-vous un distributeur (guichet) automatique de billets?
ah-vay voo uhN dee-stree-bew-tuhr (gee-sheh) o-to-mah-teek duh bee-yeh

How does one use it?
Comment s'en sert-on?
kohN-mahN sahN sehr-tohN

I'd like to make a personal loan.
Je voudrais prendre un emprunt personnel.
zhuh voo-dreh prahNdr uhN nahN-pruhN pehr-soh-nehl

I'd like to take out a mortgage.
Je voudrais prendre une hypothèque.
zhuh voo-dreh prahNdr ewn nee-poh-tehk

Attention!

If you travel with traveler's checks, make sure to keep the numbers of the checks in a separate place—just in case. Also make sure you fully understand how traveler's checks are used.

What is the time period of the loan?
Quelle est la période d'amortissement?
kehl eh lah pay-ryohd dah-mohr-tees-mahN

How much are the monthly payments?
À combien sont les paiements mensuels?
ah kohN-byaN sohN lay peh-mahN mahN-swehl

What is the interest rate?
Quel est le taux d'intérêt?
kehl eh luh to daN-tay-reh

When is it necessary to start making payments?
Quand faut-il commencer à faire des paiements?
kahN fo-teel koh-mahN-say ah fehr day peh-mahN

Culture Capsule

Although at publication time the *franc* is still the unit of currency in France, and will remain in circulation until about the year 2002, the *euro* has recently been introduced. It is currently being used for banking, credit card, and other business transactions. Many of the countries in Europe use the *euro*. It is expected that this will enhance trade between the participating countries by eliminating tariffs and trade barriers, making Europe a more efficient competitor in the world market place.

These Are My Needs

Everyone needs more money. It seems that the more you have the more you want. In Chapter 20, you learned that the verb *devoir* followed by an infinitive can be used to express need. Another way of expressing that someone *needs to* or *must* do something is to use the expression *il faut que...* (eel fo kuh)—*it is necessary that. Il faut que* and other expressions showing necessity are followed by a special verb form called *the subjunctive*.

Memory Enhancer

Use the irregular verb *devoir* + infinitive to say what you need.

The subjunctive is a mood, not a tense, and expresses wishing, wanting, emotion, and doubt. It is used after many phrases showing uncertainty and after certain conjunctions, as well. Those applications will not be treated in this book.

Since the subjunctive is not a tense (a verb form indicating time), the present subjunctive can be used to refer to actions in the present or the future. The past subjunctive will not be treated in this book, since its use is limited.

In order to use the subjunctive, certain conditions must be met:

➤ Two different clauses must exist with two different subjects.

➤ The two clauses must be joined by *que*.

➤ One of the clauses must show need, necessity, emotion, or doubt.

Here are some examples showing when you would use the subjunctive:

> Il faut que je travaille dur.
> *eel fo kuh zhuh trah-vahy dewr*
> I (I'll) have to work hard.

Il faut que nous téléphonions à notre agent.
eel fo kuh noo tay-lay-fohn-yohN ah nohtr ah-zhahN
We (We'll) have to call our agent.

Il faut qu'ils se reposent.
eel fo keel suh ruh-poz
They (They'll) have to rest.

Memory Enhancer

Note that *er* verbs do not change in the subjunctive.

Formation of the Present Subjunctive

To form the present subjunctive of regular verbs, and some irregular verbs, as shown in the following table, drop the *ent* ending from the *ils (elles)* form of the present and add these endings:

je	*e*	nous	*ions*
tu	*es*	vous	*iez*
il, elle, on	*e*	ils, elles	*ent*

The Present Subjunctive of Regular Verbs

er Verbs	*ir* Verbs	*re* Verbs
parler	finir	attendre
ils parl**ent**	ils finiss**ent**	ils attend**ent**
...que je parle *kuh zhuh pahrl*	...que je finisse *kuh zhuh fee-nees*	...que j'attende *kuh zhah-tahNd*
...que tu parles *kuh tew pahrl*	...que tu finisses *kuh tew fee-nees*	...que tu attendes *que tew ah-tahNd*
...qu'il parle *keel pahrl*	...qu'il finisse *keel fee-nees*	...qu'il attende *keel ah-tahNd*
...que nous parlions *kuh noo pahr-lyohN*	...que nous finissions *kuh noo fee-nee-syohN*	...que nous attendions *kuh noo zah-tahN-dyohN*
...que vous parliez *kuh voo pahr-lyay*	...que vous finissiez *kuh voo fee-nee-syay*	...que vous attendiez *kuh voo zah-tahN-dyay*
...qu'ils parlent *keel pahrl*	...qu'ils finissent *keel fee-nees*	...qu'ils attendent *keel zah-tahNd*

Shoe Verbs

As shown in the following table, shoe verbs and verbs that are conjugated like shoe verbs follow the shoe rule when forming the subjunctive:

The Subjunctive of Shoe Verbs

Boire	**ils boiv<u>ent</u>**
...que je boive	**...que nous buvions**
...que tu boives	**...que vous buviez**
...qu'il boive	...qu'ils boivent

Prendre	**ils prenn<u>ent</u>**
...que je prenne	**...que nous prenions**
...que tu prennes	**...que vous preniez**
...qu'il prenne	...qu'ils prennent

Manger	**ils mang<u>ent</u>**
...que je mange	**...que nous mangions**
...que tu manges	**...que vous mangiez**
...qu'il mange	...qu'ils mangent

Envoyer	**ils envoi<u>ent</u>**
...que je envoie	**...que nous envoyions**
...que tu envoies	**...que vous envoyiez**
...qu'il envoie	...qu'ils envoient

Acheter	**ils achet<u>ent</u>**
...que je achète	**...que nous achetions**
...que tu achètes	**...que vous achetiez**
...qu'il achète	...qu'ils achètent

Préférer	**ils préfèr<u>ent</u>**
...que je préfère	**...que nous préférions**
...que tu préfères	**...que vous préfériez**
...qu'il préfère	...qu'ils préfèrent

continues

The Subjunctive of Shoe Verbs (cont.)

Appeler	ils appell<u>ent</u>
...que j'appelle	**...que nous appelions**
...que tu appelles	**...que vous appeliez**
...qu'il appelle	...qu'ils appellent

Verbs Irregular in the Subjunctive

Some verbs follow no rules and must be memorized. The following table lists the verbs that will prove to be most useful.

Note: There are no changes to *-cer* shoe verbs in the subjunctive, because *c* followed by *e* or *i* always produces a soft sound.

...que je   ...que nous
commen*ce*   commen*ci*ons

Irregular Subjunctives

Aller	
...que j'aille (*ahy*)	**...que nous allions (*ah-lyohN*)**
...que tu ailles (*ahy*)	**...que vous alliez (*ah-lyay*)**
...qu'il aille (*ahy*)	...qu'ils aillent (*ahy*)

Vouloir	
...que je veuille (*vuhy*)	**...que nous voulions (*voo-lyohN*)**
...que tu veuilles (*vuhy*)	**...que vous vouliez (*voo-lyay*)**
...qu'il veuille (*vuhy*)	...qu'ils veuillent (*vuhy*)

Faire	
...que je fasse (*fahs*)	...que nous fassions (*fah-syohN*)
...que tu fasses (*fahs*)	...que vous fassiez (*fah-syay*)
...qu'il fasse (*fahs*)	...qu'ils fassent (*fahs*)

Pouvoir	
...que je puisse (*pwees*)	...que nous puissions (*pwee-syohN*)
...que tu puisses (*pwees*)	...que vous puissiez (*pwee-syay*)
...qu'il puisse (*pwees*)	...qu'ils puissent (*pwees*)

Savoir	
…que je sache (*sahsh*)	…que nous sachions (*sah-shyohN*)
…que tu saches (*sahsh*)	…que vous sachiez (*sah-shyay*)
…qu'il sache (*sahsh*)	…qu'ils sachent (*sahsh*)

Avoir	
…que j'aie (*ay*)	…que nous ayons (*ay-yohN*)
…que tu aies (*ay*)	…que vous ayez (*ay-yay*)
…qu'il ait (*ay*)	…qu'ils aient (*ay*)

Etre	
…que je sois (*swah*)	…que nous soyons (*swah-yohN*)
…que tu sois (*swah*)	…que vous soyez (*swah-yay*)
…qu'il soit (*swah*)	…qu'ils soient (*swah*)

There's So Much to Do

Do you have a million things to do this afternoon? Me too. There's no escaping the necessary hassles and chores of our daily routine. Express what these people have to do using *il faut que + subjunctive*:

Example: il/travailler Il faut qu'il travaille.

Memory Enhancer

Remember to use the subjunctive after expressions showing wants, emotions, and doubts.

1. nous/préparer le dîner

2. elle/finir son travail

3. ils/attendre un coup de téléphone

4. je/téléphone à mon bureau

5. vous/accomplir beaucoup

6. tu/descendre en ville

7. je/se lever de bonne heure

8. il/aller à la banque

9. vous/être en ville à midi

10. tu/acheter un cadeau

11. elles/prendre un taxi

12. nous/faire les courses

Un deux trois

Write a list, in French, of the things you have to do today. Say each thing in 2 ways: using *devoir + infinitive*, and then using the subjunctive.

Other Expressions of Need Taking the Subjunctive

Il faut que is a very common expression used with the subjunctive. There are, however, many other expressions that require the subjunctive. In order to speak properly, you should familiarize yourself with them, as shown in the following table:

Other Expressions Requiring the Subjunctive

It is imperative that…	Il est impératif que…	*eel eh taN-pay-rah-teef kuh*
It is important that…	Il est important que…	*eel eh taN-pohr-tahn kuh*
It is necessary that…	Il est nécessaire que…	*eel eh nay-seh-sehr kuh*
It is preferable that…	Il est préférable que…	*eel eh pray-fay-rahbl kuh*
It is urgent that…	Il est urgent que…	*eel eh tewr-zhahN kuh*
It is better that…	Il vaut mieux que…	*eel vo myuh kuh*

The Least You Need to Know

➤ French banks are modern and efficient, and provide the same services as banks in the United States.

➤ Use *devoir* (conjugated) + *infinitive* to express that the subject needs or has to do something.

➤ The subjunctive is used to express needs, wants, emotions, and doubts.

➤ To form the present subjunctive of most verbs, drop the *–ent* ending from the third person plural (*ils*) form and add the subjunctive endings: *-e, -es, -e, -ions, -iez, -ent.*

Answer Key

Chapter 2

Wow Them with Your Accent

1. ay-reek luh pahrk
2. koh-leht lah-pyehr
3. mee-shehl luh-shyaN
4. ah-laN luh-shah
5. ah-nyehs luh-loo
6. roh-lahN lah-moosh
7. pah-treek luh-buhf
8. soh-lahNzh lah-foh-reh
9. fee-leep luh-behk
10. floh-rahNs lah-vee-nyuh
11. moh-neek luh pohN
12. doh-mee-neek lah-fohN-tehn
13. dah-nyehl la toor
14. zhahN lah vahsh
15. zhahn lah-ree-vyehr
16. ew-behr lah fluhr

Chapter 3

You Understand So Much Already!

1. The blouse is orange.
2. The service is horrible.
3. The sandwich is immense.
4. The chef is excellent.
5. The client (customer) is certain (sure).

Several More

1. The pullover is rose (pink).
2. The film is important.
3. The question is unique.
4. The trip is urgent.
5. The guide is intelligent.

You've Got It!

1. The doctor helps the baby.
2. Mom prepares soup and salad.
3. The mechanic repairs the motor.
4. The family watches television.
5. The tourist reserves the room.
6. The guide recommends the café.
7. The employee sells the merchandise.
8. The child adores modern music.
9. The actor prefers Italian opera.
10. The teacher presents the program.

What Do You Think?

1. Le jardin est splendide.
2. La fontaine est superbe.
3. L'artiste est populaire.
4. La musique est splendide.
5. Le restaurant est élégant.
6. Le théâtre est ancien.
7. La cathédrale est magnifique.
8. L'acteur est fatigué.
9. L'hôtel est élégant.
10. L'opéra est amusant.

Special Tricks

hôtesse—hostess

état—state

île—isle (Island)

étrange—strange

intérêt—interest

étude—study

pâte—paste (also an English word pâte)

répondre—to respond

French Awareness

1. on the regular menu
2. in style (with ice cream)
3. have a good trip
4. that's life
5. free rein
6. stylish
7. government take over
8. cream of the crop
9. obligatory
10. newcomer to society
11. something already seen
12. team spirit
13. accomplished task
14. awkward mistake
15. lover of food
16. love of life
17. ingenuous, unsophisticated
18. art object
19. best part
20. answer, please
21. meeting
22. concerning

416

You Are Well Read

1. *The Savage*
2. *The Human Comedy*
3. *Artificial Paradise*
4. *The Stranger*
5. *The Infernal Machine*
6. *Terrible Children*
7. *The Vagabond*
8. *The Sentimental Education*
9. *The Pastoral Symphony*
10. *The Miserable People*
11. *Dangerous Affairs*
12. *The Human Condition*
13. *The Hypochondriac*
14. *Spectacle (Show)*
15. *Confessions*
16. *Nausea*
17. *Philosophical Letters*
18. *The Joy of Living*

Now You're a Pro

1. Current news: The theraputic virtues of champagne.
2. Sports: Cycling from Milan to San Remo.
3. Science and medicine: Tuberculosis is the major cause of death for adults.
4. International news: Quebec's referendum on independence: the question in question.

Chapter 4

Using Your Idioms I

Sample responses:

1. en voiture
2. en voiture
3. en taxi
4. en voiture
5. en avion
6. à pied
7. en bateau
8. en bateau
9. en bus
10. à pied

Using Your Idioms II

1. au revoir
2. tout de suite
3. en retard
4. de bonne heure
5. tout à l'heure
6. de temps en temps (de temps à autre)
7. du matin au soir
8. à demain

Using Your Idioms III

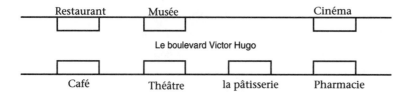

Using Your Idioms IV

Sample responses:

Bien sûr	Jamais de la vie	D'accord
Bien entendu	Tant pis	Au contraire

Using Your Idioms V

1. J'ai sommeil.
2. J'ai chaud.
3. J'ai faim.
4. J'ai soif.
5. J'ai tort.
6. J'ai trente ans.
7. J'ai raison.
8. J'ai froid.

Using Your Idioms VI

Sample responses:

1. mauvais
2. du soleil
3. beau
4. mauvais
5. frais

Chapter 5

Just Look It Up

1. feu
2. renvoyer, congédier
3. lumière
4. allumer
5. puits
6. bien
7. terre
8. atterrir
9. mieux
10. meilleur
11. jouer
12. pièce

Chapter 6

Mark Your Nouns

1. le	5. la	9. la
2. le	6. le	10. le
3. la	7. l'	11. la
4. le	8. le	12. le

Mark More Nouns

1. une	2. un	3. une	4. un	5. une	6. un
7. un	8. une	9. une	10. un	11. un	12. un

What's Their Line?

1. avocate	6. étudiant	11. patron
2. dentiste	7. chef	12. mannequin
3. coiffeuse	8. électricienne	13. pâtissier
4. facteur	9. infirmière	14. médecin
5. bouchère	10. pompier	15. ouvrier

More Than One

Je vois les boutiques.

Je vois les croix.

Je vois les restaurants.

Je vois les palais.

Je vois les automobiles.

Je vois les tapis.

Je vois les magazines.

Je vois les autobus.

Practice with Plurals

1. les châteaux	3. les gens	5. les colis	7. les ciseaux
2. les lunettes	4. les journaux	6. les palais	8. les joujoux

What Have You Learned About Gender?

1. female   2. female/male   3. female

Chapter 7

Tu or Vous?

doctor—vous   woman—vous

cousin—tu   two friends—vous

friend—tu   policeman—vous

salesman—vous   friends—vous

Who's Who?

Charles—il   La fête—ils

Lucie et Sylvie—elles   Le bal costumé—il

Berthe—elle   La musique et le décor—ils

Pierre—il   Les vêtements—ils

Luc et Henri—ils   Le travail et le coüt—ils

Robert et Suzette—ils   La cuisine et la nourriture—elles

Janine, Charlotte, Michèle, et Roger—ils   L'ambiance—elle

Paul, Roland, et Annick—ils   L'hôte et l'hôtesse—ils

Conjugation 101

1. traverse   6. présentent
2. demandent   7. réserve
3. cherchons   8. montes
4. accompagne   9. parle
5. louez   10. posent

Conjugation 102

1. finissons   5. réussit
2. réfléchit   6. choisis
3. jouissent   7. agissez
4. applaudis   8. remplissent

420

Conjugation 103

1. attends
2. descendent
3. perdons
4. répondez
5. entend
6. rends

Ask Me—I Dare You

1. Nous parlons trop?
   Nous parlons trop, n'est-ce pas?
   Est-ce que nous parlons trop?
   Parlons-nous trop?

2. Il descend souvent en ville?
   Il descend souvent en ville, n'est-ce pas?
   Est-ce qu'il descend souvent en ville?
   Descend-il souvent en ville?

3. Vous accomplissez beaucoup?
   Vous accomplissez beaucoup, n'est-ce pas?
   Est-ce que vous accomplissez beaucoup?
   Accomplissez-vous beaucoup?

4. Marie téléphone toujours à sa famille?
   Marie téléphone toujours à sa famille, n'est-ce pas?
   Est-ce que Marie téléphone toujours à sa famille?
   Marie téléphone-t-elle toujours à sa famille?

5. Tu attends toujours les autres?
   Tu attends toujours les autres, n'est-ce pas?
   Est-ce que tu attends toujours les autres?
   Attends-tu toujours les autres?

6. Les garçons jouent au tennis?
   Les garçons jouent au tennis, n'est-ce pas?
   Est-ce que les garçons jouent au tennis?
   Les garçons jouent-ils au tennis?

7. Elles écoutent le guide.
   Elles écoutent le guide, n'est-ce pas?
   Est-ce qu'elles écoutent le guide?
   Écoutent-elles le guide?

8. Luc et Anne semblent heureux?
   Luc et Anne semblent heureux, n'est-ce pas?
   Est-ce que Luc et Anne semblent heureux?
   Luc et Anne semblent-ils heureux?

421

It's All About You

Sample responses

1. Je ne fume jamais.
2. Je ne crie pas.
3. Je ne joue plus au tennis.
4. Je ne danse pas bien.
5. Je parle français.
6. Je bavarde avec des amis.
7. Je ne dîne pas tôt.
8. J'aime réussir.

Your Trip Awaits

1. Voyages de la Jeunesse
2. Loisirs et Vacances
3. Maison de Voyages
4. Sports et Loisirs

Chapter 8

Using être

1. suis en train de
2. sommes d'accord
3. sont sur le point d'
4. est à
5. êtes de retour

An Introductory Conversation

Sample responses:

1. Bonjour! Ça va?
2. Je m'appelle...
3. Très bien, merci. Et vous?
4. Je suis de...
5. Je suis professeur.

Getting the Scoop

Sample responses:

A. Robert est d'où? Il voyage avec qui? Il voyage où? Comment est-ce qu'il voyage? Ils passent combien de mois en France? Où est-ce qu'ils passent deux mois? Qu'est-ce qu'ils désirent visiter? Quand retournent-ils à Pittsburgh?

B. Tu t'appelles comment? Tu es d'où? Qu'est-ce que tu cherches? Pourquoi? Tu désires pratiquer quoi? Quand parles-tu anglais? Qu'est-ce que tu adores? Comment es-tu?

Chapter 9

A Sense of Belonging

1. La mère de Michael
2. Le père d'André et de Marie
3. Les grands-parents des jeunes filles
4. L'oncle du garçon
5. Le grand-père de la famille
6. Le frère de l'enfant

It's a Matter of Preference

Sample responses:

1. Mes actrices favorites sont…
2. Ma chanson favorite est…
3. Mes restaurants favoris sont…
4. Mon sport favori est…
5. Ma couleur favorite est…
6. Mon film favori est…

Totally Possessed

1. leur
2. sa
3. ton
4. mon
5. vos
6. son
7. ses
8. leur
9. son
10. notre

You Can Do It

Sample responses:

1. Permettez-moi de me présenter. Je m'appelle…
2. Vous connaissez mon (ma)…?
3. Je vous présente mon (ma)…
4. Je suis enchanté(e).
5. Moi de même.

Using Avoir

1. as le temps
2. a l'habitude de
3. avez de la chance
4. ont l'occasion de
5. ai l'intention de
6. a lieu

Creative Descriptions

Sample responses:

1. grande, magnfique
2. bons, intéressants
3. jeune, intelligent
4. belles, extraordinaires
5. grand, superbe

Perusing the Personal Ads

1. A charming, romantic, and cultured 25-year-old French man seeks a young French girl who likes to go out.
2. A tall, seductive, sincere, intelligent, 26-year-old American male in good financial position seeks a French girl who speaks English.
3. Francine, a 35-year-old simple, calm, devoted, charming technician and divorced mother, seeks a stable, courteous man who likes children, nature, and a quiet life.
4. A single, 27-year-old nice, dynamic, and sentimental blonde dentist seeks a young, tender girl who wants a long-lasting, serious relationship.
5. Alexis, a 30-year-old, elegant, charming, sincere, courteous, and generous engineer, seeks a single, simple, natural young woman for a lasting relationship.
6. A distinguished, refined, generous, easy-going, good-looking, 30-year-old businessman who loves the finer things in life seeks to give a gratifying, envied lifestyle to a 20- to 25-year-old woman.

Chapter 10

Airline Advice

1. For your comfort and security, take only one carry-on suitcase into the cabin. Any dangerous articles will be removed from it at the security check.
2. Choose sturdy bags that lock. Place identification on the outside and inside of all bags. Don't put anything of value in your bags that will be placed in the hold. Carry on anything important.

Customs

Sample response:

CARTE DE DÉBARQUEMENT

ne concerne pas les voyageurs de nationalité française ni les ressortissants des autres pays membres de l'UE

1. Nom de famille: <u>DUPONT</u>
   (en caractère d'imprimerie)

   Nom de jeune fille: <u>PRINCE</u>

   Prénom(s): <u>MARIE-FRANCE LUCIE</u>

2. Adresse: <u>754 Springfield Blvd.</u>
            (numéro) (rue)

   <u>Bayside Queens, NY 11364</u>
   (ville, village) (province, état) (code postal)

   <u>USA</u>
   (pays)

3. Date de naissance: <u>May 3, 1974</u>

4. Lieu de naissance: <u>NY</u>

5. Profession: <u>programmeur</u>

6. Aéroport ou port d'embarquement: <u>Paris, France</u>

7. Compagnie aérienne: <u>Air France</u>

8. Numéro du vol: <u>135</u>

9. Signature du voyageur:_____

Signs Tell It All

1. c   2. e   3. a   4. f   5. b   6. d

Where To?

1. allons   2. va   3. vas   4. vont   5. vais   6. allez

Ask for It

1. Les toilettes, s'il vous plaît.
   Où sont les toilettes?

2. Le contôle des passeports, s'il vous plaît.
   Où est le contrôle des passeports?

425

3. La douane, s'il vous plaît.
   Où est la douane?

4. Les ascenseurs, s'il vous plaît.
   Où sont les ascenseurs?

5. La sortie, s'il vous plaît.
   Où est la sortie?

6. Le bureau de change, s'il vous plaît.
   Où est le bureau de change?

Giving Commands

Verb	Tu	Vous	Meaning
aller	Va!	Allez!	Go!
continuer	Continue!	Continuez!	Continue!
descendre	Descends!	Descendez!	Go down!
marcher	Marche!	Marchez!	Walk!
monter	Monte!	Montez!	Go Up!
passer	Passe!	Passez!	Pass!
prendre (chapter 11)	Prends!	Prenez!	Take!
tourner	Tourne!	Tournez!	Turn!
traverser	Traverse!	Traversez!	Cross!

Getting from Here to There

Take the number 7 bus. When you get to town, get off at Mont-Royal avenue. Go along the avenue Mont-Royal and turn right on rue St.-Denis. Go straight, past boulevard St.-Joseph. You'll see a church on your right. After the church, turn left on the avenue Laurier. You'll go by a cinema. After the cinema, take the next right, avenue du Parc. My house is on the corner, avenue du Parc and avenue Laurier.

Chapter 11

Using quel

1. Quel train?

2. Quelle couleur?

3. Quelles blouses?

4. Quels journaux?

5. Quelle voiture?

6. Quelles cassettes?

7. Quel match?

8. Quels plats?

Off You Go

Make reservations 24 hours in advance; you must rent for 1 day; rental is based on a 24-hour period; you have unlimited kilometers; you can drop off your car at a sister agency; you are only liable for 1500 pesos in case of damage; there is an additional small fee in case of theft; there's 24-hour-road service; you must pay for your own gas; prices are subject to change.

What Did You Rent?

Air-conditioning, automatic glove compartment, anti-lock brakes, air bags, multi-function computer dashboard, electric seats, radio with loud speakers.

Renault promises the rental of a new car, unlimited mileage, multi-risk auto insurance, assistance seven days a week, for a three-week to six-month rental.

Your Number's Up?

1. quarante-cinq, soixante-sept, quatre-vingt-neuf, soixante-dix-sept

2. quarante-huit, vingt et un, quinze, cinquante et un

3. quarante-six, seize, quatre-vingt-dix-huit, treize

4. quarante-trois, onze, soixante-douze, quatre-vingt-quatorze

5. quarante et un, trente-quatre, quatre-vingts, soixante et un

6. quarante-deux, quatre-vingt-cinq, cinquante-neuf, deux

It's Movie Time

1. *Belle du jour* commence à trois heures dix, six heures moins vingt-cinq, huit heures, et dix heures vingt-cinq.

2. *Retour vers le futur* commence à trois heures moins dix, cinq heures moins vingt-cinq, six heures vingt, et huit heures cinq.

3. *Mon cousin Vinnie* commence à une heure et demie, quatre heures et quart, sept heures moins le quart, et dix heures moins vingt.

Chapter 12

Which Hotel Offers the Most?

	Hôtel Bellevue	Montréal Plaza	Le Grand Hôtel	Paris-Opéra
bar	x		x	
TV en couleurs	x			x
sauna			x	
cuisine gourmet	x	x		
téléphone direct				x
petit déjeuner compris		x		
chambre luxueuse	x	x	x	x
dîner spécial			x	
cadeau		x		
plage			x	
climatisation	x			
grande chambre	x	x	x	
casino		x	x	
garage	x			
massage			x	
transport		x	x	

Using Ordinal Numbers

1. La Tour Eiffel est dans le septième...
2. Les Invalides est dans le septième...
3. Le Forum des Halles est dans le premier...
4. Le Quartier Latin est dans le sixième...
5. La Bastille est dans le onzième...
6. Le Panthéon est dans le cinquième...

Using cer Verbs

1. commence
2. renonçons
3. remplaces
4. avance
5. annoncent

Using ger Verbs

1. range
2. déranges
3. partageons

4. nagez
5. arrangent

Using yer Verbs

1. paies (payes)
2. emploie
3. ennuyez

4. nettoie
5. essaie (essaye)

Using e+Consonant+er Verbs I

1. promène
2. appelez
3. enlève

4. jette
5. amenons

Using é+Consonant+er Verbs II

1. célèbre
2. Répétez
3. protégeons

4. espèrent
5. possède

Rate Your Hotel

VOTRE ARRIVÉE (your arrival)

Porteur (porter)

Réception (front desk)

Réservation (reservations)

Sécurité (security)

NOS SERVICES (our services)

Concierge (concierge)

Téléphones (telephones)

Messages (messages)

Caissier (cashier)

Centre d'affaires (business center)

Gouvernante (maid service)

Blanchisserie (laundry services)

Minibar (minibar)

Piscine (pool)

Gymnase (gym)

VOTRE CHAMBRE (your room)

Bien equipée (well equipped)

Espace de travail suffisant (adequate working space)

Produits d'accueil en quantité suffisante (sufficient guest amenities)

Équipement en bon état de fonctionnement (equipment in good working condition)

Chapter 13

And the Forecast Is...

Lille—Il fait froid. Le ciel est clair. Il fait un.

Reims—Il fait du vent. Il fait froid. Il fait trois.

Strasbourg—Il fait froid, mais beau. Il fait moins un.

Paris—Il y a des nuages. Il fait froid. Il fait du vent. Il fait cinq.

Tours—Il fait frais. Il y a des nuages. Il fait huit.

Nice—Le temps est variable et il fait du vent. Il fait quinze.

What's the Date?

1. le cinq août
2. le huit août
3. le quatorze août
4. le six août
5. le vingt et un août
6. le trente et un juillet

When Is It Open?

La Grillade: Open from 9 a.m. until 11.30 p.m. Closed Sundays. Music on Tuesday, Wednesday, and Friday evenings.

Using faire

1. font un voyage
2. faites la queue
3. fais venir
4. faisons une promenade

5. fait la connaissance de
6. fais des achats (emplettes)
7. fait attention
8. font une partie de

Chapter 14

I See

Je vois un défilé.

Je vois une fontaine.

Je vois des animaux.

Je vois des vitraux.

Je vois un jardin.

Je vois des fleurs.

Take Me to the Zoo

In Paris—Parc Zoologique de Paris

Closest to Paris—Parc Zoologique du Bois d'Attily

Farthest from Paris—Parc Zoologique du Château de Thoiry

Open all year—Parc Zoologique du Bois d'Attily

Open everyday—Parc Zoologique du Château de Thoiry

Picnic—Parc Zoologique de Paris

Animals roam free—Parc Zoologique du Château de Thoiry

Make Me an Offer

Sample responses:

1. On fait un pique-nique? Faisons un pique-nique.
2. On marche sur les quais? Marchons sur les quais.
3. On regarde les expositions? Regardons les expositions.
4. On fait une croisière? Faisons une croisière.
5. On va au jardin? Allons au jardin.

Your Sentiments Exactly

Sample responses:

1. C'est chouette.
2. C'est extra.
3. C'est embêtant.
4. C'est merveilleux.
5. C'est formidable.
6. Je déteste.
7. C'es génial.
8. C'est ennuyeux.
9. C'est la barbe.
10. C'est sensationnel.

Exactly Where Are You Going?

1. Je vais en Espagne.
2. Je vais en Chine.
3. Je vais au Mexique.
4. Je vais en Russie.
5. Je vais en Italie.
6. Je vais en Angleterre.
7. Je vais en Égypte.
8. Je vais en France.
9. Je vais aux États-Unis.
10. Je vais aux États-Unis.

Using y

Sample responses:

1. J'y vais.
2. J'y reste.
3. Je n'y passe pas mes vacances.
4. Je vais y descendre.
5. Je vais y dîner.
6. Je ne vais pas y penser.

Make a Suggestion

1. Voyageons-y. N'y voyageons pas.
2. Allons-y. N'y allons pas.
3. Restons-y. N'y restons pas.
4. Passons-y la journée. N'y passons pas la journée.
5. Assistons-y. N'y assistons pas.

Chapter 15

Put It On?

Sample responses:

Work—Je mets une robe, des bas, des chaussures, un bracelet, une montre, une bague, et un collier.

Beach—Je mets un bikini et des sandales.

Dinner party—Je mets une robe du soir, des bas, des chaussures, et des bijoux.

Friend's house—Je mets un jean, une chemise, des chaussettes, des tennis, et une montre.

Skiing—Je mets un pantalon, un pull, des chaussettes, des chaussures, un manteau, un chapeau, et des gants.

What Are You Looking For?

Sample responses:

Madame Paris—perfumes, beauty products, jewelry, scarfs, accessories, and leather goods

Georges Figaro—shirts of all kinds

Vivianne—large-size, ready-to-wear clothing for women, and assorted accessories

Parfumeries Pépin—perfumes

Variations—Men and women's clothing: sweaters, polos, blouses, skirts, and ensembles

Vanessa—sweaters

Chaussures de Paris—shoes for men and women

Chantal—leather goods: pocketbooks, briefcases, and luggage

Using Direct Object Pronouns

Sample responses:

1. Je l'aime.
2. Je ne les prends pas.
3. Je la choisis.
4. Je les regarde.
5. Je ne l'achète pas.
6. Je ne l'adore pas.

Using Indirect Object Pronouns

1. Offre-lui une montre.
2. Offre-leur un tableau.
3. Offre-leur des cravates.
4. Offre-leur des robes.
5. Offre-lui un bracelet.
6. Offre-lui un pull.

433

What Do You Think?

1. Cette large cravate à rayures est laide.
2. Ce short en tartan est trop criard.
3. Cette chemise à pois est abominable.
4. Ce petit tee-shirt à rayures est trop serré.

Chapter 16

Going Here and There

Je vais à l'épicerie.

Je vais à la pâtisserie.

Je vais à la boucherie.

Je vais à la fruiterie.

Je vais à la poissonerie.

Je vais au magasin de vins.

Je vais à la confiserie.

Je vais à la crémerie.

Serious Shopping

Sample responses:

1. de la viande—du jambon, du rosbif, du poulet
2. des pâtisseries—des éclairs, des choux à la crême, un gâteau
3. du pain—des croissants, des brioches
4. des légumes—des carottes, des haricots verts, des asperges
5. des fruits—des pommes, des poires, des raisins
6. de la chacuterie—du pâté, du lard, de la mortadelle

Your Likes and Dislikes

Sample responses:

1. Je déteste les fruits.
2. J'adore les légumes.
3. J'aime la viande.
4. J'adore le poisson.
5. J'aime le pain.
6. J'adore le gâteau.

Is the Fridge Bare?

Sample responses:

> deux litres d'orangeade
>
> cinq cents grammes de mortadelle
>
> une boîte de pâté
>
> un bocal de café
>
> un sac de bonbons
>
> une trance de fromage

I'd Like...

Pourriez-vous me donner _____ s'il vous plaît.

1. cinq cents grammes de jambon
2. un litre de soda
3. une tablette de chocolat
4. une boîte de biscuits
5. un sac de bonbons
6. deux cent cinquante grammes de dinde

It's a Puzzle to Me

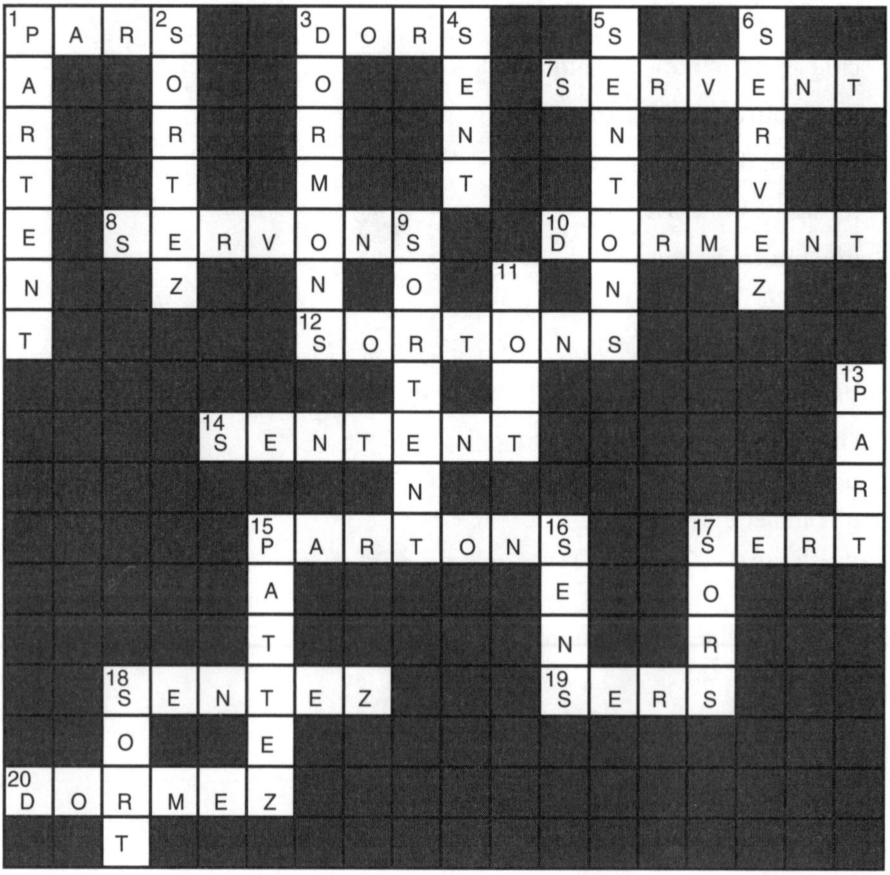

Crossword grid answers:

- 1 (across) P A R S — P A R T E N T (down)
- 3 (across) D O R S — D O R M E N T (down)
- 4 (down) S E N T
- 5 (down) S E N T
- 6 (down) S E R V
- 7 (across) S E R V E N T
- 8 (across) S E R V O N S — S O R T E Z (down)
- 9 (down) S O N T
- 10 (across) D O R M E N T — D O R M E Z (down)
- 11
- 12 (across) S O R T O N S
- 13 (down) P A R T
- 14 (across) S E N T E N T
- 15 (across) P A R T O N S — P A A T (down)
- 16 (down) S E N S
- 17 (across) S E R T — S O R T (down)
- 18 (across) S E N T E Z — S O T (down)
- 19 (across) S E R S
- 20 (across) D O R M E Z

Horizontalement

1. (leave) je
3. (sleep) you
7. (serve) ils
8. (server) rious
10. (sleep) elles
12. (go out) nous
14. (feel) ils
15. (leave) nous
17. (serve) il
18. (feel) vous
19. (serve) tu
20. (sleep) vous

Verticalement

1. (leave) elles
2. (go out) vous
3. (sleep) nous
4. (feel) il
5. (feel) nous
6. (serve) vous
9. (go out) ils
11. (sleep) il
13. (leave) elle
15. (leave) vous
16. (feel) je
17. (go out) tu
18. (go out) elle

Chapter 17

Which Restaurant Do You Prefer?

1. fine traditional cooking
2. French cooking and Lebanese specialties
3. seafood
4. Italian specialties
5. English food
6. American food, music every evening
7. French food
8. Lebanese and French specialties
9. Vietnamese and Chinese specialties
10. Vietnamese and Chinese specialities
11. Hot and cold buffet, ice cream, and pastries
12. fish, Italian specialties
13. Italian specialties
14. drinks and music
15. ice cream
16. seafood
17. businessman's special

Oh, Waiter

Il me faut une salière, une serviette, une fourchette, un couteau, une assiette, et une cuiller.

Yes or No?

1. N'en mange pas. Manges-en.
2. Prépares-en. N'en prépare pas.
3. Prends-en. N'en prends pas.
4. N'en choisis pas. Choisis-en.
5. Achètes-en. N'en achète pas.

Chapter 18

I'll Meet You There

1. Tu peux faire du tennis.　　　　Tu veux aller au court.
2. Nous pouvons faire du golf.　　Nous voulons aller au parcours.
3. Vous pouvez faire de la pêche.　Vous voulez aller à la mer.
4. Elle peut faire du base-ball.　　Elle veut aller au stade.
5. Ils peuvent faire du patin.　　　Ils veulent aller à la patinoire.

Will You Be Joining Us?

Sample responses:

C'est chouette.　　　　　　Ça dépend.

Je n'ai pas envie.　　　　　Je regrette.

C'est une bonne idée.

What About These Movies?

Blanche-Neige is being shown in French and can be seen by children.

Emmanuelle is for those 18-years old and older.

Encore is for those 13-years old and older.

Miss Daisy is shown in its original language (English) with French subtitles. It is also shown dubbed in French.

I Think...

Sample responses:

C'est émouvant.　　　　　　C'est un bon film.

Je déteste.　　　　　　　　C'est amusant.

C'est bidon.　　　　　　　　C'est toujours la même chose.

Let's Play

1. jouons au　　　　2. jouez de la　　　3. joues de la
4. jouent au　　　　5. joue du　　　　　6. joue aux

What Do You Do Well?

Sample responses:

1. Je parle français courrament.
2. Je joue mal du piano.
3. Je joue bien au golf.
4. Je cuisine parfaitement bien.
5. Je pense sérieusement.
6. Je travaille dur.
7. Je voyage souvent.
8. Je chante beaucoup.
9. Je danse assez bien.
10. Je nage peu.

Chapter 19

Dealing with Dirt

shirt

silk shirt

undershort

undershirt

pajamas

night shirt

handkerchief

socks

slip

bra

stockings/pantyhose

shorts

These Boots Were Made for Walking

He picks up and then delivers repaired shoes.

I Can't See Without Them

It promises to have your glasses ready in an hour and to sell special high-correction lenses that don't deform your face.

439

Do You Get the Picture?

It buys (at the highest rate), sells (at the lowest rate), trades, and repairs the most famous brand cameras.

Stress Relief

1. nous   2. lui/moi   3. toi   4. elle   5. eux   6. vous

You Compare

Sample responses:

> Ma soeur est plus grande que moi.
>
> Ma mère est plus vieille que moi.
>
> Moi, je suis plus jeune qu'elle.
>
> Mon mari, lui, il est plus patient que moi.

Chapter 20

What's Wrong?

Sample responses:

1. Je tousse. J'éternue. J'ai des frissons. J'ai de la fièvre.
2. J'éternue. J'ai une migraine.
3. J'ai mal à la cheville. J'ai de la douleur.
4. J'ai mal à la tête. J'ai du mal à dormir. J'ai de la douleur.

Tell It to the Doctor

See following page for sample responses.

FRÉDÉRICK A. PEREIRA
68 Rue Napoléon
Paris, France
Tél: 47 35 19 56
Fax: 47 22 80 04

FICHE MÉDICALE

Date: _____

Nom: <u>LaVache</u>_____ Prénoms: <u>Jean-Luc</u>

Adresse: <u>12 avenue Victor Hugo</u>_____

N° de téléphone: <u>99 99 99 99</u>_____

Date de naissance: <u>3 Juin 1964</u>_____ âge: <u>35</u>____

Profession: <u>Rédacteur</u>_____

Situation de famille: célibataire   _____

marié(e)   _____x_____

divorcé(e)   _____

veuf (veuve)   _____

Symptômes

<u>**Mal à la gorge, possible réaction allergique**</u>_____

_____

_____

_____

Antécédants Médicaux

Maladies subies

❑ Angine (angina)
❑ appendicite
❑ asthme
❑ attaque d''apoplexie
❑ bronchite
❑ cancer
❑ coqueluche
❑ crise cardiaque
❑ diabète
❑ dysenterie
❑ goutte
❑ grippe
❑ hépatite
❑ oreillons
❑ pneumonie
❑ poliomyélite
❑ réaction allergique
❑ rhume des foins
❑ rougeole
❑ tétanos
❑ tuberculose

❑ variole
❑ vertige

Allergies

❑ à la penicilline
❑ aux antibiotiques
❑ autres

Vaccinations

❑ coqueluche
❑ oreillons
❑ poliomyélite
❑ rougeole
❑ rubéole
❑ tétanos
❑ tuberculose
❑ variole

Me? A Hypochondriac?

1. Je tousse depuis deux semaines. Ça fait deux semaines que je tousse. Il y a deux semaines que je tousse. Voilà deux semaines que je tousse.

2. J'ai mal à la tête depuis trois jours. Ça fait trois jours que j'ai mal à la tête. Il y a trois jours que j'ai mal à la tête. Voilà trois jours que j'ai mal à la tête.

3. J'ai mal au ventre depuis un mois. Ça fait un mois que j'ai mal au ventre. Il y a un mois que j'ai mal au ventre. Voilà un mois que j'ai mal au ventre.

Using Reflexive Verbs

Sample responses:

1. Je me réveille. Je me lève. Je me déshabille. Je me lave. Je me baigne. Je m'habille. Je me coiffe. Je me maquille (Je me rase). Je me regarde dans la glace. Je me prépare.

2. Je vais me déshabiller. Je vais me laver. Je vais m'habiller. Je vais me coucher. Je vais m'endormir.

You're In Command

1. Baigne-toi. Ne te baigne pas. Baignez-vous. Ne vous baignez pas.

2. Dépêche-toi. Ne te dépêche pas. Dépêchez-vous. Ne vous dépêchez pas.

3. Rase-toi. Ne te rase pas. Rasez-vous. Ne vous rasez pas.

4. Habille-toi. Ne t'habille pas. Habillez-vous. Ne vous habillez pas.

5. Brosse-toi les dents. Ne te brosse pas les dents. Brossez-vous les dents. Ne vous brossez pas les dents.

6. Amuse-toi. Ne t'amuse pas. Amusez-vous. Ne vous amusez pas.

Chapter 21

What Do You Need?

Sample responses:

1. Il me faut des aspirines et des gouttes nasales.

2. Il me faut des aspirines.

3. Il me faut un antiseptique et des pansements.

4. Il me faut du lait de magnésie.

5. Il me faut un rasor, des lames de rasoir, et de la crème à raser.

6. Il me faut un biberon et une sucette.

You Didn't, Did You?

1. J'ai rempli... Je n'ai pas rempli...
2. Tu as répondu... Tu n'as pas répondu...
3. Tu as obéi... Tu n'as pas obéi...
4. Nous avons acheté... Nous n'avons pas acheté...
5. Elle a cherché... Elle n'a pas cherché...
6. Ils ont attendu... Ils n'ont pas attendu...

Your Past Is in Question

1. Avons-nous travaillé...?   N'avons-nous pas travaillé...?
2. A-t-elle obéi...?   N'a-t-elle pas obéi...?
3. Ont-ils perdu...?   N'ont-ils pas perdu...?
4. Avez-vous trop maigri...?   N'avez-vous pas trop maigri...?
5. As-tu trop mangé...?   N'as-tu pas trop mangé...?
6. A-t-il attendu...?   N'a-t-il pas attendu...?

Who Did What?

1. Il a fait...
2. Nous avons été...
3. Tu as vu...
4. J'ai pu...
5. Elles ont pris...
6. Vous avez lu...
7. Ils ont eu...
8. Elle a fait...
9. Je suis arrivée...
10. Nous sommes revenus...
11. Ils sont restés...
12. Tu es partie...
13. Vous êtes allés...
14. Elle est sortie...
15. Ils sont descendus...
16. Elles sont rentrées...

Chapter 22

Calling from Your Hotel Room

1. 6
2. 7
3. 1 + 16
4. 1
5. 1 + 19
6. 2 + room number
7. 5
8. 4

Insert Using a Public Phone

1. Lift the receiver.
2. Insert your card.
3. Wait for the dial tone.
4. Dial the number.
5. Speak.

Please Phone Home

Automatically—Lift the receiver. When you get a dial tone, dial 19; you'll get another tone. Give the area code for the country you are calling and the area code of the zone you are calling, and then dial the number.

With the help of a France Télécom agent—Lift the receiver. When you get a dial tone, dial 19; you'll get another dial tone. Then dial 33 followed by the code for the country you are calling. A French operator will pick up.

Minitel

You can use an electronic phone book, which allows you to find the phone number and address for everyone in France who subscribes.

I Can't Talk Now

1. Elle doit réparer...
2. Nous devons aller...
3. Tu dois sortir...
4. Vous devez faire...
5. Ils doivent travailler.
6. Je dois partir...

Making Excuses

1. Je me suis cassé le bras.
2. Elle s'est réveillée tard.
3. Nous nous sommes occupés d'autre chose.
4. Ils se sont mis à travailler.
5. Vous vous êtes levées à midi.
6. Tu t'es couchée tôt.

Chapter 23

At the Post Office

A commemorative stamp celebrating the first anniversary of the Chunnel. It will be available on the third of May.

Using Savoir and Connaître

1. savent
2. sais
3. connaissez
4. savons
5. connais
6. connaît
7. savez
8. connaissons

Formation of the Imperfect

avoir (to have)	nous avons	elle avait
boire (to drink)	nous buvons	je buvais
connaître (to be acquainted with)	nous connaissons	vous connaissiez
devoir (to have to)	nous devons	tu devais
dire (to say, tell)	nous disons	ils disaient
dormir (to sleep)	nous dormons	nous dormions
écrire (to write)	nous écrivons	elles écrivaient
faire (to make, do)	nous faisons	vous faisiez
lire (to read)	nous lisons	je lisais
mettre (to put [on])	nous mettons	nous mettions
partir (to leave)	nous partons	tu partais
pouvoir (to be able to)	nous pouvons	elle pouvait
prendre (to take)	nous prenons	ils prenaient
recevoir (to receive)	nous recevons	vous receviez
savoir (to know)	nous savons	elles savaient
sentir (to feel, smell)	nous sentons	il sentait
servir (to serve)	nous servons	elle servait
sortir (to go out)	nous sortons	tu sortais
voir (to see)	nous voyons	elles voyaient
vouloir (to want)	nous voulons	je voulais

Passé Composé or Imparfait?

1. était	9. ai dit	17. commencions
2. était	10. suis parti(e)	18. a attaqué
3. chantaient	11. sommes allé(e)s	19. a crié
4. faisais	12. nous sommes arrêté(e)s	20. s'est échappée
5. a sonné	13. sommes arrivé(e)s	21. avons passé
6. était	14. brillait	22. était
7. a demandé	15. faisait	
8. voulais	16. avons trouvé	

Chapter 24

Do You Know Your Computer?

Sample responses:

1. J'ai un P.C.
2. J'emploie un modem, une souris, et un scanneur.
3. Il a cent megabytes de mémoire.
4. La vitesse est…
5. J'emploie un programme de traitement de texte et une feuille de calcul.

Verbs Irregular in the Future

Infinitive	Stem	
avoir (to have)	aur- (*ohr*)	tu auras
devoir (to have to)	devr- (*duhv*)	nous devrons
envoyer (to send)	enverr- (*ah-vuhr*)	il enverra
être (to be)	ser- (*sehr*)	elles seront
faire (to make, do)	fer- (*fuhr*)	je ferai
pouvoir (to be able to)	pourr- (*poor*)	vous pourrez
recevoir (to receive)	recevr- (*ruh-suhv*)	nous recevrons
savoir (to know)	saur- (*sohr*)	ils sauront
venir (to come)	viendr- (*vyaNdr*)	tu viendras
voir (to see)	verr- (*vuhr*)	je verrai
vouloir (to want)	voudr- (*voodr*)	elle voudra

Predicting the Future

Aries— 1. Exceptional financial opportunities will present themselves.

Taurus— 2. You will have a very good month.

Gemini— 3. You will have tension and arguments with your colleagues.

Cancer— 4. You will be in good shape.

Leo— 5. You will concentrate on your financial affairs.

Virgo— 6. You will make an important decision concerning your professional future.

Libra— 7. You will be in harmony with your friends.

Scorpio— 8. Your ambition will serve you.

Sagittarius— 9. You will have important discussions with family members.

Capricorn— 10. Everything will go well for you.

Aquarius— 11. You will meet an important person.

Pisces— 12. You will be busy every night and will have many weekend plans.

Chapter 25

Purchasing Furniture

Your furniture will be guaranteed for five years and recovering for two years, should there be any problem with the manufacturing.

They will give a free decorating consultation and will come to give free estimates and take measurements.

You will be given a guarantee against all risks for one year.

Your old furniture will be removed.

All guarantees are free throughout continental France.

Irregular Verbs in the Conditional

Infinitive	Stem	
avoir (to have)	aur- (*ohr*)	tu aurais
devoir (to have to)	devr- (*duhv*)	nous devrions
envoyer (to send)	enverr- (*ahN-vuhr*)	il enverrait
être (to be)	ser- (*sehr*)	elles seraient
faire (to make, do)	fer- (*fuhr*)	je ferais
pouvoir (to be able to)	pourr- (*poor*)	vous pourriez
recevoir (to receive)	recevr- (*ruh-suhvr*)	nous recevrions
savoir (to know)	saur- (*sohr*)	ils sauraient
venir (to come)	viendr- (*vyaNdr*)	tu viendrais
voir (to see)	verr- (*vuhr*)	je verrais
vouloir (to want)	voudr- (*voodr*)	elle voudrait

Chapter 26

There's So Much to Do

Il faut que:

1. nous préparions…
2. elle finisse…
3. ils attendent…
4. je téléphone…
5. vous accomplissiez…
6. tu descendes…
7. je me lève…
8. il aille…
9. vous soyez…
10. tu achètes…
11. elles prennent…
12. nous fassions…

Index

455